THE DESPOTAT
1267–

THE DESPOTATE OF EPIROS 1267–1479

A contribution to the history of Greece in the middle ages

DONALD M. NICOL
Koraës Professor of Modern Greek and Byzantine History, Language and Literature, King's College, University of London

CAMBRIDGE UNIVERSITY PRESS
Cambridge
London New York New Rochelle
Melbourne Sydney

CAMBRIDGE UNIVERSITY PRESS
Cambridge, New York, Melbourne, Madrid, Cape Town, Singapore,
São Paulo, Delhi, Dubai, Tokyo

Cambridge University Press
The Edinburgh Building, Cambridge CB2 8RU, UK

Published in the United States of America by Cambridge University Press, New York

www.cambridge.org
Information on this title: www.cambridge.org/9780521130899

First published 1984
This digitally printed version 2010

A catalogue record for this publication is available from the British Library

Library of Congress Catalogue Card Number: 83–21080

ISBN 978-0-521-26190-6 Hardback
ISBN 978-0-521-13089-9 Paperback

Contents

Preface

The Fourth Crusade and the capture of Constantinople by the Latins in 1204 irreparably shattered the structure of the Byzantine Empire. One of the most enduring by-products of the disaster was the establishment of a separatist state in Epiros in the north-west of Greece. It began as a centre of resistance and a haven for refugees from the Latin invaders. It developed into a powerful political and military force whose rulers for a time claimed the title of emperors in exile. Constantinople was recovered from the Latins in 1261 and the Byzantine Empire was restored. But the rulers of Epiros stubbornly refused to recognise the new regime. Greek at first, then Italian, Serbian and Albanian, they perpetuated the autonomy of their province well into the fifteenth century, striving to maintain its identity against the competing claims of the emperors of Constantinople, the Angevin kings of Naples, the merchants of Venice and finally the Ottoman Turks. At least since the nineteenth century this defiantly independent fragment of the Byzantine world has been known as the Despotate of Epiros. In 1957 I published a work under that title in which I attempted to put together its political and ecclesiastical history from 1204 to 1267. It has long been my intention to pursue the matter to its end in the fifteenth century, when Epiros together with the rest of Greece and Eastern Europe were swept into the Ottoman Empire. This I have now tried to do and the results are set forth in the present volume.

It may be thought that I should first have corrected the faults and filled the gaps in my earlier volume on the subject, or that I should have rewritten that volume to take account of new material and research published since 1957. The latter course I considered and rejected, mainly because our knowledge of the history of Epiros in the period between 1204 and 1261 has not been substantially enriched by the discovery of new source material in the past twenty-five years. The most important addition to the literary sources for that period has been the publication of a number of previously unedited letters of John Apokaukos, metropolitan of Naupaktos. These cast some new light on the church and society of Epiros in the 1220s. Art historians have given some welcome attention to the monuments of the district and numismatists have advanced the classification of the coinage of Epiros and Thessalonica in the early thirteenth century. But the most important corrections have been made by reassessment of the existing evidence about the origin of the so-called Despotate of Epiros and about its early form and development. These new interpretations were mainly the work of Lucien Stiernon, Božidar Ferjančić and the late Père Raymond-Joseph Loenertz, O. P.; and I have attempted to incorporate them into an introductory chapter recapitulating the outlines of the history of Epiros between the years 1204 and 1267.

The empire of Nicaea, the Byzantine government in exile in Asia Minor after the Fourth Crusade, has been re-examined in a valuable study by Michael Angold; and a history of Thessaly in the thirteenth and fourteenth centuries was published by Ferjančić in 1974. But no one has so far rewritten the history of the rival government in exile in Epiros; and there is no substantial study of its survival as an independent administration after 1261. The only monograph carrying the history of Epiros from the thirteenth century to its conquest by the Turks remains that published in 1895 by the Greek scholar Ioannes Romanos, entitled *A Historical Treatise on the Despotate of Epiros*. Romanos, like every subsequent historian of mediaeval Greece, relied heavily on the encyclopaedic and gothically monumental *Geschichte Griechenlands* of Karl Hopf, published in 1867. Hopf frequently loses sight of the wood in his faithful contemplation of the trees. But in one respect at least he supplies information about the history of Epiros which can no longer be either checked or challenged. For he had access to the now lost registers of the Angevin Kingdom of Naples, which were destroyed in the Second World War. The kings of Naples claimed suzerainty over Epiros in the thirteenth and fourteenth centuries and their archives were no less important than those of Venice, whose interests in Epiros were of a different nature.

Among recent new editions of or commentaries upon the literary sources for the period from 1267 to 1479 special mention should be made of the work of Leandros Vranousis on the Chronicles of Epiros. There are also helpful commentaries on the first books of the History of George Pachymeres by Albert Failler; and a commentary, with German translation, on the History of Nikephoros Gregoras by Jan Louis van Dieten. The Chronicle of Ioannina, which narrates the history of that city for most of the last fifty years of the fourteenth century, was only imperfectly known to Hopf and Romanos. Neither knew of the existence of the Chronicle of the Tocco family, which relates the exploits of Carlo Tocco, Despot of Epiros in the first half of the fifteenth century, and which was edited by Giuseppe Schirò in 1975. The topography of

Thessaly and Hellas is admirably illuminated in the first volume of the *Tabula Imperii Byzantini* published in Vienna in 1976; and an indispensable compendium of the topography and historical geography of Epiros is the third and companion volume in the same series, entitled *Nikopolis und Kephallēnia*, which appeared in 1981.

I have interpreted the word Epiros in its literal sense of 'the mainland' and the word Despotate in its strict sense of the territory ruled by the Greek Despots and their successors. The history of the offshore Ionian Islands, which were for most of this period under Italian rule, is therefore treated only in so far as it influenced that of the mainland. Likewise, the history of Albania, which lay beyond the northern frontiers of the Despotate, is treated only in so far as the Albanians penetrated into and dominated the original territory of the Despots in northern Greece.

It is my pleasant duty to record my sincere thanks to the Society for Epirotic Studies in Ioannina, and particularly to its remarkable President, Constantine Phrontzos, for their generous help and hospitality during two extended sojourns in Epiros in recent years. My thanks are also due to my friends and colleagues at the University of Ioannina who afforded me every facility for completing my work.

London
1983

D.M.N.

Abbreviations

The following abbreviations are used for periodicals, collections of sources and reference works:

AAA	Ἀρχαιολογικὰ Ἀνάλεκτα ἐξ Ἀθηνῶν
ActAlb	*Acta et Diplomata res Albaniae mediae aetatis illustrantia*, ed. L. de Thallóczy, C. Jireček, E. de Šufflay
ActAlbVen	*Acta Albaniae Veneta Saeculorum XIV et XV*, ed. J. Valentini
AD	Ἀρχαιολογικὸν Δελτίον
AFP	*Archivum Fratrum Praedicatorum*
ASI	*Archivio Storico Italiano*
ASPN	*Archivio Storico per le Province Napoletane*
B	*Byzantion*
BF	*Byzantinische Forschungen*
BFG	Loenertz, R.-J., *Byzantina et Franco-Graeca*, I–II
BHG	*Bibliographia Hagiographica Graeca*, ed. F. Halkin
BMGS	*Byzantine and Modern Greek Studies*
BNJ	*Byzantinisch-neugriechische Jahrbücher*
BS	*Byzantinoslavica*
BZ	*Byzantinische Zeitschrift*
CFHB	*Corpus Fontium Historiae Byzantinae*
CSHB	*Corpus Scriptorum Historiae Byzantinae*
DIEE	Δελτίον Ἱστορικῆς καὶ Ἐθνολογικῆς Ἑταιρείας Ἑλλάδος
DVL	*Diplomatarium Veneto-Levantinum*, ed. G. M. Thomas and R. Predelli
EEBS	Ἐπετηρὶς Ἑταιρείας Βυζαντινῶν Σπουδῶν
Ep. Chron.	Ἠπειρωτικὰ Χρονικά
Ep. Hest.	Ἠπειρωτικὴ Ἑστία
JÖB	*Jahrbuch der österreichischen Byzantinistik*
JÖBG	*Jahrbuch der österreichischen byzantinischen Gesellschaft*

MM	Miklosich, F. and Müller, J., *Acta et Diplomata graeca medii aevi sacra et profana*
MPG	Migne, J. P., *Patrologiae cursus completus. Series graeco-latina*
NH	Νέος Ἑλληνομνήμων
OCP	*Orientalia Christiana Periodica*
PLP	*Prosopographisches Lexikon der Palaiologenzeit*, ed. E. Trapp
REB	*Revue des Etudes Byzantines*
RHSEE	*Revue historique du sud-est européen*
RSBN	*Rivista di Studi Bizantini e Neoellenici*
ThEE	Θρησκευτικὴ καὶ Ἠθικὴ Ἐγκυκλοπαιδεία
TIB	*Tabula Imperii Byzantini*, ed. H. Hunger
TM	*Travaux et Mémoires*
VV	*Vizantijskij Vremennik*
ZRVI	*Zbornik Radova Vizantološkog Instituta*

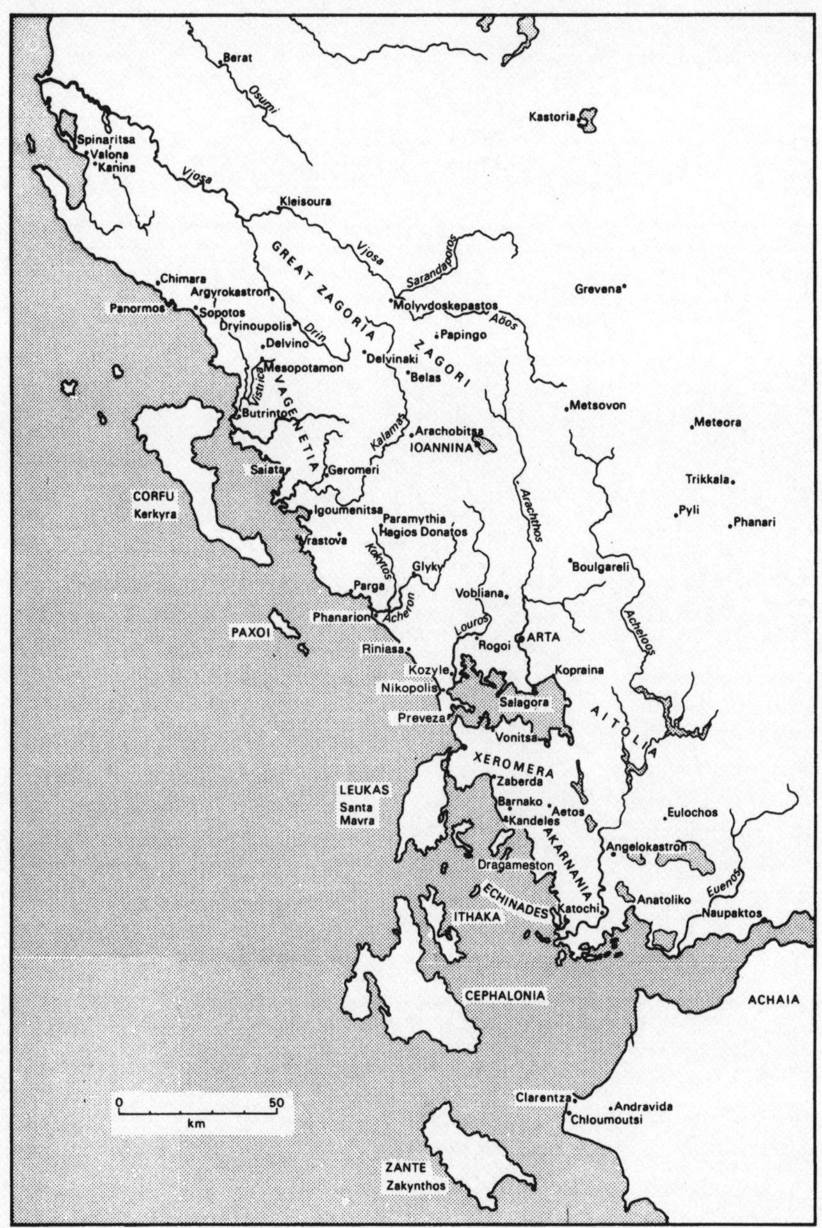

Epiros in the fourteenth century

Introduction

The history of Epiros as an independent Byzantine province in the north-west of Greece began with the Fourth Crusade. In April 1204 the crusaders and their Venetian accomplices captured Constantinople and appointed an emperor and a patriarch of their own. They then turned to the conquest of the provinces of the Byzantine Empire in Europe and in Asia Minor. Thessalonica passed to Boniface of Montferrat, the leader of the crusade; and from there he planned and directed the Latin invasion of Greece. A number of Greeks joined him. Among them was Michael Komnenos Doukas a bastard son of the *sebastokrator* John Doukas and a cousin of the Emperors Isaac II and Alexios III Angelos. Michael did not stay long in the service of the Latins. He deserted Boniface and crossed over the mountains to join his relative, the Byzantine governor of Arta. There he settled, married the governor's daughter and became the accepted leader and protector of the Greek inhabitants of Epiros.

Epiros means 'the mainland'. Surrounded by sea on the west and south and by high mountains on the north and east, its geography promotes a spirit of independence. At the beginning of the thirteenth century its independence became a fact. The rest of the Greek world was to be subjected to the Latins, to the French and Italian crusaders and their descendants. But Epiros was for a long time to remain free from their control and influence. Michael Doukas was not without experience as a provincial governor. In Epiros he took over the Byzantine administration which had been centred on the city of Arta, capital of the theme of Nikopolis. Included in his domain were the districts of Aitolia and Akarnania, Thesprotia and Ioannina, the province known as Old Epiros, whose inhabitants were mainly Greek-speaking. New Epiros lay further to the north and comprised the theme of Dyrrachion (Durazzo) and the western section of the Via Egnatia, the trunk road which had for centuries linked the ports on the Adriatic Sea with Thessalonica and Constantinople. Many of the inhabitants of New Epiros were Albanians who, by the thirteenth century, were beginning to form identifiable tribal units or clans. The offshore islands of Cephalonia, Ithaka and Zakynthos (or Zante) were under foreign rule even before 1204, having been appropriated by an Italian adventurer called Maio Orsini; while the island of Corfu was to be conquered by Venice in 1207.

Michael Doukas appointed himself as leader and defender of the mainland of Epiros against the Latins. It used to be supposed that he held the official and imperial title of Despot and was thus the founder of what later came to be called the Despotate of Epiros. This is a fallacy. None of the contemporary sources suggests that Michael held any such title. The Venetians seem to have thought that his family name of Doukas was equivalent to the Latin title of *dux*, but they never addressed him as Despot.[1] The leader of the other Greek resistance movement which arose in the ruins of the Byzantine Empire after 1204, at Nicaea in Asia Minor, soon adopted the title of emperor. By so doing he staked his claim to the throne at Constantinople in anticipation of the day when the Latins would be expelled. Nicaea came to be regarded, at least by the eastern Greeks, as the political and ecclesiastical centre of the empire in exile, the seat of the emperor and the patriarch. But it was difficult for the emperors at Nicaea to enforce their authority over the distant and isolated province of Epiros. There the spirit of independence flourished unchecked if not unchallenged for many years.

The origins of the 'Despotate' of Epiros cannot therefore be referred back to Michael Doukas. Michael was no more than a local dynast, somewhat like Leo Sgouros, lord of Argos and Corinth, or his relative Manuel Kamytzes, who had carved out his own estate in Macedonia and Thessaly before 1204. The emperor-historian John Cantacuzene, writing many years later, believed that the Greek rulers of Epiros after the Fourth Crusade held a mandate from the Byzantine emperors in Nicaea who entrusted them with an 'annual command' of the province.[2] It is certain that when Michael's brother Theodore Komnenos Doukas left Asia Minor for Epiros about 1207 he was made to swear an oath of loyalty to the emperor at Nicaea.[3] It is no less certain that that emperor and his

[1] L. Stiernon, 'Les origines du Despotat d'Epire. A propos d'un livre récent', *REB*, XVII (1959), 90–126; B. Ferjančić, *Despoti u Vizantii i južnoslovenskim zemljama* (Belgrade, 1960), pp. 49–58. Account was taken of these and other corrections in my chapter on 'The Fourth Crusade and the Greek and Latin Empires, 1204–61', in the *Cambridge Medieval History*, IV: *The Byzantine Empire*, I (Cambridge, 1966), pp. 275–330. See also D. M. Nicol, Πρόσφατες ἔρευνες γιὰ τὶς ἀπαρχὲς τοῦ Δεσποτάτου τῆς Ἠπείρου, *Ep. Chron.*, XXII (1980), 39–48. The most recent discussion of these problems is that by G. Prinzing, 'Studien zur Provinz- und Zentralverwaltung im Machtbereich der epirotischen Herrscher Michael I. und Theodoros Dukas', *Ep. Chron.*, XXIV (1982), 73–120; XXV (1983), 37–112.

[2] *Ioannis Cantacuzeni eximperatoris Historiarum libri IV*, ed. L. Schopen (*CSHB*, 1828–32), ii. 36: I, p. 520, ll. 15–20 [cited hereafter as Cantac.].

[3] *Georgii Acropolitae Opera*, ed. A. Heisenberg, I (Leipzig, 1903), p. 24, l. 23–p. 25, l. 2. George Bardanes, Metropolitan of Corfu, later tried to pretend that this had not

successors consistently regarded the rulers of Epiros as rebels with no constitutional rights of their own. In later years those rulers, whether Greek or foreign, coveted the title of Despot. But it was never hereditary and it could be conferred only by a Byzantine emperor. None of the Despots of Epiros, even in the fifteenth century, thought otherwise or presumed to take the title to themselves. Nor did it imply any imperial recognition either of a constitutional or of a hereditary right to an appanage or 'Despotate' in Epiros. The world *despotaton* was in fact Latin and not Greek in its formation, having a geographical and not a political significance; and though it passed into later Greek usage in the Chronicle of the Morea, it was a word never employed by Byzantine writers of the thirteenth century to describe the separatist or 'rebel' state of Epiros.

Other commonly held assumptions about Michael I Doukas and his career have also now been questioned. That he was never a Despot of Epiros is clear enough. It is clear too that he never used the family name of Angelos ascribed to him by modern historians. He called himself Michael Doukas or Komnenos Doukas. His contemporaries sometimes identified him merely as 'the son of John Doukas the *sebastokrator*'. The Latins knew him as 'Michalis', 'Michalitius', or 'Michael Comnianus'. Only the later Greek historians, who were hostile to him and to his successors, designated him as Michael Angelos. Neither he nor his brother Theodore liked to be known by that name. They preferred to emphasise their affinity with the more respectable imperial dynasties by styling themselves Michael or Theodore Komnenos Doukas or Komnenodoukas.[4]

By diplomacy as well as by warfare Michael I succeeded in securing the territory that he had acquired in Epiros and in enlarging its extent. In the division of the spoils among the Latins after 1204, Epiros had been allotted to the Venetians. Its coastline was familiar to their merchants and they could make good use of its northern harbours and offshore islands. In 1205 they occupied Durazzo and in 1207 Corfu. But they were never keen to press their claim by conquering the interior of the country; and in

been the case. R.-J. Loenertz, 'Lettre de Georges Bardanès, métropolite de Corcyre, au patriarche oecuménique Germain II (1226–1227 c.)', *EEBS*, XXXII (1964), 87–118 (= Loenertz, *BFG*, I [Rome, 1970], pp. 467–501), 116 (499), ll. 427–9; cf. ibid., 101–2 (482). See also J. M. Hoeck and R.-J. Loenertz, *Nikolaos-Nektarios von Otranto Abt von Casole. Beiträge zur Geschichte der ost-westlichen Beziehungen unter Innozenz III. und Friedrich II.* (Ettal, 1965), pp. 148–235.

[4] D. I. Polemis, *The Doukai. A Contribution to Byzantine Prosopography* (London, 1968), pp. 87–94; R.-J. Loenertz, 'Aux origines du Despotat d'Epire et de la Principauté d'Achaie', *B*, XLIII (1973), 360–94, especially 362–3. Loenertz here proposed some other reinterpretations of the early career of Michael Doukas and his brother Theodore, to the effect that the 'Michael' who fought and lost a battle against the Franks in Messenia in 1205 was not Michael of Epiros; and that the 'Theodore' mentioned as 'lord of Corinth and Argos' about 1210 cannot be the brother of Michael. But see M. S. Kordoses, Σχέσεις τοῦ Μιχαὴλ Ἀγγέλου Δούκα μὲ τὴν Πελοπόννησο, *Ep. Chron.*, XXII (1980), 49–57.

1210 Michael Doukas persuaded them that he could save them the trouble by consenting to govern Epiros as their agent and in their interests. He became, or pretended to become, the vassal of Venice. He made similar agreements with the crusaders who had occupied Thessaly. Not without reason did the Latins come to regard Michael Doukas as their most perfidious enemy. Within a few years he had broken all his agreements. His army invaded Thessaly, recapturing Larissa and other places. He then attacked Durazzo and Corfu, both of which he had recovered from the Venetians by 1214. When he died, probably early in 1215, it was a fact that he was master of all the land from Naupaktos in the south to Durazzo in the north. But he also controlled a large part of Thessaly; and, while Arta remained his capital, he had transformed the city of Ioannina into a second centre of administration and defence in Epiros.

Michael was succeeded by his half-brother Theodore Komnenos Doukas. Theodore was not content to be governor of a Byzantine province owing a nominal allegiance to an emperor in faraway Nicaea. His ambition was to make Epiros a base for the reconquest from the Latins first of Thessalonica and then of Constantinople itself. In 1217 he made his name more widely known by ambushing and capturing the newly appointed Latin emperor of Constantinople, Peter of Courtenay, who had rashly attempted to reach his capital by the overland route from the west. Then, in a brilliant series of military campaigns, Theodore drove the remaining Latins out of Thessaly and beat back the Bulgarians who had occupied western Macedonia. His armies encircled and laid siege to Thessalonica. Under Theodore the state of Epiros became a serious rival to the Empire of Nicaea. He proclaimed its independence in ecclesiastical as well as political affairs; and he was strongly supported by the officials of church and state whom he appointed without reference to the emperor and the patriarch in Nicaea.[5] The climax of his achievements came in December 1224 when his troops entered Thessalonica. Soon afterwards, perhaps in 1227, he was crowned emperor of the Romans by the autocephalous archbishop of Ochrida, Demetrios Chomatianos. A second Byzantine Empire in exile had been created.[6]

[5] The problem of ecclesiastical relations between Epiros and Nicaea was reconsidered by A. D. Karpozilos, *The Ecclesiastical Controversy between the Kingdom of Nicaea and the Principality of Epiros (1217–1233)* (Thessaloniki, 1973). See also the previously unpublished letters of John Apokaukos edited by Eleni Bees-Sepherles, 'Aus dem Nachlass von N. A. Bees ('Εκ τῶν καταλοίπων τοῦ N. A. Βέη): Unedierte Schriftstücke aus der Kanzlei des Johannes Apokaukos des Metropoliten von Naupaktos (in Aetolien)', *BNJ*, XXI (1971–6), Supplement, 1–243.

[6] Various alternative dates have now been proposed for Theodore's coronation in Thessalonica. L. Stiernon, 'Les origines du Despotat d'Epire (suite). La date du couronnement de Théodore Doukas', *Actes du XIIe Congrès International des Etudes*

It was a short-lived creation, but while it lasted the Empire of Thessalonica extended from Durazzo to Adrianople, from Ochrida to the Gulf of Corinth. In March 1230, when he was within striking distance of Constantinople, Theodore unwisely turned aside to invade Bulgaria. At Klokotnica on the Marica river he was defeated and taken prisoner by the Bulgarian tsar John Asen, who followed up his victory by pouring troops into Macedonia and New Epiros. Thessalonica was allowed to remain Greek under the rule of Theodore's brother Manuel, who continued to call himself emperor. But the empire which he governed was much reduced in size and dependent for its survival on the goodwill of the Bulgarian tsar.[7]

The abrupt collapse of Theodore's empire demonstrated how fragile a structure it was. But the fact that it had been created and the hope that it could be revived fired the imagination of the Greeks of Epiros for many years to come. Theodore contrived to return to Thessalonica in 1237, though not as emperor. He had been blinded during his captivity in Bulgaria. He ejected his brother Manuel and declared his own son John to be emperor in his place. Theodore's humiliation came in the end not from Bulgaria, where John Asen died in 1241, but from Nicaea. In 1242 the emperor of Nicaea, John Vatatzes, marched on Thessalonica and forced John to renounce his imperial title and to accept the lesser dignity of Despot. Four years later Vatatzes took John's brother and reluctant successor Demetrios into captivity. Thessalonica and its surroundings were now annexed to the empire ruled from Nicaea under the command of a military governor appointed from there. There was no longer a rival emperor on European soil.

The rivalry between the Greeks of Nicaea and the Greeks of Epiros had not, however, been extinguished. After Theodore's defeat in 1230 his nephew Michael II, son of the first Michael Doukas, had come back to Arta to claim his heritage. He had been exiled when his father died; and he had married Theodora of the family of Petraliphas, who was later to be revered as Saint Theodora of Arta. The Life of St Theodora, written in the thirteenth century, tells most of what is known about the early career of her husband.[8] Michael Komnenos Angelos Doukas has more claim

Byzantines, II (Belgrade, 1964), 197–202 (between June 1227 and April 1228); A. Karpozilos, 'The date of coronation of Theodore Doukas Angelos', *Byzantina*, VI (1974), 251–61 (end of 1224 or early 1225); Eleni Bees-Sepherles, Ὁ χρόνος στέψεως τοῦ Θεοδώρου Δούκα ὡς προσδιορίζεται ἐξ ἀνεκδότων γραμμάτων Ἰωάννου τοῦ Ἀποκαύκου, *BNJ*, XXI (1971–6), 272–9 (between April and August 1227).

[7] B. Ferjančić, 'Solunski Car Manojlo Angeo (1230–1237). (The Thessalonican Emperor Manuel Angelus (1230–1237))', *Zbornik filosofskog fakulteta*, XIV (1979), 93–101.

[8] L. I. Vranousis, Χρονικὰ τῆς μεσαιωνικῆς καὶ τουρκοκρατουμένης Ἠπείρου (Ioannina, 1962), pp. 49–54, demonstrates that the *Life of St Theodora of Arta* was written by Job Meles or Melias Iasites towards the end of the thirteenth century and not, as I had wrongly

than either his father or his uncle to be called the founder of what came to be known as the Despotate of Epiros. By 1246, when Thessalonica was finally incorporated into the Empire of Nicaea, the people of Epiros and of much of Thessaly had come to acknowledge him as their ruler. He began to see himself as heir to the imperial title in Europe. His ambition was encouraged by his uncle Theodore, who had retired to his castle at Vodena in western Macedonia, where lay the frontier between the territories of Epiros and those of the Empire of Nicaea. In 1251 Michael II tried and failed to cross that frontier. He was obliged to make peace with the Emperor John Vatatzes, who now removed the elderly Theodore from the scene of his earlier triumphs and took him away to end his days as a prisoner in Asia Minor.

The peace between the rival Greek states was to be confirmed by the marriage of the emperor's granddaughter Maria to Michael's son Nikephoros. At the same time both father and son were honoured with the title of Despot graciously bestowed on them by the emperor. The act was calculated to define their state of subservience to his authority.[9] The marriage of Nikephoros to the princess Maria of Nicaea was delayed until 1256, two years after the death of John Vatatzes and the accession of Theodore II Laskaris. It brought not peace but war. For Laskaris imposed certain conditions on the settlement which the Despot Michael thought to be dishonourable and unacceptable. In revenge he took to arms, inciting the Albanians to help him drive out the imperial garrisons from the towns of Macedonia. His initial success inspired him to hope that he too might add Thessalonica to his dominions and restore the rival empire.

The history of Epiros was, however, to be permanently affected by an event that occurred in 1257. In that year Manfred of Hohenstaufen, son of the Emperor Frederick II of Sicily, sent an armada across the sea from Italy and occupied a large stretch of the coast of Albania and New Epiros.[10] Durazzo fell to him as well as the ports of Valona and Kanina and the inland fortress of Berat. Before long he had seized the island of Corfu. These had been prize possessions of the rulers of Epiros. The Despot Michael had been taken by surprise. But he found a way to offset

stated, in the seventeenth century. It is therefore a more reliable authority than had been supposed.

[9] That the title of Despot was conferred on Michael II and his son Nikephoros at the same time was proposed by Ferjančić, *Despoti*, pp. 64–8. Michael may, however, have first been given the title by his uncle, the Emperor Manuel of Thessalonica.

[10] On the relations of Frederick II and Manfred with Nicaea and Epiros, see now E. Merendino, 'Federico II e Giovanni III Vatatzes', *Byzantino-Sicula*, II (1974), 1–15; idem, 'Quattro lettere greche di Federico II', *Atti dell' Accademia di Scienze Lettere e Arti di Palermo*, ser. iv., XXXIV (1974–5), part ii, 291–344; idem, 'Manfredi fra Epiro e Nicea', *Actes du XVe Congrès International d'Etudes Byzantines*, IV. *Histoire* (Athens, 1980), 245–52.

his losses while at the same time winning a powerful ally in his conflict with the Empire of Nicaea. He offered his daughter Helena in marriage to King Manfred. Since her dowry was to consist of most of the places in Epiros which he had already occupied, Manfred was pleased to accept the offer. This unexpected development established a link between Epiros and the south of Italy which was never thereafter to be broken until the Turkish conquest in the fifteenth century. Michael won the support of another foreign ally in the person of William of Villehardouin, the French prince of Achaia, to whom he gave his second daughter Anna in marriage. With the help of Manfred of Sicily and William of Achaia, Michael felt confident to go to war with the emperor of Nicaea for the possession of Thessalonica and then perhaps of Constantinople. The long rivalry between the Greeks of Epiros and the Greeks of Nicaea was now to be fought out on the field of battle.

Theodore II Laskaris, emperor at Nicaea, died in August 1258 leaving an infant son, John IV. He was succeeded first as regent and then as emperor by Michael Palaiologos, known as Michael VIII. It was he who assembled the army, under the command of his brother John Palaiologos, that was to go the defence of Thessalonica against the Despot Michael of Epiros and his foreign allies. The battle that was to determine the future of Epiros, of Nicaea and ultimately of Constantinople and the Byzantine Empire was fought at Pelagonia in Macedonia in the summer of 1259. The grand alliance on which Michael II had pinned his hopes broke up even before the fighting began. Michael and his son Nikephoros decamped by night. His illegitimate son John Doukas deserted to the enemy; and William of Villehardouin and the cavalry that Manfred had sent were cut off and captured. The army of Nicaea then invaded Epiros and Thessaly. The Despot Michael was chased from Arta to Vonitsa and took refuge on the island of Cephalonia with the Orsini family, to whom he was related. Arta, Ioannina and other towns in Epiros as far north as Durazzo were occupied by garrisons of troops from Nicaea. It looked as if the days of Epirote independence were over.

The battle of Pelagonia was the prelude to the reconquest of Constantinople from the Latins. In July 1261 a small force from Nicaea, led by Alexios Strategopoulos who had fought at that battle, entered the city almost by chance. The Latin emperor and his Venetian friends fled; and in August Michael Palaiologos took up residence in Constantinople as emperor of the restored Byzantine Empire. By then, however, Michael of Epiros had rallied. He had sailed back from his island refuge to Vonitsa and from there fought his way into his capital at Arta. His son John had repented and rejoined him with an army of Vlachs from Thessaly. His eldest son Nikephoros had been to Italy and returned with reinforcements supplied by Manfred. The soldiers of Michael VIII who had occupied Epiros were few in number and quickly dispersed. The inhabitants of Arta and Ioannina welcomed the return of their Despot. They made it abundantly clear that they would rather be governed by their native rulers than be incorporated as provincials into the revived Byzantine Empire.

After the recovery of Constantinople in 1261, Michael of Epiros obstinately refused to admit defeat or to recognise the new emperor's jurisdiction over his territory. He rose to the attack again before the year was out. He had the loyalty of his people and he had the support of Manfred of Sicily, who had lost his overseas possessions of Durazzo and Berat. Alexios Strategopoulos, sent out from Constantinople with an army, was defeated, taken prisoner and shipped as a hostage to Italy. Michael's pious wife Theodora tried to restrain her husband. She went on a mission of peace to the emperor and handed him her young son John as a security. But Michael repeatedly thwarted her efforts. In 1262 and again in 1263 the emperor's brother, John Palaiologos, the victor at Pelagonia, came west to enforce the submission of the unruly Despot. But when John was recalled to take command in Asia Minor, Michael II at once broke the peace that had been forced upon him.[11]

The emperor then resolved to deal with the matter in person and marched to Thessalonica at the head of a large army. In the summer of 1264 Michael II was chastened into accepting and signing a more formal and solemn treaty. His son Nikephoros, whose first wife had died, was to marry the emperor's niece, Anna Palaiologina. An uneasy peace was thus established between Epiros and Byzantium. Early in 1265 the emperor sent his niece with an escort to Epiros, where her marriage to Nikephoros took place in the same year. Nikephoros was invited to Constantinople and there the emperor confirmed his right to the title and rank of Despot before sending him home laden with gifts.[12] His father Michael II, the first Despot in Epiros, died some two years later, and he died at peace with the new regime in Byzantium against which he had fought so bitterly. His new daughter-in-law, Anna Palaiologina, hoped that the peace would not be disturbed. As *basilissa* of Epiros, wife of the Despot Nikephoros, Anna was to play a dominant role in its affairs for nearly half a century. She took her cue from her saintly mother-in-law Theodora of Arta, by tempering the aggressive instincts of the male members of the family into which she had married.

[11] The chronology of these events has been rectified by A. Failler, 'Chronologie et composition dans l'Histoire de Georges Pachymère', *REB*, XXXVIII (1980), 77–103.

[12] George Pachymeres, *De Michaele Palaeologo*, ed. I. Bekker (*CSHB*, 1835), iii. 26: I, pp. 242–3 [cited hereafter as Pach., *De Mich. Pal.*]; Nikephoros Gregoras, *Byzantina Historia*, ed. L. Schopen (*CSHB*, 1829–55), iv. 9: I, pp. 109–10 [cited hereafter as Greg.].

I

The restored Despotate – 1267–85

The Despot Michael II, the first of the rulers of Epiros to be so designated, died late in 1267 or early in 1268.[1] He left three legitimate sons, Nikephoros, John and Demetrios. John was in Constantinople, where he had been taken as a hostage in 1261. He had married a daughter of the *sebastokrator* Constantine Tornikios and took no further part in the affairs of Epiros. Demetrios was still a boy.[2] Michael's principal heir was his eldest son Nikephoros, who had already been created a Despot. But he had also to think of his illegitimate son John Doukas, who had more than expiated his treachery at Pelagonia before returning to his castle at Neopatras in southern Thessaly. The bastard John would not have taken kindly to being ignored in the apportionment of his father's estate.

In his will therefore Michael II, whom Gregoras describes as 'ruler of Epiros and Thessaly', divided his dominions between his two sons, Nikephoros and John. The division recognised the fact that Epiros and Thessaly were in many ways separate geographical entities cut off from each other by the Pindos mountains. Gregoras gives the fullest account of the matter, even though he expresses himself in pedantically archaic Greek terms. John Doukas inherited that part of northern and central Greece which comprised the country of the Pelasgians and Phthiotians,

[1] The exact date of his death cannot be determined, but it seems to have occurred between May 1267 and August 1268. See A. Nikarouses, Χρονολογικαὶ ἔρευναι Β΄ – Πότε ἀπέθανε Μιχαὴλ Β΄ ᾿Άγγελος ὁ δεσπότης τῆς ᾿Ηπείρου, *DIEE*, n.s., I (1928), 136–41; B. Ferjančić, 'Kada je umro Despot Michailo II Angeo? (Quand mourut le Despote Michel II Ange?)', *ZRVI*, IX (1966), 29-32; A. Failler, 'Chronologie et composition dans l'Histoire de Georges Pachymère', *REB*, XXXIX (1981), 183–4.

[2] Pach., *De Mich. Pal.*, iii. 27: I, p. 243; iv. 26: I, pp. 307–8 (*CSHB*). Greg. iv. 9: I, pp. 109–10 (*CSHB*). Gregoras errs in saying that John was still in Epiros at the time of his father's death. Cf. D. I. Polemis, *The Doukai. A Contribution to Byzantine Prosopography* (London, 1968), no. 50, p. 95 and n. 8; J. L. van Dieten, *Nikephoros Gregoras, Rhomäische Geschichte, Historia Rhomaike*, I (Stuttgart, 1973), p. 252 n. 202 [cited hereafter as Greg. (van Dieten)]. John was later to be imprisoned and blinded for making too much of a hero of himself in warfare against the Turks at Nicaea. Pach., *De Mich. Pal.*, vi. 24–5: I, pp. 485–93. *Prosopographisches Lexikon der Palaiologenzeit*, ed. E. Trapp and others, I, no. 205 [cited hereafter as *PLP*].

the Thessalians and Ozolian Lokrians, a district bounded on the north by Mount Olympos and on the south by Mount Parnassos. Nikephoros received that part of north-western Greece known as Old Epiros. It included the lands of the Thesprotians, Akarnanians and Dolopes, as well as the islands of Kerkyra (Corfu), Kephallenia (Cephalonia) and Ithaka. It was bounded on the west by the Adriatic and Ionian seas, on the north by the mountains known as Pydnos and Akrokeraunion, on the east by the river Acheloos, and on the south by Corfu and Cephalonia.[3]

Gregoras is careful to define the new Despot's territory as Old Epiros, the district covering the former Theme of Nikopolis, extending from Ioannina in the north to Naupaktos in the south, with its capital at Arta. New Epiros, the country to the north of the Akrokeraunian promontory and the bay of Valona (Avlona) included in the former Theme of Dyrrachion, was no longer within the Despotate. It had been occupied by the Byzantine army after the battle of Pelagonia. The Emperor Michael VIII in his so-called Autobiography claimed that his troops had overrun Epiros, 'both the one and the other', as well as part of Illyria, and had advanced as far as Durazzo.[4] Michael II had succeeded in expelling them from Old Epiros. But when he died they were still in control at least of Durazzo.

Nikephoros therefore inherited a dominion which could hardly be compared in size or prestige with that once ruled by his great-uncle Theodore. But it was of manageable proportions and Nikephoros, if left to his own devices, might have been content, as Pachymeres says he was, to live at peace with his neighbours.[5] He was connected with most of them by marriage. One of his sisters had married the French prince of Achaia, William of Villehardouin, whose principality lay across the water from Naupaktos. Another sister, Helena, had become the wife and was by 1267 the widow of Manfred of Sicily. His own wife, the *basilissa* Anna whom he had married in 1265, was a niece of the Emperor Michael VIII who had confirmed his right to the title of Despot.[6] Nikephoros had the blessing of Byzantium and the support of his friends in Italy whose colonial possessions on the coast of New Epiros, acquired through the marriage of Helena to Manfred, he had the good sense not to contest. His half-brother John Doukas on the other hand was far from content with the little realm in Thessaly which he had inherited. The emperor was able to pacify him for a while by bringing him into the imperial family. John's

[3] Greg. iv. 9: I, p. 110. Cf. Greg (van Dieten), I, p. 251 n. 201.

[4] 'Imperatoris Michaelis Palaeologi De Vita Sua', ed. H. Grégoire, *B*, XXIX-XXX (1959–60), p. 455, c. VII.

[5] Pach., *De Mich. Pal.*, iv. 26: I, pp. 307–8.

[6] D. M. Nicol, *The Despotate of Epiros* (Oxford, 1957), pp. 171–3. On the marriage of Anna to Nikephoros see Pach., *De Mich. Pal.*, iii. 27: I, p. 243.

daughter was married to a nephew of Michael VIII, Andronikos Tarchaneiotes; and John himself, who held no official title, was named *sebastokrator* and so given an honoured place in the Byzantine establishment.[7]

For some years thereafter there was peace between Epiros and the restored Byzantine Empire. The emperor hoped that in due course its rulers and its people would forget their obstinate claim to independence and return to the imperial fold as subjects of the government in Constantinople. His niece, the *basilissa* Anna, whom he had given in marriage to the Despot Nikephoros, might be relied upon to influence her husband in this direction. Anna Palaiologina was the third daughter of John Cantacuzene and Eirene or Eulogia, Michael VIII's favourite sister. She was devoted to the interests of her family in Constantinople and looked for ways of reconciling them with those of her husband in Epiros.[8] It was doubtless thanks to her that Nikephoros remained for so long at peace. His widowed mother, the saintly Theodora, had retired to the convent which she had founded in Arta and renounced the things of this world.[9] She too had tried to be an agent of peace and reconciliation. Her place was now to be taken by Anna who, for the next forty years, was to exercise a dominating and often soothing influence on the affairs of Epiros. But it was not easy for her to undermine the long tradition of independent sovereignty in the Despotate of which her husband was the symbol and the heir. The Epirotes, who had become accustomed to managing their own affairs, were not yet disposed to settling down as the subjects of an emperor in faraway Constantinople.

Both they and the emperor, however, were soon to be made aware that Epiros lay in the path of the most ambitious and determined enemy of the restored Byzantine Empire, Charles of Anjou. Charles, the brother of King Louis IX of France, had emerged as the pope's champion against the Hohenstaufen Manfred of Sicily. In February 1266 he defeated Manfred in battle at Benevento and became effectively king of Naples and Sicily. Manfred's widow Helena, the sister of Nikephoros of Epiros, was condemned to spend the rest of her young life as a prisoner. Two years later, at the battle of Tagliacozzo, Charles of Anjou completed his triumph in Italy by dispossessing the last of the heirs to Manfred's title.[10]

[7] Pach., *De Mich. Pal.*, iv. 26: 1, p. 308. Cf. Failler, *REB*, XXXIX (1981), 184. B. Ferjančić, *Tesalija u XIII i XIV veku* (Belgrade, 1974), pp. 103, 122; idem, 'Sevastokratori u Vizantiji', *ZRVI*, XI (1968), 180–1.

[8] D. M. Nicol, *The Byzantine Family of Kantakouzenos* (*Cantacuzenus*) ca. *1100–1460* (Dumbarton Oaks Studies, XI: Washington, D.C., 1968), no. 16, pp. 20–4.

[9] Job monachus, *Life of St Theodora of Arta*, *MPG*, CXXVII, cols. 907–8. On the author of this work (Job Melias Iasites), see Vranousis, Χρονικὰ Ἠπείρου, pp. 49–54; *PLP*, IV, no. 7959.

[10] The career of Charles of Anjou in so far as it concerned the Byzantine world is treated

Even before that event, however, he had openly proclaimed his intention to mount a campaign or a crusade for the recovery of Constantinople from the Greeks. In May 1267, in the palace of Pope Clement IV at Viterbo, a treaty was drawn up between the parties interested in this project. They were the exiled Latin Emperor Baldwin II; the prince of Achaia, William of Villehardouin; and Charles himself. It was agreed that Villehardouin should acknowledge the suzerainty of the house of Anjou over his principality, on condition that his daughter Isabelle married Charles's son Philip; and that Baldwin should cede to Charles his rights over Achaia and over the possessions of the late Manfred in Epiros and Corfu. Baldwin's reward was to be no less than his own reinstatement as emperor in Constantinople within six years.[11]

The part of the treaty relating to Epiros was signed on 27 May 1267. Baldwin made over to Charles 'all the territory which Michaelicius (Michael II) the Despot had granted... either as dowry or by any other title to his daughter Helena, widow of the late Manfred Prince of Taranto, and which the same Manfred and the late Philip Chinardo, his admiral in the said kingdom, had held as long as they lived'.[12] The Treaty of Viterbo thus affirmed that the dowry which Helena brought to Manfred at the time of their marriage in 1259 now belonged to Manfred's

especially by S. Runciman, *The Sicilian Vespers* (Cambridge, 1958) and D. J. Geanakoplos, *Emperor Michael Palaeologus and the West* (Cambridge, Mass., 1959). Charles briefly toyed with the idea of giving Helena, Manfred's widow, as wife to the Infant Henry of Castile, brother of King Alfonso. G. Del Giudice, *Codice Diplomatico del Regno di Carlo I. et II. d'Angiò*, I (Naples, 1863), no. LVI, pp. 193–6. For the subsequent tragic fate of Helena, see G. Del Giudice, 'La famiglia di re Manfredi', *ASPN*, V (1880), 299–302; G. Schlumberger, 'Le tombeau d'une impératrice byzantine à Valence en Espagne', in *Byzance et Croisades. Pages Médiévales* (Paris, 1927), pp. 74–8; M. A. Dendias, Ἑλένη Ἀγγελίνα Δούκαινα, βασίλισσα Σικελίας καὶ Νεαπόλεως, *Ep. Chron.*, I (1926), 219–94; Runciman, *Sicilian Vespers*, pp. 96–7. After the battle of Benevento she tried to escape to Epiros with her four children, but they were apprehended at Trani and incarcerated in the castle at Nocera, where Helena died in 1271.

[11] There were in fact two treaties, signed on 24 and 27 May 1267. The text of the former is published by C. Perrat and J. Longnon, *Actes relatifs à la principauté de Morée 1289–1300* (Paris, 1967), pp. 207–11. Cf. J. Longnon, *L'Empire latin de Constantinople et la principauté de Morée* (Paris, 1949), pp. 236–7; Geanakoplos, *Emperor Michael*, pp. 197–200; K. M. Setton, *The Papacy and the Levant (1204–1571)*, I: *The Thirteenth and Fourteenth Centuries* (Philadelphia, 1976), pp. 103–5.

[12] Text in G. Del Giudice, *Codice Diplomatico del Regno di Carlo I. e II. d'Angiò*, II (Naples, 1869), no. IV, pp. 30–44; C. DuCange, *Histoire de l'empire de Constantinople sous les empereurs français*, ed. J. A. C. Buchon, I (Paris, 1826), no. 23, pp. 455–63; J. A. C. Buchon, *Recherches et matériaux pour servir à une histoire de la domination française dans les provinces démembrées de l'empire grec*, I (Paris, 1840), pp. 29–37. Partial text in L. de Thallóczy, C. Jireček, E. de Šufflay, *Acta et Diplomata res Albaniae mediae aetatis illustrantia*, I (Vienna, 1913), no. 253, p. 73 [cited hereafter as *ActAlb*]. Cf. E. G. Léonard, *Les Angevins de Naples* (Paris, 1954), p. 104; S. Borsari, 'La politica bizantina di Carlo I d'Angiò dal 1266 al 1271', *ASPN*, n.s., XXXV (1956), 328–30; Geanakoplos, *Emperor Michael*, pp. 197–200; Setton, *Papacy*, I, p. 104.

conqueror, Charles of Anjou. The original extent of that dowry has been the subject of much discussion. It had certainly included the harbour of Valona and the nearby castle of Kanina, as well as the island of Corfu which Manfred had assigned to his admiral Philip Chinardo (or Chinard). Some say that it had also included Durazzo in the north and Butrinto (Bouthrotos) in the south.[13] But at the time of Manfred's death in 1266 his overseas territories had been reduced to more modest dimensions. The city of Durazzo had been occupied by the army of Michael VIII after the battle of Pelagonia in 1259. A Greek bishop, Niketas of Thessalonica, had been appointed to the see by the patriarch before the end of 1260; and Durazzo seems to have remained in Byzantine hands until 1271.[14]

Further to the south in New Epiros, however, Philip Chinardo stayed on as regent over Manfred's territories with his headquarters at Kanina, stubbornly ignoring the fact that the kingdom of Naples was under new management after 1266; while three of his sons held the inland fortress of Berat. In the last years of his life the Despot Michael II of Epiros tried to turn this situation to his own advantage. He arranged a settlement with Chinardo of the kind that he had earlier arranged with Manfred. Chinardo married a sister of Michael's wife Theodora, a widowed lady with a stormy past. Her dowry was declared to be the castle of Kanina and the island of Corfu. But the wedding was hardly over when Michael contrived to have Chinardo ambushed and shot down by assassins. This foul deed is clearly attributed to Michael II and not to his son Nikephoros. It must have been perpetrated in 1266 or early in 1267, since

[13] Sanudo has it that the dowry that Helena originally brought to Manfred in 1259 consisted of Durazzo, Valona and Corfu, which last he made over to his admiral Philip Chinardo. Marino Sanudo Torsello, *Istoria del Regno di Romania*, ed. C. Hopf, *Chroniques gréco-romanes inédites ou peu connues* (Berlin, 1873), p. 107. It is known, however, that by February 1258 Manfred was already in possession of Durazzo, Berat, Valona and the mountains of Spinaritsa. F. Miklosich and J. Müller, *Acta et Diplomata graeca medii aevi sacra et profana*, III (Vienna, 1865), pp. 239–42 [cited hereafter as *MM*]; *ActAlb*, I, no. 246, pp. 71–2. Domenico Forges-Davanzati, in his *Dissertazione sulla seconda moglie del Re Manfredi e su' loro figliuolo* (Naples, 1791), pp. 38–41, maintained that Helena's dowry consisted only of the coastline between Valona and Butrinto; Corfu and Kanina were the possessions of Chinardo, not Manfred. Del Giudice, *ASPN*, III (1878), 19 and IV (1879), 92–3, on the other hand, defines the dowry as Corfu and all the adjacent mainland of Epiros, including Valona, Kanina, Chimara, Sopotos and Butrinto. See *ActAlb*, I, no. 245, p. 71; Nicol, *Despotate*, pp. 166–7, 168 notes 18 and 19, 183 n. 5; Setton, *Papacy*, I, pp. 81–2.

[14] Niketas was appointed bishop of Durazzo by the Patriarch Nikephoros II, who died between October and December 1260. Pach., *De Mich. Pal.*, ii. 22: I, p. 126. For the dates of his patriarchate, see Failler, *REB*, XXXVIII (1980), 45–53. Kanina, Berat and Durazzo are included in the list of towns conquered by John Palaiologos and his army in Pach., *De Mich. Pal.*, ii. 11: I, pp. 106–7. The list appears to be a catalogue of all the towns captured by John Palaiologos during the whole of his campaign against Michael II of Epiros, both before and after the battle of Pelagonia. Cf. Failler, *REB*, XXXVIII (1980), 30–9.

Chinardo is referred to as deceased in the Treaty of Viterbo in May 1267.[15]

By contriving the marriage and then the murder of Philip Chinardo, Michael no doubt hoped to win back at least some of the places in New Epiros that had been appropriated by the late Manfred. To some extent he was successful. For some years after 1267 his son and heir Nikephoros seems to have controlled the coastline south of the bay of Valona and with it the harbour of Butrinto and other towns. But those whom Manfred had appointed to hold Valona, Kanina and Berat refused either to surrender or to admit that Charles of Anjou was now their lord. Valona held out against him under its castellan, Jacques of Baligny (Jacopo de Balsignano), who had been a loyal servant of Philip Chinardo. Charles retaliated by arresting his brother. But not until 1274 was Jacques persuaded to submit. He was granted some land in Italy and another French governor, Henry of Courcelles, was sent to take command of Valona and Kanina. Berat likewise resisted the new regime under the three sons of the late Chinardo; and in Corfu, although an Angevin captain-general was appointed as early as January 1267, it was not until 1272 that Charles of Anjou was fully in control.[16]

His plan was to strike at Constantinople by land, leading his army along the ancient Via Egnatia which ran across the mountains to Thessalonica by way of Berat, Ochrida and Vodena (Edessa). It was the route followed by his Norman predecessors in Italy in the eleventh and twelfth centuries. In 1185 the Normans had got as far as Thessalonica. Its southerly access from the sea was commanded by the castle of Valona, below which lay a large bay and harbour sheltered from all but the north winds. Its northerly access was through the port of Durazzo.[17] It was a

[15] Pach., *De Mich. Pal.*, vi. 32: I, pp. 508–9. The sister-in-law of Michael II, whom he gave in marriage to Chinardo, was Maria Sphrantzaina, widow of one Sphrantzes. She had earlier seduced Constantine Chabaron whom Theodore II Laskaris had appointed as commander of Albanon in 1256. George Akropolites, *Historia*, ed. A. Heisenberg (Leipzig, 1903), pp. 139–40. She was almost certainly privy to the plot to murder Chinardo; and for a while she owned some property in Kanina. See P. J. Alexander, 'A chrysobull of the Emperor Andronicus II in favor of the See of Kanina in Albania', *B*, XV (1940–1), 167–207, especially 197–201. On Chinardo and his family, see E. Bertaux, 'Les Français d'outre-mer en Apulie et en Epire au temps des Hohenstaufen d'Italie', *Revue Historique*, LXXXV (1904), 225–51, especially 241–7.

[16] *ActAlb*, I, no. 267 and pp. 76–7. K. Jireček, 'Valona im Mittelalter', in *Illyrisch-Albanische Forschungen*, ed. L. von Thallóczy, I (Munich–Leipzig, 1916), especially pp. 177–8; Bertaux, *Revue Historique*, LXXXV (1904), 247; W. Miller, 'Valona', *Journal of Hellenic Studies*, XXXVIII (1917), 186–7; Borsari, *ASPN*, n.s., XXXV (1956), 320–8; A. Ducellier, *La Façade maritime de l'Albanie au moyen âge. Durazzo et Valona du XIe au XVe siècle* (Thessaloniki, 1981), pp. 232–6. For the list of feudal lands and properties that went with the castles of Kanina and Valona in 1274, see *ActAlb*, I, no. 319, pp. 93–4.

[17] On the topography of this part of Epiros and Albania, see P. Soustal and J. Koder, *Nikopolis und Kephallēnia* (*TIB*, III: Vienna, 1981) [cited hereafter as Soustal–Koder];

well fortified city and it seemed unlikely that Charles could capture it from its Byzantine garrison. But in March 1271 Durazzo was struck by a devastating earthquake. The city was completely destroyed except for its acropolis. The survivors, among them the Greek bishop Niketas, fled, leaving the ruins to be plundered and occupied by the Albanians who lived in the neighbourhood. The Byzantine army had abandoned it and Durazzo was defenceless.[18]

The Albanian squatters in the ruins made contact with the agents of Charles at Kanina. Before long he was in control of Durazzo and had won the support of the local Albanians. In February 1272 he signed a formal treaty with them and was proclaimed king of Albania by common consent of the 'bishops, counts, barons, soldiers and citizens'. He guaranteed to protect them from their enemies and to honour all the pledges and privileges accorded to them by Byzantine emperors in times past.[19] As vicar-general of his new kingdom of Albania Charles appointed Gazo Chinardo, brother of the late Philip; though he was replaced by a French governor, Anselm of Chaus, in 1273.[20] A Latin archbishop of Durazzo was installed by September 1272.[21] The earthquake must have disrupted the commercial life of the city. The Venetians, who had been accustomed to doing business there, instructed their merchants to bypass it and to make for Arta instead. But its acropolis was intact and its harbour was usable.[22]

N. G. L. Hammond, *Epirus. The geography, the ancient remains, the history and the topography of Epirus and adjacent areas* (Oxford, 1967), especially pp. 130–1; Nicol, *Despotate*, pp. 222–3.

[18] Pach., *De Mich. Pal.*, v. 7: 1, pp. 355–8; vi. 32: 1, p. 508. The earthquake that destroyed Durazzo has often been dated to 1273. See, e.g., V. Grumel, *La Chronologie* (Paris, 1958), p. 481. The reasons for dating it to 1271 are set out in D. M. Nicol, 'The relations of Charles of Anjou with Nikephoros of Epiros', *BF*, IV (1972), 178 and n. 22. Failler, *REB*, XXXIX (1981), 214–19, argues for dating it to 1270. Ducellier, *Albanie*, pp. 176–80, wishes to date it to 1267, which appears to take it right out of the chronological context in which Pachymeres sets it. Nor is he correct in alleging that 'Kronios' in Pachymeres means July–August and not March (ibid., p. 219 n. 129). Cf. G. Arnakis, 'The names of the months in the History of Georgios Pachymeres', *BNJ*, XVIII (1960), 144–53, especially 152. The earthquake was still remembered as a catastrophic event fifty years later. An Irish pilgrim passing through Durazzo in 1323 was told that it had reduced the city to miserable proportions and buried alive 24,000 wealthy citizens beneath the ruins of their houses. *Itinerarium Symonis Semeonis Ab Hybernia ad Terram Sanctam*, ed. M. Esposito (Scriptores Latini Hiberniae, IV: Dublin, 1960), pp. 38–9.

[19] *ActAlb*, I, nos. 268, 269, p. 77 (dated 20 and 21 February 1272); R. Filangieri, *I Registri della Cancelleria Angioina, ricostruiti da Ricardo Filangieri* (Testi e Documenti di Storia Napoletana: Naples, 1950ff.), VIII, pp. 173–4, nos. 435, 436.

[20] *ActAlb*, I, no. 270, p. 77; no. 299, p. 86. Ducellier, *Albanie*, pp. 263–4. For Gazo Chinardo (or Chinard) and Anselm de Chaus, see P. Durrieu, *Les Archives Angevines de Naples. Etudes sur les registres du roi Charles Ier (1265–1285)*, II (Paris, 1887), pp. 304, 315. Cf. Geanakoplos, *Emperor Michael*, pp. 233–5.

[21] *ActAlb*, I, no. 283, p. 81.

[22] F. Thiriet, *Délibérations des Assemblées Vénitiennes concernant la Romanie*, I (Paris-La Haye, 1966), p. 35 (7 November 1272).

Durazzo was to be one of Charles's main bases for his campaign against Constantinople. Throughout the years 1272 and 1273 a series of documents emanating from the kingdom of Naples testifies to the building up of huge stocks of arms, provisions and money in Albania, especially in Durazzo and Valona.[23] Angevin troops penetrated inland as far as Berat, where Gazo Chinardo rounded up his three rebellious nephews and sent them as prisoners to Trani in Apulia. At the same time supplies were being shipped to the Morea, for the prince of Achaia was to be involved in the great enterprise. The Emperor Michael VIII in Constantinople was seriously alarmed. In 1272 he wrote to the leading Albanians of Durazzo and Berat urging them to renounce their allegiance to Charles of Anjou and his captain Chinardo. The Albanians passed the letters on to Charles who thanked them for their loyalty and warned them against the deceitful machinations of the Greek emperor.[24] The Albanians were unpredictable allies, however. Many of them had opted for the Roman Catholic faith and were thus well disposed to obey a king as pious as Charles of Anjou. Some of them felt more affinity with the Greeks than with the Latins. But most of them would prefer to enjoy their independence.[25]

The Emperor Michael's main hope of deterring Charles lay in his negotiations with the papacy. In his view the pope was the only authority able to impose moral restraint on Charles, to sanction or to forbid a holy war for the restoration of the Latin Empire of Constantinople. If the pope could be convinced that the Greeks were ready to heal the schism between the Catholic and Orthodox Churches and profess their obedience to the See of Rome then he would withdraw his support from the venture planned at Viterbo in 1267. The negotiations were long and inconclusive until, in September 1271, Gregory X was elected pope. Gregory took the emperor's proposals and promises seriously and invited him to come or to send delegates to a Council of the Church to be held at Lyons in 1274. There the Byzantine Christians could confess the error of their ways, acknowledge the primacy of Rome and be welcomed back into the fold of the Church universal. They and their emperor would then be assured of the pope's protection against their enemies. Michael VIII could see no

[23] *ActAlb*, I, nos. 273, 275, 287, 288, 291, 295, 297, 304, pp. 78–88. Geanakoplos, *Emperor Michael*, pp. 256–7; Ducellier, *Albanie* pp. 241–2.

[24] C. Minieri-Riccio, *Il Regno di Carlo I d'Angiò negli anni 1271 e 1272* (Naples, 1875), p. 81. *ActAlb*, I, no. 282, p. 80; cf. F. Dolger, *Regesten der Kaiserurkunden des oströmischen Reiches*, III² (Munich, 1977), no. 1993. Geanakoplos, *Emperor Michael*, p. 234; Ducellier, *Albanie*, p. 241; Bertaux, *Revue Historique*, LXXXV (1904), 248.

[25] Pope Innocent IV, in 1250, had been concerned to help certain priests and bishops living under Greek rule in Albania who had expressed a desire to be united to the Roman church. *ActAlb*, I, nos. 199, 200, p. 60; no. 216, p. 66. For the presence of Benedictines, Dominicans and Franciscans in Durazzo by or after 1250, see Ducellier, *Albanie*, pp. 208–9.

other way out of his dilemma. He was afraid that his army was not strong enough to beat back a determined invader from the west. Charles of Anjou was already firmly entrenched in Albania and in the Morea and in alliance with the rulers of Serbia and Bulgaria. Only by doing what the pope asked of them could the Byzantines save themselves from a repetition of the Fourth Crusade.

This clear-cut view of the alternatives before them was not shared by the majority of the emperor's subjects. The clergy and the monks in particular were loud in their condemnation of the idea of union with Rome, at least on Rome's terms. None the less a small delegation of bishops and laymen was in the end sent to the pope's council at Lyons and there, in July 1274, the reunion of the Churches of Rome and Constantinople was declared to have been accomplished. The emperor had his reward. The pope instructed Charles of Anjou to postpone his preparations. Once the news of the union of Lyons reached Constantinople, however, there was uproar. The emperor soon found that he could not impose his will on his church and people. To convince the pope that he was doing his best to enforce the union he took to persecuting and imprisoning its opponents. Not all of them were priests and monks. They included several members of his own family. Michael VIII had always had his political enemies. He had after all usurped the throne from the last of the dynasty of Laskaris to whom many were still devoted. The union of Lyons and its aftermath failed to unite Christendom; but it succeeded in uniting all the disparate elements of the opposition to the Emperor Michael VIII.

Refugees from his persecution made their way to those parts of the Byzantine world where the emperor's word was not law, to Epiros, to Thessaly and to Trebizond. His own sister Eirene, who had in her widowhood become a nun with the name Eulogia, actively encouraged her friends in the church to prepare and disseminate anti-unionist literature and propaganda. She was put in prison and so, like many others, became a martyr for the Orthodox faith. Three of her remarkable daughters followed her example. Theodora Raoulaina, herself a recent widow, was also imprisoned. Maria, wife of the tsar of Bulgaria Constantine Tich, used her influence as a foreign agent of the opposition. Eirene's third daughter was the *basilissa* Anna, wife of the Despot Nikephoros of Epiros. Her instinct had been to work for peace between Epiros and Constantinople. But she could not in conscience agree with the emperor's policy and she was horrified at the way in which he had treated her mother. The union of Lyons gave to Nikephoros and to his half-brother John in Thessaly the opportunity to pose as champions and defenders of the true Orthodox faith. Had not they and their ancestors, when face to face with the heretical Latins in Greece, fought to uphold the purity of that faith which the Emperor Michael had now betrayed? They welcomed the refugees from the capital with open arms; and they felt free and justified in making friends with any foreign powers willing and able to help in overthrowing the impious, Latinophile regime of Michael VIII.[26]

The emperor saw no reason why his negotiations with the pope should prevent him from defending his own frontiers. In the spring of 1274 he ordered his western commanders to attack the bases that Charles of Anjou had established in Albania. Berat was recaptured and became the keypoint in the Byzantine counter-offensive.[27] Michael VIII knew that Charles's hands were tied not only by the moratorium which Pope Gregory had laid on his activities but also by trouble in his own kingdom in Italy. Between 1274 and 1276 there was constant fighting in Albania and New Epiros; and the Byzantine fleet, eagerly assisted by Greek or Genoese pirate ships, made communications between Italy and the mainland increasingly difficult.[28] Durazzo and Valona, though hard pressed, remained under Angevin control, as did Corfu; and the Albanian fortress of Kroia in the mountains to the north-east of Durazzo seems to have sided with Charles of Anjou at least from 1277.[29] But the harbour of Butrinto was taken over by the Byzantine army. Butrinto lay on the mainland opposite the northern tip of Corfu, well to the south of Valona and probably well within the frontiers of Old Epiros, which the Despot Nikephoros considered to be his own domain.[30]

When Byzantine troops entered Butrinto it was their first incursion into the Despotate of Epiros. Nikephoros needed no further persuasion

[26] For the opposition of Eirene-Eulogia and her daughters and her imprisonment, see Pach., *De Mich. Pal.*, vi. 1: I, p. 427; *De Andron. Pal.*, i. 2: II, pp. 14–15. Cf. Nicol, *Byzantine Family of Kantakouzenos*, nos. 14, 15, 16, pp. 16–24.

[27] C. Minieri-Riccio, *Il regno di Carlo I° d'Angiò, dal 2 gennaio 1273 al 7 gennaio 1285*, *ASI*, ser. 3, XXIII (1876), 240 (Letter of Charles of Anjou of 24 August 1274); *ActAlb*, I, no. 323, p. 94. In January 1277 the imperial commander of Berat and Spinaritsa to the north of Valona was one Stanos *sebastos*. G. L. F. Tafel and G. M. Thomas, *Urkunden zur älteren Handels- und Staatsgeschichte der Republik Venedig*, III (Vienna, 1857), p. 182: 'Stano Savasto, capitaneo Belgradi et Spinarize pro domino imperatore...'; *ActAlb*, I, no. 368, p. 109; cf. no. 491, p. 147.

[28] For the campaigns in Albania and Epiros in 1274–6, see especially Geanakoplos, *Emperor Michael*, pp. 279–80; Ducellier, *Albanie*, pp. 242–7.

[29] *ActAlb*, I, nos. 373, 401, 403, 404, pp. 110–11, 119–21.

[30] The Byzantine capture of Butrinto may have occurred as early as 1274. But the first mention of a Byzantine governor there is in May 1277, when Butrinto is described as being an imperial fortress commanded by a captain called Lithorites. Tafel and Thomas, *Urkunden*, III, p. 243: 'Butrinto, castrum domini Imperatoris, cuius erat capitaneus quidam vocatus Lithoriti...'. K. Hopf, *Geschichte Griechenlands vom Beginn des Mittelalters bis auf unsere Zeit*, I (Leipzig, 1867) [hereafter cited as Hopf, *GG*], p. 300, supplies Lithorites with the name Theodoros. Cf. I. A. Romanos, Περὶ Βουθρωτοῦ, *DIEE*, III (1891) (reprinted in Ἰ. Ῥωμανοῦ ἱστορικὰ ἔργα, ed. K. Daphnes [Kerkyra, 1959]), p. 112; Soustal–Koder, pp. 132–4.

to throw in his lot with the foreign enemies of the Byzantine emperor. He got in touch with Charles of Anjou and with William of Villehardouin. William now held the principality of Achaia under suzerainty of Charles, and he was a brother-in-law of Nikephoros. On 12 June 1276 Charles ordered him to act as proxy in extracting an oath of homage from his relative Nikephoros Komnenos Doukas. In return for his allegiance Nikephoros was to be granted some landed property in Achaia.[31] This seems to have been the first step towards the establishment of a direct feudal relationship between the Despot of Epiros and the king of Naples. In the following year two separate embassies are known to have crossed from Epiros to Italy. The first was led by one 'Sotinos Lauros' and returned to Greece in April 1277. The second consisted of two envoys named as 'Stomatos' and 'Focinos'. They went home by way of Brindisi in October 1277.[32]

There is no record of the business done by these ambassadors. But there can be little doubt that they were empowered to discuss the terms of a formal alliance between the Despot Nikephoros and King Charles. Charles knew what he was about. He was aware that the Emperor Michael VIII had embittered many of his subjects and most of his potential allies by enforcing the union of Lyons after 1274. Angevin agents were in contact with Constantine Tich of Bulgaria whose Greek wife, the sister of Anna of Epiros, was such a bitter enemy of that union. They were also in contact with John Doukas of Thessaly, the most troublesome of all Michael VIII's Greek enemies. John had fought off a Byzantine attempt to bring him to heel in 1272–3, in the course of which he had called on the help of the French duke of Athens, John de la Roche.[33] The duke of Athens, like the prince of Achaia, was a vassal of Charles of Anjou. It was

[31] Minieri-Riccio, *ASI*, ser. 3, xxv (1877), p. 181; Filangieri, *Registri*, xiii, p. 173, no. 500. Cf. C. De Lellis, *Regesta Chartarum Italiae. Gli Atti perduti della Cancelleria Angioina*, ed. R. Filangieri, part i: *Il Regno di Carlo I*, ii, ed. B. Mazzoleni (Rome, 1942), p. 123, no. 929. Hopf, *GG*, i, p. 301, maintains that Nikephoros swore to become Charles's vassal in July 1276.

[32] Minieri-Riccio, *ASI*, ser. 3, xxvi (1877), 14, 421; Filangieri, *Registri*, xv, p. 42, no. 171 (14 April 1277); xix, p. 30, no. 110 (4 October 1277). Cf. Geanakoplos, *Emperor Michael*, p. 328 n. 89; Nicol, *BF*, iv (1972), especially 181–2.

[33] The abortive Byzantine campaign against Thessaly by land and sea is described by Pach., *De Mich. Pal.*, iv. 31 : 1, pp. 324–30; by Greg. iv. 9: 1, pp. 110–16; and by Sanudo, ed. Hopf, *Chroniques*, pp. 120–2. It is dated to 1275 by Geanakoplos, *Emperor Michael*, pp. 282–3 and by Ferjančić, *Tesalija*, pp. 105–8; and to 1271 by Setton, *Papacy*, i, pp. 423–4. For the more correct date of 1272–3, see P. Magdalino, 'Notes on the last years of John Palaiologos, brother of Michael VIII', *REB*, xxxiv (1976), 143–9; Failler, *REB*, xxxix (1981), 189–92. The daughter of John of Thessaly, Helena, subsequently married William, the younger brother of John de la Roche, a union which brought Thessaly into close alliance with the Duchy of Athens. Pach., *De Mich. Pal.*, iv. 31 : 1, p. 328; Sanudo, ed. Hopf, p. 136; *Chron. Mor. fr.* (= *Livre de la Conqueste de la Princée de l'Amorée. Chronique de Morée (1204–1305)*, ed. J. Longnon [Paris, 1911]), c. 879, p. 348.

natural that his new friend John of Thessaly should become a party to the grand alliance against the emperor in Constantinople. There is documentary proof that he did so precisely in 1273 and that he was on cordial terms with Charles of Anjou for several years thereafter. Charles addressed him as 'carissimus amicus'. The record of their dealings is in fact sparse and tells only of commercial transactions such as the purchase of horses or the sale of silk. But the Emperor Michael evidently thought that John of Thessaly was something more than an innocent friend of his enemy in Italy. The envoys whom Michael sent to Pope Innocent V in 1276 represented John as being in league with Charles and with his son Philip and they urged the pope to excommunicate him. There is no evidence, however, that he ever became a declared vassal of the kingdom of Naples. Thessaly lay somewhat off the route for the march from Albania to Constantinople.[34]

On the other hand, John of Thessaly made more political capital than his brother Nikephoros out of his real or affected moral indignation over the union of Lyons. In the winter of 1276–7 the patriarch of Constantinople, John Bekkos, called a council to confirm that union and to excommunicate all who refused to accept it.[35] Almost at the same time a council was convened in Thessaly. It was attended by about a hundred monks, a number of abbots and eight bishops, some of them undoubtedly refugees from Constantinople. They solemnly condemned as heretics the patriarch, the emperor and the pope.[36] Nikephoros seems not to have been party to this council but he was clearly in sympathy with its conclusions. For early in 1277 the emperor sent special messengers to him and to John to try to persuade them to desist from their anti-unionist activities. When he saw that they were not to be persuaded he sent each of them the sentence of excommunication laid upon all opponents of the union of Lyons.[37] The sentence was reaffirmed on 16 July 1277 with express mention of the Despot Nikephoros and the *sebastokrator* John Doukas.[38]

To be excommunicated by a patriarch whom both men regarded, or

[34] See Nicol, *BF*, IV (1972), 181 and n. 26.

[35] R.-J. Loenertz, 'Mémoire d'Ogier, protonotaire, pour Marco et Marchetto, nonces de Michel VIII Paléologue auprès du Pape Nicolas III (1278, printemps–été)', in Loenertz, *Byzantina et Franco-Graeca*, I (Rome, 1970), pp. 563 (no. 28), 564 (no. 35) (reprinted from *OCP*, XXXI [1965], 374–408). A slightly different chronology has been proposed by V. Laurent and J. Darrouzès, *Dossier grec de l'Union de Lyon (1273–1277)* (Paris, 1976), pp. 73–7, 101.

[36] Loenertz, 'Mémoire d'Ogier', p. 555, cc. 15–16; p. 563 (no. 29) ('1276–1277, automne–hiver').

[37] Ibid., pp. 552–3, cc. 6, 7; pp. 563–4 (nos. 31, 33). Cf. Dölger, *Regesten*, III², no. 2026 a.

[38] Loenertz, 'Mémoire d'Ogier', p. 565 (no. 38). V. Laurent, *Les Regestes des Actes du Patriarcat de Constantinople*, I: *Les Actes des Patriarches*, fasc. IV: *Les Regestes de 1208 à 1309* (Paris, 1971), no. 1435.

professed to regard, as the political lackey of a heretical emperor can have been no great hardship. But the emperor was infuriated by their obstinacy. Later in the year 1277 he sent an army to force them into submission. It was commanded by one of his own cousins and two of his nephews. They got no further than Thessaly. There they informed John Doukas that they had no intention of fighting him because they shared his sentiments. Instead they encouraged him to invade the emperor's territory with impunity. They were relieved of their commands, arrested and thrown into prison. New officers were sent out to replace them, but they came to grief in Thessaly largely through their own incompetence. Michael VIII had aroused so much hostility by his unionist policy that it was hard for him to find capable officers whom he could trust, even from among his own relatives.[39]

The popes became increasingly sceptical about the true nature of the union that had been proclaimed and especially about the emperor's success in making it acceptable to the Greeks. In 1278 the emperor tried to reassure Pope Nicholas III that he was doing everything in his power to silence the opposition by sending him a report drawn up by his Latin protonotary Ogerius. The report implied that the pope might lend a hand by joining in the excommunication of the anti-unionists, not least of the 'apostates and rebels' Nikephoros of Epiros and John of Thessaly. The emperor particularly lamented the fact that both were so powerfully aided and abetted in their mischief by the Latins of Athens, of Negroponte and of the Morea.[40] It was indeed a curious state of affairs that the two Byzantine 'rebels' in northern Greece should so loudly proclaim themselves protectors of the purest Orthodoxy while relying so heavily on the support of their Catholic neighbours.

The emperor tried to undermine the opposition in Epiros by dividing the ranks of the ruling family. Demetrios, the younger brother of Nikephoros, had come of age. He was no longer content to live under his brother's wing and he was known to be dissatisfied with his meagre share of his patrimony. He took to calling himself Michael as an act of piety to the memory of his father. Pachymeres implies that the emperor had already promised to make him his son-in-law. The ground had been prepared when the message reached him that the emperor would grant him the title of Despot and the hand of a princess in marriage if he would defect and come to Constantinople. Demetrios-Michael saw more prospects for his career there than in Epiros and in 1277 or 1278 he left his native land.[41] The emperor kept his promise. In November 1278 the

[39] Loenertz, 'Mémoire d'Ogier', pp. 543–5, 553, cc. 8–10; p. 565 (no. 39); Pach., *De Mich. Pal.*, v. 27: I, pp. 411–12.

[40] Loenertz, 'Mémoire d'Ogier', p. 556, c. 18.

[41] Pach., *De Mich. Pal.*, vi. 6: I, p. 439.

Patriarch John Bekkos issued a special dispensation for the marriage of Michael Komnenos, son of the late Despot Michael II Doukas, to Anna Palaiologina Komnene, daughter of the Emperor Michael VIII. The text of this document exists, unnecessary though it seems to have been. The partners to the marriage were distantly related; but, as the patriarch pointed out, a sixth degree of affinity had not constituted an impediment to marriage for partners of imperial rank since the Sixth Oecumenical Council.[42] Demetrios-Michael thus became, as it were, Despot of Epiros in exile, officially recognised as such and legitimately married to the emperor's daughter; and he took an almost feudal oath of allegiance, swearing to be 'the servant of the emperors'.[43]

The defection of his brother combined with his excommunication by the patriarch stirred Nikephoros to action. In 1278 he drove the emperor's troops out of Butrinto which they had occupied some months before.[44] At the same time he resolved to make his alliance with Charles of Anjou more formal and more effective. Charles had recently become even more of a power in the land. For when William of Villehardouin died in May 1278 his principality of Achaia passed under the direct rule of the kingdom of Naples. Thenceforth for several years it was to be administered by deputies or baillies as a colony of the Angevin empire. William had been the last hereditary Prince of Achaia. His widow Anna was a sister of Nikephoros of Epiros. Before long she was to take as her

[42] Ibid., pp. 440–1. As Pachymeres points out, the emperor's daughter Anna was a first cousin of Anna, wife of the Despot Nikephoros: while Michael and Nikephoros were brothers. The dispensation of November 1278 is published by M. Gedeon, Νέα βιβλιοθήκη ἐκκλησιαστικῶν συγγραφέων, I (Constantinople, 1903), cols. 106–8, and again in Ἀρχεῖον ἐκκλησιαστικῆς ἱστορίας, I (1911), 48–50). See Laurent, *Regestes*, no. 1441, pp. 234–5. Anna died before 1299 and in 1300 Michael married the former wife of Stephen Milutin of Serbia. Pach., *De Andron. Pal.*, iv. 13: II, p. 304; Greg. vi. 9: I, pp. 203–4. Cantac. i. 43: I, p. 211, describes him as 'one of the archons of (Neo) Patras and Thessaly'. This is surely an error. See Failler, *REB*, XXXIX (1981), 238 n. 14. Greg., I, p. 204 calls him Michael ὁ Κουτρούλης. On the name or nickname of Koutroulis, see the references collected by Polemis, *The Doukai*, no. 51, p. 96 n. 3. *Chron. Mor.* (= *Chronicle of the Morea*, ed. P. P. Kalonaros [Athens, 1940]), l. 3470, attributes the name to Nikephoros of Epiros. *Chron. Mor. arag.* (= *Libro de los Fechos et Conquistas del Principado de la Morea*, ed. A. Morel-Fatio [Geneva, 1885]), c. 53, describes the father of Nikephoros and Demetrios-Michael as '... dispot de la Arta, Quir Miqali, dicho Crutuli et senyor de la Blaquia'. For others of the same name, see A. Bon, *La Morée franque* (Paris, 1969), p. 208 n. 1, 242 ('Stephanus Cutrullus'), pp. 240, 242, 266 n. 3 (Nicholas Koutroulis). For Koutroulis meaning 'beardless' or 'bald', see H. Moritz, *Die Zunamen bei den byzantinischen Historikern und Chronisten* (Programm des K. humanistischen Gymnasiums in Landshut, II [1897–8]), p. 49.

[43] Pach., *De Mich. Pal.*, vi. 6: I, p. 441 ll. 4–5: καὶ ἦν ἐντεῦθεν ὁ μὲν Μιχαὴλ βασιλεῦσι δοῦλος ἐν ὅρκοις ....

[44] Butrinto was still in Byzantine control in May and June 1277. Tafel and Thomas, *Urkunden*, III, pp. 226, 243, 272–3. But it was evidently in the possession of Nikephoros by March 1279.

second husband the baillie of Achaia, Nicholas of St Omer.[45] Nikephoros could not make Charles of Anjou his son-in-law, as his father had done with Manfred. But he could employ somewhat similar tactics in order to promote their common cause of embarrassing the emperor in Constantinople. He could cede to the Angevin kingdom of Albania the few strategic assets that he had to offer. On 14 March 1279 Nikephoros declared himself to be the vassal of Charles and handed over to him not only Butrinto, which he had recently recaptured, but also the towns of Sopotos and Panormos. As a pledge of his goodwill he delivered his son Michael to the Angevin castellan of Valona, to be transported to Clarentza in the Morea, there to be held as a hostage.[46]

The details of the transaction were worked out in a number of diplomatic exchanges a few weeks later. The three envoys whom Nikephoros had sent to Italy to negotiate the cession of Butrinto passed through Apulia on their way home on 8 April 1279. The local harbour-masters were ordered to grant them free exit from the country with their horses as the respected ambassadors of the Despot Nikephoros Komnenos Doukas. Among them was a Franciscan Friar Giacomo, whom one is not surprised to find acting as an intermediary between Italy and Greece. The other envoys are named as 'Kirio Magulco' and 'Niccolo Andricopolo', perhaps Andritsopoulos, an Epirote family known from other sources.[47] While they were in Italy, however, Charles had sent two ambassadors of his own to Nikephoros to draft the text of a formal treaty. Their names were Roger, archbishop of Santa Severina, and the knight Ludovico de Roheriis or Royer. On 10 April Charles empowered them to receive in his name the Despot's oath of homage and his signature to the draft.[48] But Charles did not wait for the formalities to be completed. On the same day he also empowered his captain and vicar-general of Corfu, Giordano di San Felice, to secure the submission from the Despot Nikephoros not only of the castle of Butrinto but also of all the other castles, villages and lands which Manfred and Philip Chinardo had once held and which were now in the Despot's territory.[49]

[45] Longnon, *L'Empire latin*, pp. 251–8; Bon, *Morée*, p. 156.

[46] Del Giudice, *ASPN*, IV (1879), 361 n. 2. Cf. *ActAlb*, I, no. 390, p. 114 note.

[47] Minieri-Riccio, *ASI*, ser. 4, II (1878), 198. Sp. Lambros, Ἄννα ἡ Καντακουζηνή. Βυζαντιακὴ ἐπιγραφὴ ἐξ Αἰτωλίας, *NH*, I (1904), 41–2, identifies this 'Nicholaum Andracopolum' with a son or brother of Kosmas Andritsopoulos known as a writer and founder of a church at Mokista in Aitolia. See *PLP*, I, no. 940; and see below, pp. 242, 247.

[48] Minieri-Riccio, *ASI*, ser. 4, II (1878), 199. For Lodovico de Roheriis or Loys de Royer, see Durrieu, *Les Archives angevines*, II, p. 375; Filangieri, *Registri*, XX, p. 222, no. 580, and index *s.v.* Geanakoplos, *Emperor Michael*, p. 328, writes that Ludovico 'received the homage of Nikephoros for his sovereign' at Clarentza in 1278. Hopf, *GG*, I, p. 323, says that the two ambassadors went to Epiros to receive the Despot's oath of homage. Cf. Longnon, *L'Empire latin*, p. 259.

[49] Minieri-Riccio, *ASI*, ser. 4, II (1878), 199; *ActAlb*, I, no. 390, pp. 113–14; Del Giudice,

This arrangement resulted in the extension of the Angevin kingdom of Albania well into Old Epiros and the surrender by Nikephoros of a number of places on the coast to the south of the bay of Valona and the Akrokeraunian promontory. Charles of Anjou claimed with some justice that they had all once belonged to the overseas possessions of Manfred and Chinardo and that Nikephoros had reoccupied them. From north to south they were Chimara, Panormos, Sopotos and Butrinto. Chimara, now Himara in Albania, was an ancient city known for its mineral springs. It was a suffragan bishopric of the Metropolis of Naupaktos.[50] Panormos is to be identified with the port in the bay of Panermon, the modern Porto Palermo, a few miles to the south of Chimara.[51] Sopotos (or Subotum) has for long been confused with the offshore islands and port known in antiquity as Sybota, opposite the northern tip of Corfu. In fact Sopotos lay a few miles further to the south of Chimara, close to the present Albanian village of Supot.[52] Butrinto, Sopotos and Chimara were sufficiently close together for them to be placed under the command of one Angevin castellan.[53] The final details were arranged by yet more envoys from Nikephoros who set out for home from Barletta and Brindisi on 12 April 1279.[54]

Nikephoros continued to rule over most of Old Epiros, from Butrinto to the Gulf of Corinth. But he had lost status as well as territory. He was now not simply an ally but a vassal and subject of Charles of Anjou. The Despotate of Epiros had been declared to be a colony of the Angevin kingdom of Naples on much the same terms as the principality of Achaia, although under its native ruler. The whole eastern seaboard of

ASPN, IV (1879), 361 no. 6 (who gives the date as 12 April). A. Mustoxidi, *Delle Cose Corciresi* (Corfu, 1848), p. 443, who describes this document, dates it to 1278. For Giordano di San Felice (Iordanus de Sancto Felice), see Durrieu, *Les Archives angevines*, II, p. 385.

50 Soustal–Koder, pp. 136–7.

51 Ibid., pp. 224–5.

52 Ibid., p. 262. According to Hopf, *GG*, I, p. 323, one of Chinardo's men had begun to build a castle at Sopotos. See also P. Soustal, 'Sybota und Sopotos', *Ep. Chron.*, XXII (1980), 35–8, correcting Nicol, *BF*, IV (1972), 197 n. 41; Ducellier, *Albanie*, p. 217 n. 99.

53 Del Giudice, *ASPN*, V (1880), 317; *ActAlb*, I, no. 342, p. 130. The evidence for the inclusion of Vonitsa in the transaction, as indicated by Hopf, *GG*, I, p. 323, and by Geanakoplos, *Emperor Michael*, p. 328, is lacking. Léonard, *Les Angevins de Naples*, p. 134 (citing L. Halphen, *L'Essor de l'Europe XIe–XIIIe siècles* [Paris, 1932], p. 492) writes that Charles, having persuaded Nikephoros to give him Butrinto, 'puis il s'assure deux autres bases de débarquement sur la côte d'Epire, à Mourtoï (*sic*), en face de l'extrémité méridionale de l'île de Corfou, et a Vénitza (*sic*), sur le golfe d'Arta'. No source is quoted for this information. Hopf, *GG*, I, p. 323, writes of Angevin garrisons in Butrinto, Sybota and Vonitsa in 1280, under the command of one Peter de Gloriano. 'Mourtoï' could refer to Murtos, an alternative name for the modern village of Sybota to the south of Igoumenitsa. Soustal–Koder, p. 267.

54 Minieri-Riccio, *ASI*, ser, 4, II (1878), 199.

the Balkan peninsula from Durazzo down was now under suzerainty to Charles of Anjou. His network of alliances covered the northern Balkan kingdoms of Serbia and Bulgaria; and he was almost ready to mount his great offensive along the Via Egnatia from Albania first to Thessalonica and then to Constantinople.[55] Pachymeres reports that his hopes of victory were so high that his officers were beginning to divide the towns and provinces of the Byzantine Empire among themselves, as the leaders of the Fourth Crusade had done in 1204.[56]

On 13 August 1279 Charles appointed as commander-in-chief of all his Albanian and Epirote territories a knight from Burgundy, Hugues le Rousseau de Sully. His title was captain and vicar-general of Albania, Durazzo, Valona, Sopotos, Butrinto and Corfu. In the following months soldiers, weapons, horses and siege engines were shipped across from Italy in enormous quantities. The offensive was to begin with the capture, or recapture, of Berat which was still strongly garrisoned by Byzantine forces.[57] The part played in these preparations by the Despot Nikephoros is not told, nor is it recorded that he provided any soldiers as the vassal of Charles. But his support and perhaps also his advice on local conditions must have been valuable; and his messengers are known to have passed back and forth to Italy in August 1279 and again in March 1280. Nikephoros was certainly aware of what was happening to the north of his Despotate and of the aim and object of the enterprise.[58]

The emperor in Constantinople still clung desperately to the hope that his Latin enemies would be restrained by the pope. But the facade of the union of the churches had worn thin. In August 1280 Pope Nicholas III died and for six months there was no pope to impose restraint. In February 1281 Charles of Anjou secured the election of a French pope, Martin IV, who could be relied upon to bless his expedition as a crusade.[59] By then the crusade had already begun. In the summer of 1280 Hugues de Sully led his army of about eight thousand men inland from

[55] Pach., *De Mich. Pal.*, vi. 32: I, p. 509; Greg. v. 6: I, p. 146; Sanudo, ed. Hopf, pp. 129, 131.

[56] Pach., *De Mich. Pal.*, vi. 32: I, p. 509 ll. 11–14.

[57] Minieri-Riccio, *ASI*, ser. 4, II (1878), 355. For Sully and his preparations for the campaign in Albania and Epiros in 1279 and 1280, see especially Geanakoplos, *Emperor Michael*, p. 329f. and references; Setton, *Papacy*, I, pp. 135–6; Ducellier, pp. 250–5.

[58] On 15 August 1279 Charles ordered his harbour-master at Brindisi to issue an exit permit to Theodore, ambassador of the Despot Nikephoros Komnenos Doukas, returning home with his mission accomplished; and on 14 March 1280 Simone di Belvedere, vice-admiral of the coast from Tronto to Cotrone, was ordered to hold one ship ready in the harbour at Brindisi to transport 'to the Morea' the returning envoys of the Despot Nikephoros. Minieri-Riccio, *ASI*, ser. 4, II (1878), 356; III (1879), 8. Reinforcements were sent to the castles of Butrinto and Sopotos at the end of March 1280 (ibid., 9).

[59] Runciman, *Sicilian Vespers*, pp. 190–1; Geanakoplos, *Emperor Michael*, pp. 340–1; Setton, *Papacy*, I, pp. 134–5.

Durazzo to lay siege to the fortress of Berat, the gateway to Macedonia.[60] When the news reached Constantinople the emperor at once ordered reinforcements to be rushed to the scene. They were commanded by his Grand Domestic, Michael Tarchaneiotes, and the *megas stratopedarches* John Synadenos. With them went the renegade brother of Nikephoros of Epiros, Demetrios-Michael. He had little experience as a soldier; but he probably knew the terrain and he might be able to dissuade his brothers Nikephoros and John of Thessaly from collaborating with the enemy.[61]

The siege of Berat continued throughout the winter of 1280. Tarchaneiotes, who arrived there with his army early in 1281, managed to relieve the hungry garrison and inhabitants by loading food on to rafts and floating them down the river by night.[62] He hoped to avoid an open battle; and his hope was realised. For the impetuous Hugues de Sully lost patience with the Byzantine tactics and rode out to reconnoitre with only a small bodyguard. He was ambushed by some Turkish mercenaries in the Byzantine army. His horse was shot from under him and he was captured. When they heard that their commander had been taken his men at once turned and fled in panic, eagerly pursued by the Byzantine cavalry. Only those who got across the Vjosa (Booses) river in time escaped and made their way to the coast at Kanina. Most of the officers and soldiers of the Angevin army were rounded up by Tarchaneiotes and his men together with a mass of booty. They were taken in chains to Constantinople, where the giant figure of Hugues de Sully with his flaming red hair was paraded as the showpiece in a triumphal procession through the streets.[63]

The rout of the Latins at Berat in April 1281 was a famous victory. The Emperor Michael VIII was so proud of it that he had scenes of the battle painted on the walls of the Blachernai palace; and years later Pachymeres and the monk Maximos Planoudes could still recall the memorable sight of the imperial triumph in Constantinople.[64] The event was commemorated in another form nearer the scene of the victory. In the monastery church of the Virgin at Apollonia to the north of Valona are the faded vestiges of a wall-painting portraying the Emperor Michael VIII, his wife Theodora

[60] Pach., *De Mich. Pal.*, vi. 32: I, pp. 509–10, gives a vivid description of the impregnability and strategic position of Berat (Bellagrada). Cf. A. Baçe, 'Qyteti i fortifiknar i Beratit', *Monumentet*, II (1971), 43–58.

[61] Pach., *De Mich. Pal.*, vi. 32: I, p. 512. The fourth commander was Andronikos Eonopolites. Cf. Greg. v. 6: I, pp. 146–8; Sanudo, ed. Hopf, p. 129.

[62] The river was the Osumi (Asounes) which, as Pachymeres says, flows below the fortress of Berat.

[63] Pach., *De Mich. Pal.*, vi. 32: I, pp. 512–16; Greg. v. 6: I, pp. 147–8; Sanudo, ed. Hopf, p. 129. Cf. Runciman, *Sicilian Vespers*, pp. 195–6; Setton, *Papacy*, I, pp. 136–7. On the significance of the battle at Berat, see especially Geanakoplos, *Emperor Michael*, pp. 330–4; Ducellier, *Albanie*, p. 255.

[64] Pach., *De Mich. Pal.*, vi. 32: I, pp. 515–19. *Maximi monachi Planudis epistulae*, ed. M. Treu (Breslau, 1890), no. CXII, p. 151 (cf. p. 264).

and his son and heir presumptive Andronikos II. Beside the emperor stands the figure of the Theotokos holding a model of the church. This imperial portrait group is the first of its kind in Byzantine monumental art. It set a fashion for future emperors and princes. The inscription painted into the group records the privileges of the monastery of Apollonia as they had been bestowed and renewed by former emperors and now confirmed by the reigning Emperor Michael Palaiologos. It is obviously a copy of a chrysobull issued in 1281/2 by the emperor to the monastery, by way of a thankoffering for the recent victory of his army in that region. Michael VIII is entitled 'the New Constantine', the name by which he liked to be known as the restorer of the empire. The picture and its legend form a bold and proud statement of the fact that this corner of the Byzantine world was now again united with the city of Constantine.[65]

The Byzantine army followed up its victory by advancing on the Angevin bases at Valona and Kanina to the south and on Durazzo to the north. The Albanians of Kroia in the mountains behind Durazzo quickly sensed that change was in the air and sought the friendship of the Byzantine emperor. Soon after July 1281 Michael VIII rewarded them with a charter of privileges for their city and their bishopric.[66] Durazzo and Valona, though besieged, held out for some years more. In December 1281 the captain of Durazzo, John Lescot (Giovanni Scotto), sent urgent appeals to Italy for reinforcements.[67] It was reported that the emperor's son, presumably Andronikos, was on his way west with a large infantry and cavalry force.[68] Lescot's successor, Guillaume Bernard (Guglielmo Bernardi), appointed in May 1283, was a son of a former Marshal of the kingdom of Albania who knew the country well.[69] But his name disappears from the records after 1284; and by 1288 Durazzo was evidently in Byzantine control, for in October of that year the new Emperor Andronikos II renewed the privileges which his father and former emperors had granted to the Albanians of Kroia, specifically exempting them from the payment of tax on their trade with Durazzo.[70]

[65] H. and H. Buschhausen, *Die Marienkirche von Apollonia in Albanien* (Vienna, 1976), especially pp. 141–82.

[66] *ActAlb*, I, no. 456, p. 135. Cf. Dölger, *Regesten*, III², no. 2058.

[67] Minieri-Riccio, *ASI*, ser. 4, IV (1879), p. 18; *ActAlb*, I, no. 460, pp. 137–8 (cf. no. 457, pp. 135–6).

[68] *ActAlb*, I, no. 462, p. 138: '... filius Palialogi (!) scismatici inimici nostri dicebatur cum maximo equitum et peditum armatorum exercitu adventurus ...'. *ActAlb*, I, no. 461, p. 138. Cf. Geanakoplos, *Emperor Michael*, p. 334 n. 120. For Jean Lescot (Giovanni Scotto), see Durrieu, *Les Archives angevines*, II, p. 338.

[69] *ActAlb*, I, no. 473, pp. 141–2.

[70] The latest thirteenth-century document referring to an Angevin captain and castellan of Durazzo, Guillaume Bernard and Michael Sardus, is dated 20 October 1284. *ActAlb*, I, no. 494, p. 148. A Byzantine bishop (? Niketas) was reelected to the see of Durazzo by

The castellan of Valona, John of Taxis, was commended by Charles of Anjou for his continuing brave stand against the Greeks as late as September 1284.[71] In later years the court poet Manuel Philes was to attribute the reconquest of Durazzo, Kroia and Kanina to the heroic action of the *protostrator* Michael Doukas Glabas Tarchaneiotes.[72] Kanina may have been the last to fall; and there is evidence that Butrinto, which went with Corfu, was still in Angevin control as late as 1292.[73] But in the end, as Sanudo says, Kanina, Valona and Durazzo were all restored to the Byzantine Empire.[74]

The disaster at Berat forced Charles of Anjou to change his plans. The overland route to Constantinople was now closed to him. He would have to take his army by sea. For this he must have the cooperation of Venice. The Venetians were relieved that the recent Angevin interference in the straits between Italy and Albania was over. They were pleased to be invited to participate in the overthrow of an emperor in Constantinople whom they had come more and more to suspect of favouring their rivals in Genoa. Venetian trade would thrive again if Byzantium were restored to Latin management. On 3 July 1281, at the palace of Pope Martin IV at Orvieto, a new treaty was drawn up, a revised version of that made at Viterbo in 1267. The signatories were Charles of Anjou, his son-in-law, the titular Latin Emperor Philip of Courtenay, and the Doge of Venice. The purpose of the alliance was nothing less than the establishment of Philip on the throne in Constantinople that had once been occupied by his father Baldwin. The Venetians were promised rich rewards for

1289. K. Rhalles and M. Potles, Σύνταγμα τῶν θείων καὶ ἱερῶν κανόνων (Athens, 1852–59), V, p. 122. The Latin text of the chrysobull of Andronikos II for the citizens of Kroia, contained in a document of Alfonso V of Aragon and Naples dated 19 April 1457, is published by L. de Thallóczy and C. Jireček, 'Zwei Urkunden aus Nordalbanien', *Archiv für slavische Philologie*, XXI (1899), 96–8; and by A. Solovjev and V. A. Mošin, *Grčke povelje srpskich vladara* (Belgrade, 1936), pp. 316–18. For its date (October, indiction II [= 1288]), see *ActAlb*, I, no. 508, p. 151; Dölger, *Regesten*, IV, no. 2130.

[71] *ActAlb*, I, no. 488, p. 146. Other documents concerning the resistance of John of Taxis at Valona are in Minieri-Riccio, *ASI*, ser. 4, IV (1879), 14 (July 1281); 174, 176 (April and May 1282); 350 (September 1282). Hopf, *GG*, I, p. 330, writes of the appointment of Pierre d'Auteil as castellan of Valona as late as 28 August 1290.

[72] E. Miller, *Manuelis Philae Carmina*, II (Paris, 1857), pp. 240–55, especially 253 ll. 288–9: Ἐξ ὧν [sc. Ἰταλῶν] κατασχὼν τὴν πόλιν Δυρραχίου / Κροάς τε καὶ Κάννινα καὶ τὰ κυκλόθεν. . . . Cf. P. J. Alexander, *B*, XV (1940–41), 195–6, 204–7; H. Belting, C. Mango, Doula Mouriki, *The Mosaics and Frescoes of St. Mary Pammakaristos (Fethiye Camii) at Istanbul* (Dumbarton Oaks Studies, XV: Washington, D.C., 1978), pp. 11–13.

[73] Ducellier, *Albanie*, p. 261.

[74] Sanudo, ed. Hopf, p. 129: 'alla fine il detto Castello della Gianina, che è in la Vallona, e Duraccio fù restituito all' Imperador de Greci predetto'. 'Gianina' here means Kanina, which is known to have been in Byzantine control by 1307 and probably before 1294. It was reconquered by the *protostrator* Tarchaneiotes: see above, n. 72.

providing at least forty warships and troop carriers to convoy the Angevin armada from Brindisi by April 1283.[75]

Nikephoros of Epiros, who was still Charles's vassal, was evidently not a party to the Treaty of Orvieto. But a few months later another agreement was made between Charles, the Latin Emperor Philip and the Doge of Venice, with Nikephoros as an equal partner. On 25 September 1281 Charles reported to his baillie in Achaia, Philip of Lagonessa, that he had signed a treaty with the Despot Nikephoros, the Latin emperor and the Doge, for the purpose of making war on Michael Palaiologos. At the same time he instructed his baillie to release the boy Michael, son of Nikephoros, who had been held hostage at Clarentza since April 1279, and hand him back to his father or his father's representative. Whatever active part Nikephoros was expected to play in the grand alliance against Constantinople, he had now adequately proved his loyalty to his master Charles as an obedient and trusted 'friend and ally'.[76]

The grand alliance never achieved its purpose. In March 1282 the rebellion known as the Sicilian Vespers broke out at Palermo in the heart of Charles's empire. His fleet was destroyed, his army was thrown out of Sicily and his grandiose plans of eastern conquest were wrecked. Nine months later, in December 1282, the Emperor Michael VIII died. At the moment of his death he was leading an army through Thrace towards Thessalonica and Thessaly. Now that his most dangerous Latin enemy in the west had been humiliated, the emperor was determined to punish and humiliate his most perfidious Greek enemy, John Doukas of Thessaly, who had again broken his bounds and his oaths. Had this expedition been successful there can be little doubt that the emperor would then have turned his attention to John's half-brother, Nikephoros of Epiros. But it was thwarted by his death; and the wild Tatar mercenaries whom he had engaged 'to liquidate the flower of Thessaly' were disbanded and sent back to their master, the Khan Nogai of the Golden Horde.[77]

The death of the emperor who had forced his people into union with the Roman Church deprived the separatist rulers of northern Greece of their adopted role of pious defenders of the true and Orthodox faith. For almost the first act of the new emperor, Andronikos II, was to renounce the union of Lyons and to proclaim the restoration of Orthodoxy throughout his dominions. Those who had suffered persecution or

[75] Tafel and Thomas, *Urkunden*, III, pp. 287–95. Cf. Geanakoplos, *Emperor Michael*, pp. 335–8.

[76] Minieri-Riccio, *ASI*, ser. 4, IV (1879), 17. Charles here describes Nikephoros as 'dilectum amicum, fidelem nostrum'. Cf. Geanakoplos, *Emperor Michael*, pp. 339–40. No more is heard of Nikephoros's son Michael and it must be presumed that he died soon afterwards.

[77] Pach., *De Mich. Pal.*, vi. 35: I, pp. 524–32; Greg. v. 7: I, pp. 149–55.

imprisonment for their opposition during the previous reign of terror were now set free to become the heroes of the hour. Among them was the late emperor's sister Eulogia who had much influence over her nephew Andronikos.[78] Her daughter Anna, the *basilissa* of Epiros and wife of Nikephoros, had grudgingly supported her husband's dealings with Charles of Anjou so long as Michael VIII was alive. But she was quick to take the initiative in coming to terms with the new regime. As soon as she heard of her mother's release from prison, Anna set out for Constantinople. Nikephoros sent his own personal envoy to the new emperor. He was the bishop of Kozyle in Thesprotia. It was said that he had once served Philip Chinardo as a chaplain and that he had performed the funeral rites over Philip's head after his murder – his widow, acting the part of Salome, having laid the head on a golden platter.[79] In 1283 there were not many bishops about in Constantinople who could be declared free of the taint of the dogmatic controversies and compromises that had darkened the Orthodox Church in recent years. The good bishop of Kozyle, having been consecrated by the metropolitan of Naupaktos in a land free of unionists, was immaculately Orthodox. For these reasons he found himself called upon to ordain and consecrate the new patriarch of Constantinople, George or Gregory of Cyprus. George, who was a layman, had to be tonsured as a monk and ordained as a deacon in the space of five days. These offices were performed by the bishop of Kozyle. Tradition had it that patriarchs must be enthroned by the bishop of Herakleia. A monk was found to fill this see and the bishop of Kozyle installed him as bishop. Gregory of Cyprus was finally enthroned as patriarch of Constantinople on 28 March 1283. The new bishop of Herakleia presided at the ceremony assisted by the bishop of Kozyle who, after this brief and unexpected moment of glory, retired into the welcome obscurity of his remote diocese in Epiros.[80]

The *basilissa* Anna, however, whom he may well have escorted from Arta, stayed in Constantinople for a while longer. She may have been present at the synod held in the Blachernai palace in April 1283, at which the union of the Churches was formally repudiated. It is certain that she attended the synod at Adramyttion on the coast of Asia Minor early in 1284, in the company of her mother Eulogia and her sister Theodora Raoulaina, both of whom were supporters and friends of the Patriarch

[78] Pach., *De Andron. Pal.*, i. 2–3: II, pp. 14–16.

[79] Ibid., i. 14: II, p. 44.

[80] Ibid., pp. 42–5; Greg. vi. 1: I, p. 164. Greg. here records that the bishop of Dibra (Devrai) in Macedonia had also come to Constantinople. But his see came under the autocephalous archbishopric of Ochrida (Justiniana Prima). The bishop of Kozyle, on the other hand, being dependent upon Naupaktos, came under Constantinople and was therefore more suited for the task in hand. On Kozyle (or Kozile), see Soustal–Koder, pp. 186–7.

Gregory.[81] It was while Anna was there or at Constantinople that her cousin, the new Emperor Andronikos II, had words with her about the situation in Thessaly. Michael VIII had died when on his way to chastise the unruly *sebastokrator* John Doukas. Now it seemed that John's son and heir presumptive Michael was likely to prove even more troublesome than his father. The emperor therefore suggested to Anna that she might like to do him a service by kidnapping this dangerous young man and handing him over. This she promised to do as soon as she got home to Epiros. Meanwhile the emperor sent an army and a fleet to Thessaly, commanded by the hero of Berat Michael Tarchaneiotes, now promoted to the rank of *protobestiarios*. His orders were to occupy as much territory as possible and to take custody of Michael Doukas if Anna succeeded in getting hold of him. The military part of the plan was a failure. Tarchaneiotes attacked and occupied Demetrias on the coast of Thessaly. But in the course of the summer he and many of his troops died of an epidemic and the survivors withdrew with nothing achieved.[82]

Some time later, however, the deed was done by other means. Anna and Nikephoros lured the young Michael Doukas over to Epiros with the promise of marriage to one of their two daughters and then sent him under guard to Constantinople. The emperor was delighted and paid them a handsome reward for their cooperation in this rather underhand scheme.[83] Michael was held in honourable captivity at the imperial court. Andronikos II like his father believed that the problem of the separatist Greek states could be solved by marrying their rulers into his own family. He proposed that Michael of Thessaly should marry his niece, daughter of the Despot John Asen, formerly tsar of Bulgaria. But Michael's one thought was to escape. He had to be locked up in prison. In 1299 he very nearly got away with the help of his gaoler, an Englishman called Henry, who arranged for a fishing smack to carry him to Negroponte. From there he could have made contact with his sister Helena, wife of the duke of Athens William de la Roche; for by then his father John Doukas was dead. But the plan was foiled by the weather and Michael was brought back to captivity. Eight years later, in 1307, he set fire to his prison which adjoined the palace and died fighting like a tiger, hacked to pieces by the axes of the Varangian guards.[84]

[81] Pach., *De Andron. Pal.*, i. 21: II, pp. 58–9; Greg. vi. 8: I, pp. 165–7. On the dates and circumstances of the first synod at Blachernai (19–26 April 1283) and the synod at Adramyttion (8–9 April 1284), see Laurent, *Regestes*, nos. 1463, 1470, pp. 252–4, 259–60.

[82] Pach., *De Andron. Pal.*, i. 25–7: II, pp. 67–72. Ferjančić, *Tesalija*, p. 123 appears to confuse Michael Doukas, son of John, with Demetrios-Michael, son of Michael II of Epiros, who had settled in Constantinople.

[83] Pach., *De Andron. Pal.*, i. 27: II, p. 72; iii. 4: II, p. 201.

[84] Pach., *De Andron. Pal.*, i. 27: II, pp. 72–7. Pachymeres (ibid., p. 75 ll. 7–8) says that Michael's sister ruled the island of Euripos (Euboia, Negroponte). In fact she was duchess

John Doukas of Thessaly was understandably infuriated by the treachery of his brother Nikephoros. He soon retaliated by making war on the Despotate, sending an army of Greeks and foreign mercenaries over the hills and ships to raid Arta from the coast. The Venetians who did business there suffered damage to their property. In 1284 they sent an envoy to John to claim compensation. But they laid most of the blame on Nikephoros. Their consul at Corfu, who had responsibility for Arta, was ordered to suspend all commercial activities in the Despotate and to see to it that all Venetians resident in Epiros left as soon as possible.[85] Nikephoros and Anna made sure that these facts were made known in Constantinople. The Patriarch Gregory wrote a stern letter to John of Thessaly in 1285 accusing him of unchristian and fratricidal behaviour. Had he not often sworn, most recently but two years before, never to attack the emperor's friends, subjects or territory? The Despot Nikephoros, his brother, was the emperor's friend and loyal servant. It had been reported that John had been negotiating with another of the emperor's enemies, Stephen Milutin, kral of Serbia, and had sent his daughter to the Serbian court. The patriarch warned John that his perfidy and megalomania might well lead to his being excommunicated. If he did not mend his ways and abide by his oaths and treaties the emperor would put an end to him and his ambition by sending an army of godless barbarians, presumably the Tatars whom Michael VIII had proposed to let loose on Thessaly.[86]

The words of the patriarch's letter make it clear that by 1285, if not before, Nikephoros of Epiros had made his peace with the emperor and accepted his new status as imperial deputy or viceroy of an outlying province, under oath of allegiance to his sovereign lord in Constantinople. This had come about partly as a result of the change of emperors and partly through the desire and the diplomatic initiative of his wife Anna. But his constitutional position and that of his 'Despotate' were still not clearly defined. It was a sign of the times that the only terms that could be found to define them were those of western feudal society and institutions. The Despot was said to be the sworn servant or vassal of the emperor. On the other hand, although there was

of Athens and Thebes, having married William de la Roche (see above, p. 19 and n. 33). William died in 1287 and, at the time of Michael's attempted escape, his sister Helena was probably acting as regent of the duchy, as she did until her second marriage, to Hugh of Brienne, in 1291.

[85] Thiriet, *Assemblées*, I, nos. LXXXX and LXXXXI, pp. 48–9 (10 and 17 August 1284). Cf. Hopf, *GG*, I, pp. 330–1.

[86] Letter of Gregory of Cyprus to the *sebastokrator* John, ed. S. Eustratiades, Ἐπιστολαὶ τοῦ Πατριάρχου Γρηγορίου τοῦ Κυπρίου, Ἐκκλησιαστικὸς Φάρος, IV (1909), 5–11. Cf. Laurent, *Regestes*, nos. 1480, 1481, pp. 269–72. John's matrimonial dealings with Milutin of Serbia are confirmed by Pach., *De Andron. Pal.*, iii. 30: II, pp. 272–3.

room for doubt as to whether his territory was heritable, there was no doubt that in Byzantine law and custom his title of Despot was a personal distinction which he could not transmit to his heir. Only an emperor could confer that distinction. There were many anomalies about the status of the Despot Nikephoros. In 1283 he was still bound by oath to Charles of Anjou as well as to the emperor in Constantinople. The Sicilian Vespers had not caused Charles to abandon his claims and possessions in 'Romania', in Albania, Epiros and the Morea. On 5 December 1283 he responded to a plea for help from Nikephoros who felt himself threatened by the Byzantine army which was then gradually liberating Albania and New Epiros from Angevin occupation. Charles sent orders to the duke of Athens and to the baillie of Achaia to send what help they could to the Despot.[87] The agreement reached between the *basilissa* Anna and the Emperor Andronikos in Constantinople at about the same time probably relieved the pressure of Byzantine aggression on the northern borders of the Despotate.

This was the last recorded communication between Charles of Anjou and Nikephoros. Charles died on 7 January 1285. His son and heir Charles II was a prisoner of the Aragonese until July 1289. His son-in-law Philip of Courtenay, titular Latin emperor of Constantinople, had died in 1283, leaving his title to his infant daughter Catherine. Pope Martin IV also died in 1285. All the most interested parties to the Treaty of Orvieto were now gone.[88] For the moment there would be no more talk of a crusade against Constantinople. The Venetians, who were to have supplied some of the ships for that crusade, changed their policy and negotiated a ten-year treaty of their own with the Emperor Andronikos II. It was signed by the Doge in July 1285.[89] The power and the pretensions of the house of Anjou were henceforth to be limited. But neither Charles II nor his son Philip was willing to relinquish his ancestral claim to Albania and New Epiros; and both regarded the Despots of Epiros as potential friends, allies or vassals in the furtherance of that claim.

[87] Minieri-Riccio, *ASI*, ser. 4, v (1880), 361; De Lellis, *Regesta Chartarum*, I, p. 537, no. 58. Cf. D. A. Zakythinos, *Le Despotat grec de Morée*, I (revised ed.: London, 1975), pp. 59–60.

[88] Setton, *Papacy*, I, pp. 144, 146, who remarks that 'as far as the Crusade was concerned the year 1285 brought the thirteenth century to a close'.

[89] Tafel and Thomas, *Urkunden*, III, pp. 322–39. Cf. Dölger, *Regesten*, IV, no. 2104. The treaty was signed by the Emperor Andronikos II in Constantinople on 15 June and ratified by the Doge on 28 July 1285. Setton, *Papacy*, I, pp. 144–5.

2

Epiros between Italy and Byzantium – 1285–1306

Epiros was the most westerly outpost of the Byzantine world, much closer to Italy than to Constantinople. Yet its people were Greek by language and Orthodox by faith; and they were loth to lose the independence which they had enjoyed for two generations. There were those among them who favoured retaining it with the support of their friends across the water in Italy and the Morea. Such, it seems, was the policy of the Despot Nikephoros. There were others who, like the *basilissa* Anna, favoured some kind of rapport with Constantinople. In Thessaly, by contrast, there was only one ruler and one policy. The *sebastokrator* John Doukas would have no dealings with the imperial government in Constantinople; and, not without reason, he considered his relatives in Epiros to be guilty of the basest treachery to him and to the cause of independence. For most of his life John Doukas remained hostile to the Despotate. But he was dead by March 1289; and in the church of Porta Panagia which he had built six years before he is portrayed in the habit of a monk, which suggests that he had in the end escaped the anathema with which the patriarch had threatened him.[1]

He left two small sons. Constantine Doukas and Theodore Angelos. His eldest son Michael was a prisoner in Constantinople.[2] His widow retired from the world as a nun with the name of Hypomoni or Patience. She founded a convent at Lykousada near Phanari in Thessaly, for which she sought and obtained a charter from the Emperor Andronikos II in

[1] A. K. Orlandos, Ἡ Πόρτα Παναγία τῆς Θεσσαλίας, Ἀρχεῖον τῶν Βυζαντινῶν Μνημείων τῆς Ἑλλάδος, I (1935), 5–40, especially 33–5; cf. J. Koder and F. Hild, *Hellas und Thessalia* (*TIB*, I: Vienna, 1976), pp. 245–6. John is referred to as deceased in the chrysobull issued in March 1289 for the convent of Lykousada. See I. K. Bogiatzides, Τὸ Χρονικὸν τῶν Μετεώρων, *EEBS*, I (1924), 146–9; D. M. Nicol, *Meteora. The Rock Monasteries of Thessaly* (2nd ed., London, 1975), p. 51; Polemis, *The Doukai*, no. 52, p. 97; Ferjančić, *Tesalija*, p. 125; and see below, n. 3.

[2] For the names of John's sons, see M. Laskaris, Θεόδωρος Ἄγγελος, υἱὸς τοῦ σεβαστοκράτορος τῆς Θεσσαλίας Ἰωάννου, *EEBS*, III (1926), 223–4. Cf. Ferjančić, *Tesalija*, pp. 127–8.

March 1289.[3] Her husband would not have been pleased by this concession to imperial authority in his territory. Still less would he have rejoiced to know that, when his widow retired, his two sons were entrusted to the care of Anna of Epiros.[4] This arrangement must surely have been made with the consent of the emperor in Constantinople who saw fit now, or at a later date, to grant to each of them the title of *sebastokrator*.[5] By such means the emperor may have hoped to encourage the reintegration of Thessaly into his empire. It was soon to be proved that neither Thessaly nor Epiros was to be so easily accommodated in the Byzantine establishment.

In 1289 Charles II of Anjou was set free and returned to Italy as king of Naples. Before long he was scheming to reassert his father's claims in Epiros and the Morea. The principality of Achaia had of late been managed by a succession of baillies. In September 1289 Charles II made it over to its lawful heiress, Isabelle of Villehardouin, who had taken as her second husband Florent of Hainault.[6] Isabelle was a niece of Nikephoros of Epiros; and her mother Anna, sister of Nikephoros, had married the last baillie of Achaia, Nicholas II of St Omer.[7] There were strong family connexions between the Despotate of Epiros and the principality of Achaia. Charles II hoped to weld them into one. Other links in the chain were the Ionian islands offshore. Corfu remained firmly under Angevin control. But Cephalonia, Ithaka and Zante had, at least since 1264, been ruled by Richard Orsini, son of Maio Orsini, the first independent count of the islands.[8] Richard was nominally a feudatory of the prince of Achaia and so of the king of Naples, on whose behalf he acted for a while as governor of Corfu and the mainland castle of Butrinto.[9] But Charles II had no doubt that the mainland as well as the islands belonged to him; and he confidently described himself as suzerain not only over

[3] Sp. Lambros, 'Ανέκδοτον χρυσόβουλλον τοῦ αὐτοκράτορος 'Ανδρονίκου τοῦ Παλαιολόγου, *DIEE*, I (1883–4), 116–19; *MM*, V, pp. 253–6. Cf. Dölger, *Regesten*, IV, no. 2131, p. 13. On Lykousada, see Koder–Hild, *Hellas*, pp. 208–9.

[4] Pach., *De Andron. Pal.*, iii. 4: II, p. 201.

[5] Ibid., iii. 6: II, p. 206; iv. 3: II, p. 284. Cf. Ferjančić, *Tesalija*, pp. 128–30.

[6] Longnon, *L'Empire latin*, p. 263; Bon, *Morée* pp. 164–5; Setton, *Papacy*, I, p. 433. Florent was a great-grandson of the first Latin Emperor Baldwin I.

[7] Longnon, *L'Empire latin*, pp. 252–3, 257. Isabelle's first husband Philip, brother of Charles II of Anjou, died in 1277; ibid., pp. 248–9.

[8] The earliest documentary reference to Richard Orsini is in the *praktikon* of the Latin bishopric of Cephalonia of 1264. *MM*, V, pp. 16f. Cf. T. S. Tzannetatos, Τὸ πρακτικὸν τῆς λατινικῆς ἐπισκοπῆς Κεφαλληνίας τοῦ 1264 καὶ ἡ ἐπιτομὴ αὐτοῦ (Athens, 1965), p. 68. Bon, *Morée*, pp. 170–1.

[9] On 18 April 1290 Charles II transferred to Florent of Hainault the custody of Corfu and Butrinto which had earlier been granted to Richard of Cephalonia. C. Perrat and J. Longnon, *Actes relatifs à la principauté de Morée 1289–1300* (Paris, 1967), no. 15, pp. 35–6 [cited hereafter as Perrat–Longnon].

Corfu and Cephalonia but also over the principality of Achaia, the duchy of Athens and the Despotate of Epiros.[10]

The accepted method of consolidating conquests and substantiating territorial claims was by marriage. Nikephoros and Anna had one surviving son, Thomas, and two marriageable daughters, Thamar and Maria.[11] It occurred to Charles II that Thamar might be a suitable bride for one of his own sons, either for his third son Robert or for his fourth son Philip of Anjou. In June 1291 he instructed Florent of Hainault with the knight Pierre de l'Isle (Petrus de Insula) to cross over from the Morea to Arta. He gave them complete authority to discuss the possibility and the terms of such a marriage.[12] It was forty-two years since Manfred of Sicily had married Thamar's aunt Helena. That union had proved to be a mixed blessing for the Despotate. The proposal now made by Charles II, and in particular the terms of Thamar's dowry, required careful consideration. The discussions at Arta and elsewhere went on for a long time.

The proposal was very much to the taste of those in Epiros who favoured the continuing independence of the Despotate from Constantinople. But it alarmed the emperor. The coalition of Italy, Epiros and the Morea was too reminiscent of the alliance which had brought about the battle of Pelagonia. The emperor was supposed to be at peace with the Morea. In 1290, after negotiations with envoys from Florent of Hainault, he had sent a plenipotentiary to Clarentza to conclude what he hoped would be a lasting treaty. He was also in negotiation with the court of Naples and with the papacy over a plan to marry his son and heir Michael Palaiologos to Catherine of Courtenay, who had inherited the Latin title to Constantinople in 1283. This involved numerous exchanges of embassies between Italy and Constantinople, and there was even talk of arranging a 'perpetual peace'.[13] The emperor may well have felt that the only odd man out in his own chain of alliances in the west was the Despot Nikephoros, who had resumed his attacks on imperial territory even before 1290.[14] That he did

[10] Perrat–Longnon, nos. 71, 72, pp. 72–5.

[11] Their son Michael, whom they had given as a hostage to Charles I in 1279, must have died (see above, pp. 23, 29). Their son Thomas is described as being 'still a child' in 1294 and just over fifteen years old in 1303–4. Pach., *De Andron. Pal.*, iii. 4: II, pp. 200–1; *Chron. Mor. fr.*, §983, p. 385. He would thus have been born in 1288–9. Thamar was somewhat older. She was the second daughter. *Chron. Mor. fr.*, §974, p. 381. Pachymeres fails to mention her elder sister Maria, on whom see below, pp. 40, 43.

[12] Perrat–Longnon, no. 21, pp. 40, 43.

[13] A. E. Laiou, *Constantinople and the Latins. The Foreign Policy of Andronicus II 1282–1328* (Cambridge, Mass., 1972), pp. 39, 48–50; Setton, *Papacy*, I, p. 435 and n. 148; Bon, *Morée*, pp. 165–6.

[14] *Chron. Mor. fr.*, §601, p. 241; Laiou, *Constantinople*, p. 40; Bon, *Morée*, p. 166.

so against the advice and wishes of his wife Anna seems clear. The French Chronicle of the Morea speaks of the 'great tension' between the Despot and his wife.[15] Anna disapproved of the proposal for her daughter Thamar to marry a son of Charles II. She had another husband in mind for Thamar.

In 1292 the emperor, having made his peace with the Latins in the Morea, decided that the time had come to force the rebellious Despot in Epiros into submission. The military campaign that he set in motion is described only by the various versions of the Chronicle of the Morea.[16] The Byzantine historians ignore it. The account in the Chronicles is doubtless exaggerated. But it is also too factual and circumstantial to be dismissed as an invention or a romantic fiction. The date of the campaign is hard to determine. The summer or autumn of 1292 seems most probable.[17] The attack was launched on two fronts, in the north by land against Ioannina and in the south by sea against Arta. The fleet was made up of forty (or sixty) Genoese warships carrying Byzantine troops, with ten transport vessels.[18] They were to sail by way of Cephalonia and enter the Gulf of Arta through the straits of St Nicholas between Preveza and Aktion. The army is said to have numbered fourteen thousand cavalry and thirty thousand infantry, which can hardly be the truth. It was a motley collection of Greeks, Turks and Cumans.[19]

The Chronicles report that the commander of the expedition was the emperor's Grand Domestic. None of them gives him a name and the Byzantine sources are of no help in identifying who was Grand Domestic in 1292. It has been suggested that he was Syrgiannes, the father of the more celebrated Syrgiannes Palaiologos. But there is no firm evidence that he ever held this rank.[20] It is possible that the commander in Epiros

[15] *Chron. Mor. fr.*, §657, p. 262: '... si en fut grant division avec la despine sa femme ...'.

[16] *Chron. Mor.*, lines 8782–9235, pp. 353–68; *Chron. Mor. fr.*, §§607–48, pp. 243–58; *Chron. Mor. arag.*, §§456–68, pp. 100–3; *Chron. Mor. ital.*, ed. Hopf, *Chroniques*, pp. 467–8. Cf. Laiou, *Constantinople* pp. 40–1; Longnon, *L'Empire latin*, pp. 268–9.

[17] Florent of Hainault, who took an active part in the campaign, had been on a mission to Nikephoros in June 1291 (Perrat–Longnon, no. 21, pp. 39–40). He was in Italy in the first half of 1292 and left there in June (ibid., nos. 46, 47, pp. 55–6). The negotiations about the marriage of Thamar to Philip continued in May 1292 but were not resumed until June 1293 (ibid., nos. 41, 60, 61, 62, 64, 68, pp. 53–4, 66–71).

[18] The French and Aragonese Chronicles give the number of ships as 40; the Greek and Italian Chronicles give it as 60 (*Chron. Mor. fr.*, §607, p. 243; *Chron. Mor. arag.*, §456, p. 100; *Chron. Mor.*, l. 8786; *Chron. Mor. ital.*, p. 468). The French Chronicle alone adds that there were ten transport vessels to carry the horses, though later it states that they had no cavalry (*Chron. Mor. fr.*, §607, p. 243; §641, p. 255).

[19] *Chron. Mor.*, ll. 8792–3 and *Chron. Mor. fr.*, § 607 both give these figures. The latter (§631) says that the army was composed of Greeks, Turks, Cumans and 'Alemans'. *Chron. Mor.*, ll. 8787–9 says that the ships made for 'Xeromero near Arta'. Xeromera is in fact nearer to Vonitsa. For the straits and harbour of St Nicholas 'le Tort', see Soustal–Koder, p. 242.

[20] Laiou, *Constantinople*, p. 40 and n. 28, suggests that the commander was Syrgiannes. The

in 1292 held some other military rank. The Chronicles of the Morea sometimes used the title *Megas Demestikos* as a generic term to describe Byzantine generals.[21] The most likely candidate for the doubtful honour of having led the army in Epiros is the *protostrator* Michael Glabas Tarchaneiotes, the later benefactor of the Pammakaristos monastery in Constantinople. The *protostrator's* heroic exploits were praised by the poet Manuel Philes. It was Tarchaneiotes who had recaptured Durazzo, Kroia and Kanina from the Angevins in the years after the battle at Berat.[22] Philes records that he also attacked the Vlachs or Thessalians and inflicted a defeat on the *sebastokrator* Theodore.[23] This he might well have done on his way to Epiros in 1292, since the Chronicle of the Morea says that the imperial army arrived from Thessaly.[24] That Philes should have nothing to report about the great general's campaign in Epiros is not surprising, for it ended in failure.[25]

The army made straight for Ioannina and laid siege to its fortress from the landward side of the lake.[26] The Despot Nikephoros, who was in Arta, was advised by his 'barons' to appeal for help to his relative Florent of Hainault, prince of Achaia.[27] Messengers were quickly despatched over the Gulf of Naupaktos to Andravida, where they found Florent presiding

rank of Grand Domestic has been attributed to Syrgiannes only on the assumption that his wife, the mother of Syrgiannes Palaiologos, was the *megale domestikissa* called Eugenia Palaiologina, cousin of Andronikos II. S. Binon, 'A propos d'un prostagma inédit d'Andronic III Paléologue', *BZ*, XXXVIII (1938), 143–6. This assumption has rightly been called in question by J. L. van Dieten, *Nikephoros Gregoras, Rhomäische Geschichte*, II, 1 (Stuttgart, 1979), pp. 118–23. His son, Syrgiannes Philanthropenos Palaiologos, who became *pinkernes* in 1319, was never Grand Domestic and would in any case have been far too young to take command in 1292. A possible but not very probable candidate would be Alexios Raoul, who is known to have been Grand Domestic in 1303. S. Fassoulakis, *The Byzantine Family of Raoul-Ral(l)es* (Athens, 1973), no. 13, pp. 28–9.

[21] Constantine Palaiologos, for example, the brother of Michael VIII, is frequently referred to as Grand Domestic although he never held that rank. *Chron. Mor.*, ll. 4630, 4634–5, 4816, 5329, 5482–3. Alexios Philes, who was in fact Grand Domestic, is never named as such in the Chronicles.

[22] See above, p. 28 and n. 72.

[23] Miller, *Manuelis Philae Carmina*, II, p. 253 ll. 290–2: Ὁρμᾷ πρὸς αὐτοὺς τοὺς θρασεῖς πάλαι Βλάχους, / Θεόδωρον δὲ πυρπολεῖ κατακράτος / τὸν σεβαστοκράτορα τῶν ἀλλοτρίων...

[24] *Chron. Mor.*, l. 8795: Καὶ ἤλθασιν τῆς Ῥωμανίας κι ἀπέκει ἐκ τὴν Βλαχίαν. Cf. l. 9023.

[25] Philes does, however, name two places where the *protostrator* made his presence felt, Dreanoviskos and Astros; and he makes a cryptic reference to a *basilis*, a male infant and her husband (Philes, ed. Miller, II, p. 253 ll. 294–9). Dreanoviskos may be Dreanovo in the district of Ioannina (cf. *MM*, v, p. 83). Astros seems unidentifiable, though Aspros was another name for Acheloos (Soustal–Koder, p. 102). The *basilis* and her husband could conceivably be Anna and Nikephoros and the male infant their son Thomas.

[26] The Greek and French Chronicles speak of the castle of Ioannina being surrounded by a large sweet-water lake and approachable only from one side or by a bridge. *Chron. Mor.*, l. 8797 calls the lake Μέγας ὁ Ὀζερός. See Soustal–Koder, pp. 205–6.

[27] *Chron. Mor.*, ll. 8821–3. Florent's wife Isabelle (Zampea) was a niece of Nikephoros.

over a parlement.[28] They were empowered to put their case as best they could; and they found Florent in receptive mood. He put the matter to his own barons at a meeting in the church of St Sophia at Andravida. They agreed unanimously that a company of four hundred (or five hundred) knights should go to the Despot's aid, on condition that he sent them his son Thomas as a hostage and paid for the full cost of the enterprise.[29] Nikephoros, who had been uncertain about Florent's reaction, was relieved when his messengers reported back to him in Arta. He sent his son Thomas under escort over to the Morea with three (or four) months' pay for Florent's men. Thomas was to be lodged in the castle of Chloumoutsi at Clermont, which had belonged to his aunt Anna since the death of her first husband William of Villehardouin.[30] Florent did well to require a hostage and payment in advance for his cooperation. There were some who remembered how the perfidious Greeks had left their allies to fend for themselves on the field of Pelagonia.

At the same time Nikephoros also called on the help of Count Richard Orsini of Cephalonia. The conditions were much the same. Richard undertook to cross over to Epiros with one hundred knights, provided that Nikephoros paid his expenses and sent his elder daughter Maria to be held as a hostage in Cephalonia. Florent and his knights were met by Nikephoros at Lesiana in Akarnania, on the road to Arta. He had brought with him his Marshal, Nicholas III of St Omer. Richard of Cephalonia joined forces with them at Arta. Florent was housed in the Despot's palace while the rest were billeted in the castle. A council of war was held. After lengthy exchanges of compliments and pleasantries between Nikephoros and Florent as uncle and nephew, it was agreed that they should all march north on the following morning to relieve the siege of Ioannina.[31]

The 'Grand Domestic' who was in command of the siege operations had already heard it rumoured that the prince of Achaia, his Grand Marshal and the count of Cephalonia had all come to the aid of the Despot. When it was confirmed that they had assembled at Arta and were on their way north, he at once ordered the siege to be lifted and the retreat

[28] The number of messengers is given as two by *Chron. Mor.*, l. 8817, and as four by *Chron. Mor. fr.*, §610.

[29] 500 knights according to *Chron. Mor.*, l. 8844; 400 according to *Chron. Mor. fr.*, §613.

[30] *Chron. Mor.*, l. 8855, and *Chron. Mor. ital.*, p. 468, say 'three months' pay'; *Chron. Mor. fr.*, §615, says 'four months' pay'. The castle of Chloumoutsi (*Chron. Mor.*, l. 8851) at Clermont (*Chron. Mor. fr.*, §615), which the Italian Chronicle calls 'Castel Tornese' (*Chron. Mor. ital.*, p. 468), was left to Anna, together with Kalamata, by William in 1278. Cf. Longnon, *L'Empire latin*, pp. 249–50; Bon, *Morée*, pp. 152–3.

[31] *Chron. Mor.*, ll. 8864–989; *Chron. Mor. fr.*, §§616–28, pp. 246–9. The French Chronicle here anticipates the tale of Richard's later trickery of Nikephoros. For Lesiana, see Soustal–Koder, p. 194.

to be sounded. It was a curious decision. Whatever the size of the Despot's own army, his allies had brought with them no more than a total of 500 or 600 men. The Byzantine forces may not have totalled the reputed 44,000 infantry and cavalry, but they were probably superior in numbers. Yet their commander argued that, even if his emperor were there in person he could not hold out against the approaching enemy. It would be more honourable to anticipate certain defeat and ignominious flight by retreating in good order. He therefore left Ioannina without delay and led his men over the mountains towards Thessaly.[32]

The Greeks in the castle at Ioannina at once reported the news by messenger to Nikephoros and his allies. They quickened their pace and reached Ioannina in the evening. The French had been longing for a fight. They were bitterly disappointed to find that the enemy had fled. The allies passed the night in what had lately been the Byzantine camp outside the castle of Ioannina and as soon as it was light set out over the hills in pursuit of the retreating army. At the request of Florent and his Marshal, Nikephoros sent a small contingent ahead to catch up with the Grand Domestic and ask him to halt and draw up his forces on some convenient battlefield; for it was neither courteous nor honourable for a gentleman such as he to come so far in search of war and then run away without a fight. The Grand Domestic is said to have replied that if he had a Byzantine army under his command he could impose some discipline. But his troops were mainly Turks and Cumans who would obey only their own leaders.[33] They made off as fast as they could, driving their horses to exhaustion and then abandoning them with their harness to be found by their enemies. The Despot and his allies enthusiastically but vainly chased them right into imperial territory. There they plundered and took many prisoners among the surprised population who had supposed that they were protected by the army that had gone to Ioannina.[34]

Two days later word reached the Despot that the sixty Genoese warships had reached Preveza and were at the harbour of St Nicholas. Their men had gone ashore and were pillaging the towns and countryside on their way to Arta. The capital city of the Despotate was in danger. The Genoese were known to be the best crossbowmen in the world and they had the equipment to lay siege to the city. Prince Florent was informed.

[32] *Chron. Mor.*, ll. 8990–9023; *Chron. Mor. fr.*, §§629–31, pp. 250–2. *Chron. Mor. arag.*, §459, alone records that the prince and the Despot encountered the advance guard of the emperor's army at Ioannina and defeated it. The survivors fled and reported to the rest of the emperor's army that they had been routed by the Despot and the Franks and that there were many Franks in the Despot's company.

[33] *Chron. Mor.*, ll. 9084–7.

[34] *Chron. Mor.*, ll. 9024–102; *Chron. Mor. fr.*, §§632–5, pp. 252–3.

The Marshal had the trumpet sounded; and three squadrons of the fastest mounted troops, about one thousand men, were rushed south from Ioannina. The rest of the allied army would follow. Meanwhile, however, the Genoese ships had moved across from Preveza to Salagora, the harbour some distance south from Arta. There they learnt how the other part of the combined operation had failed, that the imperial army had fled from Ioannina and that the Despot and his friends were on their way to defend Arta. The Genoese captains at once decided that it would be unwise to leave their ships for fear of being cut off from them, since they had no cavalry for their protection. They therefore reloaded all the scaling ladders and tackle which they had put ashore in preparation for the siege of Arta. Some of their men, however, Greeks and Genoese, went off on a foray, setting fire to villages and capturing animals as far afield as Vagenetia. They were surprised by the advance company of one thousand horsemen from Ioannina, who killed some and took others prisoner.[35]

Nikephoros was much relieved to reach Arta and find that his enemies had done no damage there. The raid that some of them had made on the district was a comparatively small matter. Next morning he and his allies marched down to the harbour at Salagora and stationed themselves along the coast to prevent the enemy from landing to take on supplies or water. The Genoese ships then weighed anchor in the evening and made off for the district of Xeromera and Vonitsa where they put men ashore, fifty from each ship, to forage before the Despot's army had time to get there overland. They pillaged and burnt the countryside as far as Leukas (Santa Mavra) before returning to their ships. Finally they set sail for Coron in the south of the Morea on their way back to Constantinople.[36]

The Genoese and their Greek soldiers are said to have been much impressed by the discipline of the army of Florent of Hainault and by the evident superiority of western, Frankish military techniques and tactics.[37] The French had certainly been appalled by the indiscipline of the Byzantine army at Ioannina and aggrieved by what they took to be the cowardice of its commander. Florent and his Marshal may not have got the battle that they wanted but they had served the Despot well and they could now go home. Nikephoros was distressed that the enemy had caused so much damage to his territory. But he was glad that the fighting was over and suitably grateful to his allies. He entertained them in fine style; and Florent, after expressing his thanks and making pledges of undying friendship, left Arta with his men and went straight back to Clarentza by way of Naupaktos and Patras. The Despot's son Thomas

[35] *Chron. Mor.*, ll. 9103–67; *Chron. Mor. fr.*, §§636–43, pp. 253–6.

[36] *Chron. Mor.*, ll. 9168–235; *Chron. Mor. fr.*, §§644–8, pp. 256–8; *Chron. Mor. arag.*, §§462–3. The Greek Chronicle ends at this point.

[37] *Chron. Mor.*, ll. 9221–4.

was then brought from Chloumoutsi and escorted back to his father at Arta. The prince of Achaia had fully and honourably settled his accounts with the Despot of Epiros.[38]

Count Richard of Cephalonia was not so punctilious. When he returned to his island with his hundred knights he declined to honour his agreement by handing over Maria, the daughter of Nikephoros, whom he had held as a hostage. Instead he arranged that she should marry his eldest son John Orsini. The marriage was to have important and lasting consequences for the Despotate of Epiros in later years. But at the time Nikephoros was justifiably indignant and annoyed. There was little that he could do about it, for he had no fleet with which to make war on Cephalonia. Richard tried to make his peace by sending two Greek-speaking Franciscans to explain how he had been unable to find a suitable bride for his son elsewhere in Romania. He apologised for having arranged the marriage without the consent of the bride's father; and to make amends he promised henceforth to be personally at the service of Nikephoros and to defend his realm and his honour in whatever way the Despot might devise or command.[39] He promised in addition to make over to his own son either the castle of Koronoi at the southern end of Cephalonia or the whole island of Ithaka, which might enable him to keep his wife Maria in suitable style.[40]

The second of these promises was certainly never fulfilled. In January 1295 Florent of Hainault was told to look into the matter. It appears that Count Richard had also helped himself to a part of Maria's dowry. Her father, however, demanded that she and her husband should come and reside in the Despotate; and before long he found himself very taken with the young John Orsini who had been thrust upon him as a son-in-law, apparently making over to him the island of Leukas to go with the island of Ithaka, which he was supposed to have received from his father. John and Maria remained in Epiros until the accidental death of Richard Orsini in 1303, when John succeeded to the county of Cephalonia.[41]

[38] *Chron. Mor. fr.*, §§649–52, pp. 258–60; *Chron. Mor. arag.*, §§464–6.

[39] *Chron. Mor. fr.*, §§618, 653–5, pp. 246–7, 260–1; *Chron. Mor. arag.*, §§464–8, which adds that John Orsini and the Despot's (unnamed) daughter had two sons, Nicholas and John, who, after the death of his uncle the Despot Thomas, was Despot of Arta.

[40] Perrat–Longnon, no. 133, pp. 126–7 (31 January 1295). Cf. S. Lambros, Ἡ ὑπὸ τοῦ Ριχάρδου Ὀρσίνι παραχώρησις τῆς Ἰθάκης, *NH*, x (1913), 492–3; xi (1914), 414–16. This is one of the only two sources that name the Despot's daughter as Maria. For the other, see below, n. 41. For Koronoi ('castrum Coroni'), see Soustal–Koder, p. 185.

[41] *Chron. Mor. fr.*, §§655–6, pp. 261–2. That John Orsini owned the island of Leukas by 1300 is attested by Angevin documents now lost. Cf. Hopf, *GG*, I, p. 354; I. A. Romanos, Γρατιανὸς Ζώρζης αὐθέντης Λευκάδος (Kerkyra, 1870) (reprinted in Ἰ. Ῥωμανοῦ ἱστορικὰ ἔργα, ed. K. Daphnes [Kerkyra, 1959]), pp. 237–8, 317; W. Miller, *The Latins in the Levant* (London, 1908), p. 181 and n. 3. Only one of the documents cited by Hopf has been published. It refers to the construction of a fortress by John (Orsini) of

Nikephoros had meant his daughter to marry someone rather more exalted and more influential than the heir to Cephalonia.[42] He would make a better match for his younger daughter, Thamar. Recent events had greatly strengthened him in his resolve to defy the emperor in Constantinople and to preserve the independence of his Despotate. It was a policy which his wife Anna deeply deplored. Their daughter Thamar was to be the victim of their disagreement. Negotiations for her marriage to a son of Charles II of Anjou had begun in 1291. They had been conducted by Florent of Hainault. In May 1292, at which time Florent seems to have been in Naples, Charles sent two ambassadors to Epiros to make more definite proposals and arrangements. Thamar was to marry his fourth son, Philip of Anjou.[43] Discussions were resumed after the end of the fighting in Epiros. Florent had now had occasion to become better acquainted with Nikephoros and evidently thought well of him. He must also have reported favourably on the princess Thamar. In 1293 Nikephoros sent an envoy to the court of Charles II at Tarascon in the Rhone valley. He returned to Epiros by way of Lombardy, Tuscany and Apulia in June.[44] A series of diplomatic exchanges followed. Charles instructed the nobles of Negroponte to be prepared to act as trustees for the safety and property of the *basilissa* Anna, her daughter and her estate in the event that her husband Nikephoros should die before the arrangements had been concluded for the marriage of his daughter to Philip of Anjou.[45] There was some competition for the attentions of Charles II. In the summer of 1293 ambassadors from the emperor in Constantinople as well as from Nikephoros were waiting for him in Provence. The emperor was no doubt still trying to obtain the hand of Catherine of Courtenay for his son Michael.[46]

In February 1294 Philip of Anjou entered upon his knighthood and was invested as prince of Taranto by his father. It was a principality conveniently placed for communications with the Despotate of Epiros

Cephalonia at 'Lettoria' ('forteliciam quandam in terra sua lettoria'): Perrat–Longnon, no. 242, pp. 203–4. Hopf read this as 'Lettorna', which is in fact in the north of Leukas. Soustal–Koder, p. 161 (s.v. Gyra) and p. 203. The affair of Maria's dowry and her half share in all her husband's property was finally settled in 1304 in a deed sealed by John Orsini and confirmed by Philip of Savoy as prince of Achaia. J. A. Buchon, *Recherches historiques sur la principauté de Morée*, II (Paris, 1843), pp. 482–3. On the date of the death of Richard Orsini in 1303, see below, note 82.

[42] *Chron. Mor. fr.*, §657, p. 262; *Chron. Mor. arag.*, §468 (which anticipates events by saying that Nikephoros had already married his other daughter to Philip of Taranto).

[43] Perrat–Longnon, no. 41, pp. 53–4. Cf. Hopf, *GG*, I, pp. 336–7.

[44] Perrat–Longnon, no. 60, p. 66. The ambassador is named as 'Theoderus Pichridi'.

[45] Perrat–Longnon, no. 61, pp. 66–7 (25 June 1293).

[46] Both delegations left France in September 1293. The Epirote ambassadors were on their way home through Brindisi or Otranto in November. Perrat–Longnon, nos. 64, 65, p. 68 (4 September 1293); no. 68, p. 71 (11 November 1293).

and the Morea. In May Charles II relinquished to his son the suzerainty over the principality of Achaia and the duchy of Athens and also over the territories which were to constitute the dowry of his Greek bride Thamar. Arrangements for the marriage were evidently well advanced.[47] Almost at the same moment in Constantinople, in May 1294, the Emperor Andronikos II crowned his son as his co-emperor, Michael IX. Among the foreign dignitaries at the ceremony in St Sophia were envoys from Italy who had come on the matter of Michael's proposed marriage to Catherine of Courtenay.[48] They were not the only ones offering a bride for the new emperor. Anna of Epiros, in a last attempt to thwart her husband, had sent a message to Constantinople repeating her proposal that Michael IX should marry Thamar. She seems to have been aware that the proposal had already been considered and rejected by the patriarch's synod, on the ground that a sixth degree of consanguinity existed between the partners to the marriage. But Anna now implored the emperor and the patriarch to override the rules of canon law for the greater good of the empire. For if Thamar married the newly crowned emperor it would mean the reintegration into the empire of a long-lost province. Anna seemed confident that she could achieve this surrender of Epiros to Constantinople; and she was ready also to surrender herself and her son Thomas to the emperor. But her pleading did not soften the hard hearts of the patriarch and his synod. They held to the letter of the law. Thamar and Michael IX were cousins at three removes. The Church could never sanction their marriage.[49]

It is hard not to feel that the Emperor Andronikos II had his own reasons for rejecting Anna's proposal. He could have overruled his patriarch, pious though he was. He could have referred his bishops to the ruling made by the synod when his own sister Anna had married the son of the Despot Michael II in 1278. The technical impediment to that marriage had, it is true, been a sixth degree of affinity, not one of consanguinity. But the synod had on that occasion pronounced that emperors were not the same as ordinary mortals in such matters. They were answerable to no one.[50] Perhaps the emperor felt that by marrying

[47] C. Minieri-Riccio, *Saggio di Codice Diplomatico di Carlo I d'Angiò*, Suppl. I, no. LX, pp. 69–70 (4 February 1294); Perrat–Longnon, nos. 80, 81, pp. 83–5 (12 May 1294). Léonard, *Les Angevins de Naples*, p. 201; Longnon, *L'Empire latin*, p. 272; Setton, *Papacy*, I, p. 435.

[48] Pach., *De Andron. Pal.*, iii. 5: II, p. 202; Greg. vi. 7–8: I, p. 193. Cf. Laiou, *Constantinople*, pp. 50–3. For the date of Michael IX's coronation (21 May 1294) see P. Schreiner, *Die byzantinischen Kleinchroniken*, II (Vienna, 1977), pp. 213–14.

[49] Pach., *De Andron. Pal.*, iii. 4: II, pp. 201–2. Cf. Laurent, *Regestes*, no. 1564. Pachymeres makes it clear that Anna made her proposal after Michael IX had been crowned.

[50] See above, p. 22. In his dispensation for that marriage the patriarch had observed: … ἀλλ' οὐχὶ καὶ βασιλεῖς μετὰ τῶν ἄλλων προσώπων τοῖς ἐκείνων τύποις ἐναποκλείονται.

his son to Catherine of Courtenay he would in any case be in a fair way to reuniting at least the Angevin possessions in Epiros to his empire. For Catherine held the title to the Latin Empire of Constantinople; and in May 1294 Charles II had obliged her to ratify the Treaty of Viterbo with special reference to the now legendary dowry of Helena of Epiros. He had also made her swear not to marry without the consent of himself or his heirs. Charles was Catherine's uncle.[51] His wife, Mary of Hungary, was the aunt of the Emperor Michael IX. There was much to be said in favour of Michael and Catherine becoming man and wife, though the pope was none too keen about it. Andronikos II failed to find a way through this diplomatic labyrinth; and in the end Michael IX took to wife neither Catherine of Courtenay nor Thamar of Epiros. In January 1295 he married Rita or Maria, elder sister of the king of Armenia.[52]

The only reward that Anna of Epiros got for her pains was the conferment by the emperor of the title of Despot on her infant son Thomas.[53] This was some consolation, in that it implied some form of dependence of the Despotate of Epiros on Constantinople. But she could now no longer thwart her husband's plan to marry Thamar to Philip of Anjou, prince of Taranto. In July 1294, with the consent of his father, Philip effectively announced his own forthcoming marriage to Thamar by sending procurators to Greece to confirm the details of the betrothal and draw up the necessary documents. They were Roger, archbishop of Santa Severina, and Bérard of St Georges. The archbishop Roger had been that way before. It was he who had received the homage of Nikephoros to Charles I in 1279. Thamar appears to have been in the Morea at the time, and her parents were represented by two deputies from Arta, the *sebastos* John Signorinos and the *sebastos* Alexander 'Cosays'.[54]

The wedding took place at L'Aquila in the Abruzzi in August 1294.

ὑπεξήρηνται γὰρ οὗτοι, διὰ τὸ τοῦ ἀξιώματος ὑπερέχον καὶ τὸ ἐπὶ πᾶσι ἀνεύθυνον. M. Gedeon, Νέα βιβλιοθήκη ἐκκλησιαστικῶν συγγραφέων, I, (1903), cols. 106–8.

[51] DuCange, *Histoire de l'empire de Constantinople*, ed. Buchon, II, pp. 326–30; Perrat–Longnon, no. 82, pp. 85–9 (13 May 1294).

[52] Pach., *De Andron. Pal.*, ii. 18: II, p. 153; iii. 5: II, pp. 202–6. C. Marinescu, 'Tentatives de mariages de deux fils d'Andronic II Paléologue avec des princesses latines', *RHSEE*, I (1924), 139–43; G. I. Bratianu, 'Notes sur le projet de mariage entre l'empereur Michel IX et Catherine de Courtenay', *RHSEE*, I (1924), 59–63; Laiou, *Constantinople*, pp. 53–6. The younger sister of Rita-Maria of Armenia, Theophano, was affianced to one of the *sebastokrators* of Thessaly, but she died at Thessalonica on her way there. Pach., *De Andron. Pal.*, iii. 5: II, p. 206.

[53] Pach., *De Andron. Pal.*, iii. 4: II, p. 202. Pachymeres is mistaken in saying that the Despot Nikephoros was dead by the time of Thamar's marriage. D. M. Nicol, 'The date of the death of Nikephoros I of Epiros', *Rivista di Studi Bizantini e Slavi*, I (Bologna, 1981) [= *Miscellanea Agostino Pertusi*], 251–7.

[54] Perrat–Longnon, no. 103, pp. 103–4 (12 July 1294). The procurators were directed 'ad partes Romanie, ubi dicta juvenis degere dicitur'.

The archbishop of Santa Severina, accompanied by Pierre de l'Isle, escorted Thamar over to Italy. Her mother Anna was among those present. On 13 August, by two separate decrees, Charles II invested his son Philip with feudal authority over all the Angevin possessions in Greece: first, over the principality of Achaia, the duchy of Athens, the kingdom of Albania and the province of Vlachia (Thessaly), and all other mainland and island territories of Romania; second, over the island of Corfu and the castle of Butrinto and its dependencies in Epiros.[55] These were substantial claims, some of them merely theoretical. Most of the former Angevin kingdom of Albania, for example, was still occupied by Byzantine troops; and there was little reality in the Angevin claim to Thessaly. Once again, however, it was the extent of the bride's dowry that was to determine the future of the Despotate of Epiros. It had been agreed before the wedding that Thamar was to provide her husband with the sum of 100,000 *hyperpyra* a year. In addition she made over to him the fortresses of Lepanto (Naupaktos), Eulochos (near Agrinion), Angelokastron and Vonitsa, with all their dependencies. Philip of Taranto, now to be known as *Despotus Romanie*, was thus assured of control of the Gulf of Corinth, of Akarnania and of the approaches to the Ambracian Gulf and Arta.[56]

The marriage contract also contained a clause concerning the succession. The Despotate was to be regarded as the fief of Nikephoros and Anna until their death, at which time it would devolve upon their daughter Thamar with her husband Philip as Despot. If, however, her brother Thomas outlived his father, he should be allowed to retain the fief as Despot under suzerainty to Philip on condition that he ceded to Philip the castle of Hagios Donatos (Photiki) and the whole province of Vagenetia. Finally it had been agreed in advance that Thamar should be entitled to one-third of her husband's property and be assured of

[55] Perrat–Longnon, nos. 116, 117, pp. 113–15 (13 August 1294). Cf. Hopf. *GG*, I, p. 337; Longnon, *L'Empire latin*, pp. 272–3; Laiou, *Constantinople*, pp. 42–3; Setton, *Papacy*, I, p. 435. The wedding took place on or soon after 13 August 1294. On 6 September Guy of Charpigny was appointed as baillie of the territories which Philip had acquired from 'his wife' (Perrat–Longnon, no. 121, pp. 117–18). The wedding of Philip to Thamar is also recorded by Pach., *De Andron. Pal.*, iii. 4: II, p. 202; v. 30: II, p. 450; *Chron. Mor. fr.*, §§657–60, pp. 262–4.

[56] The terms of Thamar's dowry are most clearly stated by *Chron. Mor. fr.*, §658, pp. 262–3. The annuity of 100,000 *hyperpyra* is mentioned later (§976). The landed property consisted of the 'royal castles of Nepant, Blecola, Gello-Castro and Boudonnice'. 'Blecola' has been variously transcribed by modern authorities, as 'Volochos', 'Eulochos', 'Vlache', 'Vrachova', or 'Vrachori'. Cf. Hopf, *GG*, I, p. 336; Miller, *Latins in the Levant*, p. 183; R. Rodd, *The Princes of Achaia and the Chronicle of Morea*, II (London, 1907), p. 11. Romanos, *Despotate*, p. 94 (48), was almost certainly right in identifying it with Eulochos. It lay a few miles to the north-east of the modern Agrinion. Angelokastron was a little further to the south-west of Agrinion. Soustal–Koder, pp. 108, 150.

complete freedom to practice her own Orthodox religion. The same freedom was guaranteed to Philip's Greek subjects.[57]

The Despotate was now more firmly than ever joined to the kingdom of Naples. The four castles in Akarnania and Aitolia which formed Thamar's dowry were directly under French rule, and no one could pretend that this arrangement had been made under duress as had been the case when Manfred married Helena. The most important of them were Naupaktos and Vonitsa. Philip of Taranto lost no time in appointing an agent to govern his newly acquired territories, for he himself was to stay in Italy as his father's vicar-general of the kingdom of Naples. He named Guy of Charpigny, baron of Vostitsa in the Morea, as his first baillie in Akarnania. On 6 September 1294 Guy was instructed in the exercise of his new duties. Thereafter for many years the southern part of the Despotate of Epiros was to be governed by a succession of French administrators or 'vicars in the lands of the Despot'.[58]

Charles II had invested Philip with authority over the duchy of Athens and the province of Thessaly. The former was then ruled by the Duchess Helena, daughter of the late *sebastokrator* John Doukas and widow of William de la Roche. In 1291 she had taken as her second husband Hugh of Brienne. For some years she refused to do homage either to Charles or to Florent as prince of Achaia.[59] She was clearly in league with her brothers, the *sebastokrators* of Thessaly at Neopatras, Constantine and Theodore. They seem quickly to have thrown off the tutelage of Anna of Epiros said to have been imposed on them after their father's death; and they inherited their father's grudge against Epiros. Their elder brother Michael was still a prisoner in Constantinople as a result of the trickery of Nikephoros and Anna. It was going to be difficult for Philip of Taranto to assert his authority either over Athens or over Thessaly. His father therefore tried to make them direct dependencies of the crown. In April 1295 Charles II sent procurators to Greece to receive the oath of loyalty and the personal homage of the Duchess Helena and of her two brothers, 'the duke of Neopatras and (Theodore) Angelos'.[60] It seems unlikely that the procurators ever got as far as Neopatras. For only a few weeks later the *sebastokrators* Constantine and Theodore invaded Epiros, penetrating as

[57] *Chron. Mor. fr.*, §658, pp. 262–3. Minieri-Riccio, *Saggio di Codice Diplomatico*, Suppl. I, no. XLI, pp. 56–7; Perrat–Longnon, no. 21, pp. 39–40 (1 June 1291). On St Donatos ('Saint Donnat'), formerly known as Photike, near the modern Paramythia, see Soustal–Koder, pp. 236–7.

[58] Perrat–Longnon, no. 121, pp. 117–18. For the Angevin administration in southern Epiros, see below, pp. 63–8. The area covered was more or less the present *nomos* of Akarnania and Aitolia. I have called it simply Akarnania for convenience.

[59] Setton, *Papacy*, I, pp. 434–7.

[60] Perrat–Longnon, nos. 147–9, pp. 136–8: '...pro parte nobilis mulieris Helene, ducisse Athenarum, ducis Patere ac Angeli, fratrum ejusdem ducisse...'.

far as Arta, causing great damage and taking many prisoners. The new Angevin vicar of Akarnania, Ponsard of Durnay, seems to have been unable to cope with the invasion. In July and again in October 1295 Charles II ordered Florent of Hainault to go to his assistance against the 'duke of Neopatras and Angelos, his brother'.[61] According to one report the *sebastokrators* seized control of the towns of Angelokastron, Acheloos and Naupaktos, which had only recently been made over to Philip as part of his wife's dowry.[62]

The storm blew over within the year. In the summer of 1296 both sides sent ambassadors to Charles II and to Philip; and soon afterwards Constantine of Thessaly signed a peace treaty with Nikephoros, withdrew most of his army from Akarnania and surrendered Acheloos and Naupaktos.[63] The treaty was ratified by Philip of Taranto; and on 3 September 1296 Charles II informed all the Latin rulers of Romania of what had occurred and ordered them to keep the peace with the *sebastokrator* of Neopatras and avoid giving help and comfort to his enemies. His incompetent vicar of Akarnania, Ponsard of Durnay, seems to have been replaced.[64]

A few months later Nikephoros, Despot of Epiros, died.[65] His health may have been poor for some time. But he had lived long enough to see his daughter Thamar married to the sovereign lord of all Romania. His wife Anna had returned to Epiros after the wedding escorted by three warships gallantly provided by command of Charles II; and his daughter had come back to visit her parents in February 1295.[66] He had even seen fit, on the orders of his master Charles II, to provide safe conduct through his Despotate for an imperial embassy returning to Constantinople in March 1296.[67] For his master was indeed Charles II through his son Philip of Taranto; and Nikephoros had succeeded before he died in making his Despotate totally subservient to the kingdom of Naples. Its southern district of Akarnania was administered by French governors,

[61] Perrat–Longnon, nos. 155, 156, pp. 141–3 (1 July 1295); nos. 161–3, pp. 145–7 (6 October 1295).

[62] Reported only by Hopf, *GG*, I, p. 355, citing lost Angevin documents; followed by Romanos, *Despotate*, p. 95 (49). Cf. Ferjančić, *Tesalija*, p. 130. It is possible that 'Acheloos' is a misreading for Eulochos, one of the four castles of Thamar's dowry.

[63] Perrat–Longnon, nos. 183–4, p. 159 (31 August and 1 September 1296).

[64] Perrat–Longnon, no. 185, p. 160 (3 September 1296): Charles reports the news that 'inter viros nobiles dominum Nichiforum despotum, affinem nostrum carissimum, ex parte una, et Sevasto Craturam Constantinum Ducem Angelum, ex altera, pax est inita et firmata'. This is the last known document to mention Nikephoros as being still alive.

[65] Nikephoros died after 3 September 1296 and before 25 July 1298, by which date Anna was evidently a widow (Perrat–Longnon, no. 201, p. 172). See Nicol, *Rivista di Studi Bizantini e Slavi*, I (1981), 251–7.

[66] Perrat–Longnon, no. 126, pp. 120–1 (12 January 1295); nos. 135, 140, pp. 128–9, 131–2 (13 and 22 February 1295).

[67] Perrat–Longnon, no. 173, p. 153 (18 March 1296).

whose arbitrary exactions were not popular either among the Greek or the Latin inhabitants. Corfu was also under direct Angevin rule. Cephalonia, Ithaka and Zante, which had never formed part of the Despotate, were still the domain of Richard Orsini; but his family had already gained a foothold on the mainland through the shotgun marriage of his son to the daughter of Nikephoros. Such had been the price of preserving the independence of Epiros from Constantinople. It was a price which the *basilissa* Anna had never wanted to pay and one which, as a widow, she was reluctant to continue.

After her husband's death, Anna was left as regent for her son Thomas. He was already Despot in his own right, but he was not much more than six years old. Pachymeres takes pity on Anna in her widowhood as a defenceless woman. He misdates her husband's death and he misjudges her character.[68] The French Chronicle of the Morea comes nearer the truth in describing Anna as one of the cleverest women in Romania.[69] Nor was she the only woman on the scene. In the French as well as in the Greek ruling families the female line was proving stronger than the male. In August 1296 the Duchess Helena of Athens was again left a widow by the death of Hugh of Brienne. In January 1297 Isabelle of Villehardouin, the niece of Anna of Epiros, was left in charge of the principality of Achaia after the death of Florent of Hainault. For the security of Achaia it was arranged that her five-year-old daughter Matilda should marry the young Guy II (Guyot) of Athens, son of the Duchess Helena. Helena was also a niece of Anna and the sister of the troublesome *sebastokrators* of Thessaly. The marriage of her son to the infant heiress to Achaia was opposed by Charles II. There was also a canonical objection, for the parties were related in the third degree of consanguinity. But the pope was persuaded to grant a dispensation for the good of the Latin cause in Greece, and Charles was obliged to yield. The ruling houses of Achaia and Athens were thus united by marriage in 1299.[70]

In the same year Philip of Taranto, the suzerain of all Romania, was taken prisoner in war against Frederick II of Sicily. Three years were to pass before he was set free. During those years Isabelle of Villehardouin acted as personal ruler of Achaia. She appointed as her baillie Richard Orsini of Cephalonia. It ought to have been possible for the reigning princesses Anna of Epiros, Helena of Athens and Isabelle of Achaia to reach some agreement for the prevention of further warfare in Greece. They and their offspring were all related by blood or by marriage. Charles II tried to bring them all together to sign a truce with the Emperor

[68] Pach., *De Andron, Pal.*, iii. 4: II, p. 201.

[69] *Chron. Mor.fr.*, §974, p. 381: '... laquelle dame estoit adonc une des plus sachans femme de Romanie'.

[70] Longnon, *L'Empire latin*, pp. 275, 279–80; Setton, *Papacy*, I, pp. 436–7.

Andronikos II or with his deputies in the Byzantine enclave in the Morea. His intermediary was Geoffrey du Port, baillie of the Angevin lands in Epiros, in 1299. Geoffrey seems to have done the rounds of all the Angevin dependencies in Greece, and in 1300 he managed to persuade them to join in making a truce with the Byzantine emperor.[71] In the Morea at least there was to be a time of peace. Isabelle of Villehardouin felt confident enough to go off to Rome to celebrate the jubilee year of Pope Boniface VIII; and there she soon found for herself another husband. His name was Philip of Savoy and he was only half her age. But he at once assumed the title of prince of Achaia, much to the annoyance of Charles II.[72]

The truce between Charles and the Emperor Andronikos II in 1300 had been supposed to cover Epiros and Thessaly. In 1299 the emperor had had to visit Thessalonica to arrange a treaty with the kral of Serbia. While there he had taken the occasion to send messages of goodwill to his niece Anna in Epiros and to the *sebastokrators* of Thessaly. The response was predictable. Anna, who had in fact taken the initiative in goodwill, was pleased. The *sebastokrators*, who had been asked to give back some territory that they had stolen, were deviously uncooperative.[73] Not long afterwards, in 1301, they returned to the attack on Epiros. Philip of Taranto was still in captivity. But his deputy in Akarnania, Geoffrey du Port, received orders from Charles II to go to the rescue of the *basilissa* Anna. He was supported by a fleet under the command of Matthew of Gémaux, Captain of Corfu. Geoffrey du Port died in March 1301. But his successor, Rainier of Montefuscolo, with the help of the Corfiote fleet, successfully defended Anna's dominions against her nephews. They were forced in the end to surrender Angelokastron, the last of the three fortresses that they had seized in 1295.[74]

Rainier of Montefuscolo was an energetic baillie of the Angevin properties in Epiros, and he was on good terms with the *basilissa* Anna. But he looked forward to the day when his master, Philip of Taranto, would be set at liberty. Thamar worked hard to raise the necessary

[71] Perrat–Longnon, no. 219, p. 190 (31 July 1299); nos. 236, 237, 239, pp. 201–2 (18 and 20 April 1300); Dölger, *Regesten*, IV, nos. 2227, 2228. Cf. Longnon, *L'Empire latin*, p. 280; Zakythinos, *Despotat grec de Morée*, I, p. 66.

[72] Longnon, *L'Empire latin*, pp. 281–3; Setton, *Papacy*, I, pp. 151–2.

[73] Pach., *De Andron. Pal.*, iv. 3: II, p. 284. The territory in question included Demetrias on the Gulf of Volos which the emperor had offered when one of the brothers married the Armenian princess Theophano. The marriage never took place, but the *sebastokrators* had occupied Demetrias in anticipation. See above, note 52.

[74] Hopf, *GG*, I, pp. 357–8, is the only source for these events, followed by Romanos, *Despotate*, p. 98 (50). Matthew of Gémeaux, as captain of Corfu, and Geoffrey du Port are known from documents in Perrat–Longnon, nos. 213 (of 1299) and 214–22, 227–9, 232, 243 (of 1299–1300). But the series of documents published by Perrat–Longnon ends in 1300.

ransom for her husband. She is said to have pawned her golden and bejewelled crown; and in 1301 she asked her wealthy mother Anna to contribute. Anna was glad to help and got in touch with Venice, probably through the Venetian consul in Arta. The Venetians, then on the brink of war with the Byzantines, were polite but distant. Anna was also approached for money by Rainier of Montefuscolo, acting on his master's behalf. One way and another Anna seems to have done her best to effect the release of her son-in-law. She was not happy about her continuing state of subservience to the Angevins. But for the time being she needed their help and protection, and she was sorry for her daughter. In the summer of 1302 she had further cause to be thankful for their help, when Constantine of Thessaly again invaded her territory. In July Charles II wrote to the barons of Achaia and Athens ordering them to go to the aid of Anna against their common enemy.[75] Charles must have been relieved when his son Philip was finally released by his captors on 31 August 1302 and able to reassume his own responsibilities in Greece.[76]

The two *sebastokrators* of Thessaly, Constantine and Theodore, died soon afterwards. One of them left an infant son called John, but apparently no widow who might have acted as regent or guardian.[77] In his will John's father proposed that the child should be placed in the care of his cousin and neighbour, Guy II de la Roche, duke of Athens. The arrangement suited both parties. Feudal oaths were exchanged; and Guy appointed a Greek called Boutomites as his marshal in Thessaly.[78] To some of the Greeks in Epiros, if not to Anna herself, it seemed that the moment had come to take revenge for all the damage that the late rulers of Thessaly had caused them and to protect the eastern flank of the Despotate for the future. They contrived to seize and occupy the castle of Phanari (Phanarion) which lay to the south of Trikkala and near the Thessalian end of one of the mountain passes from Epiros.[79] It was an act

[75] Hopf, *GG*, I, p. 358, is again the only source. Cf. Romanos, *Despotate*, p. 99 (50).

[76] Philip of Taranto was released by terms of the Treaty of Caltabellotta which ended the war between the Angevins and the Aragonese of Sicily. For its effects on Byzantium, see Laiou, *Constantinople*, pp. 128f. Cf. Setton, *Papacy*, I, pp. 441, 446.

[77] Longnon, *L'Empire latin*, p. 283, dates their death to 1302. Others date it to 1303: e.g., Hopf, *GG*, I, p. 360; Laiou, *Constantinople*, p. 230; Ferjančić, *Tesalija*, p. 134; Nicol, *Meteora*, p. 51; idem, *The Last Centuries of Byzantium*, p. 142. Hopf, *GG*, I, pp. 360, 419 n. 26, and *Chroniques*, p. 529, followed by Romanos, *Despotate*, p. 100 (51), state that Constantine married Anna Evagionissa or Evagionesciti Doukaina, who was the mother of John II of Thessaly. So also Polemis, *The Doukai*, p. 98, and *PLP*, I, nos. 206, 212. But the only known document referring to 'Anna euagionesciti regina cominina duchisa' dates from 1317 and belongs to the *basilissa* Anna of Epiros. J. Valentini, *Acta Albaniae Veneta saeculorum XIII et XIV*, I, I (Palermo, 1967), no. 31, pp. 13–14 [cited hereafter as *ActAlbVen*]. See below, p. 78 n. 51.

[78] *Chron. Mor. fr.*, §§873–80, pp. 345–8. On Boutomites, called 'Vucomity' by the Chronicle, see Ferjančić, *Tesalija*, pp. 178–9; *PLP*, II, no. 3128.

[79] On the site of Phanari (Phanarion), see Koder–Hild, *Hellas*, p. 237.

of opportunism as well as vengeance which Anna later claimed was done without her knowledge. The young Guy II of Athens, who had just been made guardian and regent of Thessaly, regarded it as a slight on his honour. He prepared for war.

The French Chronicle of the Morea gives a long and colourful account of the consequences.[80] In 1303 Guy of Athens summoned all his vassals, the lords of Salona and of Karystos in Negroponte. He also called on the help of the Marshal of Achaia, Nicholas III of St Omer.[81] Nicholas was now answerable to the new prince of Achaia, Philip of Savoy; and he had strict instructions not to leave the Morea. But he could not forego the excitement of a battle. He set out from Andravida with eighty-nine horsemen, of whom thirteen were knights. He took them by ferry from Vostitsa (Aigion) across to Vitrinitsa near Galaxidi. There he was told of the sudden death of his father-in-law, Richard of Cephalonia; but he pressed on by way of Salona, Gravia and Siderokastron to the Spercheios valley near Neopatras. He made contact with Guy and his barons near Domoko, on the road between Lamia and Pharsala; and Guy asked him to take command of the combined forces.[82]

The French Chronicle, with customary exaggeration, reports that there were nine hundred Latin knights, six thousand Thessalian and Bulgarian (or Vlach) cavalry, divided into eighteen battalions and commanded by eighteen Greek barons, as well as thirty thousand

[80] *Chron. Mor. fr.*, §§881–918, pp. 348–62. Cf. Romanos, *Despotate*, pp. 100 (51–2); Miller, *Latins in the Levant*, p. 201; Rodd, *Princes of Achaia*, II, pp. 109–12; Longnon, *L'Empire latin*, p. 284; Setton, *Papacy*, I, pp. 438–9.

[81] Nicholas of St Omer had married Guillerma, daughter of Richard of Cephalonia and widow of John Chauderon. *Chron. Mor. fr.*, §§997–1000. Longnon, *L'Empire latin*, pp. 278, 286–7.

[82] *Chron. Mor. fr.*, §§885–94, pp. 350–3. On the topography, see Koder–Hild, *Hellas*, p. 135 (Vitrinitsa), pp. 148–9 (Domoko), p. 167 (Gravia), p. 225 (Siderokastron). Richard of Cephalonia was killed while exchanging blows with one of his knights at Clarentza. Various dates have been proposed for this event, and so for the campaign of Guy II and Nicholas III. The French Chronicle (§619, p. 247) says that Richard was murdered in the time of Philip of Savoy, 'qui princes estoit de la Morée a mil. cccj. an' (= 1301). Buchon, *Recherches Historiques*, II, pp. 478, 481, therefore accepted 1301 as the date of Richard's death. Bon, *Morée*, p. 706 (cf. p. 176 and n. 5) dates it to 1304. The chronological table at the end of the Brussels manuscript of the French Chronicle (ed. Longnon, p. 401) dates the campaign of Guy and Nicholas to June 1302 and the arrival in the Morea of Philip of Savoy to October 1302, 'indiction 1'. There is a long but inconclusive discussion of the chronology in Romanos, Γρατιανὸς Ζώρζης, p. 243 and n. 4. Longnon, *L'Empire latin*, p. 284; Setton, *Papacy*, I, p. 439 n. 170; and Bon, *Morée*, p. 176 n. 5, all follow the chronological table by dating the campaign to 1302. But the correct date is 1303. This follows from the fact that the army, having been diverted from Ioannina, made for Thessalonica, where the Empress Eirene was residing. She would not have been there in 1302 (see below, n. 85). The campaign of Guy II and Nicholas III into Thessaly and against Anna of Epiros, and consequently the death of Richard Orsini, must therefore be dated to 1303. This date affects the accepted chronology of some subsequent events.

footsoldiers. Their objective was Ioannina rather than Arta, since they had been told that that was where Anna and her army were to be found. They therefore marched north by Elassona ('Thalassino') and Trikkala to Stagoi (Kalabaka) and encamped at a place called 'Serquices' (perhaps Sarakina), which their guides assured them was only three days march from Ioannina.[83] But there they were met by messengers from Anna, bringing letters to her nephew Guy II and her cousin Nicholas III. Her scouts had reported that a large army was on its way to Ioannina. She thought it wiser to give in before they got any nearer. Her letters were full of apology and good intent. She explained that the castle of Phanari had been occupied without her consent and offered to surrender it. In addition she would pay an indemnity of 10,000 *hyperpyra* to cover the cost of the expedition, 7,000 to be paid to the duke and 3,000 to his Marshal. The Greeks of Thessaly advised Guy to accept this offer. The war against Epiros was called off. Phanari was restored to its former owners. Anna, whether innocent or not, had bought peace for her Despotate.[84]

The Greek barons of Thessaly, however, had other ideas. They soon convinced the duke and his Marshal that it would be a disgrace and a pity to have assembled so fine an army without making war on someone. The possibility was open to them to attack the Byzantine Empire in Macedonia from the south. The frontier was not far north of Trikkala. Three squadrons of Greek and Vlach cavalry were therefore sent ahead to blaze the trail while the duke's army crossed the frontier near the town of Servia. The advance guard reached the outskirts of Thessalonica, raiding the district of Pelagonia on their way. Thessalonica had recently become the residence of the Empress Eirene (Yolanda) of Montferrat, the wife of Andronikos II. Eirene had quarrelled with her husband over the inheritance of her sons and set up house as empress in her own right in the second city of the empire, soon after Easter 1303.[85] She had not expected

[83] *Chron. Mor. fr.*, §§894–903, pp. 353–6. On the topography, see Koder–Hild, *Hellas*, p. 153 ('Thalassino' = Elasson), p. 255 ('Serquices').

[84] *Chron. Mor. fr.*, §§904–7, pp. 356–7. The Thessalians are described as 'li noble homme de la Blaquie'.

[85] *Chron. Mor. fr.*, §§908–11, pp. 357–9. On the date of Eirene's arrival in Thessalonica, see Pach., *De Andron. Pal.*, v. 14: II, pp. 377–9. Her mother-in-law, Theodora, died on Monday in the second week of Lent (i.e. 4 March 1303). Eirene stayed in Constantinople for the funeral and for the marriage of Andronikos II's son John and left for Thessalonica after Easter. Cf. A. Th. Papadopulos, *Versuch einer Genealogie der Palaiologen* (Munich, 1939), p. 4; I. Ševčenko, *Etudes sur la polémique entre Théodore Métochite et Nicéphore Choumnos* (Brussels, 1962), pp. 275–9. Ferjančić, *Tesalija*, p. 134, perversely dates the event to 1304. *Chron. Mor. fr.*, §911, pp. 358–9, says that Andronikos II sent Eirene to Thessalonica because she had stood as godmother to one of his illegitimate sons. The patriarch had ruled that she could therefore no longer live in the flesh with the father of the child. But cf. Greg. vii. 5: I, pp. 233–5.

to have to face an invasion. She sent two Lombard knights and two Greek archons with letters and gifts to the duke and the Marshal in the hope that they would leave her in peace. She appealed to their chivalrous honour and reminded them of their recent truce with the emperor. They would be welcome in Thessalonica as her guests, for was she not related to them? The duke and his Marshal were moved and impressed by the words of this 'wise and noble woman'. They sent her a deputation to express their honourable affection and to announce their immediate withdrawal from her dominions. Once back in Thessaly their armies split up and went their several ways. Guy II and Nicholas III spent some days with the little John II at Neopatras, on whose behalf they had gone to a war that never happened.[86]

The Empress Eirene in Thessalonica must have suspected that the duke of Athens and his Marshal had been put up to their invasion by the Greek barons of Thessaly. She had good reason to distrust them. Her own solution to the problems of northern Greece was simple. She would spite her husband and his son Michael IX and provide for her own sons by creating separate and hereditary principalities for them in Thessaly and Epiros. Eirene proposed that her second son Theodore should marry the half-sister of Guy II of Athens, Jeannette of Brienne. Guy would then help Theodore to take over Neopatras and make himself sole ruler of Thessaly. Her plan for her elder son John was still more ambitious. He was to become prince of Aitolia, Akarnania and Epiros. Neither of her grand schemes materialised. The first was rejected by Guy of Athens; and Eirene had no means of implementing the second. She consoled herself by intriguing against her husband with the kral of Serbia.[87]

Anna of Epiros, being the cousin of Andronikos II, may well have known the Empress Eirene. But she would hardly have wanted the Despotate of Epiros to become the appanage of one of Eirene's sons. As her own son, the Despot Thomas, began to come of age and as she herself grew older, Anna felt more and more inclined to defy the kingdom of Naples and once again to offer herself and her Despotate to the Byzantine Empire. Her daughter Thamar had got little thanks for all her efforts to pay her husband's ransom. Nor had he honoured his pledge to respect her Orthodox faith. She had even been obliged to change her

[86] *Chron. Mor. fr.*, §§912–18, pp. 359–62. Eirene's claim to be related to Guy II and Nicholas III was somewhat tenuous. *Chron. Mor. fr.*, §906, p. 357, describes the former as the nephew and the latter as the cousin of Anna of Epiros. Anna was a cousin of Andronikos II and so connected by marriage with Eirene.

[87] Eirene's activities and intrigues in Thessalonica are described by Pach., *De Andron. Pal.*, v. 4: II, pp. 377–9; vi. 34: II, pp. 557–8; Greg. vii. 5: I, pp. 233–8, 240. Cf. Laiou, *Constantinople*, pp. 229–31. Greg. (I, p. 237) is wrong in saying that Eirene proposed the marriage of her son Theodore to the 'daughter' of Guy II. The bride was to have been Jeannette of Brienne, the half-sister of Guy. Miller, *Latins in the Levant*, p. 218.

name and was known as Catherine, princess of Taranto.[88] Anna therefore suggested that Thomas should marry a daughter of Michael IX, the son and heir presumptive of Andronikos II. She would settle on him and his wife the places in Epiros which had constituted the dowry of her daughter Thamar, thereby rejecting outright the claims of Philip of Taranto.[89] It was a bold proposal. But it could never have been achieved without warfare. The Angevin castles in Akarnania and Aitolia, such as Vonitsa and Naupaktos, were well garrisoned. The emperor's response is not recorded. In 1304 he had troubles enough on his hands nearer home. It was perhaps not the moment for Anna to look for comfort from Constantinople.

But Charles II seems to have known what was afoot and took action accordingly. In 1304 he wrote to Anna at Arta to remind her of the exact terms of her daughter's marriage contract. Since her husband was now dead she should either hand over Epiros to Philip of Taranto or make her son do homage to him, in which case he could hold the Despotate as a fief. Anna sent a spirited reply. Her son Thomas, she said, could not do homage to Philip because by so doing he would break his oath to his natural lord, the emperor of Constantinople, from whom he held his title and his land. By right of heredity he had succeeded to the Despotate when his father died; for he had never been disinherited by his father. By no man's law could a married sister claim possession of so great an inheritance while her brother was still alive. Thamar, and by implication Philip, must be content with the four castles and the large annuity which had constituted her dowry. They had no right to demand the inheritance of her brother Thomas, leaving him to go begging round the world. The prince of Taranto should be grateful for the portion of the Despotate which he already had and not ask for the whole of it. He could only do that if and when the Despot Thomas died without issue.[90]

Such is the account of the French Chronicle of the Morea. According to the letter of feudal law Anna was in the wrong. The marriage contract between Thamar and Philip in 1294 had stipulated that if Thomas outlived his father he should be allowed to retain the Despotate as a fief under suzerainty to Philip and on certain conditions. Thomas should therefore do homage to his lord. According to Byzantine law, on the other hand, Anna was at least partly within her rights. It was true that Thomas had received his title of Despot from the emperor, as his father and grandfather had done before him. But it was not true that the title was

[88] Pach., *De Andron. Pal.*, v. 30; II, p. 450, reports Anna's dismay over the offence being given to Thamar's faith. Hopf, *GG*, I, p. 364; Rodd, *Princes of Achaia*, II, p. 49.

[89] Pach., *De Andron. Pal.*, v. 30: II, pp. 450–1.

[90] *Chron. Mor. fr.*, §§975–6, pp. 381–2.

hereditary or that it carried with it the right to rule over and to succeed to a province of the empire. It was on precisely this issue that the Emperor Andronikos II had quarrelled with his wife Eirene and caused her to leave him. Eirene had wanted to divide what was left of the empire into hereditary appanages for the benefit of her three sons. Her husband had had to remind her that the Empire of the Romans was a single, integrated monarchy and not a polyarchy.[91] Eirene, like the French chronicler of the Morea, was a westerner and found such political theory hard to understand.

Charles II of Naples was also a westerner with a clear view of the rights and wrongs of feudal law. Anna's reply to his message infuriated him. He had also heard of her dealings with the emperor in Constantinople. He and his son would have to fight for their rights over the Despotate of Epiros. It would be a just war and an easy one, since Anna was a mere woman and Thomas was still a young man. Pachymeres has it that they retaliated by sending a fleet of twenty-four ships along the coast of Epiros to plunder the mainland.[92] The French Chronicle of the Morea tells of a more elaborate expedition planned from Italy. In 1304 Philip of Savoy, prince of Achaia, and the new count of Cephalonia, John Orsini, were ordered to invade Anna's territory.[93] The marshal of the host was Raymond of Candolle, a Provençal knight. He had two hundred horsemen and three hundred footsoldiers and he brought with him another French knight, John of Maucevrier. They sent the king's orders from Brindisi to Cephalonia and then sailed to Vonitsa. There they were joined by John Orsini with a hundred men. John seemed to have no scruples about going to war against his brother-in-law Thomas at whose court he had recently been living. Philip of Savoy meanwhile answered the summons and, bringing his own Marshal Nicholas of St Omer, crossed over to Naupaktos with some three hundred knights. In June 1304 the combined forces met at Kopraina, on the coast near Arta. Fighting on their side was a Greek landowner called Chomatianos, a

[91] Greg. vii. 5: 1, pp. 233–5; G. Sphrantzes, *Memorii 1401–1477*, ed. V. Grecu (Bucharest, 1966), p. 172. Nicol, *Last Centuries of Byzantium*, pp. 159–60.

[92] Pach., *De Andron. Pal.*, v. 30: 11, pp. 450–1. Pachymeres clearly implies that this was an act of retaliation for Anna's negotiations with the emperor.

[93] *Chron. Mor. fr.*, §§978–94, pp. 383–9. The chronological table in the Chronicle (ed. Longnon, p. 401) dates this campaign to June 1303, indiction 2. This date was accepted by Longnon, *L'Empire latin*, p. 286, and by Bon, *Morée*, pp. 176–7. For the reasons stated above (notes 82 and 85), however, it must be dated to 1304, as Hopf, *GG*, 1, pp. 364–5, and Romanos, *Despotate*, pp. 103–5 (53–5), had earlier proposed. Nicholas III of St Omer could not have been campaigning in Thessaly and in Epiros simultaneously. Bon, *Morée*, p. 177, wrongly names the count of Cephalonia as Richard. Cf. *Chron. Mor. fr.*, §980, p. 384: 'le conte Jehan estoit venu a la Bondice'. John Orsini, who had been living at Arta, went to Clarentza for his investiture as count (*Chron. Mor. fr.*, §619, p. 247).

liegeman of Philip of Taranto, who had more than two hundred horsemen.[94]

Anna had expected the worst. She had laid in stocks of provisions at the castle of Arta and had ordered that all the houses around it be demolished to give room for battle, if battle there should be. When the westerners arrived they found the town of Arta deserted and the castle well garrisoned and guarded. Anna herself had left for Ioannina. She had wanted to take Thomas with her but she had been persuaded that he was now old enough to bear arms and to lead the resistance. For about a month the castle of Arta was under siege. But the attackers began to run short of supplies and had to retreat to the port of Salagora, where their ships were waiting. When they had revictualled they decided to storm the castle of Rogoi, to the south-west of Arta. This too proved to be better defended than they had anticipated.[95]

The castle of Rogoi (or Rogous) stands on a low hill rising from the flat valley of the Louros river.[96] The river seems then to have flowed round the hill on two sides. It could not be forded, so the Marshal Raymond had a chain thrown across it and about three hundred soldiers made their way over. The hill was thickly wooded. When night fell they thought that they were safe and settled down to sleep among the trees and bushes. But the Despot's men had been spying on them; and at about nine o'clock they were surprised by a party of three hundred horsemen who had crossed the river on the other side of the hill. About eighty were killed and more than twenty drowned trying to escape. The news was quickly taken to the Despot Thomas who was waiting at the monastery of Blachernai across the river Arachthos from Arta.[97] Such was the inglorious end of the latest attempt to bring the Despotate to heel. As before, the French and their allies, for all their alleged tactical superiority, had been unable to beat the Greeks on their own ground. They blamed Raymond of Candolle for their humiliation, but above all they blamed John of Cephalonia, who knew the terrain and the enemy better than anyone.[98]

The marshal led them back to Arta where they stayed for fifteen days.

[94] *Chron. Mor. fr.*, §§979–83, pp. 383–5. The name of the Greek in their army is rendered as 'Cocomatiano'. For Kopraina (still so called), about twelve miles south-east of Arta, see Soustal–Koder, p. 184.

[95] *Chron. Mor. fr.*, §§983–4, pp. 384–5. Salagora, the harbour to the south-west of Arta, is now a village between the lagoons of Tsoukalio and Logaron. Soustal–Koder, p. 253.

[96] On the still impressive site and castle of Rogoi, see Hammond, *Epirus*, pp. 57–61 and plan 4; G. Sotiriou, Τὸ κάστρο τῶν Ῥωγῶν, *Ep. Chron.*, II (1927), 98–109; Soustal–Koder, pp. 251–2.

[97] *Chron. Mor. fr.*, §984–9, pp. 385–6. On the monastery of Blachernai or Blachernitissa, called 'Notre Dame de la Blaquerne' by the Chronicle, see A. K. Orlandos, Βυζαντινὰ Μνημεῖα τῆς Ἄρτης, Ἀρχεῖον Βυζαντινῶν Μνημείων τῆς Ἑλλάδος, III, 2 (1937), pp. 1–50; Soustal–Koder, pp. 125–6.

[98] *Chron. Mor. fr.*, §990, pp. 386–7.

But they had lost heart. The castle seemed impregnable and food was scarce. The villagers round about had disappeared to the mountains taking all their animals and belongings with them; and the Despot Thomas and his men were encamped not far away so that foraging was dangerous. It was the end of August and nearly the end of the campaigning season. Prince Philip of Savoy concluded that they had better retreat with what little honour they had left, and they set out for Vonitsa. On their way over the hills, however, they were pursued and harried by the Despot's army. His mounted archers blocked the pass of Makrynoros, above Amphilochia, and forced them to take a higher and more difficult route. The count of Cephalonia held the rearguard, forcing the Greeks to withdraw with some casualties; and finally he and the rest of the allied army got through and down to the plain of Vonitsa and Lesiana where their ships were waiting. From there Philip of Savoy and the Marshal Nicholas of St Omer sailed for the Morea. Raymond of Candolle, however, had already left with his own contingent for Acheloos, another of the Angevin castles in Akarnania. No doubt he thought that he had better redeem his reputation by seeing to the defences of the domain of Philip of Taranto against the Despot Thomas and by sending a report to Naples. John Orsini stayed with him at Acheloos for about a month before going back to Cephalonia.[99]

The report that Raymond sent to Charles II and Philip of Taranto asked for reinforcements. It was the declared intention of the prince of Achaia and his marshal to redeem their own reputation by returning to the attack in the following spring. Anna and her son Thomas were aware of their plans, but they devised a way of thwarting them. In the best traditions of Byzantine diplomacy they would bribe their enemies to stay away. It had worked before with the Marshal Nicholas and the noble duke of Athens. As her agent and intermediary Anna employed the abbot of a local monastery.[100] He was given secret instructions to go to Philip of Savoy with a money bag containing 10,000 *hyperpyra*. If the prince promised to cancel his plans for a second invasion of Epiros the money would be handed over. The prince would get 6,000 and the marshal 4,000 *hyperpyra*. Neither could resist the offer. They took the money and agreed to call off their campaign. The deal was done in secrecy. But it would surely become public if and when their lords in Naples summoned

[99] *Chron. Mor. fr.*, §§990–5, pp. 386–9. On 'Macrioros' (= Makrynoros), see Soustal–Koder, p. 200. The Chronicle here calls Vonitsa 'la Boidice', Lesiana 'la Lessyaire', and Acheloos 'la Quello'. Cf. Soustal–Koder, pp. 128, 194, 101.

[100] *Chron. Mor. fr.*, §1006, p. 392, describes him as the abbot of the abbey of 'la Starne'. This seems to be unidentifiable, though it could perhaps be Stamna on the banks of the Acheloos river south-west of Agrinion, where there are remains of two early Byzantine churches. Soustal–Koder, p. 264.

them to arms against the Despotate. They would then have to break their promise. But the marshal hit on a scheme for keeping their promise as well as their money. The prince should summon a parlement at Corinth in the spring. Every baron and every manner of man in his principality would be bound to attend it. Everyone would thus be excused from obeying a royal command to be elsewhere at the time.[101] So it came about; and it is with its account of the tournament, jousting and festivities at the parlement at Corinth in May 1305 that the French Chronicle of the Morea comes to its end.[102]

The parlement was almost the last act of Philip of Savoy as prince of Achaia. He left for Italy with his wife in November 1305. Charles II had never approved of him or of his marriage to Isabelle of Villehardouin. In October 1304 he had declared Isabelle's lands to be forfeited. The real prince of Achaia was his own son Philip of Taranto.[103] On 5 June 1306 Philip of Savoy was formally deposed for violation of feudal law.[104] Philip of Taranto arrived in the Morea soon after. He was determined to make good his claim, now publicly confirmed by his father, that he was lord of Achaia, Athens, Albania, Thessaly and all the other mainland and island territories of Romania.[105] He had already had unexpected success in Albania. Epiros could hardly hold out against him.[106]

In March 1306, shortly before Philip set out for the Morea, his father had expressed the hope that Anna of Epiros and her son Thomas would avoid any further unpleasantness by doing homage to Philip when he arrived on the scene.[107] But Anna had already told him in unambiguous language that, while she respected Philip's claim to his four castles in Akarnania, the rest of Epiros belonged to her and her son the Despot Thomas. She had survived one and nearly two attempts to make her change her mind. She had also shown that her son was capable of inspiring the spirit of resistance that had helped to create the Despotate of Epiros. Her armies were still able to outmanoeuvre and defeat the chivalry of the Morea. After their victories at Arta and Rogoi in 1304 they had even been bold enough to take the offensive; for it appears that

[101] *Chron. Mor. fr.*, §§1003–8, pp. 392–4.

[102] *Chron. Mor. fr.*, §§1009–24, pp. 394–9. The chronological sequence of events from 1303 onwards, as presented above, necessitates dating the parlement at Corinth, and so the end of the French Chronicle of the Morea, to the year 1305 (as Hopf, *GG*, I, pp. 365–6) and not 1304 (as Longnon, *L'Empire latin*, pp. 287–8; Bon, *Morée*, p. 179; Setton, *Papacy*, I, p. 440; and others).

[103] Document of 9 October 1304, reedited by Rodd, *Princes of Achaia*, II, pp. 279–82. Cf. Bon, *Morée*, p. 180.

[104] Longnon, *L'Empire latin*, p. 289; Bon, *Morée*, p. 180; Setton, *Papacy*, I, p. 153.

[105] Transfer of sovereignty to Philip of Taranto dated 9 October 1294: text in Rodd, *Princes of Achaia*, II, pp. 278–9. Cf. *ActAlb*, I, no. 570, p. 168.

[106] See below, p. 68.

[107] *ActAlb*, I, no. 579, p. 171 (24 March 1306).

Thomas's troops had recaptured Vonitsa and Naupaktos, as well as Butrinto in the north.[108]

As soon as he had established his authority in the Morea in 1306, with a preliminary and successful showing of the Angevin flag to the Greeks, Philip of Taranto set out for Epiros. The Aragonese version of the Chronicle of the Morea, the only source for these events, credits John Orsini with the initiative. It was he who convinced Philip that between them they could easily overrun and subdue the Despotate and indeed the whole of northern Greece right up to Thessalonica.[109] This may well be true. John Orsini had lived at Arta for many years and had helped to lay siege to it in 1304. He had valuable agricultural properties in the district of Xeromera behind Vonitsa, and his wife, Thomas's sister, owned vineyards at Anatoliko.[110] John possibly fancied himself as Despot in place of Thomas. But it was not to be. Thomas was well prepared for the invasion and bravely defended his territory. He was saved partly by the outbreak of an epidemic among his enemies. Philip of Taranto was forced to abandon his campaign. But he had not entirely wasted his time. Before he withdrew he managed to impose a settlement which took some of the fire out of the Epirote resistance to him. Thomas agreed to pay an indemnity in cash and also to surrender the three fortresses of Vonitsa, Naupaktos and Butrinto which he had recently, and wrongfully, occupied. It was a victory of a sort. But Philip's army had suffered heavy losses; and in the autumn of 1306 he went back to Italy to lick his wounds.[111]

There he took it out on his unhappy wife Thamar whom he rather perversely blamed for his own failure to humiliate her mother and brother across the water. Thamar had to pawn her remaining jewellery to pay for the cost of her husband's ventures in Epiros.[112] A few years later, in 1309, he found a pretext for divorcing her. She was charged with adultery and made to confess that she had deceived her husband with at

[108] See below, pp. 66–7.

[109] *Chron. Mor. fr.*, §524, p. 115.

[110] Hopf, *GG*, I, p. 359 (citing Angevin documents now lost).

[111] *Chron. Mor. fr.*, §§524–6, p. 115. Cf. Longnon, *L'Empire latin*, pp. 292–3. The epidemic is mentioned only by Ptolemy of Lucca: *Ptolemaei Lucensis Historia Ecclesiastica*, in Muratori, *RIS*, XI, col. 1232. Vonitsa and Naupaktos were clearly in Angevin control in the summer campaign of 1304 (see above). Thomas must therefore have occupied them after that campaign. John of Cephalonia had his reward. Philip called him his 'affinem carissimum' and created him 'ducem vallis Jauchie' for his help against the 'egregiam mulierem despotam soceram suam'. A. Miola, 'Notizia d'un Codice della Biblioteca Nazionale di Napoli', *ASPN*, V (1880), 406–7. 'Jauchie' is probably the 'Porto (de) Junco', 'Port de Junch' of the French and Aragonese Chronicles of the Morea, i.e. Zonklon, or Old Navarino. Rodd, *Princes of Achaia*, II, p. 294; Bon, *Morée*, pp. 668–9 and index s.v. Port-de-Jonc.

[112] Hopf, *GG*, I, pp. 366–7; Romanos, *Despotate*, p. 113 (57).

least forty of the leading barons of his court. The chief co-respondent was the count of Caserta. Though he denied the accusation and was never given a judicial hearing, he was banished. The princess Thamar, or Catherine of Taranto, retired to a convent and died soon afterwards.[113] Like her aunt Helena, who had married Manfred so many years before, Thamar had led an unhappy life in exile from her native land. Both ladies had served the purpose of conveying landed property to their husbands. Their dowries were more important than their happiness. The five children that Thamar bore to Philip were to find that they too were pawns in a game of dynastic politics. Nor were they encouraged to remember that half their roots were Greek and that their grandmother Anna the *basilissa* of Epiros had been a Cantacuzene and a Palaiologina.[114]

[113] Ptolemy of Lucca, Muratori, *RIS*, XI, col. 1232. Rodd, *Princes of Achaia*, II, p. 61 and n. 1; Longnon, *L'Empire latin*, p. 302.

[114] Thamar's children by Philip were two sons, called Charles and Philip, and three daughters, Blanche, Jeanne and Beatrice. *Chron. Mor. arag.*, §569, p. 124. Charles was betrothed to Matilda, widow of Guy II of Athens (who died in 1308), but the marriage never took place and he died in 1315. Philip married first Beatrice of Bourbon-Clermont and then Violante of Aragon; he died in 1331. Blanche married Raymond Berengar, brother of Peter III of Aragon, and died in 1328. Jeanne married King Ošin of Armenia. The third daughter, Beatrice, married Walter II of Brienne in 1325. Hopf, *Chroniques*, p. 470; Longnon, *L'Empire latin*, p. 322; M. L. Bierbrier, 'Modern descendants of Byzantine families', *Genealogists' Magazine*, XX, 3 (1980), 180.

3

French, Byzantines and Venetians in Epiros – 1294–1318

The Angevin colony which had come into being in Akarnania and Aitolia as a result of Thamar's marriage to Philip of Taranto in 1294 was never a great success. Its main centres were Naupaktos on the Gulf of Corinth and Vonitsa on the Ambracian Gulf. Even these seem to have been precariously held and inadequately defended. The *sebastokrators* of Thessaly had captured the former without much trouble in 1295. The Despot Thomas captured both in 1305. John of Cephalonia and Philip of Taranto may have thought that they could use them as bases for the conquest of the whole of northern Greece. But, as John Cantacuzene was to observe some years later, the Tarentines, for all their many invasions and devastations of Epirote territory, had never been able to conquer a single town and had always been forced to retire with heavy losses. The only towns which they controlled were those which the Epirotes had voluntarily ceded to them, such as Vonitsa, Naupaktos and Butrinto.[1]

The country between Vonitsa and Naupaktos was administered, like the Morea, by baillies and vicars-general appointed from Naples who laboured to divide it into fiefs according to the only system of tenure that they knew. Their appointments seldom lasted more than a year or two. The first was Guy of Charpigny in 1294.[2] He was followed in 1295 by Ponsard of Durnay, who was replaced in 1296 by Simon of Marzy.[3] None of them was particularly competent. In July 1298 Charles II appointed William Grosseteste, formerly captain of Corfu. Grosseteste was given orders to install able castellans and constables, to see that the towns were adequately provisioned and to repair the ravages of war occasioned by recent attacks from Thessaly. He was also to protect the interests of both

[1] *Ioannis Cantacuzeni eximperatoris historiarum libri IV*, ed. L. Schopen (*CSHB*, 1828–32), ii. 37: 1, p. 527 [cited hereafter as Cantac.].

[2] Perrat–Longnon, no. 121, pp. 117–18 (6 September 1294). Guy of Charpigny is here described as: '... balium Philippi, ... principis Tarentini, ... in terra sua parcium ipsarum sibi pro parte uxoris sue ... tradenda ...'.

[3] Perrat–Longnon, nos. 155–7, pp. 141–3 (1 July 1295). Ponsard of Durnay is described as: 'vicario in terra despoti pro parte Philippi ... Tarentini ...' (p. 143). For Simon of Marzy, see Perrat–Longnon, no. 201, pp. 171–4; and cf. Hopf, *GG*, 1, p. 337.

Greek and Latin feudatories and to maintain good relations with the Despina Anna at Arta. In consultation with her he was to appoint a *protobestiarios* and *magister maxarium* who would make a cadastral survey and census of the whole region and determine the nature and extent of all properties, with the names of their owners both Greek and Latin, whether held as fiefs or by hereditary right from decrees of the Despot and Despina.[4]

Grosseteste died before he had time to carry out these orders; and his replacement, Aimery of Poissy, made himself so unpopular that Charles II had to call for a full investigation.[5] Among the Greek victims of maladministration was the *sebastos* John Signorinos, who had helped to arrange Thamar's marriage to Philip. He protested on behalf of himself and his brother Kalodikes ('Calodicus') against the unlawful seizure by the king's agents of landed property which was theirs by hereditary right and against the abuse of privileges which had been granted to him and his forbears by the Despots. Another aggrieved party was one Chomatianos, doubtless the Greek landowner who fought with the army of Philip of Savoy in Epiros in 1304. He complained of the sequestration of his own and his nephew's property by Aimery of Poissy. Another Greek called Stasinos requested confirmation of the privileges granted to him by the Despots. But there were Latin plaintiffs too who were aggrieved by the arbitrary exactions of the administrators appointed from Naples or the Morea.[6] One was Margaret of Villehardouin, daughter of the late William II. In 1296 she complained that her property at Katochi, near Mesolonghi, had been wrongfully seized by some of the officials of Philip of Taranto. Margaret was then married to Isnard of Sabran, a blood relation of Charles II, who was indignant about the affair. Three years later, however, he seems to have changed his mind. In 1299, after Isnard's death, Margaret had married Richard Orsini, count of Cephalonia; and in August 1300 Charles wrote to Geoffrey du Port, then Philip's agent in Epiros, to the effect that the Countess Margaret's ownership of Katochi, with all its feudatories and military levies, ran contrary to the local customs and should not be permitted any longer.[7] Geoffrey du Port took over as vicar-general of the Angevin territories in 1299. It was he who negotiated the truce with the Emperor Andronikos II in July of that year. He and his successor, Rainier of Montefuscolo, gallantly assisted Anna of

[4] Perrat–Longnon, no. 201, pp. 171–4 (25 July 1298).

[5] Perrat–Longnon, no. 204, pp. 176–7 (27 November 1298).

[6] Perrat–Longnon, nos. 206, 207, pp. 178–80 (29 April 1299); no. 215, pp. 186–7 (29 July 1299).

[7] Perrat–Longnon, no. 190, p. 163 (27 September 1296); Minieri-Riccio, *Saggio di Codice Diplomatico*, Suppl., part ii (1883), no. VIII, p. 9 (9 August 1300). On Katochi, see B. Katsaros, Συμβολὴ στὴν ἱστορία καὶ μνημειακὴ τοπογραφία τοῦ χωρίου Κατοχὴ Ἀκαρνανίας, Ἑλληνικά, XXX (1977–8), 307–21; Soustal–Koder, p. 174.

Epiros to defend the Despotate against Constantine of Thessaly in 1301 and 1302. Montefuscolo was one of the more efficient of the Angevin governors. He dismissed officials who had been lax and put others in their place. He tightened control over Naupaktos and Vonitsa and stationed a garrison in Angelokastron, which he had forced the Thessalians to surrender.[8]

During the years when his son Philip was in prison, Charles II worked hard to keep the loyalty of the Epirotes, carefully attending to their many complaints against his agents. In July 1302 his court at Naples was playing host to a deputation of Greek clergy sent over by Anna.[9] Her personal envoy was Niphon, abbot of the Monastery of St Nicholas at Mesopotamon, near Delvino in the north. With him was John, bishop of Acheloos in Akarnania, and Nikodemos, abbot of the monastery of the Panagia Eremitou, in the hills between Naupaktos and Mesolonghi.[10] They had brought with them a long list of documented grievances, each of which was considered and where necessary rectified. At the request of the Abbot Nikodemos, Charles II confirmed for one Michael Nomikopoulos of Acheloos that his wife was the lawful owner of some of the property at Katochi which had been claimed by Margaret of Cephalonia. The abbot himself secured restitution of some of his monastery's goods which had been expropriated; as also did the bishop of Acheloos, whose property had been seized by a Greek official of the Angevin regime, the *sebastos* Nikephoros 'Sguillinos' (Sikelianos?). The Abbot Niphon of Mesopotamon requested and received as a fief the property of his late relative Michael Kyros in Angelokastron, which had just been recovered from the enemy. He also received some property in Acheloos belonging to his cousin Melliglavos, who had been captured by pirates in 1296.[11]

The fact that the bishop of Acheloos and the two abbots were Greeks suggests that Charles and Philip were honouring the letter of their agree-

[8] For Geoffrey du Port, see Perrat–Longnon, nos. 214, 219, pp. 185–6, 190 (28 and 31 July 1299). Hopf, *GG*, I, pp. 356–7.

[9] The only source for these transactions is Hopf, *GG*, I, pp. 358–9, followed (in part) by Romanos, *Despotate*, p. 99 (50).

[10] Hopf, *GG*, I, p. 358, describes the abbot as 'Nymphos Neradas, Abt von S. Nikolaos de Mesopotamita'. 'Nymphos' must surely be Niphon. His monastery of St Nicholas at Mesopotamon in Vagenetia was a patriarchal *stavropegion* free from the jurisdiction of its local bishop, as was to be confirmed in 1315 (see below, pp. 76–7). It produced one fourteenth-century saint, also called Niphon, who began his monastic career there before becoming a hesychast at Geromeri, a little to the south, and thence making for Mount Athos. F. Halkin, 'La vie de saint Niphon ermite au mont Athos (XIVe siècle)', *Analecta Bollandiana*, LVIII (1940), 5–27, especially 12–13. On the location of the monasteries of Mesopotamon and Panagia Eremitou, see Soustal–Koder, pp. 206–7, 223–4, and for Geromeri(on), ibid., pp. 156–7.

[11] Hopf, *GG*, I, pp. 358–9.

ment of 1294 that the local inhabitants should be allowed to practise their own religion. In 1302 this seems still to have been the case in Naupaktos, though a Latin bishop was to be installed there before long. Other Greek 'barons' whose complaints were lodged and settled at Naples in 1302 were Alexios Papadopoulos, who regained possession of his fief at Metaxa by Naupaktos, which had been taken from him by Ponsard of Durnay; Michael, formerly a cellarer in Vonitsa, who was given compensation for victuals stolen from him; and Nikephoros Longaropoulos of Acheloos, who had been wrongfully imprisoned by the baillie. It was also decreed that local magnates who had fled to the hills when the Thessalians invaded should be reinstated in their properties, while those who had volunteered to help finance the campaign against the *sebastokrator* Constantine should be exempt from payment of taxes. No taxes were to be levied in the future except for the customary tax on houses and livestock, the *kapnologion* and the *biologion*, which had been in force for the past sixty or seventy years. In August 1302 Charles II commanded that all properties seized by Ponsard of Durnay and Simon of Marzy in 1295–6 must be restored to their rightful owners. There had evidently been many abuses in the administration of the territory that made up Thamar's dowry.[12]

In the line of communications between the Latin colonies in the Morea and those in Epiros the harbour of Naupaktos was a vital link. There is no independent evidence to support the statement so boldly made by the patriarch's synod in 1365, that Naupaktos had been snatched from the Byzantine Empire by the arrogant Italians eighty years earlier, in 1285.[13] The patriarch's advisers must have misread their records. Naupaktos was a city of the Despotate and a metropolis of the church of Epiros until 1294, when it passed to Philip of Taranto as part of his wife's dowry. Philip had undertaken to respect the religion of his Greek subjects, and for a time he did so. In 1300 the *basilissa* Anna wrote to Charles II to remind him of this undertaking, since the Greek bishop of Naupaktos was being denied access to his diocese. Geoffrey du Port had declared that he had no mandate from the king to allow the bishop to officiate. On 9

[12] Ibid. On the taxes known as *biologion* and *kapnologion* (also referred to in Andronikos II's chrysobull for Ioannina in 1319), see F. Dölger, 'Zum Gebührenwesen der Byzantiner', in Dölger, *Byzanz und die europäische Staatenwelt* (Ettal, 1953), pp. 255, 256.

[13] The statement is made twice in a πρᾶξις συνοδική of the Patriarch Philotheos dated March 1365, granting to the metropolitan of Ioannina, Sebastian, the title of metropolitan of Naupaktos. *MM*, I, pp. 468–72, especially 469, ll. 17–29 and 470, ll. 7–8. Dölger, *Regesten*, IV, no. 2109; Laurent, *Regestes*, IV, no. 1482, p. 272. The reasons for rejecting the date 1285 are put by Darrouzès, *Regestes*, V, no. 2488, p. 409 crit.; by E. K. Chrysos, Ἡ προαγωγὴ τῆς ἐπισκοπῆς Ἰωαννίνων σε Μητρόπολη, Δωδώνη, V (1976), 337–48, especially 341–2; and by Catherine Asdracha, 'Deux actes inédits concernant l'Epire', *REB*, XXXV (1977), 171.

August Charles sent him orders to admit the bishop into Naupaktos and to afford him complete freedom 'according to the agreements made'.[14] The Despot Thomas had then recovered Naupaktos for a short while, until Philip of Taranto made him relinquish it in 1306. It may have been this event which led him to acquiesce in a breach of his promise to respect the Orthodox Church. For on 14 October 1307 Pope Clement V announced the appointment of a Latin archbishop of Naupaktos. He was a Dominican called Rostagnus, a brother of the knight Raymond of Candolle who had so unsuccessfully fought at Arta and Rogoi in 1304. His letter of appointment observes that the church of Naupaktos has been restored to Roman obedience and that the schismatic Greek who insolently called himself its archbishop has been removed.[15] These were harsh words to use about the successor of John Apokaukos, who had ministered to the see of Naupaktos with such distinction a hundred years before. But the presence there of a Roman prelate helped to fortify the Latin regime in Naupaktos for another seventy years, until it fell to the Albanians.

At the beginning of the fourteenth century the Despotate was hemmed in by its foreign neighbours in the south. It was also closely confined on the north. The control of New Epiros and Albania was still disputed between Byzantines and Angevins; and neither could ignore the growing pressure from the native Albanians. The kingdom of Naples had acquired its colonies in Epiros by marriage. Manfred's marriage to Helena in 1259 had legalised a robbery that had already happened; and Charles I of Anjou had not hesitated to claim Helena's dowry as the territorial base for his invasion of the Byzantine Empire. A generation later that dream had faded. But it had never died; and in 1302, after the Treaty of Caltabellotta, it was briefly revived by Charles of Valois, who had married Catherine of Courtenay, the titular Latin empress of Constantinople. Charles II of Naples was an enthusiastic accomplice in the revival. His 'kingdom of Albania' might yet prove useful in the pursuit and realisation of his father's dream.

It was a smaller kingdom than it had been before the Byzantine victory at Berat in 1281; and in 1296 Durazzo, which had been in Greek hands for about eight years, succumbed to the new conqueror on the scene, Stephen Milutin of Serbia. On 19 June of that year the Venetians lodged a complaint with Milutin about the damage done to their merchants at the time when his army seized Durazzo from the emperor of Constantinople.[16] Stephen Uroš II Milutin had captured Skoplje from

[14] Minieri-Riccio, *Saggio di Codice Diplomatico*, Suppl., part ii, no. VIII, pp. 8–9.

[15] *Acta Clementis PP. V (1303–1314)*, ed. F. M. Delorme and A. L. Tăutu (Fontes, ser. III, vol. VII, tom. I: Vatican City, 1955), no. 20, pp. 33–4. Hopf, *GG*, I, p. 364, identifies Rostagnus as a brother of Raymond of Candolle.

[16] F. Thiriet, *Délibérations des Assemblées Vénitiennes concernant la Romanie*, I (Paris-La

the Byzantines in 1282. From there he planned to extend his conquests into Macedonia and northern Greece, as well as into Albania. He had been a friend and in some sense a son-in-law of John Doukas of Thessaly. Durazzo fell to him; Thessalonica seemed to be threatened. The Emperor Andronikos II took the advice of his general Michael Glabas Tarchaneiotes and opted to avert the threat by diplomacy rather than by force. In 1299 he gave or sacrificed his infant daughter Simonis as a bride to Stephen Milutin. Her dowry consisted of all the Greek territory that he had already conquered, including presumably the city of Durazzo. This transaction, though it horrified the patriarch, brought peace between Byzantium and Serbia for some twenty years. The Serbian occupation of Durazzo was short. But it was a foretaste of things to come. Yet another ingredient was soon to be added to the ethnic melting-pot of Albania and Epiros.[17]

Durazzo was never again to belong to the Byzantine Empire. But the Angevin kingdom of Naples across the water would not let it remain in Serbian hands. After 1302, when Philip of Taranto was free to take action, measures were taken to revive the kingdom of Albania. Many of the native inhabitants were of the Roman faith, a fact which could be exploited to win them over. They would prefer to be protected by an Italian power than to live under the rule of schismatic Serbians or Greeks. In March 1304 the pope, Benedict XI, expressed his desire to help the bishops, priests and clerics of the Roman rite in the provinces of Albania and in Durazzo who were being oppressed by the Greeks.[18] Money was found for the rescue of Durazzo and in the summer of 1304 the Serbians were turned out of the city. In September Philip of Taranto rewarded its citizens for their renewed loyalty, and his generosity was confirmed by a royal charter from his father Charles II. In October Charles also confirmed that his son was lord of the kingdom of Albania. In the following year the people of Durazzo were assured of the amnesty that they had requested for what was described as their rebellion against the king's father; and in September Charles II, on behalf of his son, granted them extensive exemptions from dues and taxes. The Angevin kingdom of Albania took a new lease of life.[19]

Haye, 1966), p. 73 [cited hereafter as Thiriet, *Assemblées*]; R. Cessi, *Deliberazioni del Maggior Consiglio di Venezia*, III (Bologna, 1934), pp. 399–400; *ActAlb*, I, no. 526, pp. 155–6. K. Jireček, *Istorija Srba*, ed. J. Radonić, I (Belgrade, 1978), pp. 193–4; Ducellier, *Albanie*, pp. 327–8.

[17] Laiou, *Constantinople*, pp. 93–100; Nicol, *Last Centuries of Byzantium*, pp. 125–7.

[18] *ActAlb*, I, nos. 554–8, pp. 163–5. Ch. Grandjean, *Le Registre de Benoit XI* (Paris, 1905), no. 860, cols, 522–3; no. 867, cols. 527–8; *Acta Romanorum Pontificum ab Innocentio V ad Benedictum XI (1276–1304)*, ed. F. M. Delorme and A. L. Tăutu (Fontes, ser. III, vol. V: Vatican City, 1944), no. 153, pp. 252–5 (31 March 1304). Ducellier, *Albanie*, pp. 328–9.

[19] *ActAlb*, I, nos. 561, 568, 574–6, pp. 165–70. Ducellier, *Albanie*, p. 329.

The Byzantines, however, retained their hold on parts of New Epiros. Butrinto still went with Corfu as an Angevin possession. But Kanina and Valona, with the district of Spinaritsa, survived as outposts of empire on the Adriatic; and the inland fortresses of Berat and Kroia were still controlled by Byzantine governors and officers of the imperial army. In July 1294 the Latin bishop of Kroia was still unable to officiate in his diocese.[20] In 1297 the governor of Spinaritsa was one Kalamanos, with the title of *dux*.[21] In 1301 and for some years afterwards the governor of the district was Andronikos Palaiologos, whom western documents describe as captain of Spinaritsa.[22] His province included the coastline below the estuary of the Vjosa river and was administered and defended from Valona in the south and from Berat in the interior. The emperors in Constantinople were aware of its strategic importance and took care to supply it with competent and reliable commanders.

One curious but precious imperial document survives from this period of Byzantine government in New Epiros. It may have been the governor Andronikos Palaiologos who advised the bishop of Kanina to make a report to the emperor on the state of affairs in his diocese and to request a new charter confirming its rights and properties. The result was a chrysobull (*chrysoboullos logos*) issued by Andronikos II in June 1307 in favour of the See of Kanina. The original parchment roll, adorned with a full-length portrait of the emperor with the Virgin and Child, has come to rest in the Pierpont Morgan Library in New York.[23] The bishop of Kanina had lamented the fact that all the ancient deeds and chrysobulls of

[20] On 5 July 1294 Charles II awarded an annual pension to Romanus, bishop of Kroia. *ActAlb*, I, no. 522, pp. 154–5; Perrat–Longnon, no. 97, p. 99.

[21] *ActAlb*, I, no. 529, p. 157; B. Krekić, *Dubrovnik (Raguse) et le Levant au Moyen Age* (Paris-La Haye, 1961), no. 52, p. 17 (22 November 1297). He is described as 'in partibus Spinarice... ducas (= *dux*)... Calemanus, cognatus Straticopoli' – i.e. a relative of the Strategopoulos family. Ducellier, *Albanie*, pp. 35–6, identifies Spinaritsa with the Albanian village of Zvërnec on the south coast of the bay of Valona. But it was also a district sometimes known as the Σφηναρίτοι λόφοι. *MM*, III, p. 240.

[22] Krekić, *Dubrovnik*, no. 56, p. 176 (28 August 1301); no. 68, p. 177 (9 September 1302) (= *ActAlb*, I, no. 542, p. 159); no. 70, p. 178 (20 May 1303) (= *ActAlb*, I, no. 549, p. 162). Who was this Andronikos Palaiologos? *ActAlb*, I, no. 549 note, and Ducellier, *Albanie*, pp. 325, 351, confidently assert that he was Andronikos Asen Palaiologos, the son of John III Asen and Eirene Palaiologina, who later (in 1316) became governor of the Byzantine province of the Morea; and that he was succeeded as governor-general of Valona, Spinaritsa and Berat by his brother, Constantine Palaiologos, about 1320. But the Constantine Palaiologos in question was the emperor's son and not the brother of Andronikos Asen Palaiologos (cf. *ActAlb*, I, no. 669, p. 203). It seems more possible that Andronikos Palaiologos was the elder of the two sons of Demetrios-Michael Doukas of Epiros who had married Anna Palaiologina, sister of Andronikos II, in 1278. In 1326, having been made *protobestiarios*, this Andronikos was governor of Berat (Greg. ix. 8: I, p. 394). See below, p. 93 and n. 44.

[23] P. J. Alexander, 'A chrysobull of the Emperor Andronicus II Palaeologus in favor of the See of Kanina in Albania', *B*, XV (1940–1), 167–207. Cf. Dölger, *Regesten*, IV, nos. 2304, 2305.

earlier emperors which his church had once owned had been lost during the period of 'irregularity and confusion' that had disturbed the district some years before. Such words were regularly used in Byzantine texts as rhetorical euphemisms for the conditions created by war or enemy occupation. Kanina had been fought over by Angevin and Byzantine armies in the decade after 1281. The poet Manuel Philes recalled its reconquest for the empire as one of the heroic deeds of the *protostrator* Michael Glabas Tarchaneiotes. Together with Valona and Spinaritsa, Kanina had become a part of that Byzantine enclave on the Adriatic which John Cantacuzene was to describe in later years as 'the furthest limits of Roman hegemony'.[24]

The chrysobull of 1307 lists by name the landed and other properties in the diocese of Kanina. Not all of these can now be identified. They covered a wide area, stretching as far north as the valley of the Vjosa river at Mifoli (Hemipholon), where the church owned nine saltpans. It also possessed four saltpans and a fishing station at Valona; one thousand *modioi* of land at Risilia (Chryselios) to the north-east of Valona; a number of villages and farms; and land and water mills on the further side of the river Shushica (Sousitzes) to the east of Kanina. The document recalls the activities of one Papylas, *pansebastos domestikos*, who had requisitioned a large part of the church's property and assigned it to the inhabitants of the *kastron* of Kanina. Papylas may well have been an officer in the army of Tarchaneiotes obliged to take extreme measures to provide for the garrison in the castle of Kanina.[25] The castle is said to have contained within its walls houses and a cistern which had once been the property of a lady called Phrantzaina, though they had later been presented to the bishopric by decree (*prostagma*) of Andronikos II. The lady Phrantzaina was without doubt that Maria Sphrantzaina, sister-in-law of the Despot Michael II, who had married and probably helped to murder Philip Chinardo in 1267.[26] The cathedral church of Kanina was situated not within the *kastron* but at the village of Esochorion, presumably nearby; and here there was an annual fair or *panegyri* on the feast of the Nativity of the Virgin (8 September), the revenues of which went to the bishopric.[27]

[24] Cantac. i. 23: 1, p. 115, l. 19: ... τῶν ἄκρων ὅρων τῆς Ῥωμαίων ηγεμονίας .... The poem of Manuel Philes in praise of the exploits of the *protostrator* Tarchaneiotes is referred to above, p. 28 and n. 72.

[25] Alexander, 'Chrysobull', 196–7, tentatively identifies him with the *megas tzaousios* Papylas of Michael VIII and Andronikos II. Pach. *De Andron. Pal.*, i. 1: 11, p. 13.

[26] For Maria Sphrantzaina and Chinardo, see above, pp. 13–14. The connexions of the Sphrantzes family with Kanina are discussed by Alexander, 'Chrysobull', 197.

[27] Alexander, 'Chrysobull', 179, ll. 38–40. To the list of similar fairs in the Palaiologan period (ibid., 187) may be added that at Ioannina, which lasted from 26 October to 8 November every year. *MM*, v, pp. 86–7 (see below, p. 87).

The bishop had been anxious not only about the properties of his see but also about the extortionate or illegal demands made upon its inhabitants by some of the local Greek governors. In particular he had in mind the penalties which they imposed for murder and the *mitaton* or compulsory sale of grain to the governors at prices arbitrarily fixed by them. Blood vengeance among feuding families, described here as the *phonikon*, was no doubt endemic in this part of the world. The bishop, who might have been expected to condemn the practice, complained rather about the punishments meted out to the culprits by the governor (*doukeuon*), especially if the murderer happened to be a tenant farmer (*paroikos*) of the church or related to one of its clergy. The emperor ruled that, whereas the murderer should be punished, his neighbours in the area could not be held responsible for his crime and be made to suffer along with him, as some governors seem to have insisted. All his moveable property should be confiscated. But the church must not be made the poorer by confiscation of his landed property. The emperor also ruled that the acting governors-general (*kephalitikeuontes*) were in future to be prohibited from commandeering grain at prices below the market level whether from the farmers of land belonging to the bishop's diocese or from the people living in the whole district of Berat and Kanina.[28]

This chrysobull of 1307 is one of the few Greek documents that provide some insight into the life of Epiros at the beginning of the fourteenth century. It is comparable in some respects to the longer and more elaborate charters which the same emperor was to grant to the see of Ioannina in 1319 and 1321. But it says much for the importance which the emperor attached to this distant outpost of his dwindling dominions that he should have gratified one of its bishops with so impressive a charter.

The French colonists in Epiros, like their relatives in the Morea, had come as conquerors and settlers. The Venetians visited or resided in Epiros with a different purpose. They were more concerned with commerce than with conquest. There had often been moments when the Greek rulers of Epiros felt that they could turn to Venice to play off their other enemies. The Venetians were always interested in the commercial possibilities of a province which lay so conveniently on their trade route to the east; and they never lost the hope that one day they would regain possession of Corfu. They had claimed the harbours and markets of Epiros in the Partition Treaty of 1204 and for a while they had been fooled into believing that their treaty of 1210 with Michael I Doukas

[28] Alexander, 'Chrysobull', 180–3, ll. 70f. On the *phonikon* and *mitaton*, see ibid., 202–4; P. Charanis, 'The phonikon and other Byzantine taxes', *Speculum*, XX (1945), 331–3; G. Ostrogorsky, 'Pour l'histoire de l'immunité à Byzance', *B*, XXXVIII (1958), 247–8; Lj. Maksimović, *Vizantijska provinzijska uprava u doba Paleologa* (Belgrade, 1972), pp. 70, 95–6, 142.

would be respected. As elsewhere in Greece, they were less concerned with the interior of the country than with collecting the produce that might come from it to the ports. Of these the most lucrative to them were Durazzo, Valona and Arta. In Arta they sometimes maintained a consul. But they were quick to withdraw their merchants and their money at the first sign of trouble.

The evidence for their presence and their fortunes in Epiros in the late thirteenth and early fourteenth centuries is sparse and sporadic. In 1272, after the loss of Durazzo to Charles of Anjou, Venetian ships were authorised to take the route to Arta.[29] In 1283, there was evidently merchant traffic between Venice and Arta.[30] But in August 1284 an envoy had to be sent to Arta to investigate the theft of some Venetian merchandise; and the Despot forbade his subjects to have any further commercial dealings with Venice. Their consul at Corfu, who had responsibility for Arta, was therefore instructed to suspend all dealings with the Despotate and to advise all Venetian residents to get out as quickly as possible.[31] This embargo may not have lasted long, though the Despot Nikephoros seems to have made life difficult for Venetian traders, plundering their ships and damaging their property, despite official protests sent to him by embassies from Venice in 1289 and 1292.[32] There were, however, Venetians still doing business in Arta in 1297. Two of them were victims of the attack on the city by troops of the *sebastokrator* Constantine of Thessaly in that year. In August 1298 Venice demanded compensation from the 'duke of Neopatras' for two of her citizens, Lorenzo Mengulo and Pietro Savonario, whose property in Arta had been destroyed by his soldiers.[33]

There were also Venetian citizens who resided and owned property in Epiros and who were loyal supporters of the Despot, notably the families of Moro and Contareno. Niccolo Moro and his sons appear to have owned houses in Arta as well as ships.[34] But the best attested is Jacopo Contareno who was a landowner at Vrastova in Vagenetia, to the north of Margariti. He and his family claimed a hereditary right to their estate and persuaded the Despot Thomas to confirm this fact. In August 1303 Thomas, aping the manners of a Byzantine emperor, issued a chrysobull in favour of

[29] Thiriet, *Assemblées*, I, p. 35 (7 November 1272).

[30] Ibid., I, p. 44 (1–10 July 1283); Cessi, *Deliberazioni*, III, pp. 35, 36.

[31] Thiriet, *Assemblées*, I, pp. 48–9 (10 and 17 August 1284); Cessi, *Deliberazioni*, III, pp. 78, 79.

[32] Thiriet, *Assemblées*, I, p. 59 (21 July 1289); pp. 65, 66 (4–11 and 1 July 1292); Cessi, *Deliberazioni*, III, pp. 238, 313–19.

[33] Thiriet, *Assemblées*, I, p. 75; Cessi, *Deliberazioni*, III, p. 443 (18 August 1298). Cf. Hopf, *GG*, I, p. 331.

[34] G. M. Thomas and R. Predelli, *Diplomatarium Veneto-Levantinum*, I (Venice, 1880), p. 136 [cited hereafter as *DVL*]; *ActAlb*, I, nos. 619, 620, p. 183.

Contareno and his sons. The document has been preserved in the form of a Latin translation of the Greek original.[35] It confirms a previous edict of the Despot on behalf of Contareno; and it solemnly declares that he and his heirs shall have full proprietary rights over the domain of Vrastova, free of all levies and taxes, save for those related to the building of castles, homicide and treasure trove. Nor is any civil or military agent of the Despot ever to set foot therein. It is Contareno's own private estate in which he is at liberty to buy and sell, build churches, repair houses, plant vines and tend olives, enjoying all the rights recognised by the law relating to hereditary properties and patrimonies.

It is a pompous document which illustrates the pretensions of Thomas the Despot 'Komnenodoukas' who signed it. None of his predecessors in Epiros had presumed to issue a *chrysoboullos logos* (*sigillum aureum verbum*) as compared with a simple *chrysoboullon*. Furthermore, it lists a number of titles of functionaries, forms of taxation and legalities which were probably more imaginary than real in the circumstances of Epiros in 1303.[36] But it also illustrates how far the Despot Thomas, perhaps in contrast to his father, was prepared to go to foster the goodwill of Venice and her trade. The Venetians were to have many causes for complaint in Epiros in later years. But they were always anxious to maintain their trade; and the families of Moro and Contareno for long continued to act as brokers, moneylenders and bankers in Arta and elsewhere.

The history of Epiros in the first decade of the fourteenth century is eclipsed by the more dramatic events being enacted in the rest of Greece. The drama was caused by the activities of the Catalan Company, the army of mercenaries from the west which the emperor hired to fight the Turks in 1303. The Byzantine historians, George Pachymeres and Nikephoros Gregoras, were naturally more concerned to narrate and to account for these activities than to record events in distant Epiros. For the Catalans threatened the very heart of the empire in Constantinople. But it was in Greece that these restless adventurers finally came to roost. When driven out of Thrace, which they had reduced to a desert, the Catalans made for Macedonia in 1307. From there they moved down into Thessaly in the spring of 1309.[37]

The nominal ruler of Thessaly, or at least of its southern district

[35] P. Lemerle, 'Le privilège du Despote d'Epire Thomas I pour le Vénitien Jacques Contareno', *BZ*, XLIV (1951), 389–96 (text: 390–1). The document was known to Hopf, *GG*, I, p. 356. Lemerle, 'Le privilège', 395–6, gives the reasons for dating it to August 1303 rather than 1313. On Vrastova, see Soustal–Koder, p. 276.

[36] Lemerle, 'Le privilège', 396.

[37] For the activities of the Catalan Company in Greece, see: K. M. Setton, *Catalan Domination of Athens 1311–1388* (revised ed.: London, 1975); Laiou, *Constantinople*, pp. 134–40, 146–7, 177–83, 208–11, 220–9; Nicol, *Last Centuries of Byzantium*, pp. 137–46; Setton, *Papacy*, I, pp. 441–68.

around Neopatras, was the young John II Doukas whose father had made him a ward of Guy, duke of Athens. John had now nearly come of age. His guardian had died in October 1308. The new duke of Athens was his relative Walter of Brienne, who arrived in Greece in 1309. Walter found his duchy beset by its Greek neighbours, the Despot of Epiros as well as the lord of Thessaly.[38] He saw some use for the services of a band of mercenaries like the Catalans, whose prowess he had painfully experienced in Sicily some years before. The Thessalians would be glad to be rid of them. A deal was done; and for about six months the Catalans fought for their pay in the service of Walter of Brienne. Too late he found that they had come to stay and that he had not the means to pay them to go elsewhere. He would have to drive them out by force. On 15 March 1311 he and his army encountered the Catalans and their Turkish allies near Halmyros, north-east of Lamia. Walter was killed, his army was routed and the Catalans descended to occupy Thebes and Athens. The French duchy of Athens was at an end.[39]

The Despotate of Epiros was not much directly affected by these events. For some years the Catalans busied themselves in settling in to their new duchy and making war on their Latin neighbours to the south. Even Thessaly, though devastated by the visitation of a marauding army, was left in peace after it had moved on. The young and sickly John II of Neopatras, no longer protected by a friendly guardian in Athens, broke with the policies of his father and grandfather by making up to the emperor in Constantinople. He married Eirene, an illegitimate daughter of Andronikos II, probably in 1309.[40] He might have expected that the emperor would reward him with the title of *sebastokrator*. It seems that he may have done even better; for the epitaph on John's death written by Manuel Philes implies that he held the higher rank of Despot.[41] He liked to think that he had a claim to Athens through his relationship with the late Duke Guy II; and, though he never went there, he styled himself

[38] Ramon Muntaner, *The Chronicle of Ramon Muntaner*, translated by Lady Goodenough, II (Hakluyt Society: London, 1921), p. 575.

[39] For the site of the fateful battle of 1311, which was formerly placed by the river Kephissos in Boiotia, see now Setton, *Papacy*, I, p. 441 and n. 2, where the literature is cited.

[40] The date of this marriage is problematical. Greg. vii. 7: I, p. 249, seems to date it to 1309; but elsewhere (vii. 12: I, pp. 278–9) he says that John lived for only three years with his wife before he died in 1318. Cf. Laiou, *Constantinople*, p. 230 n. 10. Manuel Philes, who wrote an epitaph for John, says that he was married for only nine months. Philes, ed. Ae. Martini, *Manuelis Philae Carmina Inedita* (Naples, 1900), no. 87, pp. 123–5 l. 22. It has been suggested that nine 'months' should be corrected to nine 'years', which would date the marriage to 1309. Greg. (van Dieten), I, p. 293 n. 434. It is possible that Eirene was the illegitimate daughter of Andronikos II for whom his wife, also called Eirene, had stood as godmother, See above, p. 54 n. 85.

[41] Philes, ed. Martini, no. 87, p. 125, ll. 36–40.

'John Komnenos Angelos Doukas, lord of the lands of Athens and Neopatras, duke of Great Vlachia and Kastoria'.[42]

Thessaly was thus diplomatically reunited with Constantinople. The *basilissa* Anna of Epiros had always hoped that she could achieve a similar arrangement. In her declining years her hope was, however briefly, realised. Her son Thomas was persuaded to follow his mother's advice. He had been chastened by the attack on his territory in 1306 and discouraged by the ill treatment of his sister Thamar by Philip of Taranto. It was in 1303 that his mother had first suggested that he should marry into the imperial family in Constantinople. Four years later that marriage was celebrated. Thomas took as his bride Anna Palaiologina, daughter of Michael IX and granddaughter of Andronikos II. The date of the wedding is generally given, on not very substantial evidence, as 1313. It should probably be dated to the year 1307.[43] Having married a daughter to the ruler of Thessaly and a granddaughter to the ruler of Epiros, the Emperor Andronikos II had in one sense reintegrated these two provinces into his empire. In another sense he might be said to have accepted the principle of divide and rule proposed by his wife Eirene some years earlier. But Epiros and Thessaly were not quite appanages in the manner that she had proposed, for their rulers were native to the soil and hereditary and their only link with the empire was through marriage. It was soon to be shown that this was a tenuous link. But while it lasted the emperor made the most of it.

In or about 1313 the Byzantine and Epirote armies joined forces at Valona. Some modern authorities speak of an army being sent west from Constantinople under the command of one Laskaris. There is no clear evidence for the existence either of such an army or of the alleged

[42] *ActAlbVen*, I, 1, pp. 12–13: 'Çane cominino, Anzolo, ducha et segnor de le terre da thenes at patras, educha de lagran blachia e dela castoria'.

[43] The Greek sources for the marriage of Thomas and Anna are Greg. viii. 1: I, p. 283, and Cantac. i. l: I, p. 13. Neither gives any clear chronological indication. Both, however, record it in connexion with the marriage of Michael IX's second daughter to Svetslav of Bulgaria; and this seems to have occurred in 1308. F. Dölger, 'Einiges über Theodora', *Mélanges H. Grégoire*, I (Paris, 1935), 215 n. 2, 216 (reprinted in ΠΑΡΑΣΠΟΡΑ [Ettal, 1961], p. 225 n. 8). Since Anna was the elder sister it seems improbable that she should have married second of the two. The author of the *Anonymi Descriptio Europae Orientalis* (ed. Olgierd Górka [Krakow, 1916]), which was compiled in 1308, was aware that Thomas, the brother of Thamar, had 'recently' married a daughter of the emperor of Constantinople. In his account of Epiros he states: 'Partem huius provincie princeps achaye, filius regis sycylie, ratione uxoris, que est despoti filia, occupat, licet frater uterinus uxoris eiusdem principis, qui [nunc] de novo filiam imperatoris constantinopolitani duxit in uxorem, impugnet eum viriliter et proficiat multum contra eum ut dicitur' (pp. 16–17). 1307 or 1308 seems therefore to be a more correct date for this marriage, for all that the date 1313 has been generally accepted by, e.g., Polemis, *The Doukai*, no. 53, p. 98; Greg. (van Dieten), II, i, pp. 101–2; *PLP*, I, no. 197.

Laskaris.[44] More probably the Byzantine forces were sent down from Berat which was still in imperial control. Berat with Valona and Spinaritsa had been administered by Andronikos Palaiologos at least until 1303. But by 1313 Valona seems to have been controlled by one George Gantzas who called himself *prothontinus* or admiral. Gantzas used Valona as a base for plundering Corfu; and in August 1313 he was in Arta 'with some of the emperor's troops', having sailed there in two ships. While he was there a great fire broke out in the city and some of his men looted the property of a Venetian merchant called Moreto Moro. The Venetians were then on friendly terms with the Despot Thomas and with the Byzantine emperor. Their merchants were still doing regular business in Arta and Valona in 1312.[45] But they could not allow their citizens to be robbed without protest. They blamed the emperor for the misconduct of his troops at Arta and claimed compensation for the damage done to Moreto Moro. This was the first of a long list of claims for damages later to be lodged with the emperor by the Doge of Venice.

The 'irregularity and confusion' prevailing in the area south of Valona in these years is reflected in a document concerning the monastery of St Nicholas at Mesopotamon, whose abbot Niphon had gone as an emissary to Naples in 1302. Mesopotamon lay in what was called the theme of Vagenetia, on the Vistrica river not far from Delvino.[46] Its monastery of St Nicholas boasted of its foundation in the eleventh century and of its direct dependence on the patriarch of Constantinople as a *stavropegion*. In other words it was answerable to the patriarch and was free from the jurisdiction of its local bishop, as were all its landed properties and outlying sketes and hermitages. None the less, the bishop of Chimara, on the coast to the north, had taken advantage of the troubled circumstances of the time to impose his authority on the monks and their possessions. They had complained to the then patriarch, who had ordered the bishop of Chimara to be expelled from his see. In 1315 John Glykys, who had just been elected to the patriarchate, issued a decree, at the request of the monks of Mesopotamon, confirming the ancient and privileged status of

[44] See Laiou, *Constantinople*, pp. 257–8. This seems to derive from Hopf, *GG*, I, p. 418, who for once gives no source reference, but names the commander as Joannes 'Legeschera'. This might well be another variant of 'Lepischernus' or 'Pichernus', referring to Syrgiannes the *pinkernes*. A later document (of 1332) mentions a Laskaris as having formerly been 'capitaneo ... in partibus Belgradi et Avellone' (εἰς κεφαλὴν ... τοῦ κάστρου Κανίνων, τοῦ Αὐλῶνος καὶ τῶν ἄλλων ἐκεῖσε χωρῶν). *MM*, III, p. 109; *DVL*, I, p. 233; *ActAlb*, I, no. 762.

[45] *DVL*, I, no. 76, p. 135: '... Georgius Ganza, qui facit se nominari protentinus Aualone'. *ActAlbVen*, I, I, no. 48, p. 21; *ActAlb*, I, no. 619, p. 183. Ducellier, *Albanie*, pp. 354, 398. For Venetian trade with Arta and Valona, mainly in cloth, see R. Cessi and P. Sambin, *Le Deliberazione del Consiglio dei Rogati (Senato) serie Mixtorum*, I (Venice, 1960), p. 137 (Miste, III, no. 123) [cited hereafter as Cessi–Sambin, *Deliberazione*]. Cf. Hopf, *GG*, I, p. 417.

[46] Soustal–Koder, pp. 206–7. For Niphon of Mesopotamon, see above, p. 65.

their monastery and its dependencies. Not the least interesting aspect of this document is the proof that it provides for the continuing communication between the patriarchate in Constantinople and its churches and monasteries on the outer limits of the empire. The emperor had all but lost the battle to hold together the surviving pieces of his empire. But the patriarch's authority was still universally respected; and even a bishop of distant Chimara was not beyond the reach of that authority.[47]

It was about this time that the emperor appointed a new commander of the imperial forces at Berat. He was Syrgiannes Philanthropenos Palaiologos. He was only twenty-five years old when he was sent, in the words of Gregoras, to be military governor of that province of Macedonia which was next door to the Illyrians.[48] Syrgiannes was an ambitious if devious man and he soon made his presence felt in Epiros. He brought an army south from Berat and overran the district of Spinaritsa. He then made for Vonitsa, which he is said to have captured from the Angevins after a long siege in October 1314. In February 1315 he attacked Arta, causing damage to the property of another Venetian merchant, Pietro Moro.[49] No wonder that Gregoras accuses Syrgiannes of disregarding the treaties which his emperor had made and of bringing trouble on the Serbians, Aitolians and Akarnanians.[50]

The Despot Thomas had not made peace with the emperor to have his city of Arta attacked, burnt and looted by Byzantine soldiers. He now declared that peace to be at an end. The emperor in turn proclaimed Thomas to be once more a rebel and an enemy of Byzantium. Thomas retaliated by imprisoning his wife Anna, the emperor's granddaughter. The Venetians, who were anxious to keep on good terms

[47] *MM*, I, pp. 1–2, and IV, pp. vii–ix. The document is republished in H. Hunger and O. Kresten, *Das Register des Patriarchats von Konstantinopel*, I (*CFHB*, XIX/I: Vienna, 1981), no. 2, pp. 112–21 [cited hereafter as Hunger–Kresten, *Register*]. Cf. Darrouzès, *Regestes*, no. 2030, pp. 21–2 (May–July 1315); O. Mazal, *Die Prooimien der byzantinischen Patriarchatsurkunden* (Byzantina Vindobonensia, VII: Vienna, 1974), pp. 36, 141, 144, 149, 228.

[48] Greg. viii. 4: I, p. 297, ll. 4–7. A special study of Syrgiannes was made by S. Binon, 'A propos d'un prostagma inédit d'Andronic III Paléologue', *BZ*, XXXVIII (1938), 133–55, 377–407. But it takes little account of the Venetian documents, and its information on the parentage of Syrgiannes is mistaken. See Greg. (van Dieten), II, i, pp. 118–25.

[49] *ActAlbVen*, I, I, nos. 24, 48, pp. 11, 23–4 (dated February 1315); *DVL*, I, p. 136 (dated February 1314). Cf. Hopf, *GG*, I, p. 419. The captain of the emperor's army was 'Ioannes Lepischerni' or 'lopicherni' (=*pinkernes*). Some have identified him with John Angelos *pinkernes*, the cousin of John Cantacuzene (e.g., Ducellier, *Albanie*, p. 351). But he does not come on to the historical scene until 1337–8. Nicol, *Byzantine Family of Kantakouzenos*, p. 147; and see below, p. 107. It is true that Syrgiannes was not made *pinkernes* until 1319; Greg. (van Dieten), II, i, p. 125. But the Latin documents in which he is mentioned were not drawn up until 1319–20 and he is referred to by the title which he then held. Pietro Moro was questioned under oath by the Venetian consul in Arta, Marco Venerio (? Venier).

[50] Greg. viii. 4: I, p. 297: (Syrgiannes) παρασπονδῶν γὰρ πρῶτον μὲν πράγματα παρεῖχε τοῖς ὁμόροις Τριβάλλοις καὶ Αἰτωλοῖς καὶ Ἀκαρνᾶσιν.

with Constantinople, gallantly came to her rescue. Pietro Moro, who was the son of the wealthy Niccolo, lent her 500 *hyperpyra* and she borrowed another 1500 *hyperpyra* from the Contareno family bank. The settlement of these debts was later to cause some friction between Venice and Constantinople. The Venetians complained that they had never been fully repaid. At the time the emperor had gone out of his way to express his thanks to the Venetian baillie in Constantinople, Marco Minotto; and he had ordered his commander in Berat, Syrgiannes, to pay the debts incurred by his granddaughter. Syrgiannes had obeyed this order, but only to the extent of the 1500 *hyperpyra* owing to the Contareno company. Pietro Moro was still owed his 500 *hyperpyra*, although the unhappy Anna had personally written to him about the matter. In 1317 she also wrote to the Doge of Venice to explain that, so far as she was concerned, she owed nobody anything. All her outstanding debts to Venice had been paid. The Venetians were astonished when the emperor later claimed that, by lending money to his granddaughter, they had been giving comfort to his enemies. They were still demanding payment in 1320.[51]

Having failed to obtain satisfaction from the emperor, the Venetians approached Thomas and his mother Anna. In 1317 a number of envoys passed between Venice and Arta. The affair of Pietro Moro was not their only grievance. There was also the matter of the property of Lorenzo Mengulo and Pietro Savonario which had been destroyed as long ago as 1297 when the Thessalians attacked Arta. In December 1306 the Venetian Senate had taken this matter up with the *basilissa* Anna. Nine years later the claim had still not been settled. In September and October 1317 reminders were sent to Anna and Thomas.[52] Finally, in September 1318, the Venetians lost patience and announced that their merchants could no longer do business in the Despot's territory until all outstanding claims for compensation had been met.[53]

[51] These facts are derived from the petitions and claims submitted to the emperor by the Doge of Venice in 1319 and 1320 and the emperor's replies. *DVL*, I, pp. 138, 150, 163; *ActAlbVen*, I, I, no. 48, p. 26; no. 49, p. 28; no. 55, pp. 39–40. Cf. *ActAlb*, I, nos. 619–21, 625, pp. 183–4, 185; no. 657, p. 198; nos. 669, 670, pp. 202–3. Dölger, *Regesten*, IV, no. 2427. Anna's letter to the Doge of 14 May 1317 is in *ActAlbVen*, I, I, no. 31, pp. 13–14; R. Predelli, *I Libri Commemoriali della Republica di Venezia: Regesti*, I (Venice, 1876), no. 42, p. 178. Anna here styles herself 'Anna euagonesciti regina cominina duchisa'. Predelli, *Regesti*, I, no. 42, p. 178, and others have supposed this Anna to be the mother of John II of Thessaly. There is no warrant for this supposition. See above, p. 52, n. 77. 'Euagonesciti' could perhaps be no more than an attempt to transcribe the Greek word εὐγενεστάτη.

[52] *ActAlbVen*, I, I, no. 13, p. 7 (December 1306); nos. 34, 35, 37–8, pp. 15–16 (September and October 1317). Cessi–Sambin, *Deliberazione*, I, p. 120, no. 214; pp. 181–2, nos. 50, 51, 56, 58.

[53] *ActAlbVen*, I, I, no. 42, p. 20 (September 1318); Cessi–Sambin, *Deliberazione*, p. 195, no. 216.

The Byzantine intervention in the affairs of the Despotate brought more trouble than peace. The emperor had to listen to interminable tales of woe from the Venetians who had suffered as a consequence. They complained about the illegal seizure of merchant ships plying between Corfu and Valona in 1314; about the looting and destruction of Venetian merchants' houses in Valona after an incident at sea; and about the refusal of eighty men of Valona and Spinaritsa to settle their debts with Marco, Jacopo Contareno and Pietro Moro. In 1315 they had appealed to the governor of Berat, the *pinkernes* Syrgiannes, but he had not been helpful.[54] Only in the last of these cases did the emperor concede that injustice was being done; and in 1320 he ordered the new governor of the area, his son Constantine Palaiologos, to see to it that these debts were paid.[55] For the rest he replied that the Venetians must abide by the rules of war. The Despot Thomas had become an enemy of Byzantium whose land had to be devastated. Venetian residents in that land who favoured and assisted him could not complain if they got hurt. The Doge politely pointed out that not all of these incidents had happened as a result of war. At the time when George Gantzas looted Moreto's property at Arta in 1313, the Despot Thomas, 'who was crowned by your majesty as ruler of the whole Despotate', was a peaceful friend and kinsman of the emperor. It was sad that he later became a rebel and that war broke out. For merchants do much better business in conditions of peace than when there is warfare; and the Venetians who lived in Arta did so not as partisans of the emperor's enemies but as law-abiding business men.[56]

These exchanges between Venice and Constantinople took place in 1319 and 1320. By then, as the emperor was well aware, the situation in Epiros had changed. He had himself declared the Despot Thomas to be an outlaw. The Venetians had refused to do any further trade in his territory. Thomas had offended his wife and probably driven his elderly mother Anna to her grave.[57] In desperation he had turned again to his former master in Italy, Philip of Taranto, to whom he wrote in 1318. Philip was pleased at this change of heart and kindly sent Thomas some warhorses in

[54] *DVL*, I, pp. 136–8; *ActAlbVen*, I, I, nos. 23–5, 48, pp. 11, 22–6; *ActAlb*, I, nos. 621, 643, pp. 183–4, 193–4. Syrgiannes is called 'capitaneo de *Belgrado*, scilicet domino Ioanni Picherni' in 1316 (*DVL*, I, p. 138).

[55] *DVL*, I, pp. 149–50, 162; *ActAlbVen*, I, I, no. 49, p. 28: '... filio Imperii nostri felicissimo dispoto domino Constantino Paleologo, habenti potestatem generalem a nobis in locis illis'. Cf. Dölger, *Regesten*, IV, no. 2428.

[56] *DVL*, I, p. 161; *ActAlbVen*, I, I, p. 38.

[57] The last certain documentary mention of the *basilissa* or Despina Anna is in 1313 (see below, n. 59); but she could perhaps be the 'Anna euagonesciti regina' and 'Despina' mentioned in documents of May and September 1317 (*ActAlbVen*, I, I, nos. 31, 34, 35, pp. 13–15). In that case she must have died the year before her son Thomas.

June of that year.[58] But before the year was out Thomas was dead, murdered by his nephew Nicholas Orsini of Cephalonia.

A list of the rulers of Greece compiled in Venice in 1313 accords to Thomas the magnificent tile of 'Thomas Komnenos Doukas by the grace of God great Despot of Romania, Prince of Vlachia, Lord of Archangelos, Duke of Vagenetia, Count of Acheloos and Naupaktos and Lord of the royal castle of Ioannina'.[59] He would have enjoyed having his obituary so inscribed. Thomas was the last direct descendant of the family of Komnenos Doukas Angelos which had created the Despotate of Epiros. He died without issue; and with his passing the Despotate as the hereditary domain of its founding family ceased to exist. But the independence of Epiros from Constantinople had a long history. Many of its inhabitants would still prefer to live under their own separatist rulers. The political and geographical concept of a 'despotatus', though essentially western and not Byzantine, was now hellenised and it would not die with the death of the last Greek Despot. The last of the hereditary line of the *sebastokrators* of Thessaly, John II Doukas, seems also to have died in 1318. He too had no heir. Thessaly drifted into anarchy, or into the polyarchy of a number of separate domains ruled by local Greek magnates. One of them, Stephen Gabrielopoulos, was in due course to win imperial recognition as a *sebastokrator*. The Catalans moved into Thessaly from the south. The emperor claimed it as the estate of his now widowed daughter, and his army made threatening noises from Thessalonica in the north. The patriarch of Constantinople vainly exhorted the Thessalians to revert to their former and proper status within the empire. Otherwise he promised them 'horrendous penalties'. But the most ominous development for the future was the infiltration into Thessaly, and also into Epiros, of bands of marauding Albanians dislodged from their mountain fastnesses in the north.[60]

[58] Hopf, *GG*, I, p. 419, is the only source for this exchange. He names Thomas's messenger to Philip as 'Demetrios Gantzas'.

[59] Hopf, *Chroniques*, p. 178: 'Ser Thomas Dei gratia Despoti Romanie Comninus dux. Ser Thomas Dei gratia magnus Romanie Dispotus, Princeps Blachie, Archang (eli) Dominus, Dux Vigenitie, Comes Achilo et Nepanti ac Regalis Castri Ioannine Dominus'. Cf. Hopf, *GG*, I, p. 356. 'Archangeli' may be the castle of Thomokastron built by Thomas (see below, p. 115 n. 23). The list of rulers includes 'Domina Anna Christi fidelis Despina Cumnina Duccissa', which signifies that Thomas's mother, the *basilissa* Anna, was still alive in 1313. For the date of the document, see Hopf, *Chroniques*, p. xxiv.

[60] Greg. vii. 12: I, pp. 277–9; viii. 6: I, p. 318. Cf. Darrouzès, *Regestes*, no. 2091, p. 67. Conditions in Thessaly in 1325 are vividly described by Marino Sanudo in a letter to the archbishop of Capua. Tafel and Thomas, *Urkunden*, I, pp. 494–501; A. Rubió y Lluch, *Diplomatari de l'Orient Català, 1302–1409* (Barcelona, 1947), no. 229, pp. 159–61. Setton, *Catalan Domination of Athens*, p. 29 and n. 32; R.-J. Loenertz, 'Athènes et Néopatras: I', in Loenertz, *Byzantina et Franco-Graeca* (=*BFG*), II (Rome, 1978), pp. 188, 189; D. Jacoby, 'Catalans, Turcs et Vénitiens en Romanie (1305–1332): un nouveau témoignage de Marino Sanudo Torsello', *Studi Medievali*, ser. 3, xv (1974), 217–61, especially 235–8.

4

The Italian inheritance: The Orsini family – 1318–37

The Emperor Andronikos II considered the death of Thomas of Epiros in 1318 to be divine retribution. Thomas had rebelled against imperial authority. He had got what he deserved.[1] The agent of God's vengeance was Nicholas Orsini, who had succeeded his father John as count of Cephalonia in 1317. John had fancied himself as Despot of Arta. Nicholas turned the fancy into fact by murdering his uncle Thomas. His motives were part personal and part political.[2] His father had borne a grudge against Thomas for his persistent refusal to acknowledge the rights of the Orsini family over the territory in Epiros that belonged to his wife Maria. Taking a wider view, however, Nicholas could see that a political vacuum existed in Romania. There was no effective prince of Achaia. Philip of Taranto, having divorced Thamar, had in 1313 married Catherine of Valois and so acquired a share in the Latin Empire of Constantinople, the title to which Catherine had inherited six years before. Charles II of Naples had died in 1309 leaving his eldest son Robert as king. Robert and his brother Philip applied themselves to assembling a dynastic jigsaw puzzle in Romania. By tortuous negotiations they contrived that Matilda, the widow of Guy II of Athens, should marry Louis of Burgundy. Louis thus became prince of Achaia, but not for long. His title was contested by

[1] *DVL*, I, p. 146: '... cum autem contra illum (Thomas) divinum iuditium factum est et mortuus sit...'. Cf. Greg. viii. 6: I, p. 318, who regards the timely deaths of Milutin of Serbia (d. 1321), Svetslav of Bulgaria (d. 1322), Thomas of Epiros (d. 1318) and John of Thessaly (d. 1318) as clear evidence of the wonderful workings of providence.

[2] The murder of Thomas by Nicholas Orsini is recorded by Greg. viii. 1: I, 283; viii. 6: I, p. 318, by *Chron. Mor. arag.*, §628, p. 138, and by Pope John XXII. *Lettres secrètes et curiales du pape Jean XXII (1316–1334)*, ed. A. Conlon, I (Paris, 1900), cols. 669–70, no. 772: (29 November [1318?]) The pope alerts Philip of France to news recently received from Philip of Taranto: 'Comes namque Cephalonie quondam Thomasium, Romanie despotum, gladio trucidavit, cujus successio in toto despotatu predicto dictus princeps ex persona quondam principisse, consortis sue ac predicti Thomasii defuncti sororis, asserit sibi suoque primogenito, hereditario ac conventionali jure, debere defferri'. None of these sources suggests a plausible motive for the crime. The later act of the patriarch's synod concerning Ioannina (*MM*, I, no. 76, pp. 171–4) is tactfully silent on the matter of how Nicholas came to succeed Thomas.

Margaret, widow of Richard of Cephalonia, who was a Villehardouin; and in 1316 Louis of Burgundy died, leaving Matilda twice widowed. Philip of Taranto hurriedly produced a third husband for her in the person of his own brother, John of Gravina in Apulia, who thus became prince of Achaia in 1318, even though Matilda refused to live with him. It was widely rumoured that Louis of Burgundy had not died of natural causes. He had been poisoned by John Orsini of Cephalonia.[3]

The house of Orsini was well placed to take over where the Angevin and Greek rulers of Epiros might leave off. Throughout the many upheavals that had afflicted the other Latin states in Greece, the county of Cephalonia, Ithaka and Zante had remained comparatively stable. It had been held by the members of a single family ever since Maio Orsini had appropriated the islands some ten years before the Fourth Crusade. From the first, when Maio married a sister of Theodore Komnenos Doukas, the family had been connected with the rulers of Epiros. They had often looked for ways to profit from the disputes of their Greek and Latin neighbours on the mainland. By 1318 it seemed that the profits were theirs for the taking. The duchy of Athens was in Catalan hands; the principality of Achaia had never been so feeble; and its suzerain Philip of Taranto could hardly keep order there let alone in his colony in Epiros.

The court at Naples welcomed the news that the Despotate had fallen into Italian hands. Nicholas Orsini was a vassal of the prince of Achaia and had taken the oath to John of Gravina in 1318. He must now be made to do so in his new capacity as lord of Epiros. In 1319 the baillie of Achaia, Frederick of Troys (Federigo Trogisio), was instructed to see that he did. Nicholas refused to be so committed.[4] He had taken to living as the guest of his uncle at Arta. He knew the lie of the land and he felt that he could make himself master if not Despot of Epiros by winning the confidence of the Greeks. He had plenty of Greek blood in his own veins. His mother Maria was Greek and his grandfather Richard had been half Greek. He probably spoke Greek; he certainly engraved his seal in Greek; and he adopted the Orthodox faith. Having set himself up at Arta, he married Anna, daughter of Michael IX, whom he had reduced to widowhood by murdering her husband Thomas. She was his aunt, but no horrendous penalties appear to have been imposed by the church for so scandalous a union. Indeed one is left to wonder how far Anna was personally involved

[3] Miller, *Latins in the Levant*, pp. 250–61; Longnon, *L'Empire latin*, pp. 303–8; Bon, *Morée*, pp. 188–90, 193–5, 200–1; Setton, *Papacy*, I, p. 153.

[4] Hopf, *GG*, I, p. 420. Romanos, *Despotate*, p. 122 (61), however, claims that Nicholas did in fact swear an oath of allegiance, though the document which he cites does not prove the point. C. Minieri-Riccio, *Studî storici su' fascicoli angioini dell' Archivio della reggia zecca di Napoli* (Naples, 1863), p. 1: 'Nobili domino Federigo de Trogisio Regio balio... Litterae responsales de receptione homagii, et sacramenti fidelitatis... a nobili Domino Nicolao de Cefalonia...'. Cf. ibid., p. 10.

in the coup that killed her husband. Thomas had treated her far from well. She may have embraced his assassin as her liberator.[5]

Nicholas may have won the confidence of the Greeks in Arta. But in Ioannina they were of a different mind. As soon as the Despot Thomas was dead, the citizens of Ioannina declared their allegiance to the emperor in Constantinople.[6] Thomas had evidently been unpopular in Ioannina, unlike his mother who had preferred it to Arta on occasions and who owned a country retreat nearby.[7] It may have been she who persuaded its leading men of the benefits of returning to the fold of the Byzantine Empire while they had the chance. They were also no doubt influenced by the continuing presence of Byzantine troops at Berat and elsewhere to the north. They had their reward. The commander of Berat accepted the submission of Ioannina in the emperor's name. He was the *pinkernes* Syrgiannes Palaiologos whose soldiers had caused so much damage at Arta three years before. To secure his prize Syrgiannes took it upon himself to confer numerous privileges on the city and the church of Ioannina and on several of its prominent citizens.

Ioannina was a prize indeed and the emperor was impressed and gratified. He did not care for Syrgiannes. But when the citizens of Ioannina sent him a list of requests he acted accordingly. In or just before 1319 the patriarch's synod announced that, by decree of the emperor, the bishopric of Ioannina, hitherto dependent on Naupaktos, had been elevated to the rank of a metropolis. In so decreeing, the philanthropic emperor was at once celebrating the return to his empire of a prodigal son and exercising his prerogative of promoting bishops to a higher rank. The metropolitan of Ioannina would henceforth bear the exalted title of *hypertimos*.[8] Soon afterwards, in February 1319, the emperor issued a long and solemn chrysobull for the recently recovered city now dignified as a metropolis.[9] The document concerns only the city of Ioannina. But in

[5] *Chron. Mor. arag.*, §628, p. 138. G. Schlumberger, *Numismatique de l'Orient latin* (Paris, 1878), p. 374. Nicholas left his brother John to look after Cephalonia. For his adoption of the Orthodox faith, see Raynaldus, *Annales ecclesiastici*, v (Lucca, 1750), *anno* 1320, §XLVIII, p. 149: 'Neopatrensi vero archiepiscopo provinciam dedit (John XXII), ut ad Cephaloniae comitem, qui ad Graecorum schisma defecerat, ad Latinum ritum revocandum operam defigeret'.

[6] Hopf, *GG*, I, p. 419, followed by Romanos, *Despotate*, p. 119 (60), says that 'Demetrios Ganzas', governor of Valona, took over Arta in the name of Michael IX. But he cites no source for this statement.

[7] The *basilissa* Anna owned the village of Melissourgoi on Mount Tzoumerka, south-east of Ioannina. *MM*, v, p. 87 l. 3. Cf. Soustal–Koder, p. 206.

[8] Hunger–Kresten, *Register*, I, no. 62, pp. 394–9; *MM*, I, no. 51, pp. 93–5; Dölger, *Regesten*, IV, no. 2411; Darrouzès, *Regestes*, v, no. 2094; Mazal, *Prooimien*, pp. 60, 156–7. See E. K. Chrysos, Δωδώνη, v (1976), 337–48.

[9] Text in *MM*, v, pp. 77–84. Dölger, *Regesten*, IV, no. 2412. For earlier editions, see Vranousis, Χρονικὰ Ἠπείρου, pp. 54–8. Cf. E. Frances, 'La féodalité et les villes byzantines au XIIIe et au XIVe siècles', *BS*, XVI (1955), 76–96, especially 90–2; E.

the larger context of imperial policy it is eloquent of the growing tendency to grant municipal charters to the cities in the provinces. The citizens and merchants of Monemvasia had been given considerable immunities and privileges in 1316. In a way this was an admission of defeat. Andronikos II, who had earlier vetoed his wife's proposal to carve up the empire, was now conceding that the only way to hold the fragments of that empire together was by granting a measure of self-government to its cities.[10]

For Ioannina it was a large measure. The city and its people had for long been led astray but now they had seen the light and had come back to the fold of church and empire and freely submitted to their emperor. For this he rewarded them with the following privileges by chrysobull: 1. The metropolis of Ioannina was to retain in perpetuity and without let or hindrance all its existing and former rights and properties in the form of villages, vineyards, fields, mills, or other possessions such as tenant farmers (*paroikoi*) and the like, whether these were granted to it by ancient deeds or added to it more recently by charter of the emperor's relative, the *pinkernes* Syrgiannes Palaiologos.[11] 2. The citizens had particularly requested that the emperor should never make over their city to the Franks or to any others but should henceforth regard it as being indissolubly linked to the rest of his realm and empire and subject to himself and to his heirs for ever. He therefore readily agreed that neither Ioannina nor any of the other walled cities (*kastra*) recently recovered or about to be recovered would ever be so made over to anybody. 3. The imperial governors of the city were not to have the right to expel or deport citizens of whatever status and settle them elsewhere against their will, except for manifest troublemakers and rabble-rousers; since it was the governors' duty to ensure that peace and good order prevailed in the city.[12] 4. The citizens should elect for themselves a court of justice composed of the best among them who, together with the governor, would hear and try all cases except for those coming under the jurisdiction of the church. 5. The city of Ioannina should enjoy all its former fiscal immunities and exemptions and its merchants should be

Kirsten, 'Die byzantinische Stadt', *Berichte zum XI. Internationalen Byzantinisten-Kongress München 1958*, v, 3 (Munich, 1958), 36–7; Lj. Maksimović, 'Charakter der sozial-wirtschaftlichen Struktur der spätbyzantinischen Stadt (13.–15. Jh.)', *XVI. Internationaler Byzantinistenkongress, Akten*, 1/1 (Vienna, 1981), 149–88.

[10] Chrysobull for Momemvasia of 1316: text in *MM*, v, pp. 165–8. Dölger, *Regesten*, IV, no. 2383. Cf. Laiou, *Constantinople*, pp. 256–7, 259–60.

[11] *MM*, v, pp. 79–80: ...εἴ τι προσεπεδόθη αὐτῇ ἀρτίως διὰ γράμματος τοῦ περιποθήτου γαμβροῦ τῆς βασιλείας μου, τοῦ πιγκέρνη Συργιάννη Παλαιολόγου....

[12] Ibid., pp. 80–1. The governors of the city are referred to as οἱ κατὰ καιροὺς μέλλοντες κεφαλιτικεύειν, or as being εἰς κεφαλήν (or κεφαλιτικεύοντες). For the history and significance of the terms, see Zakythinos, *Despotat grec de Morée*, II, pp. 65–71; Maksimović, *Vizantijska provinzijska uprava*, pp. 70–100.

entitled to trade freely and without payment of duty (*akommerkeutoi*) in the city itself and in all the lands and cities of the empire as far as Constantinople. 6. The inhabitants (*kastrenoi*) were not to be obliged or compelled to perform military service outside their city, since only the regular soldiers enrolled in regiments (*allagia*) and in receipt of pay were so obliged to serve.[13] 7. It had been the custom in Ioannina that anyone convicted of treason or treachery should have his property confiscated and his houses destroyed and that he should be driven out of the *kastron*. At the request of the citizens this custom was to continue. 8. The military should have no prescriptive right to quarter themselves in houses without the consent of the owners. 9. The governors appointed by decree of the emperor must exercise their authority with justice and clemency. If they acted oppressively then the citizens must make a detailed report to the emperor so that the offending governor could be corrected or removed. 10. The citizens were not to suffer the imposition of taxes either within the city or outside it in their villages and estates but were to enjoy their customary immunities now and for the future. Any such impositions that had recently been proposed or implemented were now to be rendered null and void. 11. The coinage (*charagma*) of Ioannina was to be that currently in circulation and no other.[14] 12. Property owners were not to be liable to the *mitaton*, or sale of their produce to the administration at arbitrary prices, nor to any other burden; they should sell their produce freely in the way that they had always done.[15] 13. The citizens should be exempt from the levy payable for castle building (*kastroktisia*), except for the maintenance and repair of their own. 14. Those guilty of murder should be punished according to the prevailing local custom. 15. On the discovery of treasure by anyone, if it were truly reported, it should for the future be conveyed to the imperial treasury; if the report were false the matter should be brought to trial.[16] 16. There follows the list of villages

[13] *MM*, v, p. 81. Cf. N. Oikonomides, 'A propos des armées des premiers Paléologues et des compagnies des soldats', *TM*, viii (1981), 353–71, especially 353–5.

[14] I take the word χάραγμα here to mean coinage or currency. Cf. G. Rouillard, 'Le mot χάραγμα dans les actes des Paléologues', Εἰς μνήμην Σπ. Λάμπρου (Athens, 1935), 375–80, especially 376 n. 1; Zakythinos, 'Crise monétaire et crise économique à Byzance', in Zakythinos, *Byzance: état-société-économie* (London, 1973), no. xi, p. 113. For other uses of the word, see N. G. Svoronos, *Recherches sur le cadastre byzantin et la fiscalité aux XIe et XIIe siècle: Le cadastre de Thèbes* (Paris, 1959), pp. 112–16.

[15] On the *mitaton*, see above, p. 71 n. 28.

[16] The taxes relating to the building and maintenance of castles (καστροκτισία) and treasure-trove (θησαυροῦ ἀνεύρεσις) are discussed by: M. Tourtoglou, Παρθενοφθορία καὶ εὕρεσις θησαυροῦ (Athens, 1963); S. Trojanos, 'Καστροκτισία. Einige Bemerkungen über die finanziellen Grundlagen des Festungsbaues in byzantinischen Reich', *Byzantina*, i (1969), 39–57; Zakythinos, 'Crise monétaire', pp. 68, 119–20; Cécile Morrisson, 'La découverte des trésors à l'époque byzantine: théorie et pratique de l'εὕρεσις θησαυροῦ', *TM*, xiii (1981), 321–43.

which constituted the inalienable property of the city of Ioannina, including those added to it by the *pinkernes* Syrgiannes Palaiologos.[17] It is confirmed, according to the citizens' request, that none of these can be sold to a local archon or soldier, unless it be a public sale back to the citizens; nor was anyone allowed to take on another's tenant farmer (*paroikos*) as his own. Further, the said *pinkernes*, the emperor's relative, had decreed that the citizens of Ioannina should not be assessed for payment of the following taxes: the *biologion*, *kapnologion*, *nomistron*, *limnaion pakton*, *zeugologion*, *orikē*, *melissoennomion* and *choirodekatia*. These taxes had previously been imposed by their Despots. They were now no longer payable; nor would any census be taken for tax purposes (*apographē*).[18] 17. The garrison of the castle should be made up of those formerly recruited for this purpose, and the locals should not be coerced into such duties except in case of emergency. 18. The Jews in the city should live free and unhindered lives, like the rest of the inhabitants.[19] 19. Lastly, the properties granted to some of the citizens of Ioannina by decree of the *pinkernes* (Syrgiannes) were hereby confirmed.

Not long afterwards the commander (*prokathemenos*) of the city of Ioannina, called Sgouros the *sebastos*, was honoured with an imperial chrysobull granting him hereditary possession of a monastery at

[17] The twelve villages previously belonging to the city of Ioannina, all of them with a twenty kilometre radius, were: Ardichobista; Ardomista (now Longades, 8 km E. of Ioannina, on the east side of the lake); Botibista; Gardiki (now Mega Gardikion, 9 km N.W. of Ioannina); Gloxiani; Leausista (Kato Lapsista, 13 km N.W. of Ioannina); Noboseli; Pseada; Sandobitza (now Marmara, 5 km W.S.W. of Ioannina); Treabodista; Tristeanikos (? modern Drestenikos in E. Zagori, 19 km N.E. of Ioannina); Zelochobista (? Zeloba, now Vounoplagia, 6 km N.W. of Ioannina). Soustal–Koder, pp. 111, 154, 192, 254, 273, 281. The villages added to it by Syrgiannes were: Dreabopsa (? modern Dragopsa, 16 km S.W. of Ioannina); Dreanobon; Kopani (21 km S. of Ioannina); Kopantzin; Krechobon; Lipnitza; Phreastona (? Phreastana, now Kyparissia, 12 km S.E. of Ioannina. Soustal–Koder, p. 238, identify Phreastona with the modern Kato Meropi to the N. of Delvinakion; but this would be quite out of context compared with the rest of the villages here named); Psathoi; Radotobi (modern Rodotopion, 12 km N.W. of Ioannina); Sipka; Stromi; and the meadow called Skoupitza in Vagenetia (7 km N.W. of Photiki). Soustal–Koder, pp. 145–6, 184, 237, 248, 260.

[18] On the *biologion* and *kapnologion*, see F. Dölger, *Beiträge zur Geschichte der byzantinischen Finanzverwaltung besonders des 10. und 11. Jahrhunderts* (Byzantinisches Archiv, 9: Leipzig–Berlin, 1927), pp. 51–2; idem, 'Zum Gebührenwesen der Byzantiner', in Dölger, *Byzanz und die europäische Staatenwelt* (Ettal, 1953), pp. 255, 256. On the *zeugologion* as distinct from the *zeugaratikion*, ibid., pp. 257–8. The *nomistron* was a tax on pasture land; the *limnaion pakton* a tax on fishing in lakes and sweet water. Zakythinos, 'Crise monétaire', pp. 66–7. On the *melissoennomion* (tax on bees) and *choirodekatia* (tithe on pigs), see Dölger, *Beiträge*, pp. 53–4. H. F. Schmid, 'Byzantinisches Zehntwesen', *JÖBG*, VI (1957), 45–110, especially 50–3. The *orikē* (ὀρική or ὀρεική)is defined by Zakythinos, 'Crise monétaire', p. 67, as an 'impot sur les mulets', and by others as a tax on grazing land in the mountains. See P. Schreiner, 'Ein Prostagma Andronikos' III. für die Monemvasioten in Pegai (1328)', *JÖB*, XXVII (1978), 208–9.

[19] N. Bees, 'Übersicht über die Geschichte des Judentums von Janina', *BNJ*, II (1921), 159–77.

Merdeastana.[20] Finally, in June 1321, at the request of the metropolitan of Ioannina, the emperor issued a third chrysobull.[21] This document itemised and confirmed the landed properties belonging to the church and guaranteed its right to maintain its own court of law for the trial of its clergy and of others who came within its jurisdiction.[22] This covered the territory within the theme of Ioannina with its five parishes, namely those of greater Ioannina, Zagoria, Tzemernikon, Smokovo and Sestrouni, as well as its four bishoprics.[23] The church was also to benefit from the annual fair (*panegyri*) of the Archangel Michael which lasted for fifteen days, from the Feast of St Demetrios (26 October) until 8 November. Half of the proceeds of this event and its market were to go to the church and half to its clergy. The clergy were also entitled, as they had been in the past, to receive every year from the income of the church of Ioannina 300

[20] *MM*, v, p. 86 l. 15: ... μονύδριον τῶν Μηρδεαστάνων. Cf. Dölger, *Regesten*, iv, no. 2454. Its location is unknown. On the office of *prokathemenos*, see Maksimović, *Vizantijska provinzijska uprava*, pp. 101–5.

[21] Text in *MM*, v, pp. 84–7. For other editions, see Dölger, *Regesten*, iv, no. 2460; and add K. D. Mertzios, Τὸ δεύτερον χρύσόβολλον 'Ανδρονίκου τοῦ Β' Παλαιολόγου ὑπὲρ τῆς εκκλησίας τῶν 'Ιωαννίνων, *Ep. Hest.*, i, 2 (1952), 115–18. Cf. Vranousis, Χρονικὰ 'Ηπείρου, pp. 58–68.

[22] *MM*, v, pp. 84–5. The villages and properties belonging to the Metropolis of Ioannina were as follows: Aroula (to the S.S.W. of Ioannina: Soustal–Koder, p. 116); Beltsista (now Klematia, 16 km N.N.W. of Ioannina: Soustal–Koder, p. 124), with the monastery there dedicated to the Archangel Michael and two peasant farmers, Loukas and Polytechnas with their families; Goplista; half of the village of Lozetzi (now Hellenikon, 16 km S.E. of Ioannina: Soustal–Koder, p. 199); Paroikion; Poblista; Rapsista (now Pedini, 7 km S. of Ioannina: Soustal–Koder, p. 249); Sestrouni, with the peasants Markos, Tzechles, Pothetos, Vladimir and their families, and the mountain Mitzikeli (Moutzoukelis) (Sestrouni is now Strounion at the foot of Mitzikeli: Soustal–Koder, p. (258); Tobolianis, with the peasant Bogri but without the property (*stasion*) of Hasani. In addition there were various landed and other properties: in the village of Lapsista, the *metochion* dedicated to St George, with the *sigillatikion* there of the sons of Komanopoulos, with Tzamantoura and Kourtesis and the lands which they acquired there and their fishpond; the *sigillatikia* of Simon at Lozetzi, at the village of Serbiana (13 km S.S.E. of Ioannina: Soustal–Koder, p. 257), at that of Phreastana (see above n. 17), at that of Ioanista (9 km S.E. of Ioannina: Soustal–Koder, pp. 167–8) belonging to Kanakios, with its *metochion* called St Nicholas τοῦ "Ορους; the *sigillatikion* of Constantine at Momisdena; that at Baltiziston with its yields of 8 *hyperpyra* and its produce; those at Lakkos and Koukoubrikas; that at Sphonista which was abandoned (ἐξαλιμμιταῖον); that of the sons of Vlasios in Paroikion; and that of the estate of Elias. The church was also entitled to the tax payable by a number of Vlachs (στίχος Βλάχων); and it owned two mills at the village of Rasobista, three mills at Pratokai (on the lake at Lapsista) and two fishponds there as well as half a fish farm at the lake. The properties added to it by Syrgiannes consisted of half of the village of Lozetzi (presumably the other half), with its *agora* of Kasianos; and the tax payable by twenty Vlachs (Βλάχων καπνοὶ 20), together with Bisotas and Ligeros.

[23] Soustal–Koder, p. 278 (Zagoria), p. 274 (Tzemernikon, Tsumerka), p. 261 (Smokovo, Smokobon), p. 258 (Sestrouni, Sestrounion). The four bishoprics are not named, but they were probably those of Belas, Dryinoupolis, Bouthrotos (Butrinto) with Glyky, and Chimara. See C. Asdracha, 'Deux actes inédits concernant l'Epire', *REB*, xxxv (1977), 163–4; Soustal–Koder, p. 166.

modioi of mixed wheat and barley (*sitokrithon*), a full cask of wine from the *protosynkellos*, and the sum of 50 *hyperpyra* (*trikephala*).[24] The church also owned three Jews, the sons of Lamari, of David and of Samaria. In addition the chrysobull lists the properties conferred upon the church by the *pinkernes* Syrgiannes and notes the gift to it of the monastery at Merdeastana, lately granted by chrysobull to the commander of the city, Sgouros. These possessions were to be held by the church free of all public levies and taxes or any other impediments, whether from the governors or their administrators. The document ends with the matter of a village called Soucha near Dryinoupolis. Soucha had become the property of the late general (*epi tou stratou*) Kabasilas. He had obtained it by exchange for the village of Melissourgoi, which the mother of the late Thomas (the *basilissa* Anna) had owned. The emperor confirmed that Soucha also belonged by right to the church of Ioannina, as it had done before, together with its Vlach population, who were exempt from military service.[25]

In the preamble to his chrysobull of 1319 the emperor, or his secretary, dwells at some length on the features which lend to the city of Ioannina its special distinction.[26] He praises its size, its felicitous situation, its strength and its security. He extols the great number of its inhabitants and the wealth of which they justifiably boast. But its principal glory, which sets it above all other cities, is its heavenly patron and protector, the Archangel Michael, who made the place his own even before the city was founded and who has since been its ever present help in trouble, its defender and champion against all ills. The first of the separatist rulers of Epiros, Michael I Doukas, naturally receives no mention. Yet it was he who had transformed Ioannina from a small town into a walled city after 1204; and it was he who had associated it with the patronage of his namesake the Archangel and most probably built the church within the walls dedicated to the Taxiarches Michael which, in 1319, was designated as the cathedral of Ioannina.[27] The emperor's chrysobull rewrites history to show that the

[24] On the coins of Andronikos II known as *trikephala* ('perperi tre santi'), see Zakythinos, 'Crise monétaire', p. 14; M. F. Hendy, *Coinage and Money in the Byzantine Empire, 1081–1261* (Dumbarton Oaks Studies, XII: Washington, D.C., 1969), pp. 31–4; P. Grierson, *Byzantine Coins* (London, 1982), pp. 218, 296, 346.

[25] On Soucha (modern Suha in Albania), see Soustal–Koder, p. 267.

[26] *MM*, v, pp. 78–9.

[27] See the document of John Apokaukos of Naupaktos, ed. A. Papadopoulos-Kerameus, Περὶ συνοικισμοῦ τῶν 'Ιωαννίνων μετὰ τὴν φραγκικὴν κατάκτησιν τῆς Κωνσταντινουπόλεως, *DIEE*, III (1891), 451–5. Cf. L. Vranousis, 'Ιστορικὰ καὶ τοπογραφικὰ τοῦ μεσαιωνικοῦ κάστρου τῶν 'Ιωαννίνων (Ioannina, 1968), 12–15; also in Χαριστήριον 'A. K. Ορλάνδου, IV, 444–7 [cited hereafter as Vranousis, *Kastron*]. D. M. Nicol, 'Refugees, mixed population and local patriotism in Epiros and western Macedonia after the Fourth Crusade', *XVᵉ Congrès International d'Etudes Byzantines. Rapports*: I. *Histoire* (Athens, 1976), pp. 20–1.

once prosperous and populous city had fallen on hard times because, under the influence of Satan and his agents, it had cut itself off from the natural and divine order of things encompassed by the universal church of Christ and the universal empire of the Romans. Its previous rulers who had thus isolated it were sick and evil men oppressing a sickened and subject society. Now, however, its citizens had come to their senses and their sanity and elected to re-enter into the fullness of that undivided society of the Christian church and the Roman Empire. It is hard to reconcile the vaunted prosperity of Ioannina with the alleged shortcomings of its rulers. One is tempted to feel that if what the emperor says was true the Archangel Michael had been nodding for the best part of a century.

The surrender of Ioannina must have occurred about the end of 1318. The new lord of Arta, Nicholas Orsini, sensed where the wind was blowing and sought recognition from the emperor in Constantinople. He was after all now married to the emperor's granddaughter. Andronikos II granted him the title of Despot on condition that he swore to keep his hands off the city of Ioannina.[28] In other words Nicholas must accept the fact that his Despotate was confined to Arta and the south of Epiros. Neither he nor the emperor's deputy in the north expected this arrangement to last. Syrgiannes evidently had further conquests in mind. In March 1319 his troops raided and plundered the district of Vrastova in Vagenetia. This was the domain which the late Despot Thomas had bestowed by chrysobull on the Venetian Jacopo Contareno in 1303. Venice was quick to protest to the emperor and to renew her embargo on trade with the Despotate.[29] Nicholas Orsini was disappointed. He had been hoping for some support from Venice. In February 1320 he tried to mend matters by indicating to the Doge that he was prepared to settle all outstanding debts and claims for compensation to Venetian persons and property in Epiros and to reimburse the long-suffering Pietro Moro. It seems that these were not empty words. Pietro Moro was at last pacified and compensated by a gift of pearls and jewels; at least one other claim was met in full; and Nicholas added his assurance that he regarded the Republic of Venice as 'his mother'.[30]

In May 1320 he sent two ambassadors to Venice, the *sebastos* Peter Chrysoberges and Bertuccio de Mazarolo, himself a Venetian. They had

[28] *MM*, I, p. 171. An outline of the history of the city of Ioannina between 1318 and 1337 is contained in the patriarchal document of 1337–8 printed in *MM*, I, pp. 171–4. Darrouzès, *Regestes*, IV, no. 2180, dated it to 'about November 1337'. It should, however, be dated to 'between July 1337 and February 1338'. O. Kresten, 'Marginalien zur Geschichte von Ioannina unter Kaiser Andronikos III. Palaiologos', *Ep. Chron.*, XXV (1983), 120–8.

[29] *ActAlbVen*, I, I, no. 44, p. 20; no. 48, p. 24; *DVL*, I, p. 136; Cessi–Sambin, *Misti*, p. 212, no. 295; K. D. Mertzios, Τὸ ἐν Βενετίᾳ κρατικὸν Ἀρχεῖον, *Ep. Chron.*, XV (1940), 23–4.

[30] Hopf, *GG*, I, p. 420; Romanos, *Despotate*, pp. 124–5 (62–3).

full authority to negotiate a settlement. They pointed out that their master Nicholas had been on the best of terms with Venice so long as he held only the islands belonging to his county of Cephalonia. Such had been the case also with his ancestors. He hoped that Venice would now take these islands under her protection; but he hoped still more that she would extend her protection and friendship also to the whole of the mainland territory of Epiros which he now ruled and help him to extend its boundaries. He promised to swear fidelity to the Doge in respect of all his dominions, to govern them in the name of Venice, and to raise the banner of St Mark in Cephalonia and all his other lands. At his own expense he would equip one galley for every thirty put to sea by Venice. In addition, he offered to cede to Venice either the harbour of Butrinto or that of Parga. As a bait to the business men he pointed out that Butrinto brought in an annual income of 1,500 libri from its fisheries, while Parga realised 1,000 libri from its sugar cane plantations. In return for these concessions Nicholas asked for a force of four hundred soldiers and the financial resources to help him win back the territory that had formerly belonged to the Despot Thomas but which the Byzantines had now seized and occupied. There can be little doubt that he was thinking of the city of Ioannina.[31]

The Venetians were perhaps tempted by the offer of a going concern and a harbour in Epiros. They were already doing much business in Valona. But they did not want to prejudice the terms that they were then negotiating with the Byzantine emperor. Constantinople was a bigger market than Butrinto or Parga. They may even have been surprised to learn that Butrinto was in the gift of the Despot of Epiros; and they may hardly have heard of Parga. They therefore contented themselves for the time being with a polite reminder to the Despot Nicholas that, so far as his islands were concerned, his offer of homage was nothing new. For his ancestor Maio Orsini had long ago sworn 'perpetual fidelity' to Venice in return for his tenure of Cephalonia, Zante and Ithaka. Nicholas was thus already committed to the service of the Doge. As to assisting his designs on the mainland they were not yet prepared to commit themselves.[32]

Nicholas was not to be deterred. In 1320 the emperor complained of the constant and continuing aggression of the count of Cephalonia against

[31] *ActAlbVen*, I, I, nos. 51, 52, pp. 29–31; *DVL*, I, pp. 168–70, no. 81 (May 1320); Mertzios, *Ep. Chron.*, XV, 24. This is almost the first mention of Parga in a written source. It is described as being 'in acquis Villichi'. Soustal–Koder, pp. 226, 275f. In 1401 it was indeed to become a Venetian colony. See below, p. 176.

[32] Cessi–Sambin, *Deliberazione*, p. 223, no. 25; *ActAlbVen*, I, I, no. 53, p. 32 (June 1320). For Maio Orsini's treaty with Venice, see Nicol, *Despotate*, p. 34. Ithaka is described as 'Vallis compari' a name first applied to it by the Genoese writer Caffaro in the twelfth century. Another variant is 'Val di Compare'. Soustal–Koder, pp. 168–9.

the Byzantine province in northern Epiros.[33] That province now extended as far south as Ioannina. But its main strategic base was still the fortress of Berat and it included Valona and Kanina with the district of Spinaritsa on the coast. The merchants of Venice and of Ragusa (Dubrovnik) traded in Valona and the Venetians had their own commercial quarter there. For many years it seems to have been controlled by members of the family of Gantzas who, with the titles of *sebastos* and *prothontinus* (or admiral), held it in the emperor's name as an imperial city (*civitas Imperatoris Graecorum*).[34] But by 1320 the overall command of the province had changed. Syrgiannes, who had received the surrender of Ioannina in 1318, had again been arrested on suspicion of treachery and taken to prison in Constantinople. The benefactions that he had showered on that city and its leading men, though given honourable mention in the emperor's chrysobulls, may have told against him. Syrgiannes rarely did anything from altruistic motives. As so often, he talked himself out of prison and back into imperial favour. But he was not sent back to Epiros. In 1320 he was posted to Thrace.[35] The new governor-general of the western command was the emperor's second son Constantine Palaiologos, himself a Despot by rank. As such he is mentioned in 1319–20; though in the following year he was promoted to the office of governor of Thessalonica.[36]

It was against this Byzantine enclave in Epiros, the 'furthest limits of Roman hegemony', that Nicholas Orsini directed his aggression. The recovery of Ioannina was no doubt his ultimate objective. Any guilt that he may have felt about breaking his word to the emperor was soon dispelled. His wife, Anna, the emperor's granddaughter, died in 1320. He was no longer related to the imperial family. Anna's father, the junior Emperor Michael IX, died in October of the same year; and at once the sequence of events was set in motion which was to lead to the outbreak of war for the possession of the throne in Constantinople.[37] The contestants were the young Andronikos III Palaiologos, brother of the late Anna of

[33] *DVL*, I, pp. 146–7; *ActAlb*, I, no. 669, pp. 202–3; *ActAlbVen*, I, I no. 55, pp. 37–8.

[34] Cf. *ActAlb*, I, no. 739, p. 220 (December 1329): '... civitatis Aulone imperatoris Graecorum'.

[35] Greg. viii. 3: I, p. 302; Cantac. i. 2: I, pp. 19–20. Binon, *BZ*, XXXVIII (1938), 141–2.

[36] *DVL*, I, pp. 149–50; *ActAlbVen*, I, I, p. 38: '... nostro filio Imperij nostri felicissimo dispoto domino Constantino Palaeologo, habenti potestatem generalem a nobis in locis illis (sc. Aualona et Sfinaritza)'; cf. *DVL*, I, p. 162. Dölger, *Regesten*, IV, no. 2428. Greg. viii. I: I, p. 293. Dölger, *Regesten*, IV, no. 2450; Papadopulos, *Versuch*, no. 60, p. 37; Ducellier, *Albanie*, p. 351. Greg. viii. II: I, p. 355, and Cantac. i. 26: I, p. 129, indicate that Constantine Palaiologos was sent to be governor of Thessalonica and Macedonia in December 1321.

[37] Michael IX died on 12 October 1320, shortly after the deaths of his daughter Anna and his son Manuel. Greg. vii. 13: I, p. 277; viii. I: I, p. 286; Cantac. i. I: I, p. 14. Schreiner, *Chron. Brev.*, I, nos. 8/11c, 9/2, 49/2; II, p. 227.

Epiros, and his now elderly grandfather Andronikos II. In the course of this struggle for power the devious Syrgiannes was to find new openings for his ambition and new scope for his talent as a fisherman in troubled waters. When such great issues were at stake in the capital, Nicholas Orsini might be forgiven for thinking that the furthest limits of the empire would be neglected. He stepped up his invasion of Byzantine territory to the north, attacking many of the towns that were subject to the emperor. The Venetians too seem to have decided that the movement was now ripe to help him. They sent a fleet led by Giovanni Michiel to attack Valona. Many of its Greek inhabitants were killed on the spot, including the son of its admiral Gantzas; others were killed trying to escape to Corfu.[38] Nicholas meanwhile concentrated on his main objective, the city of Ioannina, laying siege to its walls with a sizeable army. But neither Valona nor Ioannina surrendered. The Byzantine garrisons held their ground.[39]

His attack on Ioannina proved to be the undoing of Nicholas Orsini. In 1323 his younger brother John took up arms against him. Nicholas was killed. The causes and the circumstances of this family vendetta are obscure. What little evidence there is suggests that the brothers had fallen out with each other for personal reasons. The Aragonese Chronicle of the Morea, with artful simplicity, reports that John Orsini left Cephalonia and took to residing at Arta as soon as he heard that Nicholas had been made Despot. He was honourably received and entertained and passed his time in hunting and other amusements; until one day he took it into his head to murder his brother and acted on the impulse. Gregoras seems also to imply that it was a direct act of fratricide. A later decree of the patriarch's synod, however, indicates that Nicholas was killed as the result of war with his brother.[40] What is reasonably certain is that the change of ruler, violent though it was, brought no change in policy. The policy of John II Orsini was no less selfish and no more considered than that of his brother. On the other hand, John had seen a way to secure possession of Ioannina for himself without further trouble. The citizens had resisted the assaults of Nicholas and his troops partly because they were loyal to the senior emperor Andronikos II and partly because they feared that they would lose all the privileges that they had recently gained from him if they submitted. John Orsini therefore secretly approached them with the proposition that they should accept him not as their lord

[38] *MM*, I, p. 171; *DVL*, I, no. 92, p. 191; *ActAlb*, I, no. 677; *ActAlbVen*, I, I, no. 60, pp. 41–2.

[39] *MM*, I, p. 171.

[40] *Chron. Mor. arag.*, §§629–30, p. 138; Greg. xi. 3: I, p. 536; *MM*, I, p. 171: ...ὁ αὐτάδελφος ἐκείνου κῦρ 'Ιωάννης ὁ Δούκας... ἐναντία φρονήσας αὐτῷ τῷ ἰδίῳ ἀδελφῷ καὶ μάχην κεκινηκὼς κατ' αυτοῦ....

and master but as their governor on behalf of the emperor. Ioannina would remain a protected city subject to Constantinople; and he swore to preserve its municipal independence and to do it no harm. On these terms and with these assurances the people of Ioannina accepted John Orsini as their governor.[41]

Having thus disposed of his brother and made himself protector if not master of Ioannina, the new ruler of Epiros assumed control of the reunited Despotate. He had first to settle his accounts with Constantinople, since he claimed to be the emperor's deputy at least in the city of Ioannina. In the year 1323 it was hard to decide which of the two contenders for the throne was in fact emperor. But it appears that it was Andronikos II and not his grandson Andronikos III who recognised the new regime in Epiros, giving John Orsini his blessing and authorising him to govern Ioannina in his name. The blessing was somewhat qualified, for the emperor seemed loth to dignify John with the title of Despot.[42] John was ready to make himself worthy of this imperial accolade. Like his late brother, he professed the Orthodox faith; and he married into the family of Palaiologos.

His wife was a daughter of the *protobestiarios* Andronikos Palaiologos, called Anna. The fact of her marriage to John is reported by only one Byzantine historian.[43] But there may be more in it than meets the eye. Andronikos Palaiologos was a son of that Demetrios-Michael of Epiros who had defected to Constantinople in 1278. In 1326 he is found as governor of Berat for Andronikos II. He may have served in that part of the empire before.[44] He was an ambitious and restless man. Cantacuzene goes so far as to say that he was the prime mover of the last phase of the civil war between the two emperors.[45] He was in league with John

[41] *MM*, I, p. 171: ...ἐπεὶ ἀνθισταμένους εἶδε καὶ τοὺς τῶν Ἰωαννίνων ἐποίκους ἐκείνῳ, τούτους προσρυεὶς καὶ ὅρκους δεδωκώς, ὥστε, εἰ δέξαιντο τοῦτον ἐν τῇ τοιαύτῃ πόλει ὡς κεφαλὴν καὶ οὐχ ὡς αὐθέντην, ἀλλ'ὡς ὅλον ὄντα τῆς ὑποχειριότητος τοῦ ἐκ θεοῦ βασιλέως....

[42] *MM*, I, p. 171. The document consistently refers to Andronikos III as the reigning emperor and to Andronikos II as his late grandfather. John Orsini is said to have been made Despot 'later': ...ὕστερον καὶ αὐτὸς δεσποτικῷ τιμηθεὶς ἀξιώματι παρὰ τοῦ κρατίστου καὶ ἁγίου μου αὐτοκράτορος (i.e. after 1328).

[43] Cantac. ii. 32: I, p. 499. On Andronikos Palaiologos and his daughter Anna, see Papadopulos, *Versuch*, nos. 50, 51, pp. 31–2.

[44] Greg. ix. I: I, p. 394; Cantac. i. 43: I, pp. 211–15. See above, p. 69, n. 22. He has been identified with the 'Komnenos Palaiologos', governor of the western provinces (ἐν τῷ τῆς δύσεως θέματι), who founded three monasteries in Epiros and issued a charter for them in 1321. D. A. Zakythinos, 'Ἀνέκδοτον βυζαντινὸν κτιτορικὸν ἐκ Βορείου Ἠπείρου, *EEBS*, XIV (1938), 277–94. See below, pp. 242–3. He also owned property in Vodena (Edessa). *Actes de Lavra*, III, ed. P. Lemerle and others (Paris, 1979), no. 146, pp. 100–4; and see below, p. 155.

[45] Cantac. ii. 32: I, p. 499 ll. 14–16. Elsewhere he bestows this doubtful tribute on Demetrios Angelos and Michael Laskaris, the sons of Theodore Metochites. Cantac. i. 43: I, p. 211.

Palaiologos the *panhypersebastos*, the nephew of Andronikos II, who was governor of Thessalonica in 1325. John was determined to make his own fortune out of the wreck of civil war. At Thessalonica he was well placed to do so. He called on the help of the kral of Serbia, Stephen Dečanski, to take over the western provinces and set up a principality of his own. He gave his young daughter as a bride to Dečanski. Andronikos Palaiologos was a party to this scheme; and he may have used his position as governor of Berat to try to win over the new ruler of Epiros by giving him his daughter in marriage. In the event the scheme was thwarted.[46] John Palaiologos died at Skoplje in 1327 and Andronikos, who had also fled to Serbia, died at Prilep a year later. Andronikos III entered Thessalonica in January 1328. In May, with the help of his friend and counsellor John Cantacuzene, he marched into Constantinople as emperor. Andronikos II abdicated and the civil war was at last over. The new governor of Thessalonica and commander of the western provinces turned out to be Syrgiannes, only recently released from another term of imprisonment for treachery. In Thessalonica he was to discover new avenues for intrigue.[47]

The change of rulers in Epiros did not for long go unnoticed in Italy. John Orsini must be made to do homage to his lord in Naples. In January 1322 King Robert of Anjou had settled the quarrel between his brothers Philip of Taranto and John of Gravina and confirmed the latter's title as prince of Achaia.[48] For some years the principality had been administered by a succession of inefficient Italian baillies and the initiative was passing to the Byzantines operating from their base at Mistra. John of Gravina would go there himself and put things right. He sent out a French knight, Nicholas of Joinville, to hold the fort until he arrived. But not until 1324 was he able to send forward his advance guard to the Morea. To finance his expedition he had to borrow from various Florentine banking families, among them the Acciajuoli, who were later to figure so prominently in the history of Greece. It had been agreed, however, that the cost as well as the gains of the enterprise would be shared with his brother Philip. For John was to go by way of Cephalonia and Epiros, where he would summon the new Despot to his presence and invest him, on behalf of Philip of Taranto, with the lordship of the dominions that he had acquired. He was also to place garrisons in various castles and to

[46] Greg. viii. 14: 1, pp. 373–4; Cantac. i. 43: 1, pp. 209–14. On John Palaiologos, see Papadopulos, *Versuch*, no. 38, pp. 23–4.

[47] Greg. ix. 1, 2, 4–5: 1, pp. 394–5, 397, 409–11, 413; ix. 10: 1, p. 440; Cantac. i. 53, 54, 55, 56; ii. 18: 1, pp. 267–72, 275–80, 285, 411–13.

[48] Longnon, *L'Empire latin*, pp. 312–13. Philip of Taranto and John of Gravina were also in dispute over claims to the moveable property of the late Nicholas Orsini. C. Minieri-Riccio, *Studii storici fatti sopra 84 registri angioini* (Naples, 1876), p. 46. Romanos, *Despotate*, pp. 128–9 (64–5).

march overland from Arta to Naupaktos, where he would rejoin his ship for the crossing to Achaia.

He finally set out from Brindisi in January 1325 with a fleet of twenty-five ships carrying 400 cavalry and 1,000 infantry. They made straight for Cephalonia. John Orsini had entrusted the care of his islands to his younger brother Guido. For some reason Guido was not on hand to greet the new prince of Achaia when he sailed in; and his castellan refused to let the prince into the castle of St George. John of Gravina was so incensed by this discourtesy that he made off for Clarentza. He took the first opportunity to have Guido arrested and a confiscation order placed on his islands of Cephalonia and Zante. But he got no further with the plan to enforce the submission of John Orsini of Epiros. Nor was John of Gravina a great success as prince of Achaia. He went back to Naples in the spring of 1326 having achieved little except an accumulation of debts to his bankers in Florence, leaving his principality to be mismanaged by a further succession of baillies.[49]

John Orsini was even less inclined than his late brother to pay homage to the kingdom of Naples. For the time being he was to be left in peace from that quarter. He must have known that it would be only a temporary respite. But while it lasted he thought it prudent to come to terms with the new emperor in Constantinople, Andronikos III. The emperor seemed willing to overlook the fact that John had been in league with his late enemies. Better that Epiros should seek recognition from him than from the Italians. He was therefore graciously pleased to confer upon John Orsini the rank and title of Despot and to send him the insignia that went with it. John's position not merely as the emperor's deputy in Ioannina but as Despot of Arta and Epiros was thus officially approved and he had his place in the Byzantine establishment.[50]

He was delighted to be so honoured. The title of Despot had come to have a special and traditional significance in the minds of the people whose land he had appropriated. It went very nicely with the names of Komnenos Angelos and Doukas, which he had also appropriated.[51] But everyone knew that only an emperor had the power to confer that title. Like most of the Despots of Epiros before him, however, John Orsini was

[49] *Chron. Mor. arag.*, §§655–6, p. 144. Hopf, *GG*, I, pp. 422–3; Rodd, *Princes of Achaia*, II, pp. 158–60; Longnon, *L'Empire latin*, pp. 320–1; Bon, *Morée*, pp. 204–6. For the castle of St George on Cephalonia, see Soustal–Koder, pp. 154–5. Hopf, *GG*, I, p. 421, states that Guido Orsini, as well as his sister Margaret, finally took refuge in Naples.

[50] *MM*, I, p. 171. On John's use of the title of Despot, see Ferjančić, *Despoti*, pp. 75–6.

[51] His court poet, Constantine Hermoniakos, dedicated his paraphrase of Homer to John Orsini thus: εἰς ἀξίωσιν δεσπότου/ Κομνηνοῦ 'Αγγελοδούκῳ/'Ιωάννου τοῦ ἥρῳου/ τοῦ τὴν δύσιν δεσποτεύων. See also his signature on his chrysobull of 1330 (below, p. 96). In Constantinople, however, he was known simply as 'John Doukas' or 'John the Count' (of Cephalonia). Greg. xi. 3: I, p. 536; Cantac. ii. 32: I, p. 495.

not over-conscientious about keeping to his agreements, whether with the emperor or with anyone else. Once he had obtained his coveted title of Despot he felt strong enough to break the oath which he had sworn to govern the city of Ioannina in the emperor's name. He could perhaps defend his perjury by the excuse that he had taken that oath to Andronikos II and not to his grandson. But he could better defend it by the fact the citizens of Ioannina supported him. They had felt some loyalty to the old emperor who had bestowed so many privileges on their city and their church. Now that he was gone they would feel safer under the direct rule of their local Despot than under oath to an emperor who had fought against their benefactor. Ioannina was therefore ready of its own free will to be reintegrated into the Despotate of Epiros and to acknowledge John Orsini as its lord.[52]

In June 1330 John rewarded the citizens of Ioannina for their trust in him by granting them a charter in the form of a chrysobull, thereby taking on himself one of the prerogatives of an emperor. He made much of his Orthodox piety which, he claimed, was of greater account than the dignity of his rank and the jewels and precious stones of his regalia as Despot. He sang the praises of the metropolis of Ioannina and of its heavenly protector and champion, the Archangel Michael. No doubt he had before him the text of the emperor's chrysobull of 1319. He confirmed and ratified all the benefactions that had been made to the metropolis in the past, in the way of dependent villages, fields and monastic foundations; and, in conjunction with his wife the *basilissa*, he added other properties to its estates, all of which were to be freehold and exempt from all forms of taxation. It was an extraordinary advertisement for the pretensions to Byzantine imperial authority of an Italian count who had made himself a big fish in a small pond. But the church and people of Ioannina were evidently content with this confirmation and restatement of their specially privileged status.[53] John Orsini might have done better to stay under the wing of Constantinople than to go it alone. By 1330 he had deluded himself that the threat of domination by the Angevins was over. If John of Gravina as prince of Achaia was the best they could do then he had little to fear. He seems even to have driven their troops out of Vonitsa. But Philip of Taranto never lost hope of reviving his colony in Epiros; and his hope was encouraged by the arrival in Naples of many Greek and Albanian refugees imploring his help and offering their cooperation to put an end to the state of insecurity in their own country. In 1328 he decided to make use of Thamar's son Philip and

[52] *MM*, I, pp. 171–2.

[53] The manuscript of this chrysobull was once in the possession of I. A. Romanos. Its contents are summarised by Romanos, *Despotate*, p. 132 (66); though its date of June 6838 indiction 13 should read 1330 and not 1329. Vranousis, Χρονικὰ Ἠπείρου, p. 65.

to send him with a fleet to the land of his mother's birth to reclaim it for the kingdom of Naples. Preparations continued into 1329 and the young Philip seems to have got as far as Naupaktos. But his heart was never in the enterprise; and when he was finally ready to embark upon the conquest of the Despotate he died, in June 1331.[54]

His father was by then increasingly alarmed at the advance of Byzantine forces towards what he considered to be his territory. Andronikos III and his Grand Domestic John Cantacuzene had reorganised the Byzantine army and made it more effective. Both Naupaktos and Corfu had been attacked. Durazzo too was threatened. Philip of Taranto could not risk allowing the Byzantines to forestall him by marching into Epiros and occupying the Despotate. But he was getting on in years and he could scarcely afford to mount yet another attempt to bring John Orsini to heel. The problem was solved for him by the action of his son-in-law, Walter II of Brienne, count of Lecce. Walter had been titular duke of Athens since 1311, when his father lost his life and his duchy to the Catalans. In 1325 he had married Beatrice, daughter of Philip of Taranto by Thamar of Epiros. In 1330 he began to prepare an expedition to recover his lost duchy and restore his family fortunes in Greece. He had an agreement with Philip's wife, Catherine of Valois; and he had the support of the pope, John XXII, who dignified the venture with the status of a crusade. King Robert of Naples realised that Walter's expedition could kill two birds with one stone. By marching through Epiros on his way to fight the Catalans he could secure the submission of the Despotate and compel the homage of John Orsini. Robert therefore granted Walter exemption from his feudal duties as count of Lecce and gave him his full support.

In August 1331 Walter of Brienne sailed from Brindisi to Corfu with an army of 800 French knights and 500 Tuscan footsoldiers. Acting as vicar-general of his father-in-law Philip of Taranto, he occupied the island of Leukas and then recaptured Vonitsa. Some say that he also captured Arta. It seems more likely that he only attacked or laid siege to it. But in either event he produced the desired effect of frightening John Orsini into submission and forcing him to acknowledge the suzerainty of the kingdom of Naples. Thirty-seven years had passed since Philip of Taranto had married Thamar of Epiros. Walter II's wife was a child of that marriage. The marriage contract had established the Angevin colony in Aitolia between Vonitsa and Naupaktos. It had also clearly laid down the conditions under which the rest of Epiros would lose its independence. The *basilissa* Anna, for the sake of her son Thomas and with some right on her side, had contested these conditions and survived the

[54] This derives only from Hopf, *GG*, I, p. 428. Cf. Romanos, *Despotate*, pp. 133–4 (67).

consequences. The Despot John Orsini, however, had no right on his side. By no stretch of the imagination could he pretend that his land or his title had come to him by inheritance. He had murdered his way to possession of the one and broken his word to the emperor who gave him the other. He was now condemned to hold his Despotate as a vassal of the king of Naples.[55]

Prince Philip of Taranto lived just long enough to rejoice at the news. He died on 26 December 1331. Before another year was out Walter of Brienne had withdrawn to the Morea. His crusade against the Catalans had failed. He had not been able either to avenge his father's death or to recover his duchy of Athens. In the summer of 1332 he sailed back to Italy. Like John of Gravina he had earned a load of debts. His only solid achievement had been to capture Vonitsa and Leukas. These he retained for many years to come, probably as fiefs held from Naples. He placed them under the command of a French knight, John de la Mandelée.[56] Arta was left under its own Despot, John Orsini, who was quick to make sure of his new, if humbler, status. He sent a personal envoy to Naples to pay his homage to King Robert. He was a knight from Cephalonia, Nicholas (or Antony) Casside. The king was pleased by this gesture and declared that he was now willing to recognise John as lawful successor and heir of the Despots of the family of Angelos and 'lord of the Despotate of Romania'. John's envoy was permitted to take some horses back to Epiros, on condition that his master would supply wheat to the principality of Achaia. It seemed after all that John Orsini had weathered the storm and that all was well between Epiros and Naples.[57]

Philip of Taranto left all his titles, including the suzerainty over the Morea, to his young son Robert under the regency of his mother Catherine of Valois. It was supposed that Catherine's title to the Latin Empire of Constantinople would in due course pass to her son. John of Gravina at first refused to accept this arrangement or to do homage to his

[55] Walter of Brienne's expedition to Epiros is described by Giovanni Villani, *Cronica*, Book x: v (Florence, 1823), pp. 240–1 (= Muratori, *RIS*, xiii, col. 717), who says that Walter '...prese la terra dell' Arta, e molto del paese, casali e ville...'. Raynaldus, *Annales ecclesiastici*, v (Lucca, 1750), *anno* 1330, c. 54, p. 495; DuCange, *Histoire de Constantinople*, ed. Buchon, ii, pp. 203–4; Longnon, *L'Empire latin*, p. 322; Bon, *Morée*, pp. 206–7; Setton, *Catalan Domination of Athens*, pp. 38–40; Setton, *Papacy*, i, p. 452.

[56] Setton, *Catalan Domination of Athens*, p. 41; A. Luttrell, 'Vonitza in Epirus and its Lords: 1306–1377', *RSBN*, n.s., i (XI) (1964), 134. The successor of John de la Mandelée as governor of Leukas and Vonitsa was Jean Clignet who, in 1343, was called to Naples to account for his maladministration. K. G. Machairas, Τὸ ἐν Λευκάδι φρούριον τῆς Ἁγίας Μαύρας (Athens, 1956), p. 15.

[57] Hopf, *GG*, i, p. 429; Romanos, *Despotate*, p. 136 (68), who mentions two other embassies from John Orsini to Robert in March and September 1332. That sent in September consisted of Demetrios Gazza(!), John Absete (? Aspietes) and Demetrios Lacimarra. C. Minieri-Riccio, 'Genealogia di Carlo II d'Angiò Re di Napoli', *ASPN*, vii (1882), 681 n. 3; cf. N. Barone, 'La Ratio Thesaurariorum della Cancelleria Angioina', *ASPN*, xi (1886), 425 n. 2.

young nephew Robert of Taranto. The dispute was resolved by a division of the spoils. In December 1332 John of Gravina consented to relinquish his claim to the Morea in exchange for the duchy of Durazzo and the 'kingdom of Albania', together with 5,000 ounces of gold. The Angevin possessions in Albania and New Epiros were thus detached from those in the islands and on the mainland of Greece. Robert of Taranto was the acknowledged prince of Achaia and so he remained until his death in 1364.[58]

The duchy of Durazzo was an isolated colony surrounded by Serbians and Albanians, as John of Gravina and his successors in the ruling family of Anjou-Duras were to discover. The other Angevin possessions in New Epiros were also constantly under threat either from the Byzantines, who still controlled Berat, Valona and Kanina, or from the Despot of Epiros; though here too the Albanians were more and more asserting their independence. Venetian documents of these years illustrate how insecure life was in the area. The Venetians had cautiously refused to assist the crusade against the Catalans, with whom they had a trade agreement.[59] They were also negotiating a renewal of their treaty with Constantinople now that Andronikos III seemed to be firmly established on the throne; and they were still doing business with the Byzantine-held ports of Epiros as well as in Arta. In 1324 they had complained to Andronikos II about damage to Venetian property caused by the emperor's army in Epiros and about debts still outstanding to some of their citizens. The debts had been incurred by the emperor's relative, the *epitrapesius* Palaiologos, when he was in Kanina.[60] They had finally ratified their treaty with Andronikos II on 30 October 1325.[61]

But the Venetians continued to find causes for complaint about the treatment of their merchants and citizens, particularly in Valona. The local Byzantine governor of Valona, Nicholas Gantzas *sebastos*, seems to have exercised a very independent and arbitrary authority. Venice sent him an ultimatum in August 1325 to the effect that unless he gave

[58] Longnon, *L'Empire latin*, pp. 322–3; Bon, *Morée*, pp. 207–8; Ducellier, *Albanie*, p. 335. The text of the agreement between Catherine of Valois and John of Gravina is in *ActAlb*, I, no. 763, pp. 226–7.

[59] The Venetian treaty with the Catalans was renewed in April 1321. Setton, *Catalan Domination of Athens*, p. 35; Setton, *Papacy*, I, p. 452.

[60] *ActAlbVen*, I, I, no. 64, pp. 43–52 (Greek and Latin texts); *MM*, III, pp. 100–5; *DVL*, I, no. 98, pp. 200–3. Dölger, *Regesten*, IV, no. 2515. The creditors were Pietro Moro of Santo Agostino, who had lent Palaiologos 3,000 *hyperpyra*; Paolo Contareno, agent for Baliano and Marino Contareno, and Stefano Baduario, agent for Jacopo Vendellino, who had lent him 2,410 *hyperpyra*, at the rate of 12 *grossi* (ducats) per *hyperpyron*, 'Gianina' here must mean Kanina and not Ioannina. I am unable to identify the Palaiologos, *gambros* of the emperor. The editors of *ActAlb*, I, p. 184 note, suggest that he was Andronikos Asen Palaiologos.

[61] *DVL*, I, no. 99, pp. 203–4. Dölger, *Regesten*, IV, no. 2530.

satisfaction Venetian merchants would no longer put in at his harbour.[62] The Contareno family still maintained their banking and money-lending business in Valona and in Arta, and frequently blamed their Greek creditors for sharp practice and default. Baliano Contareno seems to have suffered much in Valona.[63] Nicoleto and Marco Contareno complained of being robbed of 1,162½ *hyperpyra* by the former governor of Berat and Valona, whose name was Laskaris.[64] Jacopo Contareno repeatedly accused John Orsini of failing to pay his debts. In 1328 and in 1330 ambassadors from Venice arrived in Epiros to try to force a settlement and Venetian trade with Arta was again suspended. Not until 1332 did the Despot John agree to pay Contareno 2,000 *hyperpyra* and to settle the rest of his debts through the agency of the Venetian consul in Corfu. The Venetian Senate then agreed to lift their embargo on trade with Arta, though they warned the Despot that their citizens still held many grievances against him.[65]

Other wrongs done to them in Epiros were itemised in the treaty which the Venetians at last signed with Andronikos III in November 1332. In particular Jacopo Vendellino had a tale to tell about the violent seizure of some gold, silver and pearls from his nephew by Theodore Lykoudas *sebastos* of Valona and Michael Malagaris, *prokathemenos* of the castle of Kanina at Valona. These treasures had found their way into the hands of two Greek merchants from Ioannina, Spanos Stamates and Stephen Lykoudas, who had pawned them to Vendellino for 300 *hyperpyra*.[66] Lykoudas and Malagaris, together with Nicholas Gantzas and one Xenophon, all of Valona, had also been at odds with Baliano and Jacopo Contareno and Pietro Moro in 1329 and addressed themselves to the Doge for an adjudication.[67] The villain of the piece in Valona was Nicholas Gantzas, the *prothontinus* or admiral. By 1327 he had taken to calling himself *protosebastos* and *protobestiarios* ('primus reverendus et primus camerlengus et servus mei protectoris domini Andronici

[62] Cessi–Sambin, *Deliberazione*, p. 304, no. 75. Ducellier, *Albanie*, p. 352.

[63] Cessi–Sambin, *Deliberazione*, p. 343, no. 208 (August 1327); p. 422, no. 118 (July 1330).

[64] *MM*, III, p. 109; *DVL*, I, p. 233; *ActAlb*, I, no. 762, p. 226; *ActAlbVen*, I, I, no. 113, pp. 88–9. Laskaris is described as having been 'capitaneus (= εἰς κεφαλὴν)... in partibus Belgradi et Avellone'. Ducellier, *Albanie*, pp. 352–3, identifies him with Michael Laskaris Bryennios Philanthropenos, husband of Anna Komnene Kantakouzene, and founder, in 1312, of the monastery of St Nicholas at Ioannina. This is mere conjecture.

[65] Cessi–Sambin, *Deliberazione*, I, p. 370, no. 130; p. 429, no. 201; *ActAlbVen*, I, I, no. 97, p. 69 (August 1328); no. 102, p. 72 (October 1330); Cessi–Brunetti, *Deliberazione*, II, p. 69, no. 254; *ActAlbVen*, I, I, no. 112, pp. 78–9 (29 August 1332). Cf. Thiriet, *Régestes*, I, no. 24, p. 27.

[66] *MM*, III, p. 109; *DVL*, I, pp. 232–3; *ActAlb*, I, no. 762, p. 226; *ActAlbVen*, I, I, no. 113, pp. 88–9.

[67] Predelli, *I Libri Commemoriali*, II (Venice, 1878), p. 31, no. 176; *ActAlb*, I, no. 739, p. 220. Ducellier, *Albanie*, p. 353.

Paleologi imperatoris').[68] In March 1332 the Venetian Senate demanded that he pay his debts to Baliano Contareno.[69] Three years later he had still not done so. In May 1335 the Senate sent him a warning that they would withdraw all Venetians from Valona, Spinaritsa, Berat and Kleisoura (Clausura) and cease all trade and traffic until the following Christmas, under penalty of heavy fines for offenders. Gantzas ignored the threat and in September 1335 Venice sent him an ultimatum and increased the fines payable by any trading in that area.[70] It seems unlikely that Baliano Contareno was ever reimbursed. The truth was that conditions were becoming increasingly chaotic in New Epiros. The Albanians were taking the law into their own hands and raiding and plundering the districts of Berat, Valona and Kanina.[71]

Even an opportunist adventurer like the Despot John Orsini saw little scope in the confusion to the north of his dominions. The islands of Cephalonia and Zante had been seized from him by John of Gravina. He had lost Leukas and Vonitsa to Walter of Brienne. But the failure of Walter's crusade in other respects gave the Despot a chance to offset his losses in the west by some unexpected acquisitions in the east. He was tempted across the mountains into Thessaly. Since 1318, when John II Doukas died, the Catalans had overrun Thessaly from the south occupying Neopatras and other places. The northern district, however, had been held by three independent Greek archons, Stephen Gabrielopoulos, Signorinos and Melissenos (or Maliasenos). Of these Gabrielopoulos was the most successful. He had extended his barony from Trikkala up to Kastoria. In 1325 he seems to have made a deal with the emperor and received the title of *sebastokrator*. He and his colleagues were constantly at war with the Catalans. But their problems were compounded by the influx into Thessaly of hordes of Albanians who took sides with Greeks or Catalans as the mood seized them.[72]

[68] *ActAlb*, I, no. 725, pp. 215–16. For earlier Venetian complaints about him, see *ActAlb*, I, nos. 704, 708, 713, 717, 723, pp. 211, 212, 214.

[69] *ActAlb*, I, no. 758, p. 225.

[70] *ActAlb*, I, nos. 793, 796, pp. 236, 237; *ActAlbVen*, I, I, no. 118, p. 97 (dated '1334', not 1335); no. 120, pp. 98–9. Ducellier, *Albanie*, pp. 397–400. For the fortress of Kleisoura, see Soustal–Koder, p. 182.

[71] Cantac. ii. 32 : I, p. 495, who also records Albanian attacks on the fortresses of Kleisoura, Skreparion and Timoron near Berat. Marino Sanudo writes of damaging Albanian incursions into Thessaly and 'in terras Vallone Belgradi et Thessalone subiectas imperatori Graecorum' in 1327. A. Cerlini, 'Nuove lettere di Marino Sanudo il vecchio', *La Bibliofilia*, XLII (1940), 350–1.

[72] Marino Sanudo, Epist. III, ed. J. Bongars, *Gesta Dei per Francos*, II (Hanover, 1611), p. 293 (letter to the archbishop of Capua dated 1325); Epist. II, ed. A. Cerlini, *La Bibliofilia*, XLII (1940), 350–1 (letter to the archbishop of Capua and the bishop of Pozzuoli, dated February–March 1327). Signorinos ('Signorinus') may have been related to the John Signorinos of Epiros (see above, pp. 46, 64). 'Melissenus' may have belonged to the well-known Thessalian family of Maliasenos. On Stephen Gabrielopoulos, see Cantac. ii. 28 : I,

In the autumn of 1333 Stephen Gabrielopoulos died, leaving no successor. Northern Thessaly was open to the first comer. The Byzantine governor of Thessalonica and commander of the western provinces, Syrgiannes, had yet again been accused of plotting and had been removed to Constantinople to stand trial. His place had been taken by Michael Monomachos, a capable and experienced general. Monomachos saw the chance of restoring Thessaly to imperial rule, marched south with an army and took several towns and fortresses in the area to the east.[73] In the west and north-west of Thessaly, however, he had been forestalled by the Despot John Orsini. John had already led an army across the Pindos mountains and had placed his own garrisons in the towns of Stagoi, Trikkala, Phanari, Damasis and Elassona. These had formed part of the domain of the late Stephen Gabrielopoulos. Cantacuzene, the only source for these events, has it that John occupied them 'by agreement'. Having done so he returned to Akarnania.[74]

For a while part of Thessaly was united with the Despotate of Epiros, as it had been a century before. It is hard to be sure how long the union lasted. One document, or fragment of a document, survives to confirm the fact that it occurred; but it bears no date and even its signature is mutilated. The document is a chrysobull for the convent of the Theotokos Eleousa at Lykousada, near Phanari in Thessaly, which had been founded by the widow of the *sebastokrator* John I. It has been demonstrated that it was issued by the Despot John Orsini. The document must therefore belong to the period when he controlled Phanari and other parts of Thessaly.[75] The only other chrysobull that he

pp. 473–4; B. Ferjančić, 'Sevastokratori u Vizantii', *ZRVI*, XI (1968), 183–4; idem, *Tesalija*, pp. 169–72; *PLP*, II, no. 3435. Cf. Setton, *Catalan Domination of Athens*, p. 29 n. 32, p. 107; R. -J. Loenertz, 'Athènes et Néopatras, I', *BFG*, II, p. 189; D. Jacoby, 'Catalans, Turcs et Vénitiens en Romanie (1305–1332): un nouveau témoignage de Marino Sanudo Torsello', *Studi Medievali*, ser. 3, XV (1974), 217–61, especially 235–8.

[73] Cantac. ii. 28: I, pp. 473–4, naming the *polismata* of 'Golos, Kastris and Lykostomos', Koder–Hild, *Hellas*, pp. 165–6 (Golos = Volos), pp. 184–5 (Kastri), p. 208 (Lykostomion). On Monomachos, who succeeded Syrgiannes as governor of Thessalonica probably in August 1333, see F. Barišić, 'Mihailo Monomach, Eparch i veliki Konostavl', *ZRVI*, XI (1968), 215–34.

[74] Cantac. ii. 28: I, p. 474: ...ὁ τῆς Ἀκαρνανίας Ἰωάννης ὁ δοὺξ φθάσας παρεστήσατο ὁμολογίᾳ....

[75] N. A. Bees, 'Fragments d'un chrysobulle du couvent de Lycousada (Thessalie)', *Mélanges offerts à Octave et Melpo Merlier*, III (Athens, 1957), 479–86. Of the signature only the names 'Angelos Doukas' are legible. But see G. Ostrogorsky, 'Das Chrysobull des Despoten Johannes Orsini für das Kloster von Lykusada', *ZRVI*, XI (1968), 205–13. Cf. Ferjančić, *Tesalija*, pp. 193–8; Dölger, *Regesten*, IV, no. 2823. The chrysobull also mentions the Monastery of the Panagia near Arta, perhaps the Kato Panagia. Koder–Hild, *Hellas*, pp. 208–9; Soustal–Koder, p. 223. Some doubt about its attribution to John Orsini is expressed by A. Carile and G. Cavallo, 'L'inedito crisobollo di Andronico III Paleologo per il monastero di Licusada', *Atti dell' Accademia di Scienze dell' Istituto di Bologna*, Classe di Scienze morali, Rendiconti, LXVIII (1974–5), 86–7, 99–101.

is known to have issued was that for Ioannina in 1330. As with Ioannina, so with the convent at Lykousada, he was following imperial precedent set by the Emperor Andronikos II. Andronikos had granted privileges to the same convent by chrysobull in March 1289. Andronikos III was in due course to do likewise.[76]

Lykousada was not the only monastic foundation honoured by John Orsini during his reign in Thessaly. The monastery of St George at Zablantia near Trikkala and its *metochion* of the Theotokos Kalogeriane could both later recall that they had received his favours. Antonios, metropolitan of Larissa, in 1340 refers to the properties of the latter foundation as they had existed 'in the time of the *sebastokrator* (Gabrielopoulos) and the Despot (John)'.[77] In 1359 the Serbian Emperor Symeon Uroš issued a chrysobull for the monastery at Zablantia in which he refers to its immunities 'in the time of the late Despot, my father-in-law John (Orsini)'.[78] Cantacuzene gives the impression that John's stay in Thessaly was very brief. It may have been longer than he suggests. If it had lasted only a matter of weeks or months it would hardly have deserved mention in later documents as a remembered era in the recent history of Thessaly. It is possible that the 'agreement' by which, according to Cantacuzene, John had obtained control of part of Thessaly was made with Stephen Gabrielopoulos before he died. He may then have held it for the best part of a year, from 1332 until the autumn of 1333.

Michael Monomachos must have passed the news to Constantinople. As soon as he could find the time, the emperor hurried to Thessaly to take personal charge of the situation. He had an extra cause for concern. Syrgiannes, who had been brought for trial in the capital, had managed to escape while the emperor was away in Asia Minor, in August 1333. He had found his way to Galata and thence to the Venetian colony of Negroponte across the water from Thessaly. His next move was, as usual, unpredictable. It did not take the emperor and his army long to capture all the places that John Orsini had recently occupied and to drive out the garrisons that he had installed. The operation was tactfully performed. The emperor was careful to avoid bloodshed and to take no prisoners. To show his goodwill he sent all the Despot's troops home across the mountains unharmed and in safety. It looked as if most of the long-lost

[76] Dölger, *Regesten*, IV, nos. 2131, 2780.

[77] *Synodikon gramma* of Antonios of Larissa, ed. N. A. Bees, Σερβικὰ καὶ Βυζαντιακὰ γράμματα Μετεώρου, Βυζαντίς, II (1911), no. 18, p. 67. For the monastery at Zablantia and its *metochia*, see Koder–Hild, *Hellas*, p. 282.

[78] *Chrysoboullos logos* of Symeon Uroš, ed. Bees, Βυζαντίς, II (1911), no. 19, p. 76; A. Solovjev and V. Mošin, *Grčke povelje Srpskih vladara* (Belgrade, 1936), no. XXXI, p. 222, ll. 80–1. Cf. I. Bogiatzides, Τὸ Χρονικὸν τῶν Μετεώρων, *EEBS*, I (1924), 142–3; Ferjančić, *Tesalija*, pp. 197–8. Symeon married Thomais, daughter of John Orsini. See below, p. 133.

province of Thessaly had been restored to the empire without much trouble. Michael Monomachos was appointed as its governor. Before he left Thessaly, the emperor received a deputation from the Albanian immigrants, of whom there were by now about 12,000. They lived mainly in the mountains and came down to the plains only for the winter months. The winter was then coming on and the Albanians asked for the emperor's protection for fear that they might be set upon by the Greeks. In return they did homage to him and promised to be his loyal subjects.[79]

By the end of 1333 the emperor was in Thessalonica. He could congratulate himself that within a few months he had recovered most of Thessaly, dealt skilfully with the Despot of Epiros and pacified the Albanians. From Thessalonica he also made contact with the new kral of Serbia, Stephen Dušan, who entertained him for a week at Radovosdo in Macedonia and signed a pact of friendship.[80] Andronikos III went back to Constantinople feeling that he had scored a number victories. But he had failed to run to ground the fox Syrgiannes. In 1334, after almost a year in Negroponte, Syrgiannes crossed over to Thessaly. There he was well received by the Albanians as an old friend who had been good to them during his time as governor in Berat. They gave him guides to lead him to Serbia, where he was equally well received by Stephen Dušan, who gave him soldiers. Syrgiannes captured Kastoria and would no doubt have made still more conquests if the emperor had not taken immediate action.[81]

For a second time within twelve months Andronikos III set out for Thessalonica. It had been his wish that Syrgiannes should be caught alive. But the officer who volunteered to arrest him exceeded his orders by murdering him. Such was the end of the career of the *pinkernes*, former commander of the western provinces and governor and benefactor of the city of Ioannina. Dušan of Serbia, who had abetted him in his crimes and who buried his corpse with honour, at once sent messengers to make a new settlement with the emperor. Once again Andronikos III and Stephen Dušan met, this time near Thessalonica; and on 26 August 1334 they signed another treaty defining their respective frontiers in Macedonia. Kastoria and the other places that Syrgiannes had briefly occupied were restored to Byzantine rule.[82]

[79] Greg. x. 5: I, pp. 488–90; Cantac. ii. 22–4, 28: I, pp. 436–50, 473–4. For the chronology of these events, see R.-J. Loenertz, 'Ordre et désordre dans les mémoires de Jean Cantacuzène', *REB*, XXII (1964), 222–37. Cf. S. Kourouses, Μανουὴλ-Ματθαῖος Γαβαλᾶς (Athens, 1972), p. 276 n. 5; Greg. (van Dieten), II, 2, pp. 336–41.

[80] Cantac. ii. 28: I, pp. 474–5.

[81] Greg. x. 5: I, p. 490; Cantac. ii. 24: I, pp. 450–1.

[82] Greg. x. 7: I, pp. 495–501; Cantac. ii. 25: I, pp. 451–8. Syrgiannes was murdered on 23 August 1334; Stephen Dušan made his treaty with the emperor three days later.

The emperor spent that winter in Thessalonica. In the following year he was heavily engaged in warfare with the Genoese who had appropriated the island of Lesbos. He had too many distractions to be able to plan the addition of Epiros to Thessaly as a province of his empire. The opportunity was to present itself two years later, in 1337. By then John Orsini was dead. He met a violent death, as Gregoras smugly reports. Justice caught up with him in the end, as it had caught up with his predecessors. For he had come to power by murdering his brother, as his brother had come to power by murdering his mother's brother. John's wife Anna completed the cycle of violence by slipping him a dose of poison. When an illness struck her household she had come to suspect that it was the work of her wicked husband. She elected to be rid of him before he got rid of her.[83] Once again the government of Epiros was in the hands of a widow with the name of Anna and the title of *basilissa*. She was the mother of two small children: Nikephoros, who cannot have been more than twelve years old, and Thomais, who was even younger. Anna and her children were to be the last of the line of hereditary claimants to the Despotate of Epiros.[84]

Schreiner, *Chron. Brev.*, I, no. 49/1, p. 351; II, p. 245; Dölger, *Regesten*, IV, nos. 2814, 2815. Cf. Binon, *BZ*, XXXVIII (1938), 383–7; Greg. (van Dieten), II, 2, pp. 344–7.

[83] Greg. xi. 3: I, p. 536, is the only authority for the murder of John II Orsini by his wife. Cantac. ii. 32, 33: I, pp. 499, 501, prudently refrains from dwelling on the details, since his own daughter subsequently married John's son Nikephoros. The date of the murder has been variously deduced from the words of Gregoras. Romanos, *Despotate*, p. 138 (65), dated it to 1333, which seems impossible. Others have proposed 1335, 1336, or 1337 (V. Parisot, *Cantacuzène, homme d'état et historien* (Paris, 1845), p. 135). The only certainty is that it took place before the spring of 1337. Cf. Greg. (van Dieten), II, 2, pp. 377–8. Gregoras (xi. 3: I, p. 536) records lunar and solar eclipses in February and March 1337, and then inserts two events out of context, one being the marriage of the Emperor Basil of Trebizond to a daughter of Andronikos (which is firmly dated to 17 September 1335), the other being the murder of John Orsini. He then (Greg. xi. 4: I, pp. 537–8) continues to narrate the events of the year 1337. Cf. P. Schreiner, 'Zur Geschichte Philadelpheias im 14. Jahrhundert (1293–1390)', *OCP*, XXXV (1969), Appendix I, 418–22. The last will and testament of St Neilos Erichiotes of Geromeri was confirmed by John Orsini in December, indiction 5, A.M. 6845 (= December 1336). See below, p. 244. One may therefore infer that John died early in 1337.

[84] Cantac. ii. 32: I, p. 499, rightly refers to Anna as *basilissa*, the correct title for the wife of a Despot. Greg. xi. 6: I, p. 545, l. 14, calls her 'despoina'. The two historians also disagree about the age of Nikephoros. Greg. xi. 6: I, p. 545, l. 23, says that he was in his fourteenth year in 1340. Cantac. ii. 32: I, p. 500, ll. 2–3, says that he was 'not yet seven years old' in 1338. This is probably an error, since Cantacuzene's own testimony shows that Nikephoros was married in or by 1342, and he would hardly have got married at the age of eleven. Nicol, *Byzantine Family of Kantakouzenos*, no. 27, p. 130; Greg. (van Dieten), II, 2, p. 386. Greg. xi. 3: I, p. 536, further reports that Anna had 'two small children' (Nikephoros and Thomais); while Cantac. ii. 32: I, p. 501, refers to Anna and 'her daughters', implying that there were more than two children. See below, p. 113.

5

The Byzantine restoration – 1337–48

The death of John Orsini in 1336–7 proved to be a turning point in the political history of Epiros. Given the violent temperament of the Orsini family it is possible to believe, as Gregoras suggests, that Anna disposed of her husband simply because she was frightened of him and of his intentions. There may, however, have been other motives in her mind. Shortly before his death John had sent an embassy to the Emperor Andronikos III, perhaps while he was still in Thessaly. He proposed that his young son Nikephoros should be betrothed to a daughter of the emperor's Grand Domestic, John Cantacuzene. The emperor had thought well of the proposal.[1] But Anna, being a daughter of the late Andronikos Palaiologos, an avowed enemy of the emperor and of his Grand Domestic, may well have felt differently; though it is stretching the evidence to conclude that she poisoned her husband as the only way of thwarting his plans.[2] The proposal was in any case to be put into effect a few years later, whatever Anna may have done to thwart it. The problem of establishing the truth of these matters is compounded by the fact that the most detailed account of them is that given by John Cantacuzene, who was himself deeply involved in their consequences.

Cantacuzene does, however, make it abundantly clear that the death of John Orsini disclosed the political division in Epiros between those who favoured independence and those who would prefer to come to a settlement with Constantinople. What he fails to record is that the emperor at once demonstrated his support for the latter party by appointing his own governor (*kephale*) of the city of Ioannina. It was his first step towards recovering the city and the Despotate for his empire. A patriarchal document of 1337–8 describes the governor as a relative (*gambros*) of the emperor with the rank of *pinkernes*. Most probably he was the *pinkernes* John Angelos, a cousin and faithful friend of John Cantacuzene, who was later to become governor of Thessaly. Many of the

[1] Cantac. ii. 33: I, p. 502.

[2] This suggestion is made by van Dieten, in Greg. (van Dieten), II, 2, p. 385.

citizens of Ioannina were violently opposed to this enforcement upon them of Byzantine authority. Some of their priests went so far as to excommunicate those who had any dealings with the *pinkernes* in person or in writing. The patriarch's synod in Constantinople was soon to denounce this action as piling perjury upon perjury. For in the patriarch's view, when John Orsini died (and the synod keeps a discreet silence on the manner of his death), the people of Ioannina should have come to their senses and recalled the oaths that they had earlier sworn to be loyal to the emperor.[3] Large numbers of them, however, boldly hailed Anna and her son Nikephoros as their hereditary rulers. They knew that she had been associated with her husband in lavishing privileges on their city only a few years before.[4] She was their benefactress. What was true of Ioannina was presumably no less true of Arta. The late Despot's widow and her son were widely accepted as the lawful successors to sovereign authority in Epiros.

Before very long the people of Ioannina were indeed made to admit the error of their ways. They were to have pardon and absolution for their many acts of perjury thrust upon them by the patriarch of Constantinople. They were forced to do penance for their opposition to the emperor's governor. But their repentance was to some extent dictated by circumstances. In 1337 the emperor received alarming reports from his officers in the western provinces. The Albanians in the district between Balagrita and Kanina had again risen in rebellion, in spite of the privileges which the emperor had recently granted them.[5] Both Gregoras

[3] Hunger–Kresten, *Register*, II, no. 110 (= *MM*, I, p. 172). Darrouzès, *Regestes*, no. 2180, pp. 137–8, dated the patriarchal document to 'vers novembre 1337' and identified the *pinkernes* who was made governor of Ioannina as Syrgiannes. This would necessitate backdating the incident to about 1330 and conjecturing a brief interlude of Byzantine government in Ioannina during the lifetime of John Orsini, since Syrgiannes was murdered in 1334. Such was the opinion of C. Asdracha, 'Deux actes inédits concernant l'Epire', *REB*, XXXV (1977), 168 and n. 26, followed by Darrouzès, loc. cit. Cf. also Romanos, Γρατιανὸς Ζώρζης, pp. 291–2 n. 1. But see O. Kresten, 'Marginalien zur Geschichte von Ioannina unter Kaiser Andronikos III. Palaiologos', *Ep. Chron.*, XXV (1983), 120–8, who dates the document between the autumn of 1337 and February 1338 and establishes that the events described in it are presented in chronological sequence. The *pinkernes* in question cannot therefore be Syrgiannes and should instead be identified with the *pinkernes* and *gambros* of the emperor mentioned in the next document of the patriarchal register as being in Thessalonica in October 1336 (Hunger–Kresten, *Register*, II, no. 111). In a document in Chilandari monastery dated May 1339 he is given the name Angelos. L. Petit, *Actes de Chilandar*, I: *Actes grecs* (= *VV*, XVII, suppl. I: St Petersburg, 1911), no. 130, pp. 272–5. He is most probably John Angelos *pinkernes*, cousin of John Cantacuzene. See *PLP*, I, no. 204, and below, pp. 126–7.

[4] See above, p. 96 and n. 53.

[5] Cantac. ii. 32: I, p. 495. Balagrita lay in the region of Mount Tomor (Tomorit) near Berat (Ducellier, *Albanie*, pp. 349, 350). Cantacuzene probably refers here to the arrangements that Andronikos III made for the security of the Albanians in Thessaly in 1333 (see above,

and Cantacuzene deplore the unstable, revolutionary and perfidious nature of the Albanian clans and their addiction to banditry and highway robbery. They had overrun and plundered the area around Berat and Kanina; but they had broken into and occupied the three fortresses of Skreparion, Kleisoura and Timoron.[6] The Byzantine troops on the spot seemed to be outnumbered and outwitted. The emperor therefore decided to come to their rescue in the following spring and to restore order in his most westerly province. If all went well he could combine his Albanian campaign with the project that he had now conceived of enforcing the final submission of the Despotate of Epiros. It should not be too difficult. He had already appointed an imperial governor of Ioannina, whose citizens had been made to repent of their acts of disloyalty; and there is reason to think that the pro-Byzantine party in Epiros was gaining ground. Gregoras records that the Despotate was in sorry shape under the government of a widowed woman and immature children, 'floundering like an anchorless ship tossed by the winds and waves'. He also hints that the widowed woman, Anna, had already invited the emperor to come and take over her country.[7]

The emperor's prime purpose, however, was to subdue the unruly Albanians. Nothing could be done about Epiros so long as they were on the rampage in the north. His intelligence assured him that cavalry would be of no use in the campaign. The Albanians knew their mountain terrain with all its nooks and crannies where they could evade or hide from horsemen; and in the summer they took to the heights where cavalry could not operate and from which they could pelt their pursuers down below. The emperor therefore wisely engaged a force of some two thousand Turkish infantry kindly supplied, at a price, by his friend Umur, the emir of Aydin. In the spring of 1338 he led them, together with his own army, into what Gregoras calls Illyria. He made his headquarters at Berat. The Albanians were caught unawares, not by the attack but by the nature of the attackers. They had expected a cavalry force and had taken to their hills and hiding places. But the Turkish bowmen, being light-armed and agile, soon found their way among the mountains. The

p. 104). But elsewhere (Cantac. i. 55: I, pp. 279–80) he mentions the homage paid by the Albanians of Devol (Deabolis) and Koloneia while the emperor was in Ochrida; and he may also have been aware of the privileges granted or confirmed to the people of Kroia by Andronikos III in October 1333. Dölger, *Regesten*, IV, no. 2803.

[6] Kleisoura can be identified with the modern Këlcyra in Albania, to the east of Tepeleni. Soustal–Koder, p. 182. Skreparion and Timoron are probably the later Skrapari and Tomoron (Tomoritsa) in the district of Berat. Aravantinos, II, pp. 154, 165. The anonymous author of the *Descriptio Europae orientalis*, ed. O. Gorka (Cracow, 1916), p. 28, writing in 1308, speaks of the Albanian provinces of 'Clisaram et Tumurist'. Cf. Ducellier, *Albanie*, pp. 330, 349–50.

[7] Greg. xi. 4: I, pp. 538–9; xi. 6: I, p. 544.

Albanians were terrified by the unfamiliar appearance of these men from the east.[8]

The Turks did their work thoroughly, slaughtering, taking prisoners and carrying off numerous abandoned wives and children. Some of the prisoners were ransomed by their Albanian kinsmen and the emperor rescued others. But most were taken away to slavery. Huge numbers of cattle and quantities of property were also captured. It was estimated that the Greeks had rounded up 300,000 oxen, 5,000 horses and 1,200,000 sheep. The victims of Albanian depredations were allowed first pick of these, though many of the animals were later found and recovered by their owners wandering over the hills and dales. Some were sold by the soldiers at the rate of 500 sheep or 100 oxen for a gold coin. So great was the amount of booty that the customary law of war by which the soldiers gave one-fifth of their loot to the emperor and one-fifth to his Grand Domestic went by default. Each soldier helped himself to whatever he wanted as though from an inexhaustible river of treasure. The local people who had suffered so much from the Albanian bandits were delighted to see such punishment being inflicted on them. They were delighted too with the sight and the presence of their emperor; for no emperor since the time of Manuel Komnenos had ever come their way and brought them such security.[9]

In the Despotate of Epiros the emperor's presence in the north caused more apprehension than delight. He would surely not have come so far if it were not his intention to descend on Epiros either with fire and sword or with terms of submission. There was much debate between the romantics and the realists. The former wanted to take to arms to defend their cherished independence and to demonstrate their undiminished loyalty to their *basilissa* Anna and her son Nikephoros. The realists on the other hand pointed out that armed resistance would result only in the devastation of their country. Even though the emperor had disbanded his Turkish mercenaries, he still had enough troops to enforce his authority on Epiros if he were goaded into doing so; while the Epirotes had no commander to coordinate their resistance, since Nikephoros was still a boy. If they submitted without further ado they would save themselves a deal of trouble and make it possible for Anna to negotiate reasonable terms with the emperor before he imposed a humiliating surrender upon

[8] Greg. xi. 6: I, p. 545; Cantac. ii. 32: I, pp. 495–6, who says that the emperor led his army 'through Thessaly' and harried the Albanians 'as far as Epidamnos (Durazzo)'. The date of this campaign (1338) is confirmed by the Moscow Short Chronicle of 1352, ed. Schreiner, *Chron. Brev.*, I, no. 8/30, p. 80; II, pp. 248–9. Cf. Schreiner, *OCP*, XXXV (1969), 422; Greg. (van Dieten), II, 2, pp. 360, 382–3. P. Lemerle, *L'Emirat d'Aydin* (Paris, 1957), p. 111, followed by Asdracha, *REB*, XXXV (1977), 166, proposed to date it to autumn 1337.

[9] Cantac. ii. 32: I, pp. 497–9.

them. Andronikos naturally hoped that the realists would prevail. He had already sent secret messages from Berat to the leaders of the pro-Byzantine faction. He had no desire and may not even have had the power to seek a violent solution. It had always been Byzantine imperial policy to avoid the risk and expense of war when diplomacy or bribery could achieve the same object.[10]

In the end the Epirotes agreed to leave the decision to their *basilissa* and to abide by whatever course she felt to be best for them in the circumstances. Her advice was sensible. She thanked them all for thinking not only of their own welfare but also of that of herself and her son. She was against going to war. Neither she nor her son could take command, and in any event it was clear from the different opinions expressed that the resistance would not be unanimous or united. Their best course was to anticipate the emperor's next move by sending ambassadors to him with a set of specific proposals and alternatives. In the first place they should take up again the proposal that Nikephoros be betrothed in marriage to the daughter of the emperor's friend John Cantacuzene. This would establish a link between Arta and Constantinople. Then they should ask that they be left free to manage their own affairs under a government of their own choice. They would promise to supply an army to fight for the emperor if he would do the same for them. If, however, he would not accept these conditions but insisted on the total reintegration of the Despotate into his empire under his own authority, then they should still prefer surrender to the disasters of war and try to obtain the best terms that they could.[11]

It is possible to read into these proposals, and especially into the first of them, some sinister motive on the part of the Grand Domestic, John Cantacuzene. The betrothal of his daughter to Nikephoros can be seen as part of a plot to bind the offshoots of the empire to his own person and family pending the day when he wore the crown himself.[12] It is unfortunate that the only evidence for this plan comes from Cantacuzene's own pen. Here, as so often, he has proved to be his own worst enemy. Those who look for sinister motives and plots in the career of John Cantacuzene have always been able to find their proof between the lines of his own memoirs. He devotes many pages of those memoirs to the events in Albania and Epiros in the years between 1337 and 1340. He was there himself and he was in the end very largely and personally responsible for the settlement of what might be called the Epirote problem. Gregoras, who is the only other nearly contemporary source

[10] Cantac. ii. 32: I, pp. 499–500.
[11] Ibid., I, pp. 500–1.
[12] See, e.g., Parisot, *Cantacuzène*, pp. 135–6, 141–2; Greg. (van Dieten), II, 2, p. 385.

for these events, gives a comparatively meagre account and neglects to mention either the betrothal or the marriage of Nikephoros to Cantacuzene's daughter. Yet he takes the occasion to insert into his narrative not one but two eulogies of Cantacuzene and of his services to the empire in Epiros, emphasising his devotion to the emperor, his suppression of disloyal factions and his popularity with his troops.[13]

Gregoras had other reasons for being disappointed in his former friend John Cantacuzene. But he sees no sinister motive in his dealings with the Epirotes. Things may be no less simple than they seem. The idea of a marriage alliance to bind Epiros to Constantinople had been applied before. Nikephoros I had married a niece of Michael VIII. His son Thomas had married a daughter of Michael IX. In 1338 Andronikos III had no marriageable daughters, granddaughters or nieces to offer. His first minister, counsellor and companion in arms John Cantacuzene had three unmarried daughters. He could perhaps have found a better match for the eldest of them than the male heir to the Despotate of Epiros. But if he was willing to sacrifice her on this particular altar of diplomacy he must have earned the gratitude and not the suspicion of his friend the emperor.[14]

The Epirotes had agreed to abide by the decision of their *basilissa*. Ambassadors were therefore appointed to take her proposals to the emperor at Berat. His response was not encouraging. Those in favour of war had been in the minority. But many had hoped that the emperor might be persuaded to allow them to enjoy a measure of autonomy under their own rulers. This Andronikos refused. He was quite content with the proposal that the young Nikephoros should be betrothed to the daughter of John Cantacuzene. It had already been made by the late father of Nikephoros. But he could never permit the Epirotes to have an independent government. If they now declined to accept the rule of Constantinople then he would have to impose it by force, as his own imperial ancestors had so often contemplated. The autonomy of Akarnania, or Epiros, though now of long duration, was an offence against imperial order. It had from the start been wrongfully brought about through the arrogance and insolence of rebels against that order; and it was only because of their many other preoccupations that previous emperors had failed to put those rebels in their place. If the rulers and people of Epiros would now submit and surrender to their rightful sovereign all their cities and their territory without making trouble, they would put themselves in the way of many and great advantages. They would be rewarded with honours, benefits and annuities according to

[13] Greg. xi. 9: 1, pp. 552, 554.

[14] On Cantacuzene's three daughters, see Nicol, *Byzantine Family of Kantakouzenos*, nos. 27, 29, 30, pp. 130–8.

their deserts. As for Anna and her daughters, they would be looked after in a manner fitting to their rank and dignity. But she must leave Epiros and she must live out her life as a private citizen.[15]

These were the worst of the terms that Anna had envisaged. But the emperor made it clear that if her people did not accept them they had better look to their own defence. For the alternative was war. The ambassadors had been given full power to come to a settlement. They had seen that the Byzantine army was ready and poised to invade Epiros. They accepted the conditions of surrender. Soon afterwards the emperor arrived in Epiros in person to receive the voluntary submission of the army, the leading citizens and the people of the Despotate. He treated them with tactful leniency and respect. To the townspeople he granted corporate privileges, with particular honours, pensions and other rewards to those in authority. He travelled round and visited all the towns, partly out of curiosity, because he had never seen them, and partly with a view to their separate needs and welfare. (No mention was made of those places such as Vonitsa and Naupaktos which were still under Angevin rule; though there had been some diplomatic contact between Constantinople and Naples early in 1338.)[16] Finally, he arranged the betrothal of Nikephoros to Maria, eldest daughter of John Cantacuzene. The emperor had no doubt planned to take the young man with him, along with his mother, so that the betrothal could be solemnised in Thessalonica or Constantinople. But when the moment came Nikephoros was nowhere to be found. The anti-Byzantine faction in Arta had abducted him. They had persuaded his tutor, Richard, to spirit him away by night and take him to safety across the water. Nikephoros was to be made the symbol of their freedom, and for his hereditary rights they would continue the struggle.[17]

The emperor was at a loss. He did not know who had contrived and accomplished the plot. He should perhaps have guessed that his enemies in Epiros were likely to turn to Naples or Taranto for help. But he decided that the matter would have to wait. He stayed a while longer in Epiros, setting up local municipal governors and appointing the *protostrator* Theodore Synadenos as governor-general over them all.[18] In the autumn

[15] Cantac. ii. 33: I, pp. 501–2.

[16] An ambassador from Andronikos III named Demetrios returned from Naples in March 1338 with a silver cup as a gift from King Robert to the emperor. *ActAlb*, I, no. 815, p. 245; Ducellier, *Albanie*, p. 357. Thomas Magister, in his encomium of John Cantacuzene, extols his exploits among the Illyrians, the Epirotes, Ambracia and Naupaktos. F. W. Lenz, *Fünf Reden Thomas Magisters* (Leiden, 1963), p. 94 ll. 5–9. This must be poetic licence. There is no evidence that Naupaktos changed hands in 1340.

[17] Cantac. ii. 33: I, pp. 502–3.

[18] Cantac. ii. 33: I, p. 504 ll. 1–2, gives Synadenos the title of *strategos*. Greg. xi. 6: I, p. 546 l. 10, calls him *epitropos* of Epiros.

of 1338 he left for Thessalonica, taking with him the *basilissa* Anna, mother of the missing Nikephoros. It seems quite probable that she had had a hand in the abduction of her son. The emperor settled her in Thessalonica with an estate large enough to provide an income for the rest of her life. But Anna was not content to end her days there as a private citizen. Her part in the politics of Epiros was not yet finished. The mysterious disappearance of the supposed heir to the Despotate was a nuisance. Andronikos gave orders that if and when found the young man was to be sent to join his mother in Thessalonica, but without his hereditary insignia.[19] None the less, there was much to be thankful for; and the emperor duly gave thanks to God that this part of his empire, which had been severed from it since the time of Alexios Angelos, was now restored. His predecessors Michael VIII and Andronikos II had suffered much expense and many casualties in fruitless campaigns to win back the long-lost provinces of Epiros and Thessaly. Now, with very little effort and no bloodshed, it had been given to Andronikos III to reintegrate both into the Empire of the Romans.[20]

The emperor rejoiced too soon. In Thessaly his word may have been law. But in Epiros the bloodshed was yet to come. Within the year rebellion had broken out. The young Nikephoros had been carried off to the Morea, to the court of Catherine of Valois, in the autumn of 1338. Catherine, widow of Philip of Taranto, was still regent of Achaia and the other Angevin colonies in Greece on behalf of her son Robert. She was also, as Cantacuzene observes, proud to call herself empress of the Romans, as the direct descendant of Baldwin II, the last Latin emperor in Constantinople. The arrival of Nikephoros at her court was nicely timed to suit her own plans. She had just arrived in Greece to set the principality of Achaia in order. She could use Nikephoros as her agent to reimpose Angevin suzerainty over the Despotate of Epiros. She betrothed him to one of her two daughters, so ensuring that his hereditary domain if not his title would pass into her family.[21]

Meanwhile the independence party in Epiros had taken to arms. They had gained some converts as a result of the emperor's intolerance; and

[19] Greg. xi. 6: I, p. 546 ll. 3–4 ... δίχα τῶν πατρικῶν ἐπισήμων συμβόλων. Gregoras here wrongly implies that Anna had no further worldly ambitions.

[20] Cantac, ii. 33: I, p. 504.

[21] Cantac. ii. 33: I, p. 503, says that Nikephoros was taken to Taranto. But Greg. xi. 5: I, p. 546, probably more correctly, says that he escaped to Patras and took refuge with 'the wife of the late prince of the Peloponnese and Achaia', i.e., Catherine of Valois. Catherine had arrived at Clarentza in the summer of 1338 with all her family. *Chron. Mor. arag.*, §674, p. 148. She was followed by her financial adviser and reputed lover, Niccolo Acciajuoli, who left Brindisi in November. Buchon, *Nouvelles Recherches*, II, pp. 106–9, documents nos. 13 and 14. Cf. Longnon, *L'Empire latin*, p. 324; Bon, *Morée*, p. 209 and n. 2; Setton, *Papacy*, I, pp. 159–60 (whose chronology here seems to be at fault).

they looked to Nikephoros as their young pretender who would come back with foreign aid to win their cause. The leaders of the revolt were Nikephoros Basilitzes and Alexios Kabasilas. Neither had made history before, but the Kabasilas family had friends in Italy. In 1330 Philip of Taranto had granted to Alexios's son John Kabasilas and his heirs properties and *paroikoi* in Corfu. He had proclaimed John to be 'count of Aetos', knight, baron of the city and island of Corfu, marshal of the Despotate, and his own loyal friend and counsellor. On 29 December 1331 he had conferred various other properties on John and on his mother, the wife of Alexios Kabasilas. Philip's son Robert had confirmed all these deeds in 1336. Kabasilas too might therefore be considered to be an agent of Catherine of Valois in Epiros.[22]

Basilitzes seized control of Arta and arrested the recently appointed imperial governor, Theodore Synadenos. Kabasilas took over the castle of Rogoi, while forty others occupied Thomokastron on the Ionian coast. That seems to have been the extent of the rebel territory. Thomokastron is most probably the fortress above Risá, later called Riniasa, on the coast to the north of Preveza.[23] At all events, the rebellion was confined to a small district of southern Epiros, between Arta and the Ionian Sea. Cantacuzene emphasises its limited nature and lists the places that remained loyal to the emperor. They included Mesopotamon, Sopotos, Chimara, Argyrokastron, Parga, Hagios Donatos and, most significantly, Ioannina in the north; and in the south Angelokastron (Acheloos), Eulochos and Balton, the first two of which had once been Angevin property.[24]

Early in 1339 the leaders of the revolt got in touch with Catherine of Valois, who had by then arrived in the Morea. They asked her to send over the young Nikephoros with ships and an army to fight on their side. She was pleased to have her work done for her by such willing allies in Epiros. They would help her reinstate Nikephoros in his hereditary domain as her vassal and protégé. She sent him off from Patras or

[22] Mustoxidi, *Hellenomnemon* (1845), pp. 357–8; Buchon, *Nouvelles Recherches*, I, i, pp. 410–11. A. Luttrell, 'Guglielmo de Tocco, Captain of Corfu: 1330–1331', *BMGS*, III (1977), 45–56, especially 49 and 53. Hopf, *GG*, I, pp. 428, 443, suggested that Alexios was a brother of John Kabasilas. Cf. Aravantinos, I, p. 120 n. 1.

[23] For the identification of Thomokastron with Riniasa, see Soustal–Koder, pp. 250–1. Aravantinos, II, p. 66, located Thomokastron further north. Romanos, *Despotate*, p. 143 (71), states that it was formerly called Archangelos. The ruins of the castle are dramatically situated on a high rock above the sea near the modern village of Risá.

[24] Cantac. ii. 34: I, pp. 509–10. U. V. Bosch, *Andronikos III. Palaiologos* (Amsterdam, 1965), p. 137, wrongly states that these places were taken over by the rebels. This appears to be the first mention in history of Argyrokastron, on which see Soustal–Koder, pp. 111–12. Balton is unidentifiable, but it probably lay on the south-east of the Ambracian Gulf near Amphilochia. Soustal–Koder, p. 120.

Clarentza in the spring or summer of 1339 with a small fleet commanded by Loizio Caracciolo, governor of the Angevin possessions in Epiros. They sailed up to Thomokastron, and it was there that Nikephoros established himself as the figurehead of resistance to imperial subjection.[25] When the news reached Constantinople it was already the end of autumn. The emperor felt that he must go back to Epiros himself to restore order; but he had not been well and he thought it wiser to spend the winter in Thessalonica. To support the loyalists and to prevent the spirit of revolt from spreading he sent forward an army to Akarnania, under the command of the *pinkernes* John Angelos, former governor of Ioannina, and Michael Monomachos, his governor of Thessaly. Their orders were to blockade the towns in revolt and to devastate the country around them, to make life difficult for the inhabitants during the winter. When the emperor arrived in the spring of 1340 the ground had been well prepared for him. He brought with him his Grand Domestic John Cantacuzene and the rest of his army. His first concern was to reward the leading men and the people of the towns which had remained loyal to him. He then divided his army into three to lay siege to the three centres of rebellion.[26]

Thomokastron, where Nikephoros was staying, endured the siege without much hardship. It could be blockaded only from the mainland since the emperor had no ships and the defenders could get supplies and reinforcements by sea. Arta and Rogoi on the other hand could be completely surrounded; and though Basilitzes and Kabasilas had laid in stocks during the winter the inhabitants were soon reduced to near starvation. The siege of Arta was conducted by the emperor himself. Siege engines were brought up and frequent assaults were made on the walls of the castle, but to little effect. The only positive outcome was the release of the *protostrator* Synadenos. The defenders may have been afraid that his presence within the walls might lead to a plot to surrender to the emperor. Otherwise the siege of Arta dragged on until the end of the summer. The defence of the castle of Rogoi was no less stubborn. The emperor made a personal appeal to Kabasilas to persuade him to give in. Kabasilas replied that he would rather hang himself from the castle tower than be taken alive and made to serve the emperor.[27]

[25] Greg. xi. 6: I, p. 540; Cantac. ii. 34: I, p. 510. Loizio Caracciolo had formerly been in the service of Charles, son of John of Gravina, who had succeeded his father as duke of Durazzo in 1335. *ActAlb*, I, no. 811, p. 244; Hopf, *GG*, I, p. 443.

[26] Greg. xi. 8: I, pp. 550–1; Cantac. ii. 34: I, pp. 510–11. John Angelos the *pinkernes* was a cousin of John Cantacuzene: *PLP*, I, no. 204. Michael Monomachos is called John by Hopf, *GG*, I, p. 443, Romanos, *Despotate*, p. 143 (71), and others. But see Barišić, *ZRVI*, XI (1968), 225–6.

[27] Cantac. ii. 34: I, pp. 511–12.

It was at this point that the Grand Domestic John Cantacuzene took over. The long account which he gives in his memoirs of his own part in these proceedings reveals so much about the man himself and about the nature of the Epirote revolt that it may be worth paraphrasing it at some length. Brute force was evidently not going to prevail against the rebels and time was running out. Other tactics would have to be employed. Cantacuzene had a rare talent for making useful friends and contacts. They might sometimes betray him but they rarely forgot him. He recalled that, on his previous visit to Akarnania, he had been kind to Alexios Kabasilas as one who had sought his friendship and patronage. He would now put that friendship to the test. Taking a few officers with him, Cantacuzene went to Rogoi. Kabasilas saw him from the walls of the castle and shouted to him to come no nearer. He admitted that they had a bond of friendship, but he feared that if they met his personal feelings might seduce him from his sterner and more general purpose. He was, however, reluctantly persuaded to come down to the bridge over the river so that he and Cantacuzene could talk to each other from opposite ends without the close proximity which might engender emotion. Cantacuzene accused him to his face of being the prime mover of the rebellion. Kabasilas retorted that he was only doing what was best for himself and for the people of Akarnania to liberate them from imperial oppression and to restore to them the hereditary rule of the house of Angelos. He refused to discuss the matter further.[28]

Cantacuzene gave him three days to reflect. At their second meeting Kabasilas was persuaded to cross the bridge and talk man to man. Still he refused to discuss surrender. Some of his stubbornness was relaxed, however, when Cantacuzene pointed out to him that to be subject to the emperor was not really so terrible a fate and that it was wrong to prefer death to such subjection. A few days later the two men spent a whole day together outside the walls of Rogoi and Kabasilas was finally talked into surrendering himself and his castle. Cantacuzene went back to Arta to report the glad news to the emperor. On his road he stopped at a spring to eat and refresh himself, and there he saw Kabasilas hurrying after him. It was a measure of his trust in Cantacuzene that he came alone without any guarantee of his security. Cantacuzene thanked him for this evidence of their friendship and told him to return to Rogoi and await developments. The next day the emperor empowered him to go back and reward each of the men who had handed over the castle according to his own assessment of their deserts. Then, taking the most important of them with him, Cantacuzene with Kabasilas returned to Arta, where they paid homage and professed obedience to the emperor. Kabasilas laboured the point

[28] Ibid., ii. 35: I, pp. 513–14.

that his will to fight to the death had been weakened only by the eloquence of his friend Cantacuzene, who had so captivated him that he had done that which he said he would never do. This, he said, was a mystery; but one thing was clear, namely that so long as he now lived and come what might he would not again alienate himself from the goodwill of the emperor and his Grand Domestic. The emperor praised him for his good sense and showed great kindness to him, honouring him with the title of Grand Constable and granting honours proportionately to those who had fought with him.[29]

When Basilitzes and his men in Arta heard of the surrender of Kabasilas and the defenders of Rogoi, they accused them of treachery and cowardice. They themselves would never give in, not even for the promise of ten thousand benefits. A few days later, however, Cantacuzene arranged a parley with Basilitzes at the gate of the castle. He spoke of the foolishness of stubborn resistance, of the damage that warfare and the presence of a besieging army was doing to the economy and agriculture, and of the suffering being indirectly inflicted on those who had no part in the revolt. He blamed them particularly for believing that help from the Latins, even if forthcoming, would be altruistic. Rather than calling in 'the foreigners from Taranto' they should accept the rule of their Roman emperor which had been their heritage almost from the time of Caesar. Nikephoros, on whose behalf they claimed to be fighting, would never bring them their liberty. Having fled to the Tarentines he hoped with their help to expel the emperor from Akarnania. It was a fond hope. Even if it could be realised, the rebels would still be guilty of grave injustice. 'For the Angeloi did not acquire Akarnania by liberating it from barbarians, but being the subjects of the Roman emperors and having been by them entrusted with an annual command of the country, they had appropriated it to themselves as a result of the war then being waged by the Latins against the Greeks – when the Latins took over all Thrace and much of Macedonia and the Roman Empire moved to Anatolia.'[30]

This was an interesting and not too fanciful explanation of the origins of the independent state that was to become the Despotate of Epiros. It may have seemed a somewhat academic argument to put at the gate of Arta in 1340. But there was more to come. In the years after the Fourth Crusade, said Cantacuzene, the Angeloi appropriated Akarnania and there set themselves up as governors, since the Roman emperors were unable to pass through Latin-occupied Thrace and Macedonia. Eventually the Latins were driven out, with God's help, by the Palaiologoi, and their empire in Asia and Europe was joined together again. Akarnania should have been part of it. The emperors asked to have

[29] Ibid., ii. 35: 1, pp. 514–17. [30] Ibid., ii. 35, 36: 1, pp. 517–20.

it back, but in vain; and the armies that they sent to retrieve it by force were violently and unjustly resisted by its rebel rulers, who incited the foreigners round about them to fight on their behalf. The present emperor's campaign was perfectly justified, being divinely inspired by the desire to recover a part of his patrimony. For surely the Roman emperor, with his many ancestors, had a greater right to the country than Nikephoros, whose claim to it went back for only a few generations. The number of those generations was no justification. It only added further proof that the Epirotes had been at fault for far too long. Why then could they not see that further resistance was useless? If they submitted of their own free will they would reap many benefits from the emperor, on the nature of which they could consult their kinsmen and friends from Rogoi who were at hand to advise them.[31]

Once again Cantacuzene's eloquence turned the tide. The defenders of Arta discussed their position with Alexios Kabasilas and his colleagues, who had been left with them overnight. They also held an assembly to discuss it among themselves. Things were not turning out as well as they had hoped. They elected to surrender to the emperor through his Grand Domestic. On the following morning Cantacuzene reappeared at their gates and they told him the result of their deliberations. It had been their opinion that the emperor had come to restore this long detached portion of his empire and to deprive Nikephoros of his patrimony. They had therefore risen to the defence of Nikephoros. But now, seeing that the emperor was really determined to break them either by assault or by starvation and as a result of their interview with Cantacuzene, they had changed their minds. They therefore surrendered themselves and their city to him, in the knowledge that his Grand Domestic would know how to arrange matters so that submission would prove sweeter than freedom. Basilitzes and his officers were then brought before the emperor to seek and to obtain his pardon, the gate of the castle of Arta was opened and the imperial army marched in.[32]

The rebellion had now been effectively put down. But the emperor could not leave Epiros until he had rounded up the last heir to the Despotate, Nikephoros. The siege of Arta had lasted for some six months. It had taken its toll of the army's stamina. Andronikos, who had been unwell the winter before, had fallen ill again; and his troops had been affected by some kind of epidemic, possibly dysentery. Only one of the officers died of it, but it proved fatal to many of their horses and mules. Cantacuzene seems to have escaped it; and it was decided that he should lead the army to Thomokastron while the emperor convalesced in Arta. Thomokastron had been under siege for some time, but only from the

[31] Ibid., ii. 36: 1, pp. 520–2. [32] Ibid., ii. 36: 1, pp. 522–5.

landward side. This, as its defenders replied to the messages sent to them by Cantacuzene, was their strong point. They were also daily expecting help to arrive from the 'Tarentines'. Twenty-two days after Cantacuzene reached there, some help did arrive from Taranto. Thirteen ships appeared offshore, to the great joy of the besieged. But the ships rode at anchor well away from the coast and made no attempt to disembark their soldiers. They could see the enemy camp near the sea and would not risk a landing.[33]

Thomokastron was not going to be starved into surrender as Arta might have been. It would therefore have to be talked into it. Once again Cantacuzene was to put his eloquence to good use. After twenty-five days of laying siege to the castle, he suggested that they might send him one of their own company for a discussion. The discussion was, as before, largely one-sided. The messenger that they sent was Richard, the tutor of Nikephoros. To him Cantacuzene explained the fallacy in the argument of the rebels. They had revolted against an emperor who had done them no harm and they had thought to install Nikephoros as their ruler with the help and support of the Tarentines. This was an illusion. 'For the Tarentines in their greed had often made war against the Akarnanians and devastated their country. But they had never been able to capture a single town either by arms, siege or negotiation, except for those which the rulers of Akarnania had voluntarily ceded to them, namely Vonitsa, Naupaktos and Butrinto. Since they had proved so ineffective against the Akarnanians on their own, how could they expect to achieve more when the emperor was present with his whole army.' Their only hope had been that the revolt would spread to other towns; but that hope had been dashed now that the people of Rogoi and Arta had seen where their real interests lay and had benefited themselves by surrendering.

The champions of Nikephoros still believed that Catherine of Valois would help them to victory. Cantacuzene proceeded to disenchant them. He pointed out that, though she had been eager to support them at first, it had taken her a whole year to produce the few ships that were then lying offshore. Since these could not disembark their troops they would shortly sail away with nothing achieved, leaving Thomokastron to be taken or starved out. Even if a larger fleet should arrive and succeeded in driving the emperor's army out of Akarnania, the consequence would still be servitude for the Greeks. 'And what servitude to the Tarentines and to other Latins means, you know from experience better than we do.' The siege would not go on indefinitely. If the rebels did not very soon come to terms the emperor would take reprisals by making over their property

[33] Ibid., ii. 37: I, pp. 525–6. Cantacuzene here writes of thirteen Tarentine ships, ten triremes and three penteconters. Later (I, p. 530) he writes of only ten.

and that of their relatives to others who would then join in the siege until they surrendered, only to be sent with their wives and children into exile. To avoid this fate they had better give in and accept the rewards that would then come to them. Nikephoros would become the son-in-law of Cantacuzene, who would bring him up as his own son. He would be honoured by the emperor and made famous among the Greeks. His supporters would bask in his reflected glory and enjoy their share of the privileges accorded to their Despot.[34]

It is interesting that Cantacuzene should have flattered the rebels at Thomokastron by referring to Nikephoros as their Despot.[35] The title of Despot had never been conferred upon him, but Cantacuzene knew that it had long associations with Epiros. His harangue was duly reported to the defenders of Thomokastron by Richard, who returned the next day to say that they had decided to give in. He confessed that they had been disappointed in the response to their call to arms. They had thought that if they showed the way the rest of the country would follow them and restore Nikephoros to his hereditary place. But things had turned out otherwise. No doubt the threat of confiscation of their property and of exile had helped them to reach their decision. The last of the three centres of rebellion thus surrendered. Nikephoros and the other leaders were brought to Cantacuzene who took them with him to the emperor at Arta. The captains of the Tarentine ships had been able to see what was happening, and a sufficient garrison was left in Thomokastron to deter them from attempting a landing. The emperor received the rebels gladly. No reprisals were taken against them. Indeed they were handsomely rewarded for their good sense in surrendering. Nikephoros was singled out for special favour. He was invested with the title of *panhypersebastos* and treated with great respect and friendship. The title was purely honorary and it was a little lower in dignity than that of Despot. But Nikephoros was only fourteen or fifteen years old and it was assumed that he would live the rest of his life far away from the place where his father and his grandfather had ruled as Despots. Three weeks later, when he had made suitable arrangements for security in Epiros, the emperor left for Thessalonica. His Grand Domestic went with him, together with his prospective son-in-law Nikephoros. Winter was already setting in for it was the beginning of November 1340.[36]

[34] Ibid., ii. 37: I, pp. 527–32.

[35] Ibid., I, p. 530 l. 22–p. 531 l. 1 (. . .Νικηφόρος ὁ ὑμῶν δεσπότης); p. 532 ll. 11, 19. This must be by anticipation since Cantacuzene well knew that Nikephoros was not made Despot until 1347 (Cantac. iv. 5: III, p. 33). Elsewhere he is careful to refer to him as Nikephoros dux (= Doukas) or as Nikephoros, the son of the Despot. Cantac. I, p. 500 ll. 2–3; p. 503 l. 5; p. 510 l. 5; p. 511 l. 18; p. 528 l. 19; p. 534 ll. 13–14; II, p. 195 l. 5.

[36] Cantac. ii. 38: I, pp. 533–4; Greg. xi. 9: I, pp. 551–4; Schreiner, *Chron. Brev.*, I, no. 8/30,

'And thus', writes Gregoras, 'all of what used to be called the province of Old Epiros reverted to the empire of the Romans, and thenceforth there was no more opposition from that quarter. When the emperor went back to Thessalonica he took with him the son of the late count of Cephalonia. He was loth to go, but he had no further hope of succeeding to his father's inheritance. The skilful realisation of such great achievements was due to the silence of the Grand Domestic. In other men words are but the shadows of deeds. They die as soon as they have left the tongue. But in this man even his silence occasions great achievements.'[37] Silence seems a curious word to describe the torrents of eloquence with which Cantacuzene talked the Epirotes into submission. But Gregoras meant it partly as a compliment and partly as a way of showing off his own erudition. For Plutarch, who was then much in vogue among the intelligentsia of Byzantium, had told the tale of Zeno of Kition and how he alone had held his peace when his colleagues were airing their eloquence. When asked to explain his behaviour he replied: 'Go tell your friends in Athens that you have met one man who can keep his peace at a feast.'[38]

The Despotate of Epiros as a political institution seemed to have been laid to rest. Only a minority of its inhabitants had answered the final call to arms. Most of them seemed happy enough to forget the past and to settle down to enjoy the promised benefits of being subjects of the Roman *imperium*. In an encomium of Andronikos III, Nikephoros Gregoras congratulated him on having restored the Aitolians and Akarnanians to their original place in the Empire of the Romans.[39] But the ghost of the Despotate still walked. The word *despotaton* had been accepted into the Greek literary language; and in the troubled years of Byzantium after 1340 those in Epiros who had lost most by surrender found their opportunities to try to make the word become flesh once more.[40]

p. 80. On the rank of *panhypersebastos*, see J. Verpeaux, *Pseudo-Kodinos, Traité des Offices* (Paris, 1966), pp. 134–5 and index s.v.

[37] Greg. xi. 9: I, pp. 553–4.

[38] Cf. Greg. (van Dieten), II, 2, p. 393 (note 510).

[39] Νικηφόρου τοῦ Γρηγορᾶ λόγος προσφωνηματικὸς εἰς τὸν βασιλέα, ed. Westermann, *Certamina Eruditionis ... in annum MDCCCLXV. Excerptorum ex bibliothecae Paulinae Lipsiensis libris manu scriptis pars prima* (Leipzig, 1865), p. 23 ll. 49–50.

[40] Apart from the author of the Greek version of the Chronicle of the Morea, the first Byzantine writer to employ the Greek word δεσποτάτον with reference to Epiros is John Cantacuzene, in his chrysobull of 1342 for the *pinkernes* John Angelos. See below, p. 126. The author of the Life of St Niphon of Mount Athos (*floruit* 1360) related that the saint's father came from the *despotaton* that lies between Achaia and Illyricum. F. Halkin, 'La Vie de saint Niphon ermite au Mont Athos (XIVe siècle)', *Analecta Bollandiana*, LVIII (1940), p. 12. Cf. Ferjančić, *Despoti*, pp. 17–18.

6

The Serbian occupation – 1348–59

By 1340 the whole of northern Greece, Epiros, Thessaly and Macedonia belonged again to the Byzantine Empire. For a moment it seemed that the south of Greece might be added to it as well. In the summer of 1341 a deputation from the barons of the Morea came to John Cantacuzene in Thrace. They offered to effect the surrender to him or to the emperor of the places still held by the Latins in the principality of Achaia. Their only conditions were that they should retain their fiefs and pay their taxes not to 'the prince' but to an imperial governor. Some of them who had gone to Akarnania to the aid of Nikephoros had been impressed by the persuasive and authoritative manner of Cantacuzene. They would trust him to make proper arrangements for their welfare once they had surrendered.[1] The offer was made just after Catherine of Valois had left the Morea, in June 1341. She had been there for more than two years, but she had failed to win the allegiance of all her vassals. King Robert of Naples was aware that some of them were flirting with the Greeks. In December 1340 he wrote exhorting the bishops and barons of Achaia to stay loyal to their suzerain Catherine; yet one of the Latin bishops went on the deputation to Cantacuzene.[2] All was not well in the Angevin principality. Catherine or her agents had missed their opportunity in Epiros. The young heir to the Despotate, Nikephoros, who was to have become her son-in-law, had eluded her; and all that was left of the Angevin colony in Akarnania was concentrated in the two strongholds of Naupaktos and Vonitsa.

The voluntary surrender of the Morea might have revived the ailing Byzantine Empire. As John Cantacuzene said: 'If, with God's help, we win over the Latins of the Peloponnese, then the Catalans of Attica and Boeotia can hardly fail to follow their example; and so the Empire of the Romans will as before extend in an unbroken line from the Peloponnese

[1] The envoys were the bishop of Coron and John Sideros, a landowner at Skorta. Cantac. iii. 11: II, pp. 74–7; Greg. xii. 6: II, p. 596.

[2] C. Minieri-Riccio, 'Genealogia di Carlo II d'Angiò', *ASPN*, VIII (1883), 225, (24 December 1340). Zakythinos, *Despotat grec de Morée*, I, p. 76; Longnon, *L'Empire latin*, p. 326; Bon, *Morée*, p. 213.

to Constantinople and we shall have little difficulty in settling our accounts with the Serbians and our other foreign neighbours.' He began to prepare a fleet to put the matter in hand in the spring of 1342; and pending his own arrival he sent a trusted deputy to the barons in the Morea to keep the pot boiling during the winter.[3] But the opportunity was lost. The Empire of the Romans, far from being reunited, was about to divide and dismember itself in another round of civil war. The Emperor Andronikos III succumbed to his illness soon after his return from Thessalonica and he died in June 1341. His eldest son John Palaiologos was barely nine years old. Before the year was out the Byzantine world, the church, the army, the aristocracy and the people, had split into two camps: those who supported the claim of John Cantacuzene to act as regent for the heir to the throne and those who looked to the widowed Empress Anne of Savoy and the patriarch of Constantinople to form the government. Cantacuzene was proclaimed emperor by his partisans in Thrace in October 1341. In November the young son of the late Andronikos III was crowned emperor by the patriarch in Constantinople, as John V Palaiologos. A state of war was thus declared. For over six years Cantacuzene fought for what he believed to be his rights as regent or as emperor, until he entered Constantinople in February 1347.[4]

The second civil war brought Byzantium to the verge of self-destruction. Cantacuzene himself later looked back on it as a conflict that destroyed almost everything, reducing the great Roman Empire to a feeble shadow of its former self.[5] Social and political revolution broke out in the cities of Thrace and in Thessalonica; large tracts of agricultural land became devastated battlefields; the economy was ruined. But the most enduring damage was done by the neighbours of Byzantium, those 'Serbians and other foreigners', who exploited the circumstances of war and took sides in it to their own advantage or acted with impunity in the knowledge that order had broken down. The fight was over the possession of Constantinople. But the newly recovered provinces of Epiros and Thessaly could not remain unaffected. When war was declared John Angelos the *pinkernes*, who had been left as Byzantine governor in Arta the year before, at once deserted his post to join his cousin Cantacuzene in Thrace. He was there when Cantacuzene was proclaimed emperor in October 1341. Michael Monomachos, the governor of Thessaly, offered his services to the regency in Constantinople; while Theodore Synadenos, governor of Thessalonica, quickly found

[3] Cantac. iii. 11, 12: II, pp. 76, 80–1. His deputy was Jacob Broulas.
[4] Nicol, *Last Centuries of Byzantium*, pp. 191–216.
[5] Cantac. iii. 1: II, p. 12.

himself in the firing line when the anti-Cantacuzenist revolutionaries seized power and expelled him from his city.[6]

When the trouble began the *basilissa* Anna of Epiros, the mother of Nikephoros, saw her chance of escaping from her exile in Thessalonica and returning to her Despotate. She must have known that John Angelos had left Arta. She had been well provided for by the late emperor. But her lust for power, as Gregoras puts it, would not die down. 'Just as embers lurking in chaff eat into it unnoticed until they reignite the fury of the flames, so also did Anna constantly lie in wait for the fulfilment of her ambitions.'[7] Her moment came towards the end of 1341. The governor of Thessalonica, Synadenos, who was responsible for keeping guard over her, was preoccupied. She left the city and made her way in secret back to Arta. Some of the inhabitants gave her a warm welcome.[8] A flicker of hope for the future stirred in the hearts of the diehard romantics. But this was not the revival of the Despotate of Epiros. Most of the people of Epiros, like those of Thessaly, were on the side of John Cantacuzene and against his political enemies in Constantinople. If and when he became emperor they would accept his authority. Throughout the troubled years of the civil war Cantacuzene knew, and repeatedly says, that the people of the western provinces, among them the Akarnanians, were behind him. In the last resort he could always take refuge with them. Both in Epiros and in Thessaly he had friends whom he had bound to his person and his cause by past services and benefactions.[9]

Things went badly for Cantacuzene in the first years of the war. Cut off from his headquarters and his family in Thrace, and denied access to Thessalonica, he accepted the hospitality of Stephen Dušan of Serbia. Dušan's friendship was far from disinterested. It suited his purpose to keep the Greeks at war with each other. Their misfortunes would be his gain. His sights were set on Constantinople and on the creation of a Serbian–Byzantine or Slavo-Romaic empire. To this end he would take whichever side seemed to offer the greater advantage. Cantacuzene had not long been in Serbia when a deputation came to him from Thessaly asking him to be their ruler and protector. Michael Monomachos had gone and left them with no central authority any more. The district around Trikkala seems to have been briefly controlled by one Michael Gabrielopoulos, who was no doubt a relative of the former *sebastokrator*

[6] Cantac. iii. 11, 27, 28, 31, 37, 38: II, pp. 77, 167, 175, 191, 228, 233f.; Greg. xii. 14, 15: II, pp. 621, 623, 626–8. Cf. F. Barišić, 'Mihailo Monomach', *ZRVI*, XI (1968), 227–30; Lj. Maksimović, 'Poslednie godine protostratora Teodora Sinadena', *ZRVI*, X (1967), 177–85. On John Angelos, see *PLP*, I, no. 204, and above, p. 107.

[7] Greg. xiii. 6: II, pp. 657–8.

[8] Greg. xiii. 6: II, p. 658.

[9] See, e.g., Cantac. iii. 39, 50: II, pp. 239, 297; iv. 43: III, p. 318.

Stephen Gabrielopoulos. In June 1342 he granted a municipal charter to the citizens of Phanari, of which he claimed to be hereditary lord.[10] But the Thessalians wanted a single ruler who could coordinate their defence against the Catalans in the south and the restless Albanians in their midst; and their landowning aristocracy trusted Cantacuzene as the representative and champion of their own interests.

Cantacuzene was flattered and heartened by their invitation. He regretted that he was unable to come to Thessaly in person. But since their envoys had said that they would accept any governor whom he might nominate, he would send them as his deputy or viceroy his loyal and trusted cousin, the *pinkernes* John Angelos. John was known in Thessaly. He would be very acceptable.[11] Towards the end of 1342 he arrived to take up his new post. The terms and conditions of his appointment were set out in a chrysobull, the text of which is transcribed in Cantacuzene's memoirs.[12] There is much in those conditions which derives from feudal rather than Byzantine protocol. The ruling class of Thessaly had become accustomed to feudal practices. John Angelos was appointed governor of the province for life, though with no right of passing it on as an inheritance; and his powers were circumscribed by his dependence on the emperor, whose deputy he was and to whom he was bound by oath. No loophole was left for him to recreate the autonomous and separatist state that had formerly existed in Thessaly. No special title other than that of governor (*kephale*) went with his office; although John was later to receive the title of *sebastokrator* which had such long associations with the province.[13]

The chrysobull makes particular reference to the Despotate of Epiros. It is indeed the first official document in Greek in which the word *despotaton* is enshrined. Cantacuzene foresaw the day when he might elect to send his son-in-law, Nikephoros Doukas, or some other deputy to govern the Despotate. If and when he did so, John Angelos was to be at peace with his neighbour and each should respect his own rights. Any difference that might arise between them was to be referred to the emperor. Further, the boundary between Vlachia (Thessaly) and Epiros was to be that which had formerly existed, in order to avoid trouble.[14]

[10] Text in *MM*, v, pp. 260–1. Cf. K. Kyrris, 'The social status of the archontes of Phanari in Thessaly', *Hellenika*, XVIII (1964), 73–8; Ferjančić, *Tesalija*, pp. 183–9.

[11] Cantac. iii. 53: II, pp. 309–12; Greg. xiii. 3: II, p. 644, says that John was sent as governor of 'the Aitolians and the Thessalians'.

[12] Cantac. iii. 53: II, pp. 312–22. H. Hunger, 'Urkunden und Memoirentext: Der Chrysoboullos Logos des Johannes Kantakuzenos für Johannes Angelos', *JÖB*, XXVII (1978), 107–25 (text and translation, 117–23).

[13] He is so entitled in a chrysobull of Stephen Dušan dated 1348. A. Solvjev and V. Mošin, *Grčke povelje srpskich vladara*, no. XXI, p. 164 ll. 1–6 [cited hereafter as Solovjev–Mošin].

[14] Cantac. iii. 53: II, p. 321. Hunger, 'Urkunden', p. 123 ll. 94–101.

From these clauses it emerges that Cantacuzene had wasted no time in marrying his eldest daughter to Nikephoros; that he had it in mind to appoint his son-in-law as his deputy in Epiros; and that he regarded the *despotaton* as a geographical and administrative entity. Like Thessaly, it would in due course become an appanage of the crown, governed by one who was a relative of the ruling family as the viceroy of the emperor. Catherine of Valois had hoped to employ the young Nikephoros for very much the same purpose in Epiros. In fact it was to be many years before he revisited the land of his birth. When the civil war broke out he was placed in the care of Cantacuzene's wife at Didymoteichon in Thrace; and it was probably there that his wedding to Maria was celebrated in the summer of 1342. He proved to be a loyal member of the family into which he had married.[15]

John Angelos was both popular and successful as governor of Thessaly. He made the province prosperous again and he extended its southern boundaries at the expense of the neighbouring Catalans who, according to Gregoras, had degenerated into hedonists and alcoholics. The civil war was in progress elsewhere, and this made it impossible for him to refer every major decision to his master. He acted very much on his own initiative. The charter of his appointment had obliged him to respect the existing frontier between Thessaly and the Despotate of Epiros. But when the *basilissa* Anna returned to her old haunts in Arta he felt justified in overriding this obligation. Cantacuzene would surely approve of his intervention to arrest an ominous development. John took the law into his own hands, invaded Aitolia and Akarnania and captured Anna before going on to annex the whole of Epiros. He had a mind to end her ambition by putting her to death. She was a dangerous rebel. But he was moved to spare her life by family considerations. His own wife was Anna's sister. She could not be sent back to Thessalonica, for its gates were closed to all Cantacuzenists. She was therefore condemned to house imprisonment under guard, probably somewhere in Thessaly rather than in Arta where her presence might lead to further trouble.[16]

The Despotate was thus for a few years reunited with Thessaly under the rule of Cantacuzene's deputy, John Angelos. The spirit of resistance in Epiros must have lost most of its force. But any protection may have seemed better than none. For the Serbians were now rapidly advancing into Macedonia and northern Epiros. As they came they encouraged the Albanians to move south into Greece. In the autumn of 1341, before war broke out, Cantacuzene had planned to take an army to the west to

[15] Nicol, *Byzantine Family of Kantakouzenos*, no. 27, p. 130.

[16] Greg. xiii. 6: II, pp. 657–8. John's wife was, like Anna, a daughter of the *protobestiarios* Andronikos Palaiologos. Cantac. i. 54: I, p. 274 ll. 1–4. Gregoras here promises to say more about Anna, but the promise was never fulfilled.

suppress the Albanians in the region of Pogoniani and Libisda to the north of Ioannina. Every day they had been raiding and plundering the towns as far south as Akarnania and Balagrita.[17] The punishment that the Turkish mercenaries of Andronikos III had inflicted on them was soon forgotten. The Angevin duchy of Durazzo far to the north maintained its almost independent existence only by judicious deals and alliances with the leaders of the Albanian clans. But the Byzantine enclave in Berat, Valona and Spinaritsa was as good as lost by 1341.[18]

It was uncommonly unfortunate for the Byzantines that their second civil war should have coincided with the reign of the most ambitious of all the Serbian rulers of the fourteenth century, Stephen Dušan. Dušan had willingly given refuge and aid to John Cantacuzene at the start of the war. But he withdrew both as soon as Cantacuzene's fortunes began to change for the better. One of the first signs of this change was the submission to him of Thessaly late in 1342. In 1343 Dušan recalled the troops that he had lent to his protégé. He could put them to better use elsewhere. In the spring of that year he launched a great invasion of Albania. The first substantial conquest was the fortress of Kroia which surrendered to the Serbians in May or June 1343. The fact is known only from the charter which Stephen Dušan granted to its Albanian inhabitants, renewing and confirming the privileges accorded to them by Byzantine emperors of the past, whom he was pleased to regard as his honorary ancestors.[19]

From Kroia the Serbian conquest proceeded quickly but methodically. Berat, Kanina and Valona were all in Serbian hands within two years. Berat may have fallen by 1343. Valona fell between July and September of 1345. The last Byzantine outpost in the west, 'the furthest limits of Roman hegemony', bereft of help while its emperors fought each other, had been swept into the expanding Serbian empire. There is some doubt about the fate of Durazzo. But there is no doubt that by 1346 the whole of Albania was under the control of Stephen Dušan of Serbia. The Byzantine province of Berat, Valona, Kanina and Spinaritsa, which had come into being in the years after 1281, was now held by a Slav governor. His name was John Komnenos Asen. He was a brother-in-law of Dušan and a brother of the ruler of Bulgaria, John Alexander.[20]

[17] Cantac. iii. 12: II, pp. 81–2. On Pogoniani and Libisda, see Soustal–Koder, pp. 197–8, 240.

[18] Ducellier, *Albanie*, pp. 338–46.

[19] Text in L. von Thallóczy and K. Jireček, 'Zwei Urkunden aus Nordalbanien', *Archiv für slavische Philologie*, XXI (1899), 96–8; *ActAlb*, I, no. 834, p. 254. The last known Byzantine charter for Kroia had been that of Andronikos II in 1288. *ActAlb*, I, no. 508, p. 151; and see above, p. 27.

[20] On the chronology of the Serbian conquest of Albania, see especially M. Dinić, 'Za chronologiju Dušanovich osvajana vizantijskich gradova', *ZRVI*, IV (1956), 1–11; Ducellier, *Albanie* pp. 357–9. On John Komnenos Asen, see A. Solovjev, 'Un beau-frère

Serbian armies were at the same time victoriously advancing into Byzantine Macedonia. Their ultimate objective was the city of Thessalonica. Kastoria was captured and then all the towns of western Macedonia except for Berroia. In September 1345 Dušan took the city of Serres to the east of Thessalonica; and in April 1346 he had himself crowned as emperor not merely of the Serbians but 'of the Serbs and Romans'. Later in the same year he bribed the citizens of Berroia to surrender. Cantacuzene's son Manuel, who had been holding the fort at Berroia, took refuge with John Angelos in Thessaly. Thessalonica was encircled and isolated, at least by land. Dušan did not control the sea. But he had friends within the city walls, and while they did their treacherous work he could send his troops into northern Greece.[21]

The Serbian conquest of Epiros and Thessaly was complete by the end of 1348. It is impossible to be so certain about the dates and details of its accomplishment. The information haphazardly supplied by Cantacuzene suggests that the conquest of Epiros preceded that of Thessaly. In his account it follows the Serbian capture of Serres and Berroia in 1345 and 1346. A large army of infantry and cavalry then descended on Akarnania, creating havoc and destruction. The inhabitants were brought near to starvation. Many of them fled to the coast, where they became easy prey to pirates. But they would rather be carried off to life-long slavery in foreign lands than die of hunger where they were.[22] Cantacuzene made these remarks in the course of an interview that he had with Stephen Dušan in 1350. He was deliberately emphasising Dušan's iniquitous disregard for his former agreement about the frontier between Serbian and Byzantine authority. But there is no reason to doubt the truth of his words. The Serbian invasion of Epiros was violent and destructive. There were on the other hand those who did well out of it. One was the *basilissa* Anna, the widow of John II Orsini. Another is said to have been a member of the same family, John Tsaphas Orsini, whose descendants believed that he had been greatly privileged by Stephen Dušan.[23] The date of the conquest is nowhere precisely given. Ioannina may have fallen as early as 1346. Arta and the south may have been in Serbian control by 1347. In December of that year Dušan issued a chrysobull for the monastery of the Great Lavra on Mount Athos. His signature reads: 'Emperor of the Serbs and Romans and of the Despotate of the western

du Tsar Douchan', *Revue Internationale des Etudes Balkaniques*, I (Belgrade, 1935), 180–7; Ferjančić, *Despoti*, p. 166; Ducellier, *Albanie*, pp. 486–8. One Isaac, mentioned in 1344, may have been the last Byzantine captain of Berat, Valona and Spinaritsa before the Serbian occupation. *ActAlb*, I, p. 812 note 1; II, no. 4, p. 1.

[21] Greg. xv. 1: II, pp. 746–7; xvi. 1: II, p. 795. Cantac. iii. 89: II, pp. 551–2; iv. 4, 20: III, pp. 31, 147.

[22] Cantac. iv. 20: III, p. 147.

[23] See below, pp. 140–1.

lands'. The significance of this curious title has been debated. But it seems reasonable to suppose that the word Despotate implies Epiros.[24]

The violence of the Serbian invasion of Epiros suggests that it met with some resistance. The resistance must have been organised by John Angelos, who in 1347 had been rewarded with the title of *sebastokrator*. When driven out of Epiros he would have retreated to his original appanage of Thessaly. It was there that he died some months later. Cantacuzene clearly states that the Serbians seized Thessaly after their invasion of Akarnania and after the death of John Angelos.[25] John was one of the thousands of victims of the Black Death which swept through Constantinople in 1347.[26] His passing meant that Thessaly was once again bereft of leadership and open to the first comer. The Serbians marched in. The name of their commander is known. He was Gregory Preljub, one of Dušan's most capable generals. There seems to have been little opposition; and by November 1348 at the latest Thessaly like Epiros had been absorbed into the Serbian Empire. In January 1349 Stephen Dušan could proudly entitle himself: 'Emperor of Rascia and Romania, Despot of Arta and Count of Thessaly'.[27]

The Serbian conquest of Epiros happened during the last months of the Byzantine civil war. John Cantacuzene had boasted of his special relationship with its people; but in their hour of crisis he had been unable to help them. In February 1347 he finally fought his way to a triumph over ruins and entered Constantinople. In May he was crowned as the Emperor John VI. Later in the year he sent a ship to rescue his son Manuel from Thessaly.[28] That was the extent of his involvement in the protection of the northern Greek provinces whose restoration to the empire he had done so much to effect a few years earlier. At least he contrived to prevent the Serbians from conquering Thessalonica. In 1350, with the help of Turkish troops, he took it over himself, putting an end to the revolutionary regime which had controlled it for nearly eight years. Some of the other Macedonian cities then felt inspired to drive out their Serbian garrisons. But Dušan saw to it that they were quickly

[24] Solovjev–Mošin, no. XVI, pp. 116–23. Cf. M. Dinić, 'Srpska vladarska titula za vreme Tsartsva', *ZRVI*, v (1958), 9–19; Ferjančić, *Despoti*, pp. 178–9.

[25] Cantac. iv. 20: III, p. 147 ll. 21–3.

[26] This often repeated but generally unsubstantiated statement seems to be confirmed by the reference in Dušan's chrysobull of November 1348 for the monastery of Lykousada in Thessaly to 'the late Angelos, (who died) ἐν τῇ τοῦ θανατικοῦ θεηλάτου ὀργῇ". Solovjev–Mošin, no. XX, p. 158 ll. 77–8. Cf. Ferjančić, *Tesalija*, p. 226. The Black Death had spread to Coron and Modon in the Morea by February 1348. Thiriet, *Régestes*, I, no. 209, p. 63.

[27] Jireček-Radonić, *Istorija Srba*, I, p. 226. For the Serbian conquest of Thessaly in general, see G. C. Soulis, Ἡ πρώτη περίοδος τῆς σερβοκρατίας ἐν Θεσσαλίᾳ (1348–1358), *EEBS*, XX (1950), 56–73; Nicol, *Meteora*, pp. 57–60; Ferjančić, *Tesalija*, pp. 227–37.

[28] Cantac. iv. 5: III, p. 33.

reoccupied.[29] His mind was still concentrated on the capture of Constantinople and to this end he was busily courting the favour of Venice who could provide him with ships. He was granted Venetian citizenship, and in return for so great an honour he offered to make over to the Doge the Despotate of Epiros, as soon as he became emperor in Constantinople. The Despotate was his to offer. But it is doubtful if the Venetians would have wanted it. They would rather have the islands offshore.[30]

Dušan wisely recognised the fact that his subject Greek territories were naturally divided into two. Thessaly he entrusted to his relative Gregory Preljub, the man who had conquered it, and to whom he gave the title of Caesar. Preljub made his capital at Trikkala. Epiros was allotted to Dušan's half-brother Symeon Uroš.[31] It is at this point that the so-called Chronicle of Ioannina begins, to amplify and to lend life and colour to the sparse accounts of the Byzantine historians about events in Epiros in the latter part of the fourteenth century. The Chronicle was written about 1440 and was once wrongly ascribed to two monks called Komnenos and Proklos. It exists in a demotic as well as a literary version. The latter is entitled: 'The History of various Despots of Epiros and of the tyrant Thomas the Despot (called) Komnenos Preloubos'. Most of the Chronicle's lively pages are indeed devoted to recording the tyrannical deeds and general wickedness of the Despot Thomas, the son of Gregory Preljub, who became lord of Ioannina in 1367. But it is a mine of unique information about the settlement in Epiros of the Serbians and Albanians.[32]

[29] Cantac. iv. 16–22: III, pp. 108–62. Cf. Nicol, *Last Centuries of Byzantium*, pp. 234–7.

[30] Cantac. iv. 21: III, p. 152. N. Jorga, 'Latins et grecs d'Orient et l'établissement des Turcs en Europe, 1342–62', *BZ*, XV (1906), 206 and references; Thiriet, *Régestes*, I, no. 241, p. 70. Dušan offered the Venetians either the Despotate of Epiros or the Genoese colony of Pera–Galata at Constantinople. Cf. Dinić, *ZRVI*, V (1958), 14.

[31] Cantac. iv. 19: III, p. 130. Greg. xxxvii. 50: III, p. 557, errs in calling Symeon the 'son' of Dušan. Soulis, *EEBS*, XX (1950), 61–2 (though Preljub was not the 'son-in-law' of Dušan, who had no daughters); Ferjančić, *Tesalija*, pp. 228–31.

[32] The Chronicle of Ioannina [cited as *Chron. Ioann.*] was edited with a commentary by S. Cirac Estopañan, *Bizancio y España. El legado de la basilissa Maria y de los déspotas Thomas y Esaú de Ioannina*, I–II (Barcelona, 1943); vol. II contains the literary version of the text. It has been re-edited, along with the demotic version, by L. I. Vranousis, Τὸ Χρονικὸν τῶν 'Ιωαννίνων κατ' ἀνέκδοτον ἐπιτομήν, 'Επετηρὶς τοῦ Μεσαιωνικοῦ 'Αρχείου, XII (1962), 57–115 (texts: 74–101). [Page references hereafter are to this edition.] Its attribution to Komnenos and Proklos arose from a misreading of its title. L. I. Vranousis, 'Deux historiens byzantins qui n'ont jamais existé: Comnénos et Proclos', 'Επετηρὶς τοῦ Μεσαιωνικοῦ 'Αρχείου, XII (1962), 23–9. A manuscript in Oxford (Codex Aedis Christi 49, fols. 251–71) [cited hereafter as *Chron. Ioann. Oxon.*] contains the literary version of the text with some additional chronological notes to the years 1418 and 1432. Parts of this were published by Vranousis, *Kastron*, pp. 25 (457), 44 (476), 78–9 (510–11). On the other manuscripts and earlier editions of the *Chron. Ioann.*, see L. I. Vranousis, Χρονικὰ 'Ηπείρου (Ioannina, 1962), especially pp. 85–97, 225–7.

The Chronicle reports that Dušan honoured his half-brother Symeon Uroš with the title of Despot and sent him to govern 'Aitolia'. Symeon, we are told, was a 'second cousin' or 'son of the niece' of the Emperor Palaiologos. He was in fact the son of Stephen Uroš III Dečanski of Serbia by his third wife Maria, a daughter of the rebellious *panhypersebastos* John Palaiologos, who had tried to set up his own principality in Macedonia in the 1320s.[33] John Palaiologos had been a nephew of Andronikos II and a cousin of Michael IX. Only by a stretch of the imagination could he be described as a second cousin of one of the emperors of the house of Palaiologos. But such stretches were common in Byzantine usage; and Symeon Uroš felt fully justified in stressing his Byzantine connexion by adopting his mother's name of Palaiologos.[34] The Byzantine connexion was all-important if the Serbian conquerors were to be accepted by their Greek-speaking subjects. Stephen Dušan regarded this acceptance as a vital prelude to the creation of his Slavo-Romaic empire. The charters which he issued to monasteries in Thessaly were written in the sophisticated Greek of the Byzantine chancellery. The titles which he gave to his governors in northern Greece, such as Caesar and Despot, were Greek and not Slav. By such measures he advertised that he was the legitimate successor of the Byzantine emperors.

Symeon Uroš was not highly thought of in his native Serbia. The Serbian chronicles describe him not only as a half-brother of the great Dušan but also as a half-caste of limited ability with the derogatory diminutive name of Simša or Siniša.[35] But he and his family left their mark on Epiros and Thessaly. His link with the Byzantine past was strengthened by marriage. One of the last claimants to hereditary possession of Epiros was the *basilissa* Anna, mother of Nikephoros. She had been held under guard since her return and arrest by John Angelos. The Serbian invasion brought her freedom and a new lease of life. Dušan arranged for her to marry the Despot John Komnenos Asen, his governor of the now Serbian province of Berat and Kanina.[36] Her son Nikephoros had been rewarded for his loyalty during the civil war with the title of

[33] See above, pp. 93–4.

[34] The extended uses of the terms 'uncle', 'cousin' etc. by Byzantine writers are discussed by S. Binon, *BZ*, XXXVIII (1938), 146–55. On the antecedents of Symeon, see Papadopulos, *Versuch*, nos. 38–40, pp. 23–6. Chalkokondyles is mistaken in saying that Dušan entrusted Trikkala and Kastoria to one Nicholas the župan and Aitolia to Preljub. *Laonici Chalcocandylae historiarum demonstrationes*, ed. E. Darkó (Budapest, 1922–7), I, p. 25 [cited hereafter as Chalk.].

[35] Jireček-Radonic, *Istorija Srba*, I, p. 238; Jireček, *Geschichte der Serben*, I, p. 415.

[36] John Komnenos was made a Venetian citizen in 1353. *ActAlb*, II, no. 97, p. 28. He died some time after 1363 and Anna, twice widowed, went to live with her son-in-law Symeon Uroš at Trikkala. Denise Papachryssanthou, 'A propos d'une inscription de Syméon Uroš', *TM*, II (1966), 483–8.

Despot and an estate at Ainos near the Hellespont.[37] Some day the emperor might send him to govern Epiros, as he had hinted. But so long as his father-in-law was on the throne. Nikephoros would not try to fight his way back to his inheritance. Anna's daughter Thomais, however, was now of marriageable age; and Symeon, who was still young, took her to wife. Through the marriage of Symeon Uroš to Thomais some measure of the blood of the Byzantine Despots of Epiros might be made to flow in the veins of their Serbian descendants. It was true that Thomais was at least half Italian. But her husband Symeon was at least half Greek; and the three children whom they engendered were more than half Byzantine in spirit and wholly Orthodox in faith.[38]

The Greek sources have no more to tell of the early years of the Serbian occupation of Epiros. A little light is shed, however, by Italian and French documents. The Serbians seem to have been unable or unwilling to occupy Vonitsa and Leukas. Both places had remained in the possession of Walter of Brienne ever since his abortive campaign against the Catalans in 1331. He controlled them through French castellans; and when he made his will in June 1347 he arranged to provide for the constables and sergeants of his castles of Vonitsa and Santa Mavra (Leukas).[39] Walter had good friends in Venice. The Venetians saw the Serbian conquest of Epiros as a golden opportunity to acquire Corfu, which they had long coveted. It would, as they said, be very useful to the Republic, whereas it had become an expensive liability to the Angevins. In November 1348 the Senate appointed a negotiator to discuss the matter with Catherine of Valois and her son Louis. By September 1350 the negotiations had been extended to include the islands of Zante and Cephalonia as well as Corfu and Butrinto; and the price that Venice was prepared to pay had been named at 50,000 ducats. In January 1351 the Senate went so far as to nominate a Venetian captain and rector for Corfu, a castellan for Butrinto, a count for Cephalonia and a castellan for Zante.

For some reason the matter went no further and the proposal was quietly dropped. The island of Leukas, however, had not been mentioned in the deal; and this, by a circuitous route, was soon to pass into Venetian hands. Walter of Brienne had done much business with the wealthy Venetian family of Giorgio (or Zorzi). Graziano Giorgio had helped to finance his expedition against the Catalans and took part in it himself. In 1343 Walter had made him governor of Leukas, where he proved to be more successful than the French castellans before him. In October 1355,

[37] Greg. xxvi. 34, xxix. 38: III, pp. 100, 249. Cantac. iv. 5, 28: III, pp. 33, 211.

[38] *Chron. Ioann.*, c. 2, pp. 74–5.

[39] Text in C. Paoli, 'Nuovi documenti intorno a Gualtieri VI di Brienne duca d'Atene e signore di Firenze', *ASI*, ser. 3, XVI (1872), 22–62 (39–52); Hopf, *Chroniques*, pp. xxix–xxx.

the year before his death, Walter made the castle of Santa Mavra and the island of Leukas over to Graziano as a fief. They continued to be his property until 1362.[40]

In December 1354 the Emperor John VI Cantacuzene abdicated and became a monk. He had failed to bring new life to the empire, and he had made himself highly unpopular by relying on Turkish military support. Exactly a year later the great Dušan of Serbia also died. He too had failed in his mission. He had set up a vast Slavo-Romaic empire in eastern Europe, but he had not succeeded in mastering the city of Constantinople which would have been the focal point of that empire. As it was the structure collapsed as soon as he was gone. His son, Stephen Uroš V, was quite unable to hold it together. Like the successors of Alexander the Great, the other relatives and officers of Dušan proclaimed their independence in the provinces to which they had been appointed or laid claim to the throne. His half-brother Symeon at once left Epiros for Serbia to stake his claim against that of Uroš V. His mother resisted both and built up her own neutral and autonomous principality.[41] Almost simultaneously Gregory Preljub, the Caesar of Thessaly, died. He had waged what he thought was a winning battle against the Albanians. But it was they who killed him in the end.[42]

In happier circumstances the Byzantine government in Constantinople might now have stepped in without delay to retrieve the lost provinces of Epiros and Thessaly. But the Byzantines were too involved in their own internal disputes. The opportunity was taken instead by the last surviving male heir to the Greek Despotate of Epiros, Nikephoros. His father-in-law John Cantacuzene had now abdicated and Nikephoros felt no personal loyalty to the new emperor John V. In 1356 he fitted out some ships and sailed to Thessaly, leaving his wife Maria in charge of his estate at Ainos. The Thessalians welcomed him and flocked to his standard. Domination by the Serbians had not been too oppressive. But they were glad to see a relation of their friend John Cantacuzene and glad also for any reinforcements to help contain the increasingly lawless Albanian element in their country. The widow of Gregory Preljub, Eirene, fled

[40] Thiriet, *Régestes*, I, no. 216, p. 64 (8 November 1348); no. 249, p. 71 (23 September 1350); no. 251, p. 72 (30 January 1351). Thiriet, *Assemblées*, I, no. 584, p. 224 (6 February 1351). R. Predelli, *I Libri Commemoriali*, II (Venice, 1878), pp. 188–9. Cf. Romanos, Γρατιανὸς Ζώρζης, p. 320; Machairas, Τὸ ἐν Λευκάδι φρούριον, pp. 15–20; A. Luttrell, 'Vonitsa in Epirus and its Lords', *RSBN*, n.s., I, (1964), 134–5; F. Thiriet, 'Les interventions vénitiennes dans les îles Ioniennes au XIVe siecle', *Actes du IIème Congrès Panionien, 1965* (Athens, 1967), 374–85, especially 381–3. Hopf, *GG*, I, pp. 445–6, also writes of a Venetian scheme to buy Arta from Stephen Dušan.

[41] Nicol, *Last Centuries of Byzantium*, pp. 265f.; Jireček-Radonić, *Istorija Srba*, I, pp. 237f.

[42] *Chron. Ioann.*, c. 3, p. 75. Preljub's death had been foretold by St Athanasios, founder of the monastery of the Great Meteoron. Nicol, *Meteora*, p. 60.

from Trikkala to Serbia taking her son Thomas Preljubović with her. The whole of Thessaly acknowledged Nikephoros as its ruler. He then crossed over the hills to Akarnania, where his reception was even warmer. The young pretender had at last returned to claim his own. Even those who disapproved of what he stood for must have seen that the only alternatives now were occupation by the Serbians or devastation by the Albanians.[43]

While Nikephoros was being feted by the people of Epiros, the captain of his ships, a man called Limpidarios, conspired with the sailors to make off from the Thessalian coast and go back to Ainos. He persuaded them that this long and tedious expedition to Greece would bring them no profit and that by deserting their master they had nothing to lose but their chains. They sailed back to Ainos, where Limpidarios seized control, imprisoning, murdering or expropriating the Despot's supporters. Maria, the wife of Nikephoros, barricaded herself in the acropolis of the city until she was allowed to leave by boat for Constantinople. There she was comforted by the Emperor John V. John was related to her, for he had married her sister Helena, the youngest daughter of John Cantacuzene. Maria can hardly have made her next move without his knowledge and his blessing. She sailed for Thessaly to join her husband. For a time they lived together happily enough. But Nikephoros became convinced that she stood in the way of his political success. The Serbian presence was still strong in Epiros. His own sister was after all married to the Serbian Emperor Symeon Uroš. To improve his chances he decided to divorce Maria and find himself a Serbian wife. Maria Cantacuzene thus joined the unhappy society of wives rejected by the Despots of Epiros whose first member had been the saintly Theodora, wife of Michael II. She was hidden away under guard in Arta.[44]

The Serbian lady whom Nikephoros proposed to marry was the sister of the widow of Stephen Dušan. He could not have aimed much higher in the social scale. Maria was to be sent into exile in Serbia. She refused to believe in her husband's folly until it was almost too late. She was rescued by her brother Manuel Cantacuzene, then despot at Mistra in the Morea, to whom she had sent an urgent plea for help. He immediately sent a ship to fetch her and she escaped to safety in the Morea. There was no lack of accomplices to help her get away. Maria had many friends among the Epirotes and the Albanians. They respected her partly for her virtuous and generous nature but also because she was the daughter of John Cantacuzene, to whom many of them remained loyal even after his

[43] *Chron. Ioann.*, c. 3, p. 75; Greg. xxxvii. 50; III, pp. 556–7; Cantac. iv. 43: III, pp. 314–15. The only documentary evidence for Nikephoros's rule in Thessaly is a reference to his benefaction to a monastery in a charter of Symeon Uroš dated August 1359. Solovjev–Mošin, p. 220, ll. 2–3.

[44] Cantac. iv. 43: III, pp. 315–17.

abdication. Nikephoros had in fact blundered. By rejecting Maria he made himself highly unpopular. People said that he had exchanged gold for brass. The Albanians in Epiros made the scandal a pretext for rebellion. They proclaimed their devotion to the Cantacuzene family and they declared that they would go to war unless the Despot recalled his wife. At length, either from fear of this threat or because he realised his mistake, Nikephoros renounced his Serbian marriage and summoned his lawful wife to come back. She was so much in love with her husband that she was ready to forgive his sins and she made ready to return from the Morea. But before she set out the news reached her that he was dead. He had gone to crush the rebellious Albanians before she arrived, for he did not want people to think that his authority over them depended on their devotion to her. With the help of some Turkish pirates who chanced to be raiding the coast of Thessaly he attacked the Albanians near Acheloos; and there in the spring of 1359 his whole army was destroyed and he himself was killed in battle.[45]

Nikephoros was the last hereditary claimant to the Greek Despotate of Epiros. The future of the Despotate was to be determined by those who had brought his downfall, the Serbians with whom he had flirted and the Albanians who had killed him. The story of his brief success and failure in Epiros and Thessaly is told almost as a piece of family history by Cantacuzene. The reader may wonder whether the Albanians were really stirred to rebellion and war by their emotional loyalty to that family. Rather more significant is the evident fact that by 1359 the Albanians were settled and organised in sufficient numbers as far south as Acheloos in Akarnania to be able to annihilate their opponents. Maria, whom they had made a widow, wisely decided not to put their devotion to the test by returning to Arta. Her brother Manuel looked after her during her time of mourning for her husband's death. She then went to Constantinople where she passed the rest of her life in the convent of Kyra Martha with her mother, the former Empress Eirene Cantacuzene. Her only child, if indeed he was her son, became a monk among the rocks of the Meteora in Thessaly.[46] The Despot Nikephoros was the very last of the line of the Komnenos–Doukas–Angelos dynasty which had created the Despotate of Epiros. As a child he had been its figurehead for about a year at Thomokastron. As a man he had held it for three years and two months, from 1356 to 1359.[47]

[45] Cantac. iv. 43: III, pp. 317–19; *Chron. Ioann.*, c. 4, pp. 76–7.

[46] Cantac. iv. 43: III, p. 319. On Antonios Cantacuzene, who may have been her son, see Nicol, *Byzantine Family of Kantakouzenos*, no. 28, p. 133.

[47] The length of the reign of Nikephoros is given as three years and two months by *Chron. Ioann.*, c. 4, pp. 76–7. The date there given for his death is A. M. 6866 (= A. D. 1357–8). This is almost certainly wrong. The battle of Acheloos is to be dated between February

There is little record of what Nikephoros achieved in his short reign in Epiros. The Chronicle of Ioannina says that the country was depopulated, the Greeks having fled to escape from the wicked Albanians, and that the Despot sought to recall them and restore their lands to them.[48] He also encouraged the Greeks of Leukas to rise in rebellion against their new Venetian master, Graziano Giorgio. In January 1357, in answer to Giorgio's appeal for protection, Venice agreed to send some ships to Leukas on the understanding that they could collect provisions there. But in March, before they arrived, the Greeks, incited by Nikephoros, had seized part of the island. In April Nikephoros sent them reinforcements who captured some Venetian merchants as well as all the provisions collected for the Venetian ships. Graziano Giorgio was disappointed. He had thought that the Greeks liked him. Not until May did the promised ships arrive from Venice. He borrowed a hundred men from their captain, Pietro Soranzo, and, taking his brother Nicholas, went to war. The Greeks were said to number forty horsemen and 500 footsoldiers. Graziano was taken captive and delivered over to Nikephoros. At that point the Venetian captain thought that he had done all that he could; and leaving a force of thirteen men to help Graziano's brother Bernardo to defend Santa Mavra he sailed away. The Senate advised all Venetians to get out of the island; though they promised to try to effect the release of Graziano from the Despot's clutches.[49]

In the event he escaped and returned to his island, probably after the death of Nikephoros in 1359. For in the summer of that year he was reported to be attacking Vonitsa and causing great damage to its fisheries, its land and its people. The complaint was made to Venice by Jean d'Enghien, who had succeeded to the titles of his late uncle Walter of Brienne, among them the lordship of Vonitsa. Graziano was supposed to be his vassal; he was also a Venetian citizen. The Venetians prevaricated.[50] They seemed uncertain of their policy. Two years earlier Nikephoros had approached them about his title to the county of Cephalonia. He had doubtless heard that Venice had put in a bid to buy the island from the kingdom of Naples. He was told that he must accept the appointment of a Venetian rector over his domain; though he could fly the banner of St Mark wherever he liked, since he was a Venetian citizen.[51] Much the same reply had been given to his uncle, Nicholas

and August 1359. R. Mihaljčić, 'Bitka kod Acheloja (La bataille d'Acheloos)', *Zbornik filosofskog fakulteta*, XI (Belgrade, 1970), 271–6; Greek translation by K. Sotiriou, in Ἐπετηρὶς Ἑταιρείας Στερεοελλαδικῶν Μελετῶν, III (1974), 365–71.

[48] *Chron. Ioann.*, c. 4, p. 76.

[49] Romanos, Γρατιανὸς Ζώρζης, pp. 320–2; Machairas, Τὸ ἐν Λευκάδι φρούριον, pp. 21–4; Luttrell, 'Vonitsa', 137.

[50] Luttrell, 'Vonitsa', 137–8; Romanos, Γρατιανὸς Ζώρζης, pp. 322–3.

[51] Thiriet, *Régestes*, I, no. 317, p. 86 (5 September 1357).

Orsini, in 1320. The Venetians still liked to think that the counts of Cephalonia were their vassals. For once they seem to have been behind the times. Nikephoros would have done better to address himself to Naples. There he would have been surprised to discover that his title had just been bestowed on someone else.

In May 1357 Robert of Taranto invested his friend and seneschal Leonardo Tocco as count of Cephalonia and Zante, thus unburdening himself of yet another costly responsibility. The Tocco family, originally from Benevento, had served the Angevins faithfully and well for many years. Leonardo's father, Guglielmo Tocco, had governed Corfu for Philip of Taranto in the 1330s. He had married a sister of John II Orsini, the father of Nikephoros. Leonardo Tocco reaped the reward of his family's loyalty to the house of Anjou and Naples; and it was through him and his own family that the Italian claims to the Despotate of Epiros were to be revived in the years to come.[52] The island of Cephalonia was to be their base for adventures on the mainland, as it had been for the Orsini family; and before long both Leukas and Vonitsa were in their control.[53] The fate of the Despotate was no longer in the hands of its Greek inhabitants or its Byzantine protectors. It lay with the Serbians, the Albanians and the new Italian counts of Cephalonia.

[52] Miller, *Latins in the Levant*, p. 292; Luttrell, 'Vonitsa', 136; G. Schirò, 'Il Ducato di Leucade e Venezia fra il XIV e XV secolo', *BF*, v (1977), 353–78, especially 353–6; idem, *Cronaca dei Tocco di Cefalonia di anonimo* (*CFHB*, x: Rome, 1975), pp. 10–12.

[53] As late as 1375 Bernardo, son of Graziano Giorgio, was complaining to Venice about the unlawful seizure of his hereditary domain of Leukas by Leonardo Tocco. Thiriet, *Régestes*, I, no. 558, p. 138. Machairas, Τὸ ἐν Λευκάδι φρούριον, pp. 24–6; Schirò, *Cronaca dei Tocco*, p. 26.

7

The Serbian Despotate of Ioannina and the Albanian Despotate of Arta – 1359–84

The Despot Nikephoros II had lost his land and his life to the Albanians. But it was the Serbians who came to claim his inheritance. Symeon Uroš had left Epiros in 1356. He had gone to Kastoria and there gathered a large following of Greeks and Albanians and an army of four to five thousand men. They proclaimed him to be their emperor in succession to Stephen Dušan, and he was on his way to Serbia to prove the point when he heard of the defeat and death of Nikephoros. It might be easier to become an emperor in northern Greece than to fight his way to the throne in Serbia. Symeon changed his plans and made south for Thessaly with his army. He had no trouble in taking over Trikkala, where Gregory Preljub had ruled as Caesar. He then sent for his wife Thomais to come from Kastoria with their two children. By August 1359, if not earlier, Vlachia or Thessaly was again firmly under Serbian hegemony. In that month Symeon rewarded the monks of the monastery of St George at Zablantia for their cooperation with a chrysobull endorsing all the privileges granted to them by former princes and emperors in Thessaly, by Andronikos III, by his own father-in-law the Despot John Orsini, by his uncle John II of Thessaly and by Stephen Gabrielopoulos. Stephen Dušan had styled himself Emperor of the Serbs and Greeks (or Romaioi). Symeon signed his first chrysobull as Symeon Palaiologos, Emperor of the Greeks and Serbia. It was a subtle change of emphasis. Having failed to become emperor in Serbia he would be content to reign as emperor in Greece over the lands which he had recently ruled as Despot.[1]

In the autumn of 1359 he went to reclaim the rest of those lands in Epiros, leaving Thomais and her children in Trikkala. The people of Arta and Ioannina and elsewhere are said to have welcomed him as their emperor. They had perhaps come to know by now that every change of ruler brought a new round of gifts and benefactions to their leading citizens. They were not disappointed. But while Symeon was away

[1] *Chron. Ioann.*, c. 5, p. 77. Solovjev–Mošin, no. XXXI, pp. 216–22; N. A. Bees, Σερβικὰ καὶ Βυζαντιακὰ γράμματα Μετεώρου, Βυζαντίς, II (1911), no. 19, pp. 73–80.

another claimant to the province of Thessaly arrived on the scene. He was a Serbian noble called Radoslav Chlapen who had taken over Berroia and other Byzantine towns in western Macedonia; and he had recently married Eirene, widow of Gregory Preljub, the late Caesar of Thessaly. According to Serbian law, as codified by Stephen Dušan, Eirene was entitled to inherit her deceased husband's property, including Thessaly. Chlapen was therefore legally justified in accusing Symeon Uroš of trespass. He led his army into Thessaly to right the wrong done to his wife, bringing with him his stepson Thomas Preljubović. The news brought Symeon hurrying back from Epiros. A deal was done which would meet the claims of all parties. It was arranged that Thomas Preljubović should be betrothed to Symeon's daughter Maria. Since she was only ten years old the wedding would have to wait for two years. But there was great rejoicing in the city of Trikkala. The betrothal ceremony was performed by the metropolitan of Larissa. Preljubović went off to his castle at Vodena (Edessa) and his stepfather Chlapen retired to Kastoria. Honour had been satisfied all round, and Symeon Uroš was left in peace as undisputed Emperor of the Greeks and Serbians in Thessaly and Epiros.[2]

The only document that survives from the brief period of Symeon's rule over Epiros is one that creates more problems than it solves; for there is no little doubt about its authenticity. It is a chrysobull in Greek issued by Symeon Palaiologos as emperor of the Greeks and Serbians in favour of a rich and powerful landlord, John Tsaphas Orsini, in January 1361.[3] Symeon describes Orsini as his 'father and relative' (πατὴρ καὶ σύντεκνος) and entitles him *megas kontostavlos*. He could have been godfather to one of Symeon's children. Some say that he was a son of Guido Orsini of Cephalonia and so a nephew of the Despots Nicholas and John Orsini.[4] If this were true he would have been a cousin of Thomais, Symeon's wife. He claimed that he had been privileged by a chrysobull from Stephen Dušan; and it could have been Dušan who gave him his title of Grand Constable. At all events, he seems to have made his fortune out of collaborating with the Serbian invaders of Epiros. According to his story, all his family papers and archives had been destroyed in a great fire in Arta. He therefore requested the Emperor Symeon to provide him with a document to replace the charters from previous emperors and despots which had been among those papers. This Symeon was pleased to do. The list of landed properties itemised in the chrysobull was presumably drawn up by the beneficiary, John Tsaphas Orsini. It is a very extensive list and covers huge acreages of territory in Epiros. It

[2] *Chron. Ioann.*, cc. 6–7, pp. 77–8.

[3] Text in Solovjev–Mošin, no. XXXII, pp. 230–9; also in *MM*, III, pp. 126–9; Aravantinos, II, pp. 311–15.

[4] Hopf, *Chroniques*, p. 529; Romanos, Γρατιανὸς Ζώρζης, p. 309.

included the castle of Rogoi with all its land as far as the coast, as well as properties inside and outside Arta. These he claimed to have received from Dušan. He also claimed possession of Santa Mavra with Leukas and a number of places in the 'theme' of Xeromera south of Vonitsa; of still more places in the 'theme' of Ioannina; and more still in the 'theme' of Vagenetia, some of which he had given as dowry to his son-in-law the *protospatharios*, others by *pronoia* to his nephew, John Tsaphas Orsini. Symeon graciously confirmed that all these estates properly belonged to Orsini and his heirs, inalienably and in perpetuity, free of all let or hindrance and exempt from all taxes and imposts.

There are many reasons for suspecting the authenticity of this document, at least in its present form. Symeon may have been a half-caste but he knew the difference between a chrysobull and a *prostagma* and he would not have issued such a hybrid charter as a *chrysoboullon prostagma*.[5] In addition, Orsini's alleged claim to Santa Mavra and Leukas could scarcely be made let alone justified. In 1361 Leukas was still in the possession of the Venetian Graziano Giorgio, to whom Walter of Brienne had given it in 1355; and when he died in 1362 the island passed not to any Orsini but to Leonardo Tocco, count of Cephalonia and Zante, though Leonardo had some claim to the Orsini inheritance through his mother. Suspicions are also aroused by the sheer extent of the alleged Orsini property, running from the villages of Glina and Soter, near Argyrokastron in the north, through Vagenetia and down to Arta, Rogoi and Leukas in the south. Many of the places listed appear for the first time in any known source, among them Igoumenitsa; and many cannot be identified at all. It is also curious that Rogoi should be named as an Orsini property when it is known that Symeon was about to make it over to an Albanian, if he had not already done so. Finally, the document claims that Orsini gave a whole village, called Phiatsa, to his nephew by *pronoia*. If this were true, it would be the unique exception to the rule that properties could be given by *pronoia* only by the head of state and never by one of his vassals, however great. One has the impression therefore that this 'chrysobull' was concocted in later years, with many place names that were then current, to support the claims or the vanity of latterday members of the Italian family of Orsini. The impression is reinforced by the odd history of the transmission of the text of the document which, like the document itself, poses many questions.[6]

[5] Solovjev–Mošin, p. 232 ll. 6–7. The editors have corrected this to read '*chrysoboullos horismos*' at pp. 234 l. 45, 236 ll. 63, 75.

[6] G. Ostrogorsky, *Pour l'histoire de la féodalité byzantine* (Brussels, 1954), pp. 208–10, discusses this chrysobull at length, noting some of its peculiarities, but appears to accept it as genuine. The earliest edition of the document, the manuscript of which does not survive, is in a seventeenth-century work entitled *Risposta di Iacopo Grandi... a una*

Symeon soon decided that he preferred the plains of Thessaly to the mountains of Epiros. He divided his realm into two. In other words, as the Chronicle of Ioannina puts it, he abandoned 'the whole of Aitolia' to the Albanians. It was an admission of defeat in face of the fact that the Albanians had become too numerous and too powerful to be moved. They had proved it by their victory over the Despot Nikephoros at Acheloos in 1359. Symeon would rather have them organised as a client state of his own empire behind the barrier of the Pindos mountains than allow them to run free all over northern Greece. His decision was to have great consequences for the future of Epiros. The Despotate was to be split into two appanages graciously conferred on their rulers by the emperor of the Greeks and Serbians. The district of Acheloos and Angelokastron was to be the appanage of Gjin Boua Spata. It may have been he who led the Albanians to victory at Acheloos. His father Peter Boua had earlier made himself lord of Angelokastron.[7] Arta and Rogoi were assigned to another Albanian lord, Peter Losha. In his case Symeon may simply have recognised an accomplished fact, for the Chronicle of Ioannina implies that Losha had already appropriated both places.[8] In his capacity as emperor, and to emphasise his suzerainty over them, Symeon bestowed on each the title of Despot. The southern part of Epiros was thus divided into a Despotate of Aitolia and a Despotate of Akarnania, both under Albanian rule. This arrangement, or concession, made it possible for Symeon Uroš Palaiologos to call himself emperor not only of the Greeks and Serbians but also of 'All Albania', as he did in 1366.[9]

It would be interesting to know how the people of Arta reacted to the imposition upon them of an Albanian Despot. But the only source for these events is the Chronicle of Ioannina whose author was naturally concerned with the history of that city. The people of Ioannina reacted vigorously against the very idea of being incorporated into an Albanian Despotate. They refused to accept such a fate. Ioannina was the home of numerous prosperous and well-bred Greeks and many of their kind had packed up and left the smaller and more vulnerable towns in Vagenetia to

lettera del ... Alessandro Pini ... sopra alcune richieste intorno Santa Maura e la Preuesa (Venice, 1686). The fullest account of its history and authorship is in Vranousis, Χρονικὰ Ἠπείρου, pp. 69–85, who expresses grave doubts about the authenticity of the document. See also Polemis, *The Doukai*, no. 212, p. 186.

[7] *Chron. Ioann.*, c. 8, p. 79. The demotic version here calls Acheloos 'Aspropotamon'. G. Schirò, 'La genealogia degli Spata tra il XIV e XV sec. e due Bua sconosciuti', *RSBN*, XVIII–XIX (1971–2), 67–85, especially 69.

[8] *Chron. Ioann.*, c. 8, p. 79. The demotic version does not make the distinction between the words ἐκληρώσατο and ἐσφετερίσατο. It also adds Amphilochia to the dominions of Peter Losha.

[9] Chrysobull of Symeon Uroš for the monastery of St George at Zavlantia in Thessaly, dated May 1366. Bees, Βυζαντίς, II (1911), no. 20, pp. 80–4; Solovjev–Mošin, no. XXXIV, pp. 250–7.

take shelter behind its walls. The locals and the newcomers banded together and sent a deputation to Symeon to beg him to find them a lord and leader of their own to preserve them from the Albanians. Symeon was glad to help them and he assigned the city and district of Ioannina to his son-in-law Thomas Preljubović. Messengers were sent to put the proposition to Thomas at his residence at Vodena. He accepted without hesitation; and in 1367 he arrived in the historic city of Ioannina with a large army and with his young wife Maria Angelina Palaiologina, the daughter of Symeon and Thomais. The citizens welcomed him. They little knew, says the chronicler, that they had brought a greater evil upon themselves than the yoke of Albanian servitude which they had thus escaped.[10]

The Chronicle of Ioannina is deeply prejudiced against Thomas Preljubović. This may explain why the chronicler is so grudging about according him any title, at least until he acquired that of Despot from a respectable Byzantine emperor in 1382. He does on the other hand speak of the Albanian rulers of Acheloos and Arta as Despots, even though they received their titles from a self-styled Serbian emperor.[11] It is inconceivable that Thomas should have consented to become lord of Ioannina without any official title or at any point lower in the social scale than the Albanian Despots. One can reasonably assume that he was officially known as Despot of Ioannina from 1367.[12] The assumption that he felt himself to be entitled also to the imperial family name of Palaiologos seems, however, to be unfounded. The Chronicle of Ioannina would obviously not dignify him with such an honourable name. The only document so far known which bears his name describes him simply as 'Thomas Despot Komnenos Preljub', though his wife is named as 'Maria basilissa Angelina Doukaina Palaiologina'. But she had a right so to call herself, being a daughter of Symeon Uroš Palaiologos. Whatever his other faults, it appears that Thomas Preljubović did not wilfully adopt the imperial name.[13]

The welcome given to him by the citizens of Ioannina in 1367 was not unanimous. Thomas had to take stern measures to impose his authority.

[10] *Chron. Ioann.*, cc. 8–9, pp. 79–80.

[11] Only three times does the *Chron. Ioann.* refer to Thomas as Despot before 1382, at cc. 14, 16, 24, pp. 84 l. 15, 86, l 32, 92 l. 6.

[12] Ferjančić, *Despoti*, pp. 80–1.

[13] For the document, of May 1375, see below, p. 155 and n. 55. The idea that Thomas appropriated the name Palaiologos seems to have originated or to have been reinforced by a misreading of the inscription on an icon which he presented to the monastery of the Great Meteoron (on which, see below, p. 154). G. Ostrogorsky and P. Schweinfurth, 'Das Reliquiar der Despoten von Epirus', *Seminarium Kondakovianum*, IV (1931), 165–72; followed by G. C. Soulis, 'Byzantino-Serbian Relations', *Proceedings of the XIIth International Congress of Byzantine Studies* (Oxford, 1967), p. 61. Cf. Vranousis, *Kastron*, p. 506 (74).

Some of the archons of the city declined to serve him and had to be imprisoned. Among them were Constantine Vatatzes and the *kaballarios* Myrsioannes Amirales, who was probably a westerner. The former was eventually exiled, but Amirales was honourably reinstated. Others fled from the city, and a few fortified towns in Epiros declared their independence and offered asylum to the refugees. At Hagios Donatos (Photiki) one Bardas held out as a rebel, while Arachobitsa was seized by John Kapsokovades.[14] The chronicler describes the particularly barbaric manner in which Thomas punished one of the wealthy citizens of Ioannina, Elias Klauses, whose money and property the avaricious Despot was determined to acquire. He also lists the names of some who shamelessly collaborated with Thomas either to save their skins or to save their fortunes. Especially dishonourable mention is made of Koutzotheodoros, Manuel Tziblos and Michael Apsaras. Apsaras, who was of a well-known archontic family in Epiros, was rewarded with the title of *protobestiarios* and earned his master's special favour by denouncing his own first cousin, Nikephoros Batalas, who was as a result blinded and exiled with his family.[15]

These measures were only a foretaste of the horrors to come under the tyranny of Thomas Preljubović. If the Chronicle is to be believed, Thomas directed peculiar venom against the church of Ioannina. The Metropolitan Sebastian, whom the patriarch had appointed only two years before, was hounded into exile. The revenues and properties of his diocese were taken over for the benefit of the Serbians and his palace was turned into warehouses.[16] Sebastian appears to have taken himself off to a monastery in Thessaly where he was still living in 1371. The patriarch, who can have known little of the hardships of life in Ioannina, ordered him either to return to his see or to present himself in Constantinople. Sebastian chose the latter course; and before long he was transferred to the safer diocese of Kyzikos.[17] The see of Ioannina appears thereafter to have been vacant, until in 1381 the patriarch appointed Matthew as its metropolitan.[18]

[14] Arachobitsa was some 17 km north-west of Ioannina. Soustal–Koder, p. 110. The demotic version of the *Chron. Ioann.* (p. 81) adds to the name of Kapsokavades those of Makrys and Constantine Longades.

[15] *Chron. Ioann.*, cc. 10–11, pp. 80–2.

[16] *Chron. Ioann.*, c. 10, pp. 80–1. The demotic version, which frequently confuses Serbians with Bulgarians, has it that the church's goods were made over to the 'Bulgarians and Turks' in Thomas's company. In March 1365 Sebastian, as the new metropolitan of Ioannina, had been given the title also of Naupaktos with jurisdiction over both dioceses, so long as Naupaktos remained in Latin hands. *MM*, I, pp. 468–72; Darrouzès, *Regestes*, V, no. 2488, pp. 408–10.

[17] *MM*, I, p. 587; Darrouzès, *Regestes*, V, no. 2629, pp. 531–2. Asdracha, *REB*, XXXV (1977), 171–2.

[18] *Chron. Ioann.*, c. 26, p. 93. *MM*, II, pp. 23–4; Darrouzès, *Regestes*, VI, no. 2714, pp. 34–5.

In 1368, the first year of Thomas's reign, Ioannina was struck by the plague, a misfortune which the chronicler confidently ascribes to the Despot's wickedness. As soon as it had passed, he married off the Greek widows of its victims to Serbian husbands, thus alienating their property and ensuring the prosperity of the Serbian ascendancy. At the same time he raised taxes and imposed new levies increasing the price of wine, corn, meat, cheese, fish and vegetables. The sale of the necessities of life became a state monopoly exercised either by Thomas himself or by his complacent archons. Taxes were also imposed on the most skilled craftsmen, while the unskilled worked as serfs for no pay and no reward. 'Paltry is all wickedness compared to that of Thomas', observes the chronicler of the pitiable city of Ioannina. The statement occurs like a refrain in his narrative.[19] But surely he exaggerates. The church and the city of Ioannina had been spoilt by the generous attentions of previous rulers courting their goodwill and treating them as exceptional cases. They had been cocooned in privileges by Andronikos II in 1319 and 1321 and again by John Orsini in 1330. They had even been awarded special penances for their treachery by the patriarch in 1337. They must have been disappointed to get rougher treatment from Thomas Preljubović; and no doubt he made himself unpopular with the Greeks by bringing a large Serbian element into the church and the administration. He may have been a tyrant but he was perhaps not the demoniacal monster portrayed by the chronicler. The people of Ioannina had appealed for a leader to protect them against the Albanians. Thomas did his best to fulfil that role. But to pay for the cost of almost continuous warfare he had to impose taxes on citizens who had for long regarded exemption from taxation as their right. The Chronicle of Ioannina scathingly reports that Thomas's army was composed of or augmented by bands of robbers, brigands and pirates.[20] Whoever his soldiers were, and many of them must have been Serbian, they had to be paid; and without them Ioannina would have fallen to the Albanians.

Every year between 1367 and 1370 the Albanians attacked and blockaded the city. They were led by Peter Losha, whom Symeon had made Despot of Arta and Rogoi, supported by the clans of the Mazarakaioi and Malakassaioi, some of whom Andronikos III had encountered in Thessaly in 1333.[21] Thomas persuaded them to make

[19] *Chron. Ioann.*, c. 12, pp. 82–3.

[20] *Chron. Ioann.*, c. 16, p. 85. Cf. M. C. Bartusis, 'Brigandage in the late Byzantine Empire', *B*, LI (1981), 386–409, especially 402–3.

[21] Cantac. ii. 28: 1, p. 474, writes of the Albanian clans of the Malakasioi, Mpouioi and Mesaritai, so called from their chieftains. G. C. Soulis, Περὶ τῶν μεσαιωνικῶν ἀλβανικῶν φύλων τῶν Μαλακασίων, Μπουίων καὶ Μεσαριτῶν, *EEBS*, XXIII (1953), 213–16; T. Jochalas, 'Über die Einwanderung der Albaner in Griechenland', *Dissertationes*

peace in 1370 by proposing that his own daughter Eirene should be betrothed to Losha's son. Eirene can have been only an infant since her parents were not married until about 1361. But the Albanians were satisfied with the arrangement and Ioannina was spared their attacks for a few years. In 1374, however, Peter Losha died during an epidemic in Arta and the Despot of Acheloos, Gjin Boua Spata, promptly moved in and united under his single rule the two Despotates of Arta and Acheloos. He was not bound by any arrangement with the Despot of Ioannina. His troops laid siege to the city and ravaged the country round about. Gjin Boua Spata was held in high esteem by the chronicler of Ioannina as a man distinguished in word, deed and appearance. Almost anyone set to do down the evil Thomas was a hero in the eyes of the chronicler. But if it is true that Thomas had broken his truce with the Albanians and had filled Ioannina with Albanian children taken as hostages, then he got what he deserved. In 1375, however, he bought peace once again by promising his sister Helena as wife to Gjin Spata. His poor little daughter Eirene, the bride to be of the son of the late Despot Peter Losha, died during a second outbreak of the plague in Ioannina in the same year.[22]

Nevertheless, sporadic and often savage warfare continued between Ioannina and the Albanians. On 14 September 1377 a chieftain called Gjin Phrates at the head of some of the Malakassaioi attacked the city. He was defeated and paraded in triumph through the streets. Those taken captive were sold into slavery. This was Thomas's first victory over the Albanians, though they got away with much plunder.[23] His second and more spectacular victory came in 1379. In February of that year the Malakassaioi returned to the attack, assisted by a traitor within the city.[24] The Albanians had always made their assaults on the landward side of Ioannina. But on this occasion, directed by the traitor, they arrived unexpectedly and under cover of darkness by boat from the lake side, which was undefended. Two hundred of them swarmed up the rock and occupied the northern acropolis of the city with its tower. The rest waited on the island in the lake. For three days and nights the Albanians encircled the city and those on the acropolis attacked the tower with all

Albanicae (Munich, 1971), 93–5. The demotic version of the *Chron. Ioann.* (p. 84) says that the 'Dryinopolitans' joined the Albanians in their assaults on Ioannina.

[22] *Chron. Ioann.*, cc. 13–16, pp. 84–6; Chalk. (ed. Darkó), I, p. 198. On the proposed marriage of Helena Preljubovna to Gjin Boua Spata, see Schirò, *RSBN*, XVIII–XIX (1971–2), 75–6.

[23] *Chron. Ioann.*, c. 17, p. 86. The demotic version gives the total number of Thomas's army as 15,000 and his casualties as 2,568 as against 6,393 Albanian casualties. But the figures are surely fictitious. Gjin Phrates is otherwise unknown, and not to be confused with the Gjin Losha invented by Hopf, *GG*, II, p. 38. Schirò, *Cronaca dei Tocco*, p. 16 and n. 1.

[24] The traitor's name is given as Nikephoros Perates the deaf (τὸν κωφὸν Νικηφόρον τὸν Περάτην). *Chron. Ioann.*, c. 18, p. 87.

their might, yelling their warcry. Finally, those on the island sailed across to complete the business. But the citizens went out to meet them with only two ships and a few rowing boats; and battle was joined on the waters of the lake. Victory went to the people of Ioannina, heartened by the timely intervention of the Archangel Michael on whom they had called for help. The raiders were turned back in confusion; and those on the acropolis surrendered.[25]

The Chronicle of Ioannina attributes this great triumph solely to the citizens and the Archangel. The Despot Thomas receives no credit and no mention, at least until after the event, when his brutal treatment of the captured Albanians can be held against him. The pick of them he put in prison for ransom; the rest he divided among the archons and the people to be sold as slaves. Those who were rounded up on the island were also sold. But the Bulgarians and Vlachs who had been fighting with them had their noses cut off. The whole of Ioannina ran with blood. It seemed indeed as though Thomas had found his chance to fulfil his wish to go down in history as the Albanitoktonos, the slayer of Albanians. In May of the same year Gjin Spata came back to devastate the vineyards and fields of Ioannina and Thomas was given the opportunity to slay still more Albanians and to treat still more barbarously those who had the misfortune to fall into his hands. Some he hung from the city's towers. Others had their limbs cut off or their eyes gouged out and sent as gruesome presents to their leader, until he was persuaded to withdraw.[26]

By 1379 Gjin Spata had good cause for thinking that he was the equal of the Despot of Ioannina, for he had scored a notable victory in his own Despotate of Arta. Of the three towns once held by the Angevins in Akarnania and Aitolia, only Vonitsa remained in Italian hands. It had been occupied in 1362 by Leonardo Tocco, count of Cephalonia, and he had added Leukas to his domains. He had no clear warrant other than self-interest for taking possession either of Vonitsa or of Leukas. But he saw himself as heir by default to the Angevin dominions on the mainland and to the Orsini dominions in the islands. When he died in 1375–6, his widow Maddalena Buondelmonti was left with two infant sons, Carlo and Leonardo Tocco. She thought it wise to entrust the defence of Vonitsa to the Knights Hospitallers of Rhodes, to whose care the principality of Achaia had just been transferred by Queen Joanna of Naples. The new Grand Master of the Order was Juan Fernandez de Heredia, nominated by Pope Gregory XI in September 1377. He left Italy for the Morea at the

[25] *Chron. Ioann.*, cc. 18–19, pp. 87–8. The details and the topography of this Albanian attack on Ioannina are thoroughly examined by Vranousis, *Kastron*, pp. 449–57 (17–25). The 'upper tower' referred to in the Chronicle is the smaller acropolis of the city, where the Mosque of Aslan Pasha (the Demotic Museum) now stands.

[26] *Chron. Ioann.*, cc. 20–1, pp. 88–90.

end of the year, putting in at Vonitsa on his way. While there he was tempted to invade the Albanian Despotate and to attack Arta. It was a rash venture that ended in disaster. Heredia was ambushed by Gjin Spata, captured and sold to the Turks along with several of his companions.

Had the Albanian Despot known any of the history of his country he might have compared himself to his predecessor Theodore, who had ambushed and captured the Latin Emperor Peter of Courtenay in 1217. He put a high price on the head of so distinguished a prisoner as the Grand Master of the Knights of Rhodes; and his achievement brought him, as it had brought Theodore, to the notice of a wider world. The news of Heredia's capture was known in Florence by the end of September 1378. About eight months later the necessary ransom had been found to buy him back from his Turkish captors and he was safely at Clarentza in the Morea. With his share of the ransom money, amounting to eight thousand florins, Gjin Spata provided a dowry for his daughter Eirene. She married one of the barons of the Morea, Marchesano of Naples, who had served as a somewhat incompetent baillie of the principality of Achaia. They were married before April 1381, and Marchesano took his bride to live at Naupaktos, where he was still to be found in 1386.[27] This happy arrangement confirms the fact that Gjin Spata was already in possession of Naupaktos, presumably by conquest; for in September 1380 he sent a bishop, Matthew of Kernitza in the Morea, to the emperor and patriarch in Constantinople to tell them that this was so.[28] Vonitsa, however, remained in the hands of the Tocco family, as the last surviving Latin foothold on the mainland of Epiros.

[27] *Chron. Ioann.*, c. 17, p. 86. R. -J. Loenertz, 'Hospitaliers et Navarrais en Grèce', *OCP*, XXII (1956), 319–60 [= *BFG*,I, pp. 329–69], especially 331–5 [340–1, 345]. Cf. Hopf, *GG*, II, p. 11; Miller, *Latins in the Levant*, p. 309; Setton, *Catalan Domination of Athens*, pp. 122–3; *Chron. Ioann.*, ed. Estopañan, I, p. 145; A. K. Eszer, *Das abenteuerliche Leben des Johannes Laskaris Kalopheros* (Wiesbaden, 1969), pp. 70–2; Bon, *Morée*, pp. 253–4. All these authorities accept the story that Heredia also wrested Naupaktos from Gjin Spata, who regained it in 1379 or 1380. The only evidence for this is the often fanciful history of the Order of St John by Giacomo Bosio, *Dell' Istoria della sacra religione et illustrissima militia di San Giovanni Gerosolomitano*, II (Rome, 1630), as reconstructed by J. Delaville le Roux, *Les Hospitaliers à Rhodes jusqu'à la mort de Philibert de Naillac, 1310–1421* (Paris, 1913), pp. 202–3. But see A. Luttrell, 'Aldobrando Baroncelli in Greece: 1378–1382', *OCP*, XXXVI (1970), 273–300 (especially 280, 284–5); idem, 'Interessi fiorentini nell' economia e nella politica dei Cavalieri Ospedalieri di Rodi nel trecento', *Annali della Scuola Normale Superiore di Pisa*, ser. II, XXVIII (1959), 322–4; idem, 'The Principality of Achaia in 1377', *BZ*, LVII (1964), 340–5; idem, 'Vonitza', *RSBN*, n.s., I (XI) (1964), 140–1; G. Schirò, *Cronaca dei Tocco*, pp. 31–2. Luttrell, *OCP*, XXXVI (1970), 288–90, established the true identity of Marchesano (the 'Myrsi Makatzanos' of the *Chron. Ioann.*). See also Schirò, *RSBN*, XVIII–XIX (1971–2), 74. The rather garbled account of these events given by Chalkokondyles, I, pp. 197–8, tells of a siege of Arta by the Italians and of the capture of 'Prealoupas' (Preljub) by the Albanians.

[28] *MM*, II, pp. 11–18; Darrouzès, *Regestes*, VI, no. 2708, p. 31 (September 1380).

Thomas Preljubović was not impressed by the exploits of his Albanian neighbour. The Chronicle of Ioannina briefly records the invasion of Arta by the 'Megas Maistor' and his capture by Gjin Spata, but rather by way of digression from its main purpose of cataloguing the iniquities of the Despot Thomas.[29] We are told that Thomas, whose wickedness knew no bounds, had sunk so far into depravity as to believe the vile insinuations made by his favourite Michael Apsaras about his young wife Maria Angelina. He had repudiated her and given himself up to sodomy. In 1379 he rounded up a number of the leading men of Ioannina who had dared to speak out against him. John Boulgaris was hanged, Theocharis was executed, and Grastitziotes was dragged round the town by horses. Others, most of them innocent, were blinded, exiled or imprisoned; and many took to flight of their own free will for fear of being denounced to the tyrant on empty rumour or mere suspicion.[30]

A reign of terror prevailed and with it corruption, in all of which Thomas was abetted by the treacherous Apsaras. He raised the duty on wine, monopolised the markets, multiplied the taxes and enforced penalties on defaulters. Houses and properties were seized from law-abiding citizens to be bestowed on foreigners, on Thomas's Serbian friends. Later, with the help of one Chouchoulitzas, Thomas took to incarcerating the most influential citizens. One of them was his first secretary, Manuel Philanthropenos. He was held for two months in gaol, restored to favour for a while and then poisoned. The commander (*prokathemenos*) of Ioannina was imprisoned for six years, blinded, driven into exile and finally murdered for his alleged crime of treason. Many more were killed, tortured and gaoled; and the number of exiles was such that the city was empty and the countryside full. But even beyond the city the tyrant's lash was felt. The good abbot of Metsovon, Esaias, was imprisoned as a criminal; and though there were godly men who paid the sum of two hundred *aspra* to save the sight of his eyes, the avaricious Thomas had him blinded and sold into slavery none the less.[31]

Thomas's behaviour as a tyrant is at least understandable. His behaviour as a statesman is less easy to interpret. It is said that a delegation came to him from Kastoria in December 1379 asking him to take over the castle of Servia on the borders of Thessaly and Macedonia. Servia had once belonged to Thomas's father Gregory Preljub, who had stoutly defended it against John Cantacuzene.[32] It might be thought that

[29] *Chron. Ioann.*, c. 17, p. 86.

[30] *Chron. Ioann.*, c. 17, p. 86. The demotic version (p. 89) here turns the name 'Grastitziotes' into 'Gastritsa' and invents a tale about the persecution of the abbot of the monastery at Kastritsa at the south end of the lake of Ioannina. See the comments of Vranousis, *Chron. Ioann.*, pp. 112–13.

[31] *Chron. Ioann.*, cc. 21–23, pp. 89–91.

[32] Cantac. iv. 19: III, pp. 130–3.

he had some interest in its protection. But he would have nothing to do with it. Instead he clapped both of the emissaries in prison in the hope of raising a ransom on them.[33] They had almost certainly been seeking protection against the Turks, who by 1379 were well established on European territory. Their monumental victory over the Serbians at the Marica river in 1371 had opened the gates for them to advance into Macedonia. The Ottoman general Lala Shahin, who had been an agent of that victory, was rewarded with the title of Beglerbeg or commander-in-chief of the Ottoman forces in Europe.[34] It may well be that Thomas was prepared to let Servia, and even Kastoria, fall to the Turks if they would help him fend off the Albanians. For the Chronicle of Ioannina reports that he compounded all his other crimes by calling on the help of the godless Turks to do battle against the Albanians; and that on 2 June 1380 a Turkish commander called Isaim captured Belas and Opa and blockaded the Malakassaioi and the Zenevesaioi in a place called Politzai.[35]

It has been suggested that Isaim was the Beglerbeg Lala Shahin himself. Alternatively he was Shahin Pasha, allegedly an Albanian renegade.[36] The army that he commanded, having invaded Albania, probably then descended on the country to the north-west of Ioannina, where Thomas enlisted Shahin as an ally. Belas (Vellas), which he is said to have occupied, is only some thirty kilometres north of Ioannina in the valley of the Kalamas river. Opa may be identified with Lachanokastron, to the south-west of Konitsa. But Politzai, where Shahin blockaded the Albanians, is a good distance further north, on the western slope of Mount Nemerčka.[37] At all events it is clear that Shahin's operations relieved the Albanian pressure on Ioannina. Thomas used the respite to add a number of places to his dominions, among them Boursina, Kretzounista, Dragomi, Beltsista and Arachobitsa. All of these lay in the

[33] *Chron. Ioann.*, c. 22, p. 90. The demotic version here says that he raised 3,000 florins. The names of the emissaries were Theophylact and Chontetzes.

[34] Lala Shahin is said to have been the first Ottoman holder of the title of Beglerbeg, conferred on him by Murad I after the capture of Adrianople. V. L. Ménage, 'Beglerbegi', *Encyclopedia of Islam*, 2nd ed., I (London–Leiden, 1960), pp. 159–60.

[35] *Chron. Ioann.*, c. 23, pp. 90–1.

[36] Hopf, *GG*, II, p. 39, has it that 'Isaim (Sayn, Schahin)' was an Albanian renegade from Liaskovic and that he was buried in Berroia. So also Aravantinos, I, p. 145 and n. 1; K. Papageorgiou, Οἱ δύο τουρκικὲς κατακτήσεις τοῦ Γιαννιωτικοῦ κάστρου, *Ep. Hest.*, IV (1955), 419. G. T. Dennis, *The Reign of Manuel II Palaeologus in Thessalonica, 1382–1387* (Rome, 1960), p. 106, identifies him with Lala Shahin. So also Vranousis, *Chron. Ioann.*, p. 113; G. C. Chionides, Ἱστορία τῆς Βεροίας, II (Thessaloniki, 1970), pp. 55–6; *PLP*, IV, no. 8279. Cf. F. Babinger, *Beiträge zur Frühgeschichte der Türkenherrschaft in Rumelien: 14–15. Jahrhundert* (Südosteuropäische Arbeiten, 34: Munich, 1944), p. 78.

[37] For the topography, see Soustal–Koder, pp. 123–4 (Bela), 191 (Lachanokastron), 240 (Politzai).

area to the west of Ioannina and all had presumably been occupied by Albanians before the Turks arrived.[38] Arachobitsa had earlier held out against Thomas under John Kapsokavades, who had declared his independence from Ioannina in 1367. At that time the castle of Hagios Donatos (Photiki) had also refused to recognise Thomas as Despot. It had then been held by one Bardas, but it had changed hands in the course of the years. For in 1380 Thomas is said to have bought it from its lord 'Myrsi Robertos', or Robert. He was surely a westerner, but no other clues are offered to his identity or about how he came to succeed Bardas as lord of Hagios Donatos.[39]

In 1382 the Turks came back and gave Thomas further support. Helped by one Kostes with a band of forty Turks, he overcame the Zoulanaioi, an Albanian clan in the region of Konitsa.[40] On 5 May of the same year Shahin Pasha returned and captured the fortress of Revnikon, not far to the south-west of Konitsa.[41] Thomas was then able to enforce the submission of the Zenevesaioi and to take over the districts of Belas, Dryinoupolis and Vagenetia as well as part of the lands of the Malakassaioi up as far as Katounai; though before the year was out Shahin relieved him of Dryinoupolis by capturing it himself.[42] Meanwhile Gjin Boua Spata, the Despot of Arta, came north to see what was afoot. Perhaps he was afraid that Thomas's Turkish friends might be turned loose on his own Despotate. He advanced as far as a place called Aroula, somewhere to the south of Ioannina, and from there he sent forward his Italian son-in-law, Marchesano, as his ambassador. Thomas received his foreign guest with great honour and filled him full of tales of the proposal, originally made in 1375, that a marriage alliance was to be arranged. Gjin Spata was to be offered the hand in marriage of Thomas's sister Helena, thus securing a lasting peace between the Despotates of Arta and Ioannina. Marchesano reported back to his father-in-law. The alliance was never sealed, for Helena died soon afterwards. Gjin Spata then arrived in person to claim the dowry that had been promised with her hand; but Thomas was equal to the occasion and bribed him to go away.[43]

[38] Ibid., pp. 110 (Arachobitsa), 124 (Beltsista), 131–2 (Boursina), 141 (Dragomi), 188 (Kretzounista).

[39] *Chron. Ioann.*, c. 23, pp. 90–1. The demotic version adds many colourful and fanciful details to the narrative at this point. Cf. Aravantinos, I, p. 146.

[40] Hopf, *GG*, II, p. 39, says that Kostes was a renegade Albanian.

[41] *Chron. Ioann.*, cc. 24, 25, pp. 92–3. Soustal–Koder, p. 250 (Revnikon).

[42] Soustal–Koder, p. 175 (Katounai, south-east of Argyrokastron).

[43] *Chron. Ioann.*, c. 25, pp. 92–3; Chalk. IV: 1, p. 198. Aroula is difficult to locate (Soustal–Koder, p. 116). The chronicler's description of Marchesano as 'Myrsi Makatzanos' has led to various speculations. But see above, p. 148 and n. 27. He was the second husband of Eirene Spata. Her third was to be Esau Buondelmonti. *PLP*, III, no. 5969.

Thomas must have been grateful to the Turks for helping him to clear so much of his Despotate from Albanian occupation. But he must also have realised that their help was far from altruistic, as Shahin's seizure of Dryinoupolis had shown. For many years there had been little hope of support or recognition from the Byzantines. But in 1382 Manuel II Palaiologos, son of John V, had left Constantinople and set himself up as emperor in his own right in Thèssalonica. Within a few months he had scored an unexpected and dramatic victory over the Turks. Manuel planned to make Thessalonica, the second city of the Byzantine Empire, a rallying point for all who, like himself, preferred resistance to appeasement of the Turks. He hoped that the rulers of Thessaly and of Epiros would cooperate with him.[44] In Thessaly the days of Serbian rule were already over. Symeon Uroš had died about 1371. His wife Thomais had died before him. Their son John Uroš reigned at Trikkala for not much more than a year; and though he styled himself John Uroš Doukas Angelos Komnenos Palaiologos, emperor of the Greeks and Serbians, his heart was set on the true glory of the angelic life. He abdicated and took the monastic habit. As the monk Joasaph, John Uroš became the second founder of the monastery of the Great Meteoron, not far from his capital at Trikkala.[45] His place in Thessaly was taken not by a Serbian but by a Greek, Alexios Angelos Philanthropenos, who had married a niece of Thomas Preljubović. Alexios held the Byzantine title of Caesar, the title which Thomas's father Gregory had held. But whereas Gregory had received it from Serbia, there can be no doubt that Alexios was made Caesar by a Byzantine emperor. For in 1382 he recognised Manuel II in Thessalonica as his overlord.[46]

The Chronicle of Ioannina has little to say about affairs in Thessaly. But there was probably some coming and going between Trikkala and Ioannina. The emperor-monk John-Joasaph Uroš was the brother-in-law of Thomas Preljubović; and Thomas and his wife presented an icon to his monastery of the Great Meteoron. In 1382 Thomas followed the example set by the Caesar Alexios and sent an embassy to the emperor Manuel in Thessalonica. It was led by Gabriel, abbot of the monastery of the Dormition or the Archimandreion in Ioannina.[47] He came back

[44] See, especially, G. T. Dennis, *The Reign of Manuel II Palaeologus in Thessalonica*, pp. 60–76.

[45] On John-Joasaph Uroš, See especially M. Laskaris, 'Byzantino-serbica saeculi XIV. Deux chartes de Jean Uroš, dernier Némanide (Novembre 1372, indiction XI)' *B*, XXV–XXVII (1955–7), 277–323; Dennis, *Manuel II*, pp. 103–4; Nicol, *Meteora*, pp. 64–5, 102–12; Ferjančić, *Tesalija*, pp. 259–64.

[46] On Alexios Angelos Philanthropenos, who married a daughter of Radoslav Chlapen, see R. -J. Loenertz, 'Notes sur le règne de Manuel II à Thessalonique – 1381/82–1387', *BZ*, L (1957), 390–4; Dennis, *Manuel II*, pp. 104–6; Nicol, *Meteora*, pp. 65–6; Ferjančić, *Tesalija*, pp. 265–72.

[47] Aravantinos, II, p. 244, identifies the Archimandreion with the monastery of the

accompanied by an archon called Mankaphas who brought the regalia of a Byzantine Despot, with which Thomas was then invested. The investiture was solemnised by a liturgy conducted by the new metropolitan of Ioannina, Matthew, whom Thomas now grudgingly recognised as the successor to Sebastian. Matthew had been appointed by the patriarch in March 1381 and installed in Ioannina on 8 September 1382. He quickly fell foul of Thomas who drove him to live in exile at Arta.[48] But the investiture ceremony at which Matthew assisted confirmed that the Despotate of Ioannina had no more formal links with Serbia. In ecclesiastical as well as political matters Thomas Preljubović had acknowledged himself to be a creature of the Byzantine establishment and bound to the cause of a Greek emperor at Thessalonica.[49]

The fact that he was now properly ordained as Despot seems not to have made Thomas any more popular in Ioannina. Nor did it please the Turks, who were enraged by Manuel's courageous stand at Thessalonica. In 1384 Timurtash, successor of Lala Shahin as Beglerbeg, attacked Arta with a large army and took many prisoners. Gjin Spata was so alarmed that he sent the exiled bishop Matthew to Ioannina to propose that the two Despotates should join forces against their common enemy. It was a sensible proposal. But Thomas would have none of it. His only reply was to arrest Matthew's companion, whose name was Kalognomos, and to have the unfortunate bishop removed to another place of exile. The church of Ioannina, whose revenues Matthew had at first been permitted to enjoy, was made over to one Senacherim. That was Thomas's last recorded act of wickedness. On 23 December of the same year 1384, at the fifth hour of the night, he was murdered by his bodyguard. The Chronicle of Ioannina lists the names of his assassins as in a roll of

Dormition and says that it was destroyed in 1852. See also P. G. Oikonomos, Ἡ ἐν Ἰωαννίνοις Ἐκκλησία (Athens, 1966), pp. 75–6.

[48] Matthew combined in his title if not in practice the See of Naupaktos with that of Ioannina. He had formerly been metropolitan of Kernitza in the Morea, which ceased to be a metropolis when he was transferred to Ioannina in March 1381. *MM*, II, pp. 23–5; Darrouzès, *Regestes*, VI, no. 2714, pp. 34–5. Cf. Dennis *Manuel II*, pp. 103–8.

[49] The *Ekthesis Nea*, a manual of protocol of the Byzantine chancellery of 1385 and later, indicates the correct mode of address for the patriarch when writing to a Despot who is not the son of an emperor. A distinction is made between a Despot who is a Romaios and one who is a *barbaros*. In the latter category come 'the Despots of Vlachia and of Albanon', (οἱ τῆς Βλαχίας δεσπόται καὶ οἱ τοῦ Ἀλβάνου). J. Darrouzès, 'Ekthésis Néa. Manuel des pittakia du XIVe siècle', *REB*, XXVII (1969), 5–127, especially 56 ll. 30–4. There were in fact no 'Despots of Vlachia (= Thessaly)' after 1385. The last was Nikephoros who was killed in 1359. Alexios Angelos Philanthropenos held the title of Caesar, as did his son or brother Manuel, who is known to have been in Thessaly in 1392–3. The author of the *Ekthesis* probably meant Epiros rather than Vlachia; and his reference would therefore be to Thomas Preljubović or to his successor Esau Buondelmonti. The 'Despots of Albanon' must be the Albanian Despots Peter Losha of Arta and Gjin Spata of Acheloos. Cf. I. Djurić, 'Svetovni dostojanstvenici u "Ektesis Nea" (The laic nobles in the "Ekthesis Nea")', *ZRVI*, XVIII (1978), 189–211, especially 194–6.

honour. One of them was a Frank called Antonios. As the news of the tyrannicide went round, the citizens of Ioannina gathered in the cathedral and with one voice acclaimed as their natural sovereign, the *basilissa* Maria Angelina, the disprised wife of Thomas, who had shared their sufferings during his reign. In the middle of the night she was brought before them and received their obeisance. She summoned two loyal counsellors, Theodore Apsaras and Meliglavos, and invited her brother, Joasaph Uroš, to come from Thessaly; and the people joined in providing for their late and unlamented Despot what, in the end, was an honourable burial.[50]

His marble tomb was discovered in 1795, when Ali Pasha was laying the foundations of his seraglio in the south-eastern acropolis of Ioannina, by the Fethiye mosque. The tomb may originally have stood in the cathedral church of the Archangel Michael where previous Despots had perhaps been laid to rest, but of which there is now no trace. It carried a Greek inscription in which at least the words 'Thomas Prealipos Despotes' were legible. The tomb, like the cathedral, is now lost.[51] But Thomas's name is recorded in two other inscriptions in his city of Ioannina. One is in brick, high up on the tower to the right of the entrance into the fortress. It now consists of no more than the single word Thomas. The other is inscribed on three fragments of stone found on the acropolis at Ioannina and now in the Demotic Museum. It has been plausibly reconstructed to read: 'Thomas known also as the Albanian-killer' ([Θω]μᾶς ὁ καὶ Ἀλβανητ[οκτόνος ἐπικλ]ηθείς).[52]

No doubt Thomas would be happy to be remembered as the Slayer of Albanians, as the Chronicle of Ioannina suggests. Yet, for all his faults, or perhaps because of them, Thomas advertised his Christian piety by making generous gifts to monasteries and churches. The reliquary icon of Christ and the Virgin and Child, which he gave to the monastery of the Great Meteoron, still exists.[53] The monastery of Vatopedi on Mount

[50] *Chron. Ioann.*, cc. 27, 28, pp. 93–4. The demotic version (p. 94) says that the assassins came one from Kastoria, the other from Pelagonia or Bitoli. It dates the murder to May 1382 and records that Maria Angelina fled to Vodena two months later, with her two sons. All of this is pure fiction. See Vranousis, *Chron. Ioann.*, p. 115.

[51] Vranousis, *Kastron*, pp. 49–63 (481–95).

[52] Ibid., pp. 64–74 (496–506).

[53] The reliquary diptych icon which Thomas and Maria gave to the Great Meteoron is now in the cathedral of Cuenca in Spain. What may have been the artist's prototype for its left leaf is still in the Great Meteoron monastery. See *Chron. Ioann.*, ed. Estopañan, I, pp. 1–32; Nicol, *Meteora*, p. 176; A. Xyngopoulos, Νέαι προσωπογραφίαι τῆς Μαρίας Παλαιολογίνας καὶ τοῦ Θωμᾶ Πρελιούμποβιτς, Δελτίον Χριστιανικῆς Ἀρχαιολογικῆς Ἑταιρείας, ser. 4, IV (1964–5), 53–70; P. Mijović, 'O ikonama s portretima Tome Preljubovića i Marije Paleologove (Les icones avec les portraits de Toma Preljubović et de Marie Paléologine)', *Zbornik za likovne umetnosti*, II (Novi Sad, 1966), 183–95.

Athos possesses a chalice bearing the name of 'Thomas Despot Komnenos Preloubos';[54] and the only surviving original document of his reign is a deed of gift which he and his wife Maria drew up in May 1375 in favour of the monastery of the Great Lavra on Athos.[55] This unique charter recalls how Thomas and Maria had built a church dedicated to the Virgin Gaballiotissa at Vodena at the time when they were lords of that district. Later, after they had acquired their 'hereditary Despotate' of Ioannina, they thought to protect their foundation for fear of their own premature death. They therefore made it over to the abbot and monks of the Lavra, together with all its landed and moveable property. It is interesting to note that the land on which their church at Vodena was built had come to them by inheritance from their great-grandfather, the late *protobestiarios* Andronikos Palaiologos, a man who had many investments in western Macedonia and Epiros.[56] The document itemises the buildings, gardens, vineyards, fields, mills and villages which constitute the property; while a second document lists the icons, relics, books, vestments and other objects in the church of the Gaballiotissa.[57] In addition to the property in Vodena, Thomas made over to the Lavra a village called Sousitza in the district of Servia in northern Thessaly where his father Gregory Preljub had been Caesar. He had acquired it as a patrimony confirmed by chrysobulls of the Serbian Emperors Stephen Dušan and Stephen Uroš V, which were handed over to the monks of the Lavra as their title deeds. The deed of gift was drawn up at Ioannina by the notary of the metropolis, Nicholas, in May 1375.[58]

The date may be significant in view of the apprehension expressed about the possible premature death of the donors. It was in 1375 that Ioannina suffered its second outbreak of the plague. The daughter of Thomas and Maria died of it, and they may well have thought that some act of piety was in order. It may also be significant that in all but one of the known works of piety or charity that Thomas performed his wife Maria

[54] Alexandros Vatopedinos, Ἐπιγραφαὶ ἱερᾶς Μονῆς Βατοπεδίου, Μεσαιωνικὰ Γράμματα, II (1934–5), 219.

[55] *Actes de Lavra*, III: *de 1329 à 1350* (Archives de l'Athos, x), ed. P. Lemerle, A. Guillou, N. Svoronos, Denise Papachryssanthou (Paris, 1979), no. 146, pp. 100–4. See L. Mavromatis, 'A propos des liens de dépendance en Epire à la fin du XIVe siècle, *ZRVI*, XIX (1980), 275–81.

[56] On Andronikos Palaiologos, see above, Chapter 4, pp. 93–4. His daughter Anna Palaiologina was the wife of John II Orsini and mother of Thomais. He was therefore the great-grandfather of Maria Angelina, Thomas's wife.

[57] *Actes de Lavra*, III, no. 147, pp. 105–7.

[58] The village of Sousitza is described as being ἐν τῇ τοποθεσία τῆς Σερβίας (p. 104, ll. 43–4), which the editors of the document take to mean the 'district of Servia in Thessaly'. Mavromatis, *ZRVI*, XIX (1980), 277–80, however, argues that the village was that of Sušica in Serbia.

was associated with him by name. To the Chronicler of Ioannina Maria was 'the most pious *basilissa*'. Perhaps it was she who influenced her evil husband to take out a number of insurance policies in anticipation of the day of reckoning for his sins. There were others who said that she herself was not untainted by sin. But she had a hard life with Thomas Preljubović; and for all his faults she gave him an honourable funeral and a marble tomb.

8

The Italian Restoration: Esau Buondelmonti and Carlo Tocco – 1384–1411

The news that Thomas was dead brought the Albanians hurrying north. Gjin Spata laid siege to Ioannina once more. It was an anxious moment. Maria was in despair and sent some of her jewellery and valuables over the hills to the safe keeping of the monks of the Great Meteoron.[1] But her brother, the emperor-monk Joasaph Uroš, had already been summoned from his monastery to take charge in Ioannina and to form a council of state. They resolved that Maria must marry again without delay, since she could not cope with the emergency on her own. Her new husband was to be Esau Buondelmonti who was then living in Cephalonia. Esau was the brother of Maddalena Buondelmonti, widow of Leonardo Tocco, who had become count of Cephalonia in 1357 and had added Leukas and Vonitsa to his domains before his death in 1375. In 1384, when the Despot Thomas died, Maddalena was acting as regent for her infant son Carlo Tocco.[2]

The Buondelmonti family came from Florence and were connected with the wealthy banking family of the Acciajuoli. Esau was young and adventurous and he seems to have been glad to be invited to seek his fortune on the mainland of Greece and to do so by marrying the *basilissa* Maria Angelina. There is a strong suspicion that they were already more than mere acquaintances. The Chronicle of Ioannina breathes no word of scandal about its pious heroine, except to record the vile insinuations of the traitor Apsaras. But another account has it that Esau had helped her to accomplish the murder of her Serbian husband. It is alleged that Esau had been taken prisoner by Thomas during the siege of Arta by 'the Italians', presumably the assault launched from Vonitsa by Fernandez de Heredia in 1377. No other source confirms that Thomas was fighting on the side of the Albanians of Arta on that occasion, and indeed it would be a unique instance of cooperation if it were so. Esau is said, however, to have

[1] N. A. Bees, Σερβικὰ καὶ Βυζαντιακὰ γράμματα Μετεώρου, Βυζαντίς, II (1911), no. 5, pp. 20–3; Solovjev–Mošin, no. XXXIX, pp. 290–7.

[2] *Chron. Ioann.*, c. 29, p. 94. The literature on Esau Buondelmonti is collected in *PLP*, IV, no. 8147.

been taken off to captivity in Ioannina and there held to ransom; and it was in the palace at Ioannina that Maria Angelina first saw him, fell madly in love with him and became his mistress, for 'she had gone with other men before and was of licentious nature'. Between them she and Esau plotted the murder of Thomas in his bedroom.[3]

There may or may not be some truth in this scandalous tale. It squares ill with the version of Thomas's murder and of Maria's virtue in the Chronicle of Ioannina. But at the time, in December 1384, the proposal that Esau should marry Maria found favour with all parties. On 31 January 1385 he entered Ioannina to the unanimous applause of the citizens who acclaimed him as their new Despot. His engagement to Maria was announced and arrangements were made for the wedding. Maria had no female relatives of her own to act as her sponsor (*paranymphos*). She therefore sent for the wife of Alexios Angelos, the Caesar of Thessaly, who was a relative by marriage; and the *kaisarissa* was escorted to Ioannina by Maria's younger brother, Stephen. The wedding ceremony was then performed, to the great delight of the citizens who celebrated the occasion with joyful festivities.[4]

Maria's brother Joasaph seems to have stayed in Ionnina for a time as an adviser, and the chronicler writes in glowing terms of the beneficent administration and the reforms of the triumvirate of Esau, Maria and Joasaph. Those who had collaborated with the tyrant Thomas were given their just deserts. The notorious *protobestiarios* Michael Apsaras was imprisoned with his family before being blinded and sent into exile. Those who had been banished were welcomed back and all political prisoners were set free. Esau recalled the exiled Metropolitan Matthew and restored to him all the property of his church. The prisons were emptied, the torture chambers destroyed. Taxes were lowered and penalties mitigated. The *mitaton*, the enforced levy for the maintenance of the army, was abolished. All hereditary properties were restored to their rightful owners. It was like the calm after the storm of the tyranny of Thomas Preljubović; and so it seemed not only to the people of Ioannina but also to the Albanians beyond the walls. Gjin Spata, who had abandoned his siege of the city when Esau arrived, returned to the attack between February and August 1385. But Esau persuaded him to withdraw and to make a treaty of peace.[5]

Esau Buondelmonti was even more of a foreigner in Epiros than his

[3] Chalk. I, pp. 198–9 (ed. Darkó). Esau participated with his brother Francesco in Heredia's campaign. See Luttrell, 'Interessi fiorentini', 323–4.

[4] *Chron. Ioann.*, cc. 29–30, pp. 94–5. The anonymous '*kaisarissa* of Vlachia' in the Chronicle was identified by M. Lascaris, 'Byzantinoserbica', *B*, XXV–XXVII (1955–7), 313; Nicol, *Meteora*, p. 107.

[5] *Chron. Ioann.*, cc. 29, 31–2, pp. 94–6.

predecessor had been. A Florentine himself, with no admixture of non-Italian blood, he was now lord of a little realm with a population of Greeks, Serbians and Albanians. He had surely adopted the Orthodox faith. But he knew that his political authority required the seal of approval which could be obtained only from a Byzantine emperor. The Chronicler of Ioannina, in his euphoria over the death of Thomas, designates Esau as Despot from the moment of his marriage to Maria in January 1385. But not until he was established in Ioannina did Esau apply to the proper quarter to have the title conferred upon him. By then it was too late to seek such favours from an emperor in Thessalonica, as Thomas had done. Thessalonica was under siege by the Turks and the beleaguered Emperor Manuel II was having small success in rallying the fighting spirit of its apathetic citizens. Esau therefore applied to Constantinople, and towards the end of 1385 a Byzantine official of the Emperor John V arrived in Ioannina with the regalia of a Despot. Esau's coronation and investiture were performed by the bishops of Belas and Dryinoupolis, assisted by the restored Metropolitan Matthew.[6] By May 1386 Maria Angelina, now once again the *basilissa* of a properly ordained Despot, felt confident enough to retrieve from the monks of the Meteoron the valuables which she had deposited with them five months before; though she allowed them to keep some of the church plate and also a cross which had belonged to her uncle Nikephoros.[7]

Matthew, metropolitan of Ioannina, died before the end of 1385. On 1 January 1386 the Despot Esau, whom he had helped to install, nominated as his successor the monk Gabriel, abbot of the Archimandreion. The Serbians in the city had hoped that the see would be left vacant so that they could again lay their greedy hands on its property. But Esau was a pious Christian who knew his duty to the church. Gabriel served as bishop-elect of Ioannina for two years before travelling to Constantinople for his consecration by the patriarch. In the troubled circumstances of the time such delays were common enough. Even the nomination of bishops by local rulers or authorities had become accepted practice. Gabriel, however, had the misfortune to reach Constantinople at a moment when there was no patriarch to give him his blessing. He had to wait there until the appointment of Patriarch Antonios IV in January 1389; and it was eleven months before he got back to his see in Ioannina, on 21 March 1389.[8]

[6] *Chron. Ioann.*, c. 32, p. 96. The Byzantine official was called Palaiologos Vryonis. Cf. Ferjančić, *Despoti*, p. 81. Esau's investiture must have occurred before 1 January 1386, the date of the nomination of Matthew's successor as metropolitan of Ioannina. The 'year' specified by the Chronicle ran from September 1385 to August 1386.

[7] See above, note 1.

[8] *Chron. Ioann.*, cc. 33, 34, pp. 96–7. Gabriel left Ioannina for Constantinople on 23 April 1388. Darrouzès, *Regestes*, VI, no. 2850, p. 146.

Esau may have been the pious Christian depicted by the Chronicle of Ioannina. But he soon realised that his Despotate could be saved only by coming to some arrangement with the Turks. The peace that he had made with the Albanian Despotate of Arta would not last for long. There were other Albanian clans to the north and west of Ioannina waiting for their moment to strike. As Thomas Preljubović had discovered, the Turks were the only people who could frighten them into submission. With the hindsight of history it is easy to say that the latterday Despots of Epiros, like the Despots of the Morea, should have known that to invite the temporary help of the Turks was to encourage the permanent subjugation of their own countries to the Ottoman Empire. The Christian Despots of Greece, as the Chronicle of Ioannina so vividly demonstrates, lived from year to year and crisis to crisis, often with naive hopes for the morrow but with little thought for the longer term.

In 1385 the Turks advanced as far as the Albanian coast. Balša Balšić, who in 1371 had become Serbian lord of Valona, died in battle against them in September of that year. Under their new Beglerbeg, Hayr ad-Din Pasha, other Turkish forces penetrated into Macedonia and northern Thessaly. In 1386 they occupied Kitros and Larissa.[9] Esau prudently decided to forestall their advance into Epiros. The Chronicle of Ioannina baldly reports that the Despot went to see the emir, adding that there was a great thunderstorm in Ioannina in which fourteen souls were struck down by lightning.[10] The chronicler resists the temptation to connect these two events. Nor does he mention the major event which shocked the world beyond the confines of Ioannina and Epiros. In April 1387 the Emperor Manuel II finally despaired of turning the citizens of Thessalonica into heroes and sailed away, leaving them to their fate. As soon as he was gone they opened their gates to Hayr ad-Din and his troops; and the second city of the Byzantine Empire was in Turkish hands. The surrender had been voluntary and the city was for that reason spared the horrors of pillage and massacre.[11] But to the Christian inhabitants of Thessaly and Epiros the fall of Thessalonica must have seemed ominous; and it was quickly followed by the fall of the city of Berroia, in May 1387.[12] The emir whom Esau went to see was Murad, the first of the Ottoman rulers to adopt the title of sultan. It was Murad who broke the last concerted resistance of the Serbians at the battle of Kossovo in June

[9] F. Taeschner and P. Wittek, 'Die Vezirfamilie der Ǧandarlyzade', *Der Islam*, XVIII (1929), 74–5; Sp. Lambros, Ἐνθυμήσεων ἤτοι συλλογὴ σημειωμάτων, I, *NH*, VII (1910), 145, nos. 77, 78. Dennis, *Manuel II*, p. 128; Jireček-Radonić, *Istorija Srba*, I, p. 319.

[10] *Chron. Ioann.*, c. 33, pp. 96–7.

[11] Dennis, *Manuel II*, pp. 151–6; Nicol, *Last Centuries of Byzantium*, pp. 297–9.

[12] Schreiner, *Chron. Brev.*, I, nos. 58/4, 63/3, 64/3, 72/4; II, p. 334. Lambros, *NH*, VII (1910), 146, no. 79 (dating the capture of Berroia to 1386).

1389. Fighting on his side were various Christian princes who had been forced to become his vassals. It seems likely that Esau Buondelmonti had been obliged to do the same as a result of his interview with the sultan; though he was clearly not present at Kossovo. Murad was killed in that battle, but his place as sultan and commander-in-chief of the Ottoman army was at once assumed by his son Bajezid.[13]

The capture of Thessalonica and then the Turkish victory at Kossovo isolated Epiros from the rest of the eastern Christian world. As an Italian, Esau may have hoped for some support from the Christians of the west, especially from the Venetians, since he was a citizen of their Republic. But the Venetians were more obstructive than helpful and Esau soon fell foul of them. In 1386, after long negotiations, they had at last acquired possession of Corfu, and with it the mainland castle of Butrinto. It came to the notice of the Venetian Senate that the Despot of Ioannina had rebuilt and refortified a ruined tower at Saiata some miles to the south of Butrinto and that he had constructed some saltpans there which were doing a brisk trade. The Senate considered this to be intolerable and unfair competition with their own salt industry in Corfu; and in June 1387 they ordered the rector of the island to send men over to destroy the Despot's little business enterprise and to dismantle his tower. They argued, rightly or wrongly, that Saiata had formerly been Venetian, that it came under the jurisdiction of Corfu, and that it had been fraudulently taken from them. In 1394, however, for all the blusterings of Venice, Esau or his agents were still in business at Saiata; and in 1399 the Senate suggested that he might be willing to sell the place and its tower as a going concern. If not it must regrettably be destroyed.[14] It was an affair of no great consequence. But it gave Esau little encouragement to hope for support from his countrymen in the west. The Venetians were not much interested in the Despotate of Ioannina. If it were to be preserved from the Albanians then it must be done with Turkish help.

On 7 July 1389 Gjin Spata, the Albanian Despot of Arta, again attacked and laid siege to Ioannina. He must have known that Esau had come to some arrangement with the Sultan Murad. The sultan had been killed at Kossovo in June and Ioannina was thus deprived of its Turkish protector. Some of the Albanians further north sensed the same opportunity. The Malakassaioi joined Spata in destroying the vineyards of Ioannina and captured Beltsista, a place about twelve miles north-west of the city. The bishop of Belas was so alarmed that he came to terms with Spata and allowed the Albanians to occupy a small fortress in his diocese which the

[13] Nicol, *Last Centuries of Byzantium*, pp. 299–302.

[14] *ActAlbVen.*, I, 2, no. 334, p. 50 (8 June 1387), no. 543, pp. 243–4 (15 May 1394); I, 3, no. 764, pp. 125–6 (1 September 1399). Thiriet, *Régestes*, I, nos. 729, 850, 968.

Despot Esau had given him.[15] When driven back on the landward side of the city, Spata then attacked Ioannina from the lake, sinking one of Esau's boats. But he had misjudged the Despot's new relations with the Turks. On the orders of the Sultan Bajezid, a Turkish officer called Melkutz arrived from Thessalonica and chased Spata's army away.[16]

The price of his intervention had now to be paid. Esau was summoned to the sultan's presence. The Caesar Alexios Angelos of Thessaly, who had come to Ioannina with Melkutz, had received the same summons. In October 1389 Esau and Alexios, the Despot of Ioannina and the Caesar of Thessaly, were conducted together to Bajezid's camp, perhaps at Adrianople. One year and two months passed before they were allowed to return. The Chronicle of Ioannina gives the impression that they spent the time residing with the sultan as his guests. They must, however, have answered his call to go and do their duty to him as his Christian vassals. It seems likely that Melkutz left a Turkish force to protect Ioannina when he escorted Esau to the sultan. For there is no record of Albanian attacks on the city during the fourteen months of the Despot's absence. When he came back it was with a Turkish army commanded by one of the most experienced Ottoman generals, the Ghazi Evrenos Beg. They marched by way of Acheloos and Arta, to receive the submission of Gjin Spata, and reached Ioannina on 4 December 1390. Thereafter, says the chronicler, Ioannina enjoyed four years of peace and prosperity under the beneficent care of the good Despot Esau, assisted by the bishop, to whom he was devoted, and by wise counsellors of noble birth whom he appointed.[17] What the chronicler omits to say is that the four years of peace were made possible only by the favour of the Turks. In the Byzantine Morea the same truth was to be revealed, that only the Turks could stop the Christian rulers from fighting each other.

The end of the years of peace in Ioannina was heralded by the sad event of the death of the pious *basilissa* Maria Angelina Doukaina Palaiologina, on 28 December 1394. The whole city mourned the passing of the widow of the tyrant Thomas and the wife of the benevolent Esau. He too

[15] *Chron. Ioann.*, c. 34, p. 97. On Beltsista (modern Klematia), one of the villages listed as belonging to the metropolis of Ioannina in 1321, and on the bishop's property at Bribia or Bribiani, see Soustal–Koder, pp. 124, 130.

[16] *Chron. Ioann.*, c. 35, pp. 97–8.

[17] Ibid. *PLP*, III, no. 5955 (Evrenos Beg). Local tradition in Ioannina has it that the arrival of Evrenos inaugurated the first Turkish occupation of Ioannina, which was to last for almost seven years, from 1390 to 1396. Evrenos is said to have transformed the church of Hagia Triada near the western end of the *kastron* into a *teke*. Evlija Celebi, who visited Epiros about 1670, reports that Evrenos was the first Turkish conqueror of Ioannina and that mosques were built in the time of Bajezid I in Arta, Ioannina, Paramythia, Konitsa and Argyrokastron. K. Papageorgiou, Οἱ δύο Τουρκικὲς κατακτήσεις τοῦ Γιαννιωτικοῦ κάστρου, *Ep. Hest.*, IV (1955), 419–26; N. G. Ziangos, Φεουδαρχικὴ Ἤπειρος (Athens, 1974), pp. 184–5.

lamented his loss and observed the proper period of mourning. But after twelve months had passed he was persuaded by his archons that he could solve one of the recurrent problems of his Despotate by marrying Eirene, the daughter of Gjin Spata. Eirene had already been married twice, first to an Albanian by whom she had two sons, and then to the Italian baron Marchesano of the Morea, who gave her another son. The chronicler describes her as being courageous, intelligent, beautiful and virtuous. At worst she must have learnt some western manners from her second husband. She married Esau on 4 January 1396.[18]

A marriage between the ruling families of Ioannina and Arta had been proposed before. This was the first time it had been realised. It had been a sensible proposal in times past, and there was still much to commend it. But now it was almost too late. Only a few days after the wedding, Evrenos Beg with another Turkish commander called Yahshi Beg, who had been fighting the Zenevesaioi around Dryinoupolis, were met by Gjin Spata in the district of Driskos, between Ioannina and Metsovon. The Turks, who were not more than three hundred in number, were at first driven back as far as Phaneromeni; but then they turned on their pursuers, inflicting many casualties near a place called Pratokai, to the north-west of Ioannina. Evrenos and his colleague escaped unharmed. It was true that the attack had been led not by the Despot Esau but by Gjin Spata. But the Turks cannot have been pleased that the two were now united by a marriage alliance.[19]

Spata, whose only daughter had now married a second Italian husband, had become almost respectable. But the Albanian clans of the Malakassaioi, the Mazarakaioi and especially the Zenevesaioi from around Argyrokastron, Dryinoupolis and the mountains of Great Zagori, had yet to be tamed. It was Gjin Zenevesi, chieftain of his clan, who led their raids. In April 1399 Esau assembled all his army for a campaign against them. He got as far as Mesopotamon, but near there, in bad weather, the Albanians came down from the hills. Esau and his officers were surrounded and taken prisoners by Gjin Zenevesi on 9 April 1399.[20] It may not have been so spectacular an event as the capture of the Grand Master of the Knights Hospitallers by Gjin Spata. But it served a similar purpose in bringing the southern Albanians to the attention of a wider world; and Zenevesi demanded the highest possible ransom for the

[18] *Chron. Ioann.*, cc. 36–8, pp. 98–100. *PLP*, III, no. 5969 (Eirene Spata).

[19] *Chron. Ioann.*, c. 38, pp. 99–100. On Yahshi Beg (called 'Iaxes' in the Chronicle), see *PLP*, IV, no. 7954. I take the Γκιόνη of the Chronicle here to be Gjin, chieftain of the Zenevesaioi, and not Gjin Spata. For the topography, see Soustal–Koder, pp. 146 (Driskos), 233 (Phaneromeni) 241 (Pratokai).

[20] *Chron. Ioann.*, c. 39, p. 100. Esau was captured somewhere between Dibre and Mesopotamon. Soustal–Koder, p. 142. On Gjin Zenevesi, see *PLP*, III, no. 6521.

release of his distinguished prisoner. The news of Esau's misfortune was soon known in Florence and the Acciajuoli bankers, to whom he was related, set about raising the ransom money and seeking the good offices of Venice. On 30 May 1399 the Venetian Senate considered the friendly request of Florence and agreed to try to act as intermediaries with the Albanian '*sebastokrator*', Gjin Zenevesi, to effect the liberation of one who was, after all, a Venetian citizen.[21] None the less four months passed before Esau was set free through the combined efforts of the Florentines and the Venetian governor of Corfu. Zenevesi was the richer by ten thousand florins, though he stubbornly refused to relinquish to Venice the saltpans at Saiata, which he had acquired as a consequence of his victory. Esau was released and sent from Argyrokastron to Corfu, where he spent a few days before going on to Leukas. From there he crossed to Arta, to a warm welcome from his father-in-law, Gjin Spata. He arrived home in Ioannina on 17 July 1399.[22]

Two months later, on 29 October 1399, Gjin Spata died. He had no son and heir. The government of Arta was at once taken over by his brother, Sgouros Boua Spata, who had been among the welcoming party for Esau. But only a few days afterwards an independent adventurer called Bokoi (Bongoes) descended on and seized the city, chased out Sgouros and brought in a reign of terror.[23] It is at this point that the Chronicle of Ioannina comes to its somewhat abrupt end, with a lament for the sad fate of the city of Arta and a prayer for better times to come. Where the Chronicle of Ioannina ends, however, the Chronicle of the Tocco family takes over.[24] Both refer to the usurpation of Arta by the mysterious Bokoi. The former describes him as a 'Serbian-Albanian-Bulgarian-Vlach' (Serbalbanitoboulgarovlachos) which may be the name that he adopted to win the allegiance of the various racial components of

[21] *ActAlbVen*, I, 3, no. 750, pp. 115–16 (30 May 1399). It is unclear how he came by the title of *sebastokrator* by which the Venetians addressed him ('albanensem Jahannem seuastokratora'). He is probably to be identified with the *sebastokrator*, lord of the '*staria*' (= mainland) opposite Corfu who , in 1414, became a vassal of Venice. *ActAlbVen*, II, 7, no. 1890, p. 136; Thiriet, *Régestes*, II, no. 1543. Cf. Hopf, *GG*, II, p. 102; and see below, p. 189, n. 35.

[22] *Chron. Ioann.*, c. 40, pp. 100–1. Esau is said to have passed through τὰ μέρη Γυροβολέας (= Gyra on Leukas). Soustal–Koder, p. 161. Venetian dealings with Gjin Zenevesi over the control of Saiata are documented in C. N. Sathas, Μνημεῖα Ἑλληνικῆς Ἱστορίας. *Monumenta Hellenicae Historiae. Documents relatifs à l'histoire de la Grèce au moyen âge*, II (Paris, 1881), no. 257, pp. 45–6 (20 September 1401) [cited hereafter as Sathas, *Monumenta*]; *ActAlbVen*, I, 2, no. 543, pp. 243–4; I, 3, nos. 764, 793, 815, 817, 887, 910, 1044, pp. 147, 174, 175–6, 244–5, 263–5, 400. Zenevesi is variously named in these documents as '*geonius*' or 'Geomi Zenevessi'.

[23] *Chron. Ioann.*, c. 41, p. 101.

[24] G. Schirò, *Cronaca dei Tocco di Cefalonia di Anonimo. Prolegomeni, testo critico e traduzione* (*CFHB*, X: Rome, 1975). [Hereafter the text of the Chronicle is cited as *Chron. Tocco*, and the editor's commentary as Schirò, *Cronaca*].

the society which he hoped to govern. He may have called on the Turks to help remove Sgouros Spata. He seems to have succeeded, but only briefly. He was in his turn removed by the grandson of the late Gjin, Muriki Spata, who made himself lord of Arta about December 1399. Sgouros retired to Angelokastron in the south. Bokoi disappears from history.[25] The Chronicle of Tocco declares that with the death of Gjin Boua Spata the Albanian clan or family of Spata went into decline. It is true that the family never again produced so commanding a figure as Gjin who, for twenty-five years (1374–99), had so successfully and aggressively ruled over Arta and Akarnania, constantly threatening the Despotate of Ioannina in the north and the Ionian islands in the west. His brother Sgouros was not his equal. But his daughter Eirene was a forceful character and something of his spirit lived on in the two sons of her first marriage, Muriki Spata and Yaqub Spata.[26]

The Chronicle of Ioannina tells the tale of a city over a period of fifty years, even though it concentrates on the brutal tyranny of the Serbian Thomas. The Chronicle of the Tocco family by contrast is a verse epic that tells the heroic deeds of two men, Carlo Tocco and his younger brother Leonardo. Like the Chronicle of Ioannina it was written by a patriotic citizen of that city, over which Carlo was, in due course, to rule as Despot. With its opening chapters, however, the scene changes. The city of Ioannina is not at first the centre of events. The world of the Tocco family, the cradle and the nursery of Carlo and Leonardo, was the island of Leukas and the adjacent mainland of Akarnania in the southern part of the original Despotate of Epiros. The author of the Chronicle, which appears to have been completed by June 1429, is anonymous. He was patently a Greek or a Romaios and proud to be so. But it is a mark of the multi-racial nature of the ruling class of Epirote society at the time that he is no less proud of the character and the exploits of his Italian hero; and he can even extend a measure of praise for some of the Albanian chieftains who figure in his narrative.[27]

Carlo and Leonardo were the sons of that Leonardo Tocco who in 1357

[25] *Chron. Ioann.*, c. 41; *Chron. Tocco*, I, cc. 14–15. Schirò, *Cronaca*, pp. 34–6; the identity of Bokoi is discussed at p. 35 n. 1. Cf. Schirò, 'La genealogia degli Spata', *RSBN*, XVIII–XIX (1971–2), 76–7, 83–5. It is unfortunate that there is a lacuna in the text of the *Chron. Tocco* at this very point. Hopf, *GG*, II, pp. 103, describes Bokoi as 'Bongo Zardari, son-in-law of Paul Materango of Gora'. Hopf, ibid., also invents a brother of Gjin Spata called 'Morikios Bua Sgouros (1400–1418)', who never existed. Cf. Schirò, *Cronaca*, p. 57; and see below, n. 64.

[26] Eirene's second husband was the Baron Marchesano, by whom she had a son called Carlo Marchesano. Her third husband was Esau Buondelmonti of Ioannina, by whom she had a daughter called Maddalena. *PLP*, IV, no. 8147.

[27] The date and authorship of the Chronicle are discussed by Schirò, *Cronaca*, pp. 123–42. Elisabeth A. Zachariadou, in a recent article in *Ep. Chron.*, XXV (1983), proposes a rearrangement of the first 1,000 verses of the text.

had been made Palatine count of Cephalonia, Ithaka and Zante by Robert of Taranto. By 1362 he had annexed Leukas and Vonitsa and liked to be known as duke of Leukas and count of Cephalonia. He married Maddalena Buondelmonti, sister of the Despot Esau of Ioannina.[28] At the time of his death, in 1375–6, Carlo and Leonardo (II) were both infants, probably no more than three or four years old. Their mother refused the many offers of remarriage which she received and determined to bring up her sons on her own. In 1376 she took them to Italy to have their heritage confirmed by royal authority in Naples.[29] Leonardo I Tocco, for all his grand titles, left little mark on history. He had been content to govern his island dominions and to protect them from the Albanians and from the principality of Achaia. His widow Maddalena aspired to do the same, though she was ambitious for her sons. In 1377 she made over their only mainland possession, the castle of Vonitsa, to the Knights Hospitallers. Their tenure appears to have been brief. The Chronicle of Tocco makes no mention of them and describes the defence of Vonitsa by a castellan appointed from Leukas or Cephalonia.[30] During the long regency of Maddalena, Vonitsa as well as Leukas came under repeated attack from the Albanians of Arta and Acheloos led by Gjin Spata. They caused much damage but made no permanent conquests. The chronicler records that it was their aggressive behaviour that bred in the young Carlo Tocco a lasting hostility to the Albanian clan of Spata and a deep desire for vengeance. It was not enough to fortify the castles of Santa Mavra on Leukas and Vonitsa on the mainland and wait for the Albanians to come. He must turn the tables on them by taking the war into their own territory.[31]

The Chronicle of Tocco leaves untold many details of the early life of

[28] Schirò, *Cronaca*, pp. 10–12. Maddalena was the daughter of Manente and Lappa dei Buondelmonti Acciajuoli. She also had three daughters, Petronella, Giovanna and Susanna; Petronella married first Niccolo dalle Carceri and second Niccolo di Antonio Venier. Ibid., p. 25 n. 2.

[29] *Chron. Tocco*, I, cc. 1–3. Schirò, *Cronaca*, pp. 25–9. The 'king' of Naples referred to in the Chronicle was in fact Queen Joanna of Naples, who was dispossessed by Charles III of Anjou and Durazzo in 1381. The Chronicle relates how Maddalena and her children were nearly lost at sea on their return voyage. Schirò, *Cronaca*, pp. 25–6, proposes 1374–5 as the date of Carlo's birth. He would thus have been only thirteen or fourteen at the time of his marriage in 1388. The Chronicle (I, c. 1, l. 4) says that he was a βρέφος μικρόν at the time of his father's death in 1375–6, i.e. an infant rather than a baby. It would be reasonable to suppose that he was married at the legal age of sixteen, in which case he must been born about 1372.

[30] *Chron. Tocco*, I, cc. 6–8. Schirò, *Cronaca*, p. 30 and n. 1. See above, p. 148, n. 27. The Hospitallers had left by 1381. In the same year Jacques des Baux, prince of Achaia, conferred the title of 'Count of Cephalonia and Zante' on John Laskaris Kalopheros. Luttrell, 'Interessi fiorentini', 324; A. K. Eszer, *Das abenteuerliche Leben des Johannes Laskaris Kalopheros* (Wiesbaden, 1969), pp. 79–80.

[31] *Chron. Tocco*, I, cc. 4–5.

Carlo Tocco, not least the event of his marriage to Francesca, second daughter of Nerio Acciajuoli of Florence. It was Nerio who put an end to the Catalan occupation of central Greece in 1388, adding Athens to the cities of Corinth and Megara which he had already appropriated. In 1394 he was formally invested with the title and dignity of duke of Athens by Ladislas of Naples, who still claimed suzerainty over Achaia. His daughter Francesca Acciajuoli is said to have become the bride of Carlo Tocco and so duchess of Leucadia in 1388.[32] She was a remarkable woman who gave her husband every support in his political and military ventures. She was proud to be known as the wife of a Despot, even long before her husband had acquired that title. As early as 1394 she signed a letter in the imperial cinnabar ink as *Vasilissa Romeorum*.[33] She was her father's favourite daughter and when he died, in September 1394, he left her most of his property, the castles of Megara, Sikyon (Basilicata) and Corinth, as well as a large sum of money. Her sister Bartolomaea, the wife of Theodore Palaiologos, despot of Mistra, got almost nothing from her father's estate. She incited her husband to contest the will, especially with regard to Corinth.[34] Theodore laid siege to it. The defence of Corinth was ably conducted by Francesca in person, until her husband arrived from Cephalonia. He invited the Turks, who were by now well established in Thessaly, to come and help him; and an Ottoman army arrived led by Evrenos Beg. The quarrel between the two brothers-in-law was soon over. Perhaps it was the intervention of the Turks that brought them to their senses. Carlo Tocco sold Corinth to Theodore for 6,000 ducats with an annual rent of 600 ducats. This was Carlo's first but not his last adventure on the mainland of the Morea.[35]

The Chronicle of his exploits is also silent on the subject of Carlo's

[32] Hopf, *GG*, II, p. 49; Hopf, *Chroniques*, pp. 476, 536; Setton, *Catalan Domination of Athens*, pp. 170–1, 194, 197; Bon, *Morée*, p. 269.

[33] Buchon, *Recherches historiques*, II, pp. 483–4; Buchon, *Nouvelles Recherches*, II, pp. 253–4 (letter to her brother Nerio of 28 September 1394). Three other documents signed by Francesca in Greek as βάσισσα or βασύλισσα Ῥωμαίων and in Latin as *Vasilissa Romanorum* are to be found in Buchon, *Recherches historiques*, II, pp. 488, 490, and *Nouvelles Recherches*, II, pp. 283–4, 285–6 (a letter to her brother Nerio of April 1424, and a deed of gift of a slave to Nerio dated December 1424). The third is in *MM*, III, pp. 253–4 (Greek text of a donation which she made to one Giuliano Zaota, an archon of Cephalonia, in May 1428). Cf. Schirò, *Cronaca*, p. 77 n. 1; *PLP*, III, no. 6505.

[34] The text of Nerio's will is in Buchon, *Nouvelles Recherches*, II, pp. 254–61; F. Gregorovius, Ἱστορία τῆς πόλεως Ἀθηνῶν, translated by Sp. Lambros (Athens, 1906), III, pp. 146–52. Cf. Setton, *Catalan Domination of Athens*, pp. 195–8; Bon, *Morée*, p. 270.

[35] Ch. Maltezou, Οἱ ἱστορικὲς περιπέτειες τῆς Κορίνθου στὰ τέλη τοῦ ΙΔ αἰῶνα, Σύμμεικτα, III (Athens, 1973), 17–23; J. Chrysostomides, 'Corinth 1394–1397: Some new facts', *Byzantina*, VII (1975), 81–110. Theodore sold Corinth to the Knights Hospitallers in 1396. Cf. Miller, *Latins in the Levant*, pp. 350–3; Longnon, *L'Empire latin*, pp. 345–6; R.-J. Loenertz, 'Pour l'histoire du Péloponnese au XIVe siècle', in Loenertz, *BFG*, I, pp. 227–65, especially pp. 253–4.

early dealings with Venice. Now that Corfu was theirs, the Venetians were anxious to make sure that the other Ionian islands remained friendly. They were pleased to remind Carlo Tocco that he was a citizen of Venice by terms of the charter granted to his father Leonardo in 1361. They were irked that the Genoese also claimed him as a citizen.[36] But when in 1390 he demanded, among other things, that their ships using the channel of Santa Mavra should pay him a toll, they thought that the time had come to cut him down to size. They informed him that Santa Mavra belonged by right to the Venetian family of Giorgio, and they refused to declare their neutrality in Carlo's conflict with the Albanians on the mainland. Carlo angrily retorted by resigning his Venetian citizenship, whereupon the Venetians imposed an embargo on trade with his islands. None of their ships was to go anywhere near him.[37] The Venetians never liked losing business. They explored all avenues of reconciliation. They even offered Carlo's mother Maddalena, who disapproved of his overtures to Genoa, a grace and favour residence in Venice. Maddalena, upstaged by her new daughter-in-law, preferred to live and to die in Zante.[38] In 1396, after five years of economic blockade, Carlo gave in, agreeing to pay for the damage he had done to Venetian property during his campaign in the Morea. He was re-enrolled as a citizen of Venice. The embargo was lifted.[39]

A year later his wife, the Duchess Francesca, played hostess at Cephalonia to a distinguished group of battered warriors on their way home to France. They were the survivors of the disastrous crusade of Nikopolis, who had been captured by the Turks in 1396 and ransomed after months of harsh imprisonment. Among them were the count of Nevers, the future duke of Burgundy, and several distinguished French knights. Froissart tells how they were made welcome when they put in at Cephalonia. Francesca and her court of fair ladies in the castle of St George were thrilled to have the pleasure of such civilised company. Their only visitors as a rule were Venetian and Genoese merchants whose manners were not so refined as those of the chivalry of France. Froissart was led to believe that Cephalonia was ruled by lovely ladies who, under the benevolent guidance of Francesca Tocco, spent their time making embroideries and silken coverlets so fine and beautiful that they were

[36] Thiriet, *Régestes*, I, nos. 764, 767. Cf. Hopf, *GG*, II, pp. 103–4.

[37] *ActAlbVen*, I, 2, no. 413, pp. 116–17; Thiriet, *Régestes*, I, nos. 782, 787, 822.

[38] Thiriet, *Régestes*, I, nos. 803, 829. The Florentine traveller Cristoforo Buondelmonti was related to Maddalena and says that she was buried in Zante. *Christoph. Bondelmontii, Florentini, Librum Insularum Archipelagi*, ed. L. de Sinner (Leipzig–Berlin, 1824), p. 60; *Description des Iles de l'Archipel par Christophe Buondelmonti. Version grecque par un anonyme*, ed. E. Legrand (Paris, 1897), I, pp. xii–xiii, 12.

[39] Thiriet, *Régestes*, I, nos. 883, 886, 905. He even offered to sell Corinth and Megara to Venice. Cf. Chrysostomides, *Byzantina*, VII (1975), 92–3.

beyond compare. It is a pleasant glimpse of tranquillity and gracious living in an enchanted island.[40] But Francesca was not always at her silks and samplers, as her behaviour in the defence of Corinth had shown; and her husband was not a man to be tempted into a life of idleness by such idyllic surroundings.

When he had settled his accounts in the Morea and with Venice, Carlo Tocco began to plan his offensive against the Albanians in Akarnania and Aitolia. He recruited a large army. The county of Cephalonia was rich and he had married money. He could afford to pay mercenaries higher rates than his competitors and he could entice them to serve him by the promise of properties and lands in *pronoia* on the island of Leukas. They came to him in large numbers, Franks, Greeks, Serbians, and especially Albanians, among them many belonging to the clan of Spata. He was soon able to turn a defensive operation into a war of aggression against the mainland Albanians who had done him so much damage.[41] It began about 1399. Carlo's army was commanded by an Italian officer, Galasso Peccatore, who established a bridgehead opposite Leukas by attacking Zaberda on the coast to the south of Vonitsa. Many Albanian prisoners were taken and brought back to be held as hostages in Santa Mavra. It was in the course of this action that Gjin Spata died, on 29 October 1399. Before the year was out his grandson Muriki Spata had set himself up as lord of Arta.[42]

It is hard to be sure whether Carlo Tocco saw himself from the start of his career as a future Despot of Arta and Ioannina. His feudal ties with the principality of Achaia were officially severed in 1396, when Ladislas of Naples declared Cephalonia and Leukas to be independent. The fact was confirmed on 1 April 1400; and Carlo, though still a vassal of the kingdom of Naples, must have felt that he was now more free to make his own fortune.[43] But his first and immediate concern was to protect Leukas by driving the Albanians back in Akarnania. The Albanians were far from being united in common cause. Sgouros Spata, having been dispossessed at Arta, had set up house at Angelokastron. His son Paul, his son-in-law Lalthi, and his nephew Peter Spata controlled various places in the neighbourhood.[44] But they were at daggers drawn with the clan of Boua,

[40] Froissart, ed. K. de Lettenhove, *Oeuvres de Froissart : Chroniques*, XVI (Brussels, 1871), p. 53; ed. J. A. Buchon, *Les Chroniques de Jean Froissart* (Collection des chroniques nationales françaises), XVI (Paris, 1826), pp. 57–8. Miller, *Latins in the Levant*, pp. 371–2; Longnon, *L'Empire latin*, p. 349.

[41] *Chron. Tocco*, I, cc. 9–12.

[42] Ibid., I, cc. 13–14. On Zaberda (modern Palairos), see Soustal–Koder, p. 278. The only surviving monument of Gjin Spata's reign seems to be an inscription on a column of the ruined church of the Pantanassa near Philippiada. See below, p. 240.

[43] Hopf, *GG*, II, p. 105; Miller, *Latins in the Levant*, pp. 370–1; Longnon, *L'Empire latin*, p. 349; Schirò, *Cronaca*, p. 29.

[44] Lalthi or Lalthis is also called Lanthi(s). Schiro, *Cronaca*, p. 38 and n. 2.

whose leaders were Muriki and his brother Dimo. Carlo had the wit to turn this rivalry to his own advantage. He bribed Muriki Boua to join him in war against the Spata family and gave one of his cousins in marriage to Dimo Boua.[45] The chronicler narrates, often in vivid detail, the campaigns of his hero in Akarnania, first his capture, or recapture, of Katochi in the far south and then his daring though fruitless attack on Angelokastron one Easter Sunday (1401–2).[46]

These were by way of preliminary skirmishes fought, as the chronicler says, on the threshold of the enemy's territory; and it seems that many of them had to be refought. The castle of Katochi changed hands several times. Carlo had to recapture it from Peter Spata who fled to his uncle at Angelokastron, leaving his wife to be taken prisoner. Carlo complained to Venice that her baillie in Corfu and her castellans of Coron and Modon were actually assisting and supplying his Albanian enemies.[47] But little by little they were driven inland and encircled. The castle of Barnako near Kandeles on the coast to the south of Zaberda was taken from them, and then Kandeles itself. As governor (*kephale*) of this corner of his new dominions Carlo appointed a Sicilian, Mano Meliaresi; and from here he was able to besiege and capture the castle of Aetos, whose Albanian castellan was taken prisoner.[48] Sgouros Spata, ever more isolated at Angelokastron, sank his pride and called on the help of his grandnephew Muriki Spata, who had turned him out of Arta. Muriki came to his rescue, defeating an attack led by Galasso Peccatore, and then went on to recover Katochi. But Sgouros died from a wound sustained in this encounter, leaving his dwindling dominions to his son Paul in 1403.[49]

The death of Sgouros Spata made the Italian conquest of Akarnania easier. Paul Spata soon lost heart in its defence. In 1404–5 Carlo's soldiers made an audacious and successful night attack on Dragameston on the coast to the south of Kandeles. It had been commanded by Lalthi, son-in-law of the late Sgouros. He got away, but his wife was captured and sent over to Leukas to be held to ransom. In the following year Carlo sent a fleet led by Matteo Landolfo of Naples to attack and conquer Anatoliko, on the coast to the south of Angelokastron.[50] At the same time

45 *Chron. Tocco*, I, c. 16; III, c. 22.

46 Ibid., I, cc. 17–23.

47 Ibid., III, c. 15. Sathas, *Monumenta*, II, no. 328, p. 114 (20 July 1403); *ActAlbVen*, I, 3, no. 1046, pp. 401–2; Schirò, 'Il Ducato di Leucade e Venezia', *BF*, V (1977), 367 and n. 41. The wife of Peter Spata was held at Santa Mavra until her ransom was paid.

48 *Chron. Tocco*, III, cc. 6, 17–20. Mano Meliaresi is mentioned, together with Rocco (? Rosso) and Guido, as being among the companions of Carlo Tocco by Chalk., I, p. 196 l. 13 (ed. Darkó). See below, p. 209 n. 33. Schirò, *Cronaca*, pp. 32–3. Soustal–Koder, p. 170 (Kandeles and Barnako).

49 *Chron. Tocco*, III, cc. 23–8.

50 Ibid., I, cc. 24–5, 28. Carlo's occupation of Dragameston was later to be contested by Philip, son of the Venetian nobleman Francesco Foscari. He claimed that Dragameston

he and his brother, joined by Muriki Boua, raided the plain of Arta. Their troops, moving in from Kopraina on the coast, wrecked the commercial quarter and market area outside the town, destroyed the vineyards and devastated the crops.[51] Arta was well defended by Muriki Spata and not so easily to be taken. But the loss of Dragameston and then of Anatoliko seriously weakened the Albanian hold on Akarnania, for these two places were the coastal lifelines of Angelokastron. The feeble Paul Spata could think of only one remedy, the last resort of a Christian scoundrel. He invited the Turks to help him; and the Ottoman commander of Thessaly, Yusuf Beg, crossed the mountains into Akarnania with an army allegedly of 20,000 men. The Acheloos river was in full spate and many of the Turks were drowned trying to cross it. The survivors marched north to besiege Vonitsa, but they were driven off with the loss of many dead and many prisoners. The outcome was not what Paul Spata had intended. Yusuf Beg made his peace with Carlo Tocco and signed a treaty. Paul was now powerless. Even his relative Muriki Spata declined to come to his rescue. In desperation he ceded Angelokastron to the Turks in 1406 and slipped away with his family to the greater safety of Naupaktos.[52]

For some years the Venetians had had their eyes on Naupaktos, or Lepanto. Its commercial and strategic importance was too great for it to be allowed to fall either to the Turks or to Carlo Tocco, for all that he was nominally a Venetian citizen. His acquisition of nearby Anatoliko, with its lucrative fisheries and saltpans, caused much concern in Venice. As early as February 1402 the Senate had begun negotiations to buy Naupaktos from the Albanians for fear that they would otherwise make it over to the Turks. The news that Paul Spata had abandoned Angelokastron to the Turks spurred Venice to secure possession of Naupaktos without further

had been given to his late father by Sgouros Boua Spata as dowry with the hand of his daughter Sterina about 1386. The matter became a *cause célèbre* between Venice and Tocco, involving the papacy and the court of Naples, between 1425 and 1428. It was still unresolved when Carlo died and his son Ercole inherited the lordship of Dragameston. See documents in K. D. Mertzios, Μια ἀνέκδοτη ἐπιστολὴ τοῦ Καρόλου Α' τοῦ Τόκκου πρὸς τὸν Δόγην Βενετίας γραφεῖσα ἐξ 'Ιωαννίνων τὸ 1425, Πεπραγμένα τοῦ Θ' Διεθνοῦς Βυζαντινολογικοῦ Συνεδρίου (Θεσσαλονίκη, 1953), II (= 'Ελληνικά, pt 9: Athens, 1956), 556–9; idem, 'Trois lettres inédites de Charles Tocco en 1427, 1428 et 1432', *Akten des XI. Internationalen Byzantinistenkongresses* (Munich, 1960), pp. 352–4; Ch. Maltezou, Προσωπογραφικὰ βυζαντινῆς Πελοποννήσου καὶ ξενοκρατουμένου ἑλληνικοῦ χώρου (μὲ ἀφορμὴ τὸν φάκελο Foscari τῆς Βενετίας), Σύμμεικτα, v (1983), 1–28; and see below, p. 194.

[51] *Chron. Tocco*, I, cc. 26–7. The μπόριο or ἐμπόριο of Arta was the market and commercial centre outside the city walls. Cf. Ducellier, 'Aux frontières de la Romanie', *TM*, VIII (1981), 115.

[52] *Chron. Tocco*, I, cc. 29–37. Angelokastron was for a while occupied by Baraq, the son of Evrenos (Ibid., I, c. 36). The Venetians knew that Paul Spata had given it to the Turks by May 1407. Sathas, *Monumenta*, II, no. 407, pp. 172–3; *ActAlbVen*, I, 5, no. 1254, p. 29; Thiriet, *Régestes*, II, no. 1262.

delay. The decision was taken on 27 May 1407, and by July 1408 at latest the deal had been done. Paul sold Naupaktos to the Venetians for 1,500 ducats, half the price that had originally been proposed.[53] Carlo Tocco was not so accommodating about the possession of Anatoliko. There were protracted discussions with Venetian agents to try to define where the boundary might lie between the adjoining properties of Anatoliko and Naupaktos, or to achieve some form of condominium. Venice had repeated cause to complain that Carlo was not a one for keeping his word. But in 1409 it was agreed that he should retain the fortified tower of Anatoliko while the Venetians reaped the profits from its fisheries.[54] Meanwhile Carlo seems to have rounded off his conquest of Akarnania by occupying Angelokastron. The text of the Chronicle is silent, or rather defective, about the circumstances. But Venetian documents make it clear that Angelokastron was in Tocco's hands at latest by July 1408; and later the Chronicle records that he entrusted it, together with Acheloos and Katochi, to his loyal Albanian ally and subject Dimo Boua. By 1408 the whole of Akarnania, from Vonitsa in the north to Anatoliko in the south, was owned by the Tocco family.[55]

Carlo's ambitions of conquest, however, were no longer confined to Akarnania. Early in his career of adventure he acquired the fortress of Riniasa (Thomokastron) on the coast of Epiros north of Preveza. It came to him not by force of arms but by purchase from a Greek archon called Pinkernes (or Pikernaios) whom he settled in Leukas with his brother and family.[56] Riniasa changed hands more than once; but its position by the

[53] *ActAlbVen*, I, 3, no. 932, pp. 293–4 (14 February 1402); no. 951, p. 307 (20 April 1402); no. 952, p. 308 (22 April 1402); no. 953, p. 309 (5 May 1402); no. 960, pp. 313–14 (1 June 1402); no. 1048, pp. 402–4 (11 August 1403); I, 5, no. 1254, pp. 29–34 (27 May 1407); no. 1367, p. 159 (20 July 1408). Sathas, *Monumenta*, I, no. 1, pp. 1–2 (20 April 1402); II, no. 407, pp. 172–3 (27 May 1407); no. 415, p. 180 (15 July 1407); no. 424, p. 186 (13 September 1407). Thiriet, *Régestes* II, nos. 1052–3, 1262, 1284. An intermediary in the early stages of the negotiations was the Venetian Francesco Foscari who had married a daughter of Sgouros Spata and was thus a brother-in-law of Paul Spata; see above, n. 50. Cf. V. Lazzarini, 'L'acquisto di Lepanto (1407)', *Nuovo Archivio Veneto*, XV (1898), 267–87; Schirò, *Cronaca*, pp. 40–1; Maltezou, Σύμμεικτα, V (1983), 10–14.

[54] Schirò, *Cronaca*, pp. 41–2; Hopf, *GG*, II, p. 105. A sister of Carlo, Petronella, wife of Niccolo Venier, acted as go-between. Sathas, *Monumenta*, II, nos. 424–5, pp. 186–9 (13 September 1407); I, no. 27, p. 31 (16 November 1408); II, no. 461, pp. 220–1 (15 March 1409); I, no. 32, pp. 34–6 (27 September 1410), where the Venetians admonished Carlo 'quod observari debeant pacta et conventiones ac promissiones et obligationes existentes inter nostram dominationem et suam Magnificentiam'. Thiriet, *Régestes*, II, nos. 1284, 1285, 1328, 1345, 1392. For other complaints about Carlo's unreliability, see Sathas, *Monumenta*, II, nos. 531, 535, pp. 264–6, 268 (5 October 1411 and 17 March 1412); Thiriet, *Régestes*, II, nos. 1437, 1447.

[55] *Chron. Tocco*, IX, c. 6. *ActAlbVen*, I, 5, nos. 1285, 1367, pp. 60–1, 159. Schirò, *Cronaca*, pp. 43–4.

[56] *Chron. Tocco*, III, c. 13. The brothers 'Pikernaioi' are said to have been renowned throughout the Despotate as warriors who had fought with Carlo's army (ibid., I, c. 27, ll.

sea made it a useful base from which to invade the Epirote mainland. Carlo also had dreams of returning to the attack in the Morea. The second book of the Chronicle describes his brief occupation and plunder of Clarentza, the capital of the principality of Achaia, in 1407–8. His excuse for this act of piracy was that the prince, Centurione II Asen Zaccaria, had been sending raiding parties across to Cephalonia. The fact is confirmed by Neapolitan as well as Venetian documents. The expedition of reprisal was led by Leonardo Tocco, whose soldiers, Greeks and Albanians, were so carried away by the opulence of the city of Clarentza that they did their work of plundering with irrepressible violence. It remained in Leonardo's hands for about six months. Carlo never fulfilled his intention of joining him there, perhaps to make it his base for an invasion of the Morea. Thirteen years later Clarentza was indeed to become a part of his dominions. But in February or March 1408 Leonardo and his soldiers sailed away and left it to its rightful owner.[57]

The next stage in the career of Carlo Tocco and so in the history of the Despotate was determined by the death of Esau Buondelmonti, Despot of Ioannina, in 1411. Esau was Carlo's uncle. He had not much approved of his nephew's activities, for they tended to upset the tenuous balance of power that existed between his own Despotate of Ioannina and the ruling Albanian clan of Spata. In 1396 Esau had married Eirene, daughter of Gjin Spata and mother of Muriki and Yaqub. In 1402 he divorced her and married a Serbian lady, Eudokia Balšić.[58] Muriki might have resented this unfriendly act; but at the time he needed the help of Esau to combat Carlo Tocco's raids on Arta and Akarnania. Esau was quite ready to help since he regarded Carlo's activities as dangerous. He made an alliance with Muriki, strengthened by the betrothal of his son Giorgio to Muriki's daughter. The arrangements were concluded in Ioannina about 1410, and between them the contracting parties worked out a division of the spoils in anticipation of their defeat of Carlo Tocco. Muriki would have

351–2). Schirò, *Cronaca*, p. 33 and n. 3, suggests that they may have been descendants of the *pinkernes* John Angelos. The Italian notary, Nicholas de Martoni, when sailing up the coast from Leukas to Corfu in 1395, took refuge at 'Arevessa' (probably Riniasa), whose captain at that time was a Neapolitan. L. Legrand, 'Relation du pèlerinage à Jérusalem de Nicolas de Martoni notaire italien (1394–1395)', *Revue de l'Orient latin*, III (1895), 566–669, especially 665.

[57] *Chron. Tocco*, II, cc. 1–13. Schirò, *Cronaca*, pp. 45–7; Longnon, *L'Empire latin*, pp. 349–50; Bon, *Morée*, pp. 283–4.

[58] Eudokia was a daughter of George Balšić, one of the three Serbian brothers who ruled over Zeta, and half sister of Mrkša Zarković, who became lord of Valona and Berat in 1391. C. Jireček, 'Die Witwe und die Söhne des Despoten Esau von Epirus', *BNJ*, I (1920), 1–16; G. Schirò, 'Evdokia Balšić Vasilissa di Gianina', *ZRVI*, VIII, 2 (= *Mélanges G. Ostrogorsky*, II: 1964), 383–91; *PLP*, III, no. 6230. The date of her marriage to Esau is provided by *Chron. Ioann. Oxon.*, fol. 269^{v} (6 August 1402); Vranousis, *Kastron*, p. 78 (510).

Vonitsa and Esau would have Leukas.[59] But Carlo outmanoeuvred his uncle by making his own arrangement with Muriki. He was afraid that the Turks would take over Arta before he did. He proposed that one of his illegitimate daughters should marry Muriki's half-brother, Carlo Marchesano. The wedding took place at Rogoi in February 1411. It was hoped that it would mark the beginning of a lasting peace between Carlo Tocco and Muriki Spata.[60]

The hope was shattered almost at once. During the marriage feast at Rogoi news came from Ioannina that the Despot Esau had died, on 6 February 1411. A message was at once sent to Carlo.[61] He is said to have grieved at his loss, for Esau was his uncle. But he also foresaw the awful possibility that Muriki would now appropriate the city of Ioannina for himself, bereft as it was of its Despot. Esau's son Giorgio was only seven years old and he was betrothed to Muriki's daughter. The family of Spata might force their claim to inherit the legacy of Esau. Carlo immediately sent a trusted agent to Ioannina to dissuade its citizens from surrendering to the Albanians. This was probably his first direct intervention in the affairs of Ioannina. Had he known its people better he would have realised that they needed no dissuasion, since they had for long regarded the Albanians as their natural enemies. Events moved quickly after Esau's death. His widow, the Serbian Eudokia Balšić, assumed control and, for a few weeks, behaved like the tyrant Thomas Preljubović. She arrested or exiled those whom she disliked and made their property over to fellow Serbians. Among her victims were the Greek governor of Ioannina, Symeon Strategopoulos, and a Florentine noble called Matteo Libardi, who had served the late Esau. Both found their way to the court of Carlo Tocco at Leukas.[62]

Within days, if the chronicler tells the truth, Strategopoulos was back in Ioannina, persuading the citizens to swear allegiance to Eudokia and to her young son Giorgio, as they had promised to do before Esau died.

[59] *Chron. Tocco*, III, cc. 3–5. The Chronicle (l. 720) certainly tells of a marriage, not a betrothal. But if Giorgio was the first son of Esau by Eudokia, married in 1402, he could not have been more than seven or eight years old at the time of his wedding. Cf. Schirò, *Cronaca*, pp. 53–4; Jireček, 'Die Witwe'. Esau had a daughter by Eirene Spata, called Maddalena, who was killed when an archway of the castle of Ioannina collapsed on 6 January 1402. *Chron. Tocco*, III, c. 3, ll. 707–8. The date of this sad event is recorded in *Chron. Ioann. Oxon.*, fol. 269ʳ, and also in a note added to the text of the *Epirotica* (or *De Rebus Epiri*) [= *Chron. Ioann.*] printed in *Historia politica et patriarchica Constantinopoleos* (*CSHB*: 1849), p. 238. Cf. Vranousis, *Kastron*, pp. 25–7 (457–9).

[60] *Chron. Tocco*, III, cc. 29–30. Carlo Marchesano was the child of Eirene Spata's marriage to the Baron Marchesano (see above, p. 148). He was thus the half-brother of Muriki and Yaqub Spata.

[61] *Chron. Tocco*, IV, c. 1. The messenger was Matteo Landolfo of Naples, who had escorted the bride to Rogoi (ibid., III, c. 30).

[62] *Chron. Tocco*, IV, cc. 1–4.

Muriki Spata meanwhile threatened to take them over by force and, assisted by Gjin Zenevesi of Dryinoupolis, ravaged their fields and vineyards beyond the walls. The *basilissa* Eudokia made some attempt to mend her ways and to make herself more popular and acceptable. It had after all been agreed that her only authority stemmed from the fact that she was the mother of the new lord of Ioannina, Esau's heir. But since he was only a child there was an air of unreality about the agreement. The crisis broke when it was revealed that Eudokia had sent to Serbia to find herself a new husband. The people of Ioannina would not tolerate another Serbian master. They took the law into their own hands, swarmed up to the acropolis of the city and drove out the *basilissa* and her children. The chronicler expresses his amazement at their clemency. They might well have thrown her down from the city walls. As it was, Eudokia was sent into exile and found refuge at the court of Gjin Zenevesi.[63]

The Oxford manuscript of the Chronicle of Ioannina dates this revolution and the exile of Eudokia Balšić to 26 February 1411, exactly twenty days after the death of Esau Buondelmonti.[64] Much had happened in those three weeks and it was the intervention of Carlo Tocco which had precipitated events. At the start of his career of conquest Carlo may perhaps have seen the day when he would be lord of Arta. But for one who was heir to a county and duchy of islands it must have seemed improbable that he would one day be master of a city so far inland as Ioannina. He was always a one for acting as opportunities presented themselves. His hour had now come to achieve the improbable. The clear message transmitted by the people of Ioannina was that they disliked the Serbians almost as much as they loathed the Albanians, and that if they must have a foreign master they would prefer an Italian. After long years of rule by the Orsini family and then by Esau Buondelmonti they knew where they were with Italians. One of the last acts of Esau as Despot had been to issue a chrysobull, in March 1408, confirming the privileges and the properties

[63] Ibid., IV, cc. 5–10. She was later to be found in Ragusa. Krekić, *Dubrovnik*, nos. 741, 748, 750, 754, 755, 757 (dated 1427–8). Schirò, 'Evdokia Balšić', 383–91; Jireček, 'Die Witwe', 7–11.

[64] *Chron. Ioann. Oxon.*, fol. 270r. Vranousis, *Kastron*, p. 78 (510). The problem of fitting so many events into the space of twenty days, thus reconciling the narrative of *Chron. Tocco* with the chronology given by the Oxford Chronicle, is recognised but not resolved by Schirò, *Cronaca*, p. 54 and n. 5. He suggests that Eudokia had already taken control and driven Strategopoulos out of Ioannina before her husband Esau died. Hopf, *GG*, II, pp. 103–6, and *Chroniques*, p. 531, followed by Romanos, *Despotate*, pp. 167–9 (84–5), and Miller, *Latins in the Levant*, pp. 372–3, gives a largely fictitious account of events following the death of Esau, which he dates to 1403. In particular, he invents a brother of Gjin Spata called 'Morikios Bua Sgouros' who is said to have been Despot in Ioannina from 1403 to 1418. The evidence now provided by the *Chron. Tocco* refutes almost all the account of these years given by Hopf and his followers. See Schirò, 'Genealogia', 69–71; Schirò, *Cronaca*, p. 57.

of the church of Ioannina on the basis of an investigation by its bishop Joseph of all its previous charters and deeds.[65] Esau had made himself popular in Ioannina; and Carlo Tocco, although an unknown quantity, was his nephew. He was also rich and able to buy his way into the favour of the leading men in the city.

The governor of Ioannina, Symeon Strategopoulos, had already been befriended by Carlo. He and his son Paul took charge of affairs after Eudokia had been driven out; and he invited Carlo's agent, who had returned to the city, to attend the meeting of civic leaders at which the future was to be debated. The agent served his master well. He assured the assembled dignitaries that untold material benefits would come their way if they accepted Carlo Tocco as their lord. The vote in his favour was unanimous and a delegation was sent to Leukas with a formal invitation. They had to travel through Paramythia to Parga and thence by ship, for the roads south from Ioannina were blocked by the Albanians. Parga had become a Venetian protectorate in 1401, but the more southerly fortress of Riniasa had been temporarily occupied by Muriki Spata, who was keen to prove himself a friend to Venice by raising the banner of St Mark on its battlements. Indeed, Muriki and his ally Zenevesi were so incensed by the news from Ioannina that they laid siege to it for a while.[66]

As the delegates from Ioannina made their way to Parga they were joined by about fifty other persons, coming from as far afield as Papingo and Zagoria as well as from Hagios Donatos, all of them eager to be early recipients of the largesse which Carlo Tocco was expected to distribute. They were welcomed and entertained in Leukas and, when the invitation had been confirmed, Carlo at once made preparations for his journey to Ioannina. His brother Leonardo got ready the ships and about a hundred troops and horses were embarked for Parga. It would have been imprudent to attempt to force their way north by land. But Carlo did not burn his boats behind him. He left Leonardo well equipped to create a diversion at Arta in the event that Muriki Spata might attack Ioannina.[67]

[65] Esau's chrysobull for the metropolis of Ioannina, dated March, indiction 1, A.M. 6916 (=A.D. 1408), is known only from Romanos, *Despotate*, pp. 168–9 (84), in whose possession it once was. Cf. Vranousis, *Kastron*, p. 29 (461).

[66] In 1395 Parga was subject to the Despot of Arta, Gjin Spata, although Phanarion, only a short distance to the south, was already Venetian. Legrand, 'Relation du pèlerinage ... de Nicolas de Martoni', 665. Documents relating to the occupation of Parga by the Venetians are in: *ActAlbVen*, I, 3, nos. 869, 911, pp. 229–30, 265–6 (23 April and 20 September 1401); Sathas, *Monumenta*, II, nos. 240, 258, pp. 29, 45–6; Thiriet, *Régestes*, II, nos. 1015, 1029. The Venetians knew that Riniasa ('Larnasa') was in Albanian hands in 1410, when Muriki Spata and Carlo Tocco both sent envoys to seek their support. Sathas, *Monumenta*, II, no. 490, pp. 234–6; I, no. 32, pp. 34–6 (15 March and 27 September 1410); Thiriet, *Régestes*, II, nos. 1368, 1392; *ActAlbVen*, I, 5 no. 1600, pp. 86–9. Cf. Ducellier, TM, VIII (1981), 115.

[67] *Chron. Tocco*, V, cc. 1–11. The castle of Hagios Donatos marked the frontier between

Carlo's journey through the mountains from Parga to Ioannina had its triumphal moments. He sent Matteo Landolfo ahead to announce his impending arrival. At Hagios Donatos the people and their bishop were waiting for him with the keys of their castle; and the Albanians of the district and from further afield, the Malakassaioi from Zagoria, came to pay him homage. As he approached Ioannina the army marched out to acclaim him as their 'Despot', led by their captain, Stephen Voisavos, who was a son-in-law of the governor Strategopoulos. After a short halt at Arachobitsa, Carlo reached Ioannina on 1 April 1411, to be greeted and hailed by the leading men of church and state, the bishop and the clergy all decked out in their finest vestments and carrying lighted lamps and candles. His first act, a symbolic and popular gesture, was to go up to the cathedral and pay his respects at the shrine of the Archangel Michael, patron of the city. He then sent word to his wife and his brother to tell them that he had arrived safely. Those who had unanimously voted to accept Carlo as their lord were not disappointed. He rewarded them with gifts of clothes and money, ducats and florins. Symeon Strategopoulos, who had done so much to pave the way, was granted a castle as his hereditary property. Voisavos was honoured with the rank of *protostrator* of the army. Paul Strategopoulos and others were enriched as *megistanes* or magnates of the city of Ioannina.[68]

Once he had settled in, Carlo summoned Leonardo to join him and together they discussed future plans with the archons of the city. They agreed that their policy should be to restore the boundaries of their territory to their original extent.[69] The territory in question was presumably that of the Despotate of Ioannina as it had been geographically defined in the days of Thomas Preljubović, its first and original Despot. The possibility of reuniting Ioannina with Arta, Epiros with Akarnania, into one single territory or Despotate had not yet arisen. Carlo Tocco had been accepted as their lord and protector by the clergy, the people and the army of Ioannina, on the understanding that he would defend their city and its lands against the Albanians. The Chronicle of Tocco dwells upon the many talents and virtues of its hero. But it is hard to see him as much more than an adventurer with an eye to the main chance. One of his talents was a readiness to seize whatever opportunities were offered him by fate or fortune. But there was little method in his opportunism. Having made himself master of the mainland

Greek and Albanian territory. The Albanian Mazarakaioi had in fact declared for Carlo Tocco, and he sent Matteo Libardi to tell them to join him at Parga. Schirò, *Cronaca*, pp. 54–6.

[68] *Chron. Tocco*, V, cc. 12–17; *Chron. Ioann. Oxon.*, fol. 270^v. Vranousis, *Kastron*, p. 78 (510); Schirò, *Cronaca*, pp. 56–8.

[69] *Chron. Tocco*, V. c. 18.

opposite his island of Leukas, logic might have suggested that his next objective should be the city of Arta, to complete the conquest of the Albanian Despotate of Arta and Acheloos. Fortune had offered him instead the city of Ioannina and he had been unable to resist the temptation, even though he knew that his only line of communication with it was by sea and that it was isolated from his other dominions by Albanians who bitterly resented his presence.

9

The reunited Despotate – 1411–29

Until the death of Esau Buondelmonti in February 1411 there had been a precarious understanding between the various rulers of Epiros, Esau himself in Ioannina, Muriki Spata in Arta and Gjin Zenevesi in Dryinoupolis and the north. Now that Esau was gone and Carlo Tocco, who already controlled Akarnania and the islands, was master of Ioannina, both Albanian leaders felt threatened. Natural enemies though they were, they joined forces in common cause against the new Italian interloper in their midst. Muriki gave his daughter in marriage to Zenevesi's son Simon. It was not their aggression, however, that provoked open warfare. They were even ready to discuss the changed situation. They were not given the chance, for Carlo Tocco was determined on war. He could still rely on his old Albanian ally Muriki Boua, and there were other Albanians willing to fight on his side. He was too confident of success. From his camp at Pratokai in the valley to the north of Ioannina he led plundering raids on Lachanokastron and other places in the territory of Zenevesi; he also invaded Muriki's lands to the south.[1]

The Albanians responded by sending out the rallying cry to all their clansmen to unite in battle against the enemy.[2] The battle was fought in the spring or summer of 1412. Carlo had sent his brother forward to station his troops at a vantage point in the mountains from which he could estimate the size of the Albanian army. It was a daunting sight. The rallying cry had been heard and answered. Leonardo was outnumbered four to one. He brought his men down to the plain at Kranea, to the south of Mesopotamon, and there they were surrounded and almost annihilated. Symeon Strategopoulos was wounded and barely escaped capture;

[1] Lachanokastron, now Oraiokastron, lies some 9 km north-east of Delvinaki. Pratokai was on the former lake of Lapsista to the north of Ioannina. Soustal–Koder, pp. 191, 241. Schirò, *Cronaca*, p. 59 n. 2, following Aravantinos, II, p. 133, mistakenly places 'Pratoka' between Driskos and Metsovon.

[2] The call went out 'to Mouzakea and to all places inhabited by Albanians'. *Chron. Tocco*, VI, c. 6 l. 1682.

but many of his officers, Greeks and Franks, were taken prisoner, among them his own son Paul and a nephew of Tocco called Ziassa. Leonardo got away and went back to Ioannina to report to his brother.[3]

The battle at Kranea was a major disaster for the Tocco family. Their army had been destroyed. The fate of Ioannina hung in the balance. The Albanians had been led by Gjin Zenevesi. Muriki Spata had played a minor part. His contribution to the discomfiture of Carlo Tocco was to enter into alliance with the prince of Achaia, Centurione Zaccaria. He reminded the prince of the damage that Leonardo had done to Clarentza four years before. He assured him that the culprit had now been defeated, that he had been driven back to his islands and that the moment had come to blockade him and be done with him. The pact between the Albanians and the prince of Achaia is confirmed by Venetian sources.[4] Their plan was first to attack Leukas, which they assumed would be undefended, and then the other islands. But they miscalculated. The Duchess Francesca, Carlo's wife, manfully saw to the defence of Leukas, and there were garrisons in the islands. Carlo meanwhile sent to Venice to ask for help. The Venetians were not keen on becoming involved, especially since both Carlo and Centurione were citizens of their Republic. In the end, however, they agreed to send an armed galley to Corfu which might, if need arose, lend support to Carlo's fleet. By a happy chance, as the chronicler puts it, a large armed vessel put into Zante, where Leonardo was equipping his own ships, and sailed with him to confront the navy of Centurione. A battle was fought off Clarentza and the victory went to Leonardo and the Venetians. Centurione's ships were put to flight. Some months later, on 12 July 1414, a truce of three years was arranged between Carlo Tocco and the prince of Achaia.[5]

This victory at sea was some compensation for the defeat on land at Kranea in the previous year. But the Albanians had not suffered from it, nor did it make any difference to Carlo's desperate plight at Ioannina. Thomas Preljubović and Esau Buondelmonti had each in his turn acknowledged the fact that, in the last resort, the Ottoman Turks could be

[3] *Chron. Tocco*, VI, cc. 1–13. Other prisoners taken were two brothers, Nicolafranco and Giacomo Scrofa: ibid., c. 12. The chronicler makes much of Zenevesi's barbarous ill-treatment of them. Schirò, *Cronaca*, pp. 58–61, tentatively identifies Kranea, the site of the battle, with Krania to the north-east of Metsovon (p. 60 n. 2). Since Tocco's army had been operating in the area of Lachanokastron, however, Kranea is much more likely to be the modern Krane in Albania, on the west bank of the Vistrica river to the south of Mesopotamon. Soustal–Koder, p. 187.

[4] *Chron. Tocco*, VI, cc. 14–16. *ActAlbVen*, I, 7, no. 1823, pp. 74–6; Sathas, *Monumenta*, I, no. 39, pp. 43–4; Thiriet, *Régestes*, II, nos. 1498, 1500 (July and August 1413). Schirò, *Cronaca*, pp. 61–4.

[5] *Chron. Tocco*, VI, cc. 16–18. *ActAlbVen*, I, 7, no. 1885, pp. 125–6; Sathas, *Monumenta*, III, no. 616, pp. 63–4; Thiriet, *Régestes*, II, nos. 1535–6. Schirò, 'Il Ducato di Leucade', 370–1.

useful allies. Carlo Tocco was now forced to the same conclusion. As a rule, the author of the Chronicle disapproved of such tactics, correctly observing that those who flirt with the Turks will sooner or later be smothered by them.[6] His hero was an exception to the rule. In the chronicler's eyes Carlo Tocco could do no wrong. He had no option. To ask for Turkish support was in fact a wise move and further evidence of Carlo's diplomatic talent. It was the only way in which he could redress the balance of his defeat at Kranea and humiliate Gjin Zenevesi. The Ottoman leader to whom he turned was the Emir Musa, who had supplanted his brother Suleiman at Adrianople in 1410. By whatever means an alliance was arranged. Musa married one of Carlo's daughters. She was illegitimate, for Carlo and Francesca had no children of their own, but she was beautiful; and the Emir Musa became the friend and protector of the Tocco family. He at once sent orders to Zenevesi to release the prisoners whom he had taken at Kranea; and he lent Carlo a small contingent of Turkish troops, the only soldiers that seemed capable of striking fear into the Albanians. This happy alliance of Italians and Turks must have occurred in 1412 or early in 1413. It eased the problem of the defence of Ioannina, but not for long. For in 1413 Musa's brother Mehmed went to war against him and Musa was killed. The final battle between them was fought in Serbia. The Albanians quickly discovered that Carlo had lost his new Turkish son-in-law and protector and resumed their hostilities. They underestimated Carlo's resourcefulness, for they did not know that he was also on good terms with Musa's conqueror Mehmed.[7]

Mehmed's victory in July 1413 brought many advantages to the Byzantine Empire. Once established as sultan at Adrianople, Mehmed made his peace with the emperor, a peace which he honoured and respected until his death in 1421.[8] Carlo Tocco was also a beneficiary of the new sultan's benevolence. The chronicler fails to explain how Carlo came to be so well connected with both of the rivals for power in the Ottoman world. But it appears that the connexion was not new, for four of his illegitimate sons had been sent to serve at the sultan's court and one of them was still there in 1413. Mehmed was graciously pleased to accept the profession of loyalty and the *haradj* or tribute which Carlo offered to pay him, and formally recognised his status as lord of Ioannina. The link was strengthened by the marriage of Carlo's daughter, the widow of

[6] Contrast the chronicler's remarks about the recourse of Paul Spata to the Turks. *Chron. Tocco*, I, c. 30 ll. 425–8, c. 36 ll. 496–7. Schirò, *Cronaca*, pp. 64, 135–6.

[7] *Chron. Tocco*, VI, cc. 19–20.

[8] Mehmed's final defeat of Musa took place on 5 July 1413. He died on 21 May 1421. Schreiner, *Chron. Brev.*, I, nos. 72a/18, 91/7, 97/3; II, pp. 401, 412. Nicol, *Last Centuries of Byzantium*, pp. 342–7.

Musa, to one of Mehmed's officers, Hamza Beg; he was the brother of Bajezid Pasha, to whom the sultan was particularly devoted.[9] Perhaps the chronicler was right to praise Carlo's diplomatic talent. Certainly these developments frightened the Albanians in Epiros and promoted discord among them. Muriki Spata fell out with Gjin Zenevesi, who seemed prepared to accept Carlo's offer of friendship. At the same time Muriki's half-brother, Carlo Marchesano, who had married Tocco's daughter, offered to make over to his father-in-law his castle of Riniasa on the coast. Tocco was delighted to accept the offer, even though the people of Riniasa at first refused to submit for fear of Albanian reprisals. Muriki Spata found himself more and more isolated. Carlo and Leonardo were optimistically planning a joint land and sea campaign against him when he fell ill and died, probably in 1414.[10]

The city and former Despotate of Arta were left in the hands of his mother, Eirene Spata, the disprised wife of Esau Buondelmonti and mother, by her second marriage, of Carlo Marchesano. Muriki's widow, a Serbian called Nerata, was not popular, and he had no sons to succeed him. He had, however, a brother, Yaqub Spata. Yaqub had hitherto played no part in the affairs of Epiros. He had been brought up among Turks and was a Muslim by faith. But when he heard of his brother's death he hurried to Arta to claim the succession. The same thought had occurred to Carlo Tocco, who had hopes of getting a foot in the door of Arta by pressing the claim of his son-in-law, Carlo Marchesano. He contrived to capture a key position in the hills to the north-west of the city. It was the castle of Vobliana (Bompliana), an ancient fortress by the village of Kastri above Ammotopos; and it controlled the approach to Arta from the north.[11] He stationed a garrison there commanded by a loyal Greek from Ioannina called Michael Kapsokavades, whose orders were to make daily raids on the plain of Arta. In the end it was the elderly Eirene Spata, mother of the late Muriki and of Yaqub, who settled the question of the succession. With the consent of the leading citizens she proposed that Yaqub should be lord of Arta and Carlo Marchesano lord of Rogoi. Muriki's widow Nerata was exiled. Tocco was at first pleased to hear of this arrangement, since Marchesano was his son-in-law. But he was quickly disappointed. The new lords of Arta and Rogoi wanted nothing to do with him and were united in their determination to drive his garrison out of Vobliana.[12]

[9] *Chron. Tocco*, VII, cc. 1–6.

[10] Ibid., VII, cc. 7–11.

[11] Vobliana (Βομπλιανά) is to be identified with the Hellenistic settlement and fortress by the village of Kastri, to the west of Ammotopos. Hammond, *Epirus*, pp. 154–9; Soustal–Koder, pp. 126–7.

[12] *Chron. Tocco*, VII, cc. 11–17. On Michael Kapsokavades, see Schirò, *Cronaca*, p. 33 n. 4; *PLP*, V, no. 11590.

Since Esau's death in 1411 there had been no ruler in Epiros bearing the title of Despot, the title which only a Byzantine emperor could confer. As the chronicler observes, it had in the past been customary for ambassadors to be sent to Constantinople to receive the Despot's crown from the emperor's hands and to bring it back with them. Thomas Preljubović and Esau Buondelmonti had each been invested in this manner. Carlo coveted the title and the insignia that would legalise his acquisitions and give him a dignity which his Greek subjects could understand. In the summer of 1415 the Emperor Manuel II, profiting from his treaty with the Sultan Mehmed, visited the Morea. His purpose was to supervise the reconstruction of the Hexamilion wall across the isthmus of Corinth, against the day when the Turks ceased to be so amenable. With the Byzantine emperor so near at hand, Carlo decided to pay his respects and to seek imperial recognition of his status as lord of Ioannina. The sultan had already recognised him as such. But only the emperor could grant him the title that had given its name to the Despotate of Epiros.

Leonardo was therefore despatched to the Morea to do homage to the Emperor Manuel and to remind him of the many services which the Tocco family had rendered to the Byzantine Empire in the past. Some element of fiction may have coloured this interpretation of events. But the emperor was impressed. He rewarded Leonardo with the title of Grand Constable and he honoured Carlo with the rank and the crown of a Despot. The chronicler remarks that he was persuaded to do so 'because the dominion which Carlo had, by God's grace, obtained was the Despotaton'. It is questionable whether the Emperor Manuel himself thought in these terms. To him, as to all his imperial predecessors, the title of Despot bound its holder in a certain relationship to the crown. It had no territorial significance. In Carlo's case the link with the crown was emphasised in a unique fashion; for the chronicler records that the Tocco brothers were enrolled as 'Kantakouzenatoi', as honorary blood relations of the imperial family. Manuel II was a grandson of the Emperor John VI Cantacuzene, whose name was well known in Epiros. By conferring that distinguished name on the new ruling family of Epiros, the emperor must have meant to give them a special sense of belonging to the Byzantine establishment. The crown and insignia of his new rank were taken to Carlo at Ioannina; and there, in August 1415, he was invested as Despot. The people rejoiced that they had once more a true Despot at their head.[13]

[13] *Chron. Tocco*, VIII, cc. 1–3. The date is given in *Chron. Ioann. Oxon.*, fol., 271ʳ. G. Schirò, 'Manuele II Paleologo incorona Carlo Tocco Despota di Gianina', *B*, XXIX-XXX (1959–60), 210–17; Zakythinos, *Despotat grec de Morée*, I, pp. 167–70; J. W. Barker, 'On the chronology of the activities of Manuel II Palaeologus in the Peloponnese in 1415', *BZ*, LV (1962), 39–55; idem, *Manuel II Palaeologus* (New Brunswick, 1969), pp. 311–14, 346

The chronicler, who was one of them, knew what an honour it was. Until this point in his narrative he had scrupulously refrained from calling his hero anything more exalted than 'the duke' or 'the lord' (*doukas* or *aphentes*). Henceforth Carlo Tocco will be described with some pride as 'the Duke and Despot'.[14]

Only a man of Ioannina could have declared that Carlo's dominion in 1415 constituted the 'Despotaton'. A man of Arta, the original capital of the Despotate of Epiros, would never have agreed. At the time that he was made Despot, Carlo's territory consisted of the islands of Cephalonia, Ithaka, Zante and Leukas with the castle of Vonitsa. On the mainland he had acquired most of Akarnania and a large part of Epiros, from Parga to Hagios Donatos to Ioannina. Parga itself had become Venetian in 1401, but the castle of Riniasa further south was in Carlo's hands. The administration of these scattered possessions was entrusted to his brother, his sons and various Italian or Albanian dependants, each of whom was given a hereditary title to his property. Carlo himself was Despot in Ioannina and district. His second son Torno ruled the area between Parga and Hagios Donatos, where lived the Albanian Mazarakaioi. One of his nephews held Riniasa. Leonardo, now Grand Constable, commanded the islands and Vonitsa; though his normal and favourite residence was Zante, and Vonitsa was defended by his deputy, Giovanni Presa. In Akarnania, Matteo of Naples held the town of Barnako and the country around Kandeles. Angelokastron with Acheloos and Katochi were at first governed by the loyal Albanian, Dimo Boua; although later it seems that Carlo's eldest son, Ercole, who had married a daughter of the late Sgouros Spata, was given command of Angelokastron and the region of Acheloos as far south as the now Venetian city of Naupaktos.[15] It appears that very few of Carlo's governors or commanders were Greek. Symeon Strategopoulos, who had been *kephale* of Ioannina for Esau Buondelmonti, is an exception. His captain at Vobliana was Michael Kapsokavades and his constable there was one Papadopoulos. The evidence presented by the Chronicle is not complete;

n. 89; Nicol, *Byzantine Family of Kantakouzenos*, pp. x–xi; Schirò, *Cronaca*, pp. 67–9. By September 1416 it was known in Ragusa that Leonardo Tocco was Grand Constable. Krekić, *Dubrovnik*, no. 626.

[14] Schirò, *Cronaca*, p. 67. His wife Francesca, who had long before taken to calling herself *basilissa*, was addressed in 1418 as 'dignissima ducissa dela Luchata, comitissa Cephalonie palatina, domina Jaline (Ioannina)'. Krekić, *Dubrovnik*, no. 647 (11 July 1418).

[15] *Chron. Tocco*, IX, cc. 6, 10. About 1397 Carlo had made over Zante to Leonardo as his hereditary appanage, a deed confirmed by Ladislas of Naples on 1 April 1400. N. Jorga, *Notes et extraits pour servir à l'histoire des croisades au XVe siècle*, v (Paris, 1900), p. 80 Ercole's wife's name was Petronella; he was to be found at Angelokastron in 1436. See Maltezou, Σύμμεικτα, v (1983), 8; and below, p. 206. The Venetians were on the whole very patient with Carlo's insistence that Naupaktos really belonged to him. Cf. Sathas, *Monumenta*, III, no. 616, pp. 63–4 (12 July 1414); Thiriet, *Régestes*, II, no. 1536.

but its author was proud to be a Greek and he would surely have recorded the names of any Greeks appointed to more responsible positions. Carlo was romantic enough to give three of his bastard sons the classical names of Ercole, Menuno and Torno (Hercules, Memnon and Turnus). But he seems to have preferred to import Italians as his deputies.[16]

To add substance to his title of Despot Carlo now turned to the conquest and annexation of Arta. The arrangement by which Yaqub Spata and Carlo Marchesano shared Arta and Rogoi between them rapidly proved unworkable. The people of Arta suspected that it was Yaqub's intention, since he was a Muslim, to hand them over to the Turks. They chased him out and invited Marchesano to take his place. Yaqub went straight to the sultan and returned with a Turkish army commanded by one Ismail to right the wrong thus done to him. All the clan of Spata was on his side. Even Muriki Boua, the faithful friend of Carlo Tocco, joined his cause. Marchesano and his supporters were arrested and Yaqub became lord of Arta once again. This petty squabble between the sons of Eirene Spata was observed from the distant heights of Vobliana by Carlo's troops, who continued their daily raids on the plain of Arta. Yaqub was determined to put a stop to their nuisance. Battle was about to be joined between Italians and Albanians for the possession of Arta.[17]

The events of the campaign which was to bring victory to Carlo Tocco are narrated by the chronicler in a rather disjointed manner, interspersed with episodes from an earlier period telling of the heroic deeds of Carlo's sons. He describes with verve the first taste of battle of the young Ercole, against a company of four hundred Turks who had come over to Angelokastron from Levadia by way of Salona and Lidoriki. Ercole had only about sixty men but he led them over the river Phidares (Ophidares) and put the Turks to flight, taking many prisoners.[18] He relates how Torno was surrounded and nearly captured by the Albanian clan of the Alkadii but fought his way out to join his father at Vathy, on the road between Arta and Ioannina.[19] He tells how Carlo and his brother reoccupied Riniasa.[20] But the most important part of his narrative centres

[16] *Chron. Tocco*, VII, cc. 1–5. The fourth of Carlo's bastard sons, Triano, was unknown to Hopf; but he listed two others, one perhaps called Antonio, the other Orlando, lord of Riniasa, neither of whom appears in the *Chron. Tocco*. Hopf, *Chroniques*, p. 530; cf. Schirò, *Cronaca*, pp. 27 and n. 4, 66. Schirò seems inclined to dismiss Orlando as a figment of Hopf's imagination. But a Venetian document of 20 August 1463 refers to 'domino *Rolando* de *tocho* olim domino *Renesse*'. *ActAlbVen*, III, 25, no. 7448, pp. 184–5.

[17] Carlo's troops captured the castle of Sestrouni, on the eastern slopes of the Souli mountains. Soustal–Koder, p. 257.

[18] *Chron. Tocco*, IX, c. 10. Soustal–Koder, p. 218 (Ophidares river).

[19] *Chron. Tocco*, IX, cc. 8–9. On the clan of the Alkadii, see Schirò, *Cronaca*, p. 72 n. 2.

[20] *Chròn. Tocco*, IX, c. 11.

on the operations of Carlo against Arta from the north and of Leonardo against Rogoi from the south. Leonardo scored his first victory over Yaqub and the Malakassaioi at a place called Mazoma between Rogoi and Nikopolis. He then laid siege to the castle of Rogoi. It was strongly fortified but undermanned and even its patron saint seems to have despaired. The chronicler, who was evidently an eye-witness, tells the strange tale of how the defenders of Rogoi placed part of their most holy relic, the sceptre of St Luke, on the battlements and how it fell down into the ranks of the besieging army. The relic was taken to the Despot and its fall was interpreted as a clear sign that Rogoi would soon surrender.[21]

Meanwhile Carlo and his army rampaged over the fields and vineyards of Arta. They pillaged the market town outside the city and fought a battle with Yaqub and Muriki Boua before returning to Ioannina.[22] In the end Yaqub was outwitted by trickery. The constable of Vobliana, Papadopoulos, fooled him into believing that the castle was defended by a mere handful of soldiers and that it was his for the taking. Yaqub's troops were surrounded when trying to enter Vobliana by night. He himself was captured and put to death on 1 October 1416.[23] The way to Arta was open to Carlo Tocco. Marchesano, who might have fought for it, had fled and made for Parga, where Leonardo apprehended him when he was trying to escape by sea. He and his wife were sent to live out the rest of their days in Cephalonia.[24] The people of Arta now had no alternative but to submit to Carlo Tocco, who came down through the pass called Dema and encamped on the edge of the plain at Stribina.[25] He sent a messenger to persuade the archons of the city to surrender rather than be destroyed. Once again the decision was taken after consultation with Eirene Spata, the mother of Muriki and Yaqub. Her liberty and that of Yaqub's widow, a daughter of Muriki Boua, were to be guaranteed, as well as all the rights

[21] Ibid., IX, cc. 12–13. The relics of St Luke the Evangelist were housed in the church dedicated to him in the castle of Rogoi. They are said to have been taken there from Constantinople after 1204. Ciriaco of Ancona saw and revered them when he visited Rogoi in October 1448. Five years later, after the Turkish conquest of Arta, they are said to have been removed to Smederevo on the orders of the Serbian Despot George Branković. G. Sotiriou, Τὸ κάστρο τῶν ῾Ρωγῶν, *Ep. Chron.*, II (1927), 98–109, especially 102f.; E. Ziebarth, Κυριακὸς ὁ ἐξ ᾿Αγκῶνος ἐν ᾿Ηπείρῳ, *Ep. Chron.*, I (1926), 110–19; Jireček-Radonić, *Istorija Srba*, I, p. 427.

[22] *Chron. Tocco*, IX, cc. 14–16. Carlo came down into the plain from Topoliana and encamped by the river Kataphoro (Arachthos). Soustal–Koder, pp. 116, 271.

[23] *Chron. Tocco*, X, cc. 1–11. Schirò, *Cronaca*, pp. 75–7. The exact date of Yaqub's death is supplied by *Chron. Ioann. Oxon.*, fol. 271^r^. Vranousis, *Kastron*, p. 79.

[24] *Chron. Tocco*, X, cc. 13–15. For reasons which the chronicler does not explain, Marchesano was on his way to take refuge not with the Turks but with the emperor (l. 2899). Schirò, *Cronaca*, pp. 76–7.

[25] Stribina is the modern Kambi near Philippiada, 10 km north-west of Arta. Soustal–Koder, p. 265.

and privileges of the people of Arta. On those terms they would submit. There was little else that they could do. Some of them were already waiting cap in hand at Carlo's camp in hopeful expectation of the largesse that he would distribute when they surrendered. Only four days after the death of Yaqub, on 4 October 1416, Carlo Tocco entered Arta as Despot and raised his banner on the castle tower. At the same time, Leonardo, summoned from Leukas, accepted the submission of Rogoi and gave it a new garrison before joining his brother at Arta to celebrate their achievement.[26]

The nature of the achievement is presented by the chronicler in terms that might have seemed strange to the Tocco brothers themselves. The reunification of Arta with Ioannina, he writes, signified the reunification of all the Greek inhabitants of Epiros. The two cities had been separated since the foundation of the Despotate; but now they were united and, together with the islands, constituted a single dominion (ὅλα μοναφεντία) under the rule of one Despot. The Greeks of the Despotate were glad to feel a common loyalty as his subjects and they were guaranteed the possession of their hereditary properties with a security that they had not enjoyed for some two hundred years.[27] The chronicler's knowledge of the history of his country did not go very far back. He was evidently unaware that the division of Epiros into a Despotate of Ioannina and a Despotate of Arta dated no earlier than the Serbian conquest of 1348; and he was over-optimistic about the beneficial consequences of its reintegration. The 'single dominion' was a superficial structure. Its one Despot, Carlo Tocco, was well pleased with his success in making himself master first of Ioannina and then of Arta. But he had no gifts of statesmanship equal to the tasks of administering so large a territory or of creating a unified society out of its multi-racial constituents.[28]

The family of Spata which had for so long dominated the regions of Arta and Acheloos was now eliminated. Yaqub had been its last representative and he had no sons. The other Albanians were naturally suspicious of and hostile to the victorious Despot of Epiros. Carlo understood this. He sent gifts to Gjin Zenevesi and to Muriki Boua to allay their fears and to persuade them that they would do well to cooperate against the common enemy of all the Epirotes, the Turks. He also sent gifts to the Sultan Mehmed and to Bajezid Pasha, to whom he was related by marriage. The Sultan was no doubt annoyed that Arta had passed out of Muslim hands, but he confirmed that Carlo could keep it,

[26] *Chron. Tocco*, x, cc. 16–21.
[27] *Chron. Tocco*, x, c. 22.
[28] Cf. Schirò, *Cronaca*, pp. 106–7.

provided that he paid the *haradj* for the privilege.[29] Carlo was rightly apprehensive of the intentions of his Ottoman friends and allies. But in 1416 they were preoccupied with another power struggle among themselves and he was allowed time to see to the affairs of his Despotate.[30]

He nominated his brother Leonardo as lord of Arta, reserving Ioannina for himself. The chronicler of Tocco's exploits firmly believed that the centre and the root of the Greek world in Epiros was the city of Ioannina. For him it was and always had been the capital of the Despotate. The Despots might choose to reside in Arta in the winter or during the hunting season. But Ioannina was their headquarters.[31] This was the opinion of a local patriot. It was not shared by Carlo Tocco. It was true that Ioannina had always managed to keep the Albanians beyond its walls. In the early fifteenth century it was probably more Greek in character than Arta, where the long Albanian occupation must have reduced the size and influence of its Greek population. Carlo took to calling himself Despot of the Greeks, or Romaioi. He signed his documents in Greek and in the red ink of a Byzantine emperor. But he would not have offended the historical sensibilities of the Greeks of Arta by declaring Ioannina to be the first city of his Despotate.[32]

The chronicler speaks highly of Carlo's success in restoring peace and confidence in Arta after the long years of war and uncertainty. Its leading men were honoured; wealth and prosperity returned; the streets were cleaned and widened; and by land and sea it was once more safe to travel. There were no more raids and incursions; agriculture revived; and everywhere there was a new feeling of security and stability.[33] The remaining Albanian chieftains, however, had still to be persuaded that a new age had dawned. Muriki Boua had proved to be a treacherous friend, but Carlo forgave him and bound him to keep the peace by yet another bond of kinship. His third son Menuno married Muriki's daughter and took her off to Akarnania, to the district of Xeromera, where he was

[29] *Chron. Tocco*, XI, cc. 1–2.

[30] *Chron. Tocco*, XI, c. 3, gives a brief outline of the struggle for power between Mustafa and the Sultan Mehmed I in 1416. Mustafa, who claimed to be a son of the Sultan Bajezid, was abetted by the Byzantine emperor and given asylum in Thessalonica. Doukas, *Historia*, ed. V. Grecu (Bucharest, 1958), pp. 157–61; Schreiner, *Chron. Brev.*, I, no. 72a/20; II, pp. 405–6. Barker, *Manuel II*, pp. 340–4; Schirò, *Cronaca*, p. 78.

[31] *Chron. Tocco*, XI, cc. 5, 7; cf. V, c. 14; XII, c. 10.

[32] For Carlo's signature in Greek in red ink, see Krekić, *Dubrovnik*, no. 722 (8 May 1425). The Venetians at first called him the duke of Cephalonia 'qui se intitulat Dispotum Romanie'. *ActAlbVen*, II, 10, no. 2247, p. 24 (24 May 1418); Sathas, *Monumenta*, I, no. 78, p. 119; III, no. 730, p. 174; Thiriet, *Régestes*, II, no. 1693. Schirò, *Cronaca*, pp. 78–9. His wife Francesca adopted the title of *basilissa* of the Romaioi long before. See above, p. 167.

[33] *Chron. Tocco*, XI, c. 4.

appointed as lord of Aetos.[34] Gjin Zenevesi, the victor at Kranea, was an older and less tractable enemy. He still dominated the mountains and valleys around Dryinoupolis and Argyrokastron and he was capable of descending upon Ioannina at any time. But fate was again kind to Carlo Tocco. Zenevesi died in 1418.[35]

Carlo had tried to convince him that his real enemies were the Turks. That truth was now to be revealed. The news of Zenevesi's death promoted an immediate Turkish invasion of his territory. An army, said to have been thirty thousand strong, marched on Dryinoupolis. Its leader was Hamza, a son-in-law of Carlo. Zenevesi had a son and heir in the person of Simon, who had married a daughter of Muriki Spata. But he was young and he soon gave up the struggle to defend his heritage. In the summer of 1418 the Turks captured Dryinoupolis and most of the lands of the Zenevesaioi. All the prisoners taken were decapitated. Simon escaped and tried to take refuge in Ioannina. But the people there had bitter memories of his father's depredations and they turned him away.[36] The Turks went on to lay siege to Argyrokastron. It was a long and difficult operation, but Simon Zenevesi relieved them of their trouble. Turned away from Ioannina, he went back to Argyrokastron and, in October 1418, voluntarily made it over to the Turks. Then, having collected his goods and his wife, he fled to Corfu where he committed suicide – a fitting end, as the chronicler says, for one who had betrayed a Christian city to the infidel. The Albanians who survived the siege and occupation of Argyrokastron made south for the Morea, where their services as mercenaries were much in demand.[37]

The Despot Carlo was glad to see the end of the clan of Zenevesi but uncertain about what the Turks might do next. As a precaution he summoned Leonardo to bring reinforcements up from Arta to Ioannina.

[34] Ibid., XI, c. 6. Soustal–Koder, pp. 102–3 (Aetos).

[35] *Chron. Tocco*, XI, c. 8. A Venetian document of 26 April 1419 reveals that the late '*Jannj* Sauastocratora' (? Gjin Zenevesi) had deposited some money, jewellery and silver with the baillie of Corfu, Niccolo Foscolo, to be distributed among his heirs when he died. His heirs are named as his two sons and his two sisters, Maria, wife of the Corfiote Perotto de Altavilla, and '*chiure*' (or 'Chivre'), whom Hopf, *GG*, II, p. 102, identifies as Kyranna, who married Andreas III Musachi. *ActAlbVen*, II, 10, no. 2320, pp. 118–19; Sathas, *Monumenta*, III, no. 751, pp. 198–9; Thiriet, *Régestes*, II, no. 1736.

[36] *Chron. Tocco*, XII, cc. 1–3. Schirò, *Cronaca*, pp. 79–80. On Simon (or Symeon) Zenevesi, see *PLP*, III, no. 6522. The identity of the 'Zenebisas' of Chalk. II, p. 96 (ed. Darkó) is problematical. He is said to have been lord of the land from Argyropolichne (Argyrokastron) to Kastoria, where he was defeated and captured by Therizes (? Firuz), Turkish governor of Berroia, in about 1418. He may have been the other son of Gjin Zenevesi. *PLP*, III, no. 6524; IV, no. 7699. Schirò, *Cronaca*, p. 80. Hopf, *GG*, II, p. 102, describes him as 'Bua Zenevesi', a loyal ally of Venice, who died in battle against the Turkish governor of Berroia, 'Sfaridsche Pasha', a few years after 1430.

[37] *Chron. Tocco*, XII, cc. 4, 7–8. For the date of the fall of Argyrokastron, see Schirò, *Cronaca*, p. 81; Schreiner, *Chron. Brev.*, I, nos. 60/12, 64/4; II, p. 408.

The Chronicle records how Leonardo was on hand to rescue the people of Papingo from a Turkish attack on their fields just when they were about to begin the harvest. Another Turkish force invaded the plain of Ioannina, but only in pursuit of retreating Albanians. Carlo could have gone out to fight them; but he trusted the word of their commander Hamza, his son-in-law, that no damage would be done to his property. He was wise to be patient with the Turks and to see that his best policy was one of appeasement.[38]

Some time after the fall of Argyrokastron, in 1418 or early 1419, Leonardo Tocco died at Zante, where he had gone for relaxation. The chronicler makes much of the passing of this 'second Achilles', the lion Leonardo, whose bearing and prowess had so impressed the great rulers of the world, King Ladislas, who had received him on a visit to Naples, and the Byzantine emperor, who had made him Grand Constable. He left a young son to whom he had given the name of Carlo, though he seems also or originally to have been called Leonardo.[39] It had been agreed in advance that this young man should in due course inherit the Despotate, since Leonardo's brother had no legitimate sons of his own. He had been brought up in Naples but the Despot and the *basilissa* Francesca had adopted him. The castle of Riniasa was allotted to him as his domain; and he married the daughter of Nerata, the Serbian widow of Muriki Spata, who had found asylum in Corfu. His nomination as heir apparent was almost bound to cause resentment among the bastard sons of the Despot Carlo. But so long as their father lived they served him loyally and well.[40]

The last chapter of the Chronicle of the Tocco family as it now survives tells of events in the Morea and has little bearing on the history of Epiros. In 1418 the city of Clarentza, the capital of Achaia, which Leonardo had briefly held in 1408, had been seized by an Italian condottiere, Franco Oliverio. In 1421 Oliverio was forcibly persuaded to sell it to Carlo Tocco.[41] Once again the Tocco family had a foothold in the Morea. This time they meant to keep it. In defiance of the prince of Achaia, Centurione II Zaccaria, and of the Byzantine despot of Mistra, Theodore II Palaiologos, Carlo's troops occupied most of the province of Elis in the north-west of the Morea. His eldest son Ercole directed the campaign, assisted by his brother Torno. The prince of Achaia became the ally if not the vassal of the victorious Carlo Tocco, who began to see his way to

[38] *Chron. Tocco*, XII, cc. 5–6.

[39] Ibid., XIII, cc. 1–8. Matteo Landolfo seems to have taken charge at Arta after Leonardo's death. He is mentioned in a Ragusan document of 1424 as 'Mateus de Nandolfi, capitaneus Arthe, factor domini despothi'. Krekić, *Dubrovnik*, no. 704. See below, p. 232.

[40] *Chron. Tocco*, IX, cc. 18–23.

[41] Ibid., XIV, cc. 1–6. Schirò, *Cronaca*, pp. 85–92; Zakythinos, *Despotat grec de Morée*, I, p. 184; Bon, *Morée*, pp. 286–8.

further conquests in the Morea. With this in mind, he applied to his friends the Turks to provide him with reinforcements. They were delighted to do so since, as the chronicler observes, the Turks were always gratified when the Christians were divided.[42]

The Chronicle is silent about the Ottoman storming of the Hexamilion wall at the isthmus of Corinth and the devastating invasion of the Morea by Turachan Beg and his army in May 1423.[43] But the Tocco family must take their share of the blame for causing this disaster. The text of the Chronicle is incomplete. As it stands, its narrative runs out in a rather breathless and inconsequent series of deeds of daring and valour conducted against the Greeks of the Morea by the brothers Ercole and Torno and the bold Matteo Landolfo of Naples.[44] The facts and the truth about how this adventure ended are to be found in other sources. For a time there was a truce between Carlo's occupying force at Clarentza and the Despot Theodore II. The Venetians helped to arrange it, which was generous of them considering that they were simultaneously protesting against Carlo's illegal activities near Naupaktos in the south and at Parga in the north.[45] But the truce was broken in 1426. The news brought the emperor, John VIII Palaiologos, hurrying to the scene from Constantinople, to take personal charge of affairs and put a stop to Tocco's nuisance. He marched straight from Mistra to Clarentza and laid siege to it by land and sea. In a naval battle off the Echinades islands Tocco's fleet, led by Torno, was decisively defeated. Such was the end of Carlo Tocco's third and last attempt at conquest in the Morea.[46]

Some of his dignity was saved, however, by a diplomatic arrangement. His niece Maddalena, daughter of Leonardo, married Constantine Palaiologos, brother of the Emperor John VIII and the Despot Theodore II. Clarentza and the other Tocco acquisitions in the Morea were said to constitute her dowry. The wedding took place in July 1428, by which date the emperor's faithful servant, the historian George Sphrantzes, had already taken over Clarentza in his master's name.[47] Constantine Palaiologos was to cover himself with immortal glory as the last Byzantine

[42] *Chron. Tocco*, XIV, cc. 7–12; c. 12, l. 3738: Οἱ Τοῦρκοι πάντα ἠγαποῦν τῶν Χριστιανῶν τὸ σχίσμα.

[43] Zakythinos, *Despotat grec de Morée*, I, p. 196; Barker, *Manuel II*, p. 371.

[44] *Chron. Tocco*, XIV, cc. 13–22. Schirò, *Cronaca*, pp. 92–100.

[45] *ActAlbVen*, II, 11, no. 2690, pp. 188–9; no. 2689, pp. 199–200 (4 and 28 February 1423); Sathas, *Monumenta*, I, no. 83, p. 127 (24 February 1423); III, nos. 809, 811, pp. 242, 245 (the latter misdated to '31 February 1422'). Thiriet, *Régestes*, II, nos. 1867, 1871, 1873, 1877. Bon, *Morée*, p. 289.

[46] Miller, *Latins in the Levant*, pp. 385–8; Zakythinos, *Despotat grec de Morée*, I, pp. 198–204; Bon, *Morée*, pp. 290–1.

[47] Sphrantzes, *Chron. Minus*, XVI. 1, 3: p. 24; *Chron. Majus*, II. 2: pp. 266–8 (ed. Grecu). Schreiner, *Chron. Brev.*, I, no. 34/3; II, pp. 435–6.

emperor, who died fighting the Turks at the walls of his city in 1453. But the good Maddalena, known to the Greeks as Theodora, was to be his wife for only a few months. She died in November 1429.[48] Like so many of the daughters of the ruling families in Epiros, she had served her purpose and solved a problem created by the ambition of her menfolk. Her uncle Carlo Tocco, whose particular purpose she had served, did not live to lament her passing. He had been in poor health for some time and had made his will in June 1429. He died at Ioannina a month later.[49]

Maddalena-Theodora had married above her station, and her death was, as a matter of form, mourned in stylised epitaphs by two of the Byzantine literati of the age, John Eugenikos and Bessarion of Nicaea.[50] The death of Carlo Tocco passed unnoticed in such circles. It was not an event that moved the court poets of Mistra or of Constantinople to compose their excruciatingly elaborate verses; and the cities of Arta and Ioannina had long since ceased to breed men of letters in the old Byzantine style of rhetoric. The Chronicle of Tocco, though it breaks off seven years before he died, must stand as the encomium and the epitaph of Carlo Tocco. Bessarion would not have approved of its vulgar language and its lack of finesse. But in its simple way it is more eloquent of the truth of Carlo's life and of the people whom he conquered and ruled than the sophistries and artificialities of the numerous encomia and epitaphs produced by more polished and learned Byzantine writers of the age. One of them, Isidore of Kiev, author of a lengthy panegyric of John VIII Palaiologos, devotes four of his sixty-seven pages to the achievements of Carlo Tocco. He was,

[48] Sphrantzes, *Chron. Minus*, XX. 9: pp. 46–8; *Chron. Majus*, II. 9: p. 296. Zakythinos, *Despotat grec de Morée*, I, p. 211.

[49] Carlo writes of his ill-health in a letter to Francesco Loredano on 5 May 1428. His will was drawn up by his notary and secretary Ser Ambrogio on 4 June 1429. Mertzios, 'Trois lettres inédites de Charles Tocco', 353 (see above, p. 171 n. 50); Schirò, *Cronaca*, pp. 149–50. Only two sources date his death with any precision: (1) Sphrantzes, *Chron. Minus*, XX. 6: p. 46. ll. 25–6: Ἔν τε δ' αὐτῷ Ἰουλίῳ μηνὶ τοῦ αὐτοῦ ἔτους ἀπέθανε καὶ ὁ δεσπότης ὁ Κάρουλος εἰς τὰ Ἰωάννινα. Cf. Sphrantzes, *Chron. Majus*, II. 9: p. 296. (2) Schreiner, *Chron. Brev.*, I, no. 34/4: τὸ αὐτὸ ἔτος (1430) ἀπέθανεν ὁ δεσπότης Κάρουλος καὶ ἐπῆραν τὰ Ἰωάννινα οἱ Τοῦρκοι . . . The year in question in Sphrantzes is unspecified. Hopf, *GG*, II, p. 107, and *Chroniques*, p. 530, dated the event to 4 July 1429, probably taking the third word of the Sphrantzes passage to be the Greek numeral 'four' instead of the particle δέ. Aravantinos, I, p. 163, dated it to June 1430, for which there seems to be no warrant. Schirò, *Cronaca*, p. 149, and others before him accepted Hopf's dating of 4 July 1429. Schreiner, *Chron. Brev.*, II, p. 441, on the other hand, argues for accepting 1430 as the correct date. Venetian documents, however, make it clear that Carlo II had succeeded his uncle at latest by June 1430. *ActAlbVen*, II, 14, nos. 3327, 3375, pp. 30–1, 80–1; Jorga, *Notes et extraits*, I (Paris, 1899), pp. 513–15; Thiriet, *Régestes*, II, nos. 2186, 2201 (March and June 1430). If therefore one accepts the statement of Sphrantzes that Carlo I died in the month of July, then the year must be 1429.

[50] Sp. P. Lambros, Παλαιολόγεια καὶ Πελοποννησιακά, I (Athens, 1912), pp. 117–22; IV (1930), pp. 94–5.

says Isidore, a man of action, well trusted by the emperors and honoured by them with the title of Despot. His ancestral realm was insular, comprising the islands of Ithaka, Zakynthos, Leukas and Cephalonia. Little by little he added to it the Epirote portion of the Aitolians as far as the lands of the Thesprotians and the Molossians, and the area from Acheloos up to the Euenos river. The coastal parts of this territory, writes Isidore, eager to show off his erudition, are inhabited by Hellenes; but the interior and upper regions are peopled by barbarians... (among whom) are the Albanians, an Illyrian race of nomadic and wretched lifestyle, with no cities, castles, villages, fields or vineyards. The cities of Epiros, however, are still of pure Hellenic stock: Ambrakia (Arta), on the Gulf of that name, and the other (Ioannina) a city founded by one John, which stands on the Acherousian Lake and may have been the Ephyra of the ancient Thesprotians.[51]

The last Byzantine historian, Laonikos Chalkokondyles, describes, with various inaccuracies, the rise to power of Carlo Tocco, the Italian from the islands who drove the Albanians out of Akarnania and Aitolia. In the north he succeeded to the former Serbian hegemony over Ioannina and in the south he conquered the land as far as Acheloos and Aetos and Angelopolichne (Angelokastron), up to Naupaktos which is opposite Achaia; and he married the daughter of the lord of Athens and Corinth. He was, says Chalkokondyles, a man second to none of the rulers of his time in administrative and military ability.[52] The chronicler of the Tocco family would no doubt have approved of this verdict on his hero. Carlo's military prowess as a condottiere on foreign soil is attested by his achievements in the way of conquest. But his talents as an administrator are not so evident; and those who had to do business with him were frequently made aware of his volatile and untrustworthy nature. He was a citizen of Venice, yet the Venetians never knew where they were with him. For many years, between 1411 and 1417, their agents patiently tried to make him admit his liability for the seizure of one of their ships.[53] In 1417 they accused him of violating the principle of free trade by forbidding the export of grain from Arta without his permission. They

[51] Ibid., III (1926), pp. 194–5. The panegyric goes on to describe the activities and the ultimate defeat of Carlo and Torno in the Morea and how he became the relative instead of the enemy of the emperor, through the marriage of his niece to John VIII's brother Constantine (ibid., pp. 196–7). For its ascription to Isidore, see G. Mercati, *Scritti d'Isidoro il cardinale Ruteno* (Studi e Testi, 46: Rome, 1926), pp. 6–7. Cf. I. Bogiatzides, Συμβολὴ εἰς τὴν μεσαιωνικὴν ἱστορίαν τῆς Ἠπείρου, *Ep. Chron.*, I (1926), 72–80.

[52] Chalk. IV: 1, pp. 196–200 (ed. Darkó).

[53] Sathas, *Monumenta*, II, nos. 531, 535, pp. 264–9; III, nos. 572, 617, 642, 673, 713, pp. 34, 65–6, 94, 120–1, 156–7; Thiriet, *Régestes*, II, nos. 1437, 1447, 1506, 1536, 1566, 1590, 1650.

rightly suspected that this measure was designed to favour the merchants of Ragusa, who were actively interested in buying salt from Arta and Leukas instead of from Corfu or Saiata.[54] The Venetians disliked those who undercut their own free trade. They were alarmed too by his readiness to make compromises with the Turks for his own advantage. They warned him against the dangers of such tactics.[55] None the less, because he was a friend and a citizen of Venice, they were ready to grant his request for a letter of recommendation to the pope;[56] and they ranked him third in importance among the potentates of Romania with whom they had to deal, after the emperor of Constantinople and the prince of Achaia.[57]

In 1423 they had further cause to complain about his sharp practices. He had again broken his agreement about the saltpans at Naupaktos, where his son Ercole was creating havoc, and he had also appropriated some Venetian property at Parga.[58] What finally made Venice despair of Carlo was the long-standing question of his right to possession of Dragameston, which he had taken by conquest in about 1405. This was raised from time to time on behalf of the heirs of the late Francesco Foscari, who claimed that it had come to him by marriage to a daughter of Sgouros Spata. In June 1428 the Venetians lost patience and threatened to seize the goods of Carlo and his subjects if he persisted in refusing to submit the matter to independent arbitration.[59] This and many other problems remained unresolved at the time of Carlo's death. He had lived from moment to moment and when he died the Despotate which he had almost accidentally recreated was quickly proved to be an illusion. Neither in Arta nor in Ioannina is there any sign or monument of his rule. An inscription in the charming little monastery church near Monodendri

[54] *ActAlbVen*, II, 8, no. 2183, pp. 386–9 (9 July 1417); Jorga, *Notes et extraits*, I, p. 266; Thiriet, *Régestes*, II, no. 1660. Krekić, *Dubrovnik*, pp. 50, 97; Ducellier, *TM*, *VIII* (1981), 120.

[55] *ActAlbVen*, II, 11, nos. 2712–13, pp. 233–7 (18 April 1423), nos. 2807, 2811, pp. 326–8, 331–3 (13 August and 1 September 1423); Thiriet, *Régestes*, II, nos. 1901, 1904.

[56] *ActAlbVen*, II, 9, no. 2247, p. 24 (24 May 1418); Sathas, *Monumenta*, III, no. 730, p. 174; Thiriet, *Régestes*, II, no. 1693.

[57] *ActAlbVen*, II, 12, p. 195: '...nomina in quibus nostra dominatio se Compromittere contentantur sunt hec videlicet. Imperator *Constantinopolis*, Princeps *Achaie*, Despotus *Janine*...'.

[58] *ActAlbVen*, II, 11, no. 2690, pp. 188–9, no. 2689, pp. 199–200 (4 and 28 February 1423); no. 2811, pp. 332–3 (1 September 1423); Sathas, *Monumenta*, III, nos. 809, 811, pp. 242, 245; Thiriet, *Régestes*, II, nos. 1867, 1873. On 7 July 1424, however, the Venetians were pleased to accept Carlo's proposal that someone should be sent from Corfu to fix an agreed boundary line between the Despotate of Arta and Venetian territory at Anatoliko and Naupaktos. Sathas, *Monumenta*, III, no. 844, p. 268; Thiriet, *Régestes*, II, no. 1946.

[59] *ActAlbVen*, II, 13, no. 3154, pp. 69–71 (14 June 1428); Sathas, *Monumenta*, III, no. 921, pp. 333–4; Thiriet, *Régestes*, II, no. 2092. See above, p. 170 and n. 50. The affair of Dragameston was only resolved by the Turkish conquest. Maltezou, Σύμμεικτα, V (1983), 8–10.

in Zagori records that it was founded in 1413–14 by the 'voivode' Michael Therianos in the reign of the most exalted Despot Karoula the Duke. It seems to be the sole surviving memorial to the long and colourful career of Carlo Tocco, who made so much stir but left so little mark on the history of Epiros.[60]

[60] L. Politis, Ἡ κτιτορικὴ ἐπιγραφὴ τῆς μονῆς Ἁγίας Παρασκευῆς Βίτσας καὶ ἡ χρονολογία της, *Hellenika*, XX (1967), 421–6; Vranousis, *Kastron*, p. 80 (512), n. 1. Cf. Soustal–Koder, p. 125 (s.v. Besetza).

10

The Turkish conquest and the end of the Despotate – 1429–79

The history of the last years of the Despotate of Epiros has to be pieced together from isolated documents and sources. Apart from a fragmentary chronicle purporting to be a summary history of the early Ottoman sultans, which contains an account of the Turkish conquest of Ioannina, there is no historical text that provides a connected narrative of events.[1] The Greek historians Sphrantzes and Chalkokondyles give some information; and this can, with due caution, be supplemented by the Italian or Greco-Italian chroniclers of the sixteenth century, notably Stefano Magno of Venice and Theodore Spandounes or Spandugnino. Spandounes composed a treatise on the origins and customs of the Ottoman Empire which was in its final form by 1538.[2] Extracts from it were incorporated into the highly fanciful history of his family written by Giovanni Musachi in the sixteenth century.[3] Musachi called himself 'Despoto d'Epiro'. He claimed that his ancestor, Andreas II Musachi, had been granted the title and the arms of a Despot by the emperor of Constantinople, John V, about 1372. But Spandounes had correctly noted that the rank of Despot was not an office that passed by succession from one generation to another; it could only be bestowed at the benevolent discretion of the emperor on his brothers, sons, kinsmen or other great lords.[4]

[1] *Epirotica. De Rebus Epiri Fragmentum III*, in *Historia politica et patriarchica Constantinopoleos*, ed. I. Bekker (*CSHB*, 1849), pp. 240–6. Cf. Vranousis, Χρονικὰ Ἠπείρου, pp. 89–93.

[2] Stefano Magno: *Estratti degli Annali Veneti di Stefano Magno*, ed. Hopf, *Chroniques*, pp. 179–209; *Evènements historiques en Grèce (1479–1497). Extraits d'un recueil sous le nom de Stefano* Magno: in Sathas, *Monumenta*, VI (Paris, 1885), pp. 214–43. Theodore Spandounes: *Theodoro Spandugnino, Patritio Constantinopolitano, De la origine deli Imperatori Ottomani, ordini de la corte, forma del guerreggiare loro, religione, rito, et costumi dela natione*, in Sathas, *Monumenta*, IX (Paris, 1890), pp. 133–261. Cf. Nicol, *Byzantine Family of Kantakouzenos*, pp. xv–xvii.

[3] Giovanni Musachi: *Breve Memorie de li discendenti di nostra casa Musachi*, ed. Hopf, *Chroniques*, pp. 270–340 (the extracts from Spandounes are at pp. 315–35). Cf. Hopf, *Chroniques*, pp. xxxiii–xxxv.

[4] Musachi, ed. Hopf, p. 281. Cf. Dölger, *Regesten*, V, no. 3132; Ferjančić, *Despoti*, pp. 14, 78–9. Spandounes, ed. Sathas, p. 150, ll. 5–9.

Thus defined, Carlo I Tocco was the last true Despot in Epiros. The Despotate as a territorial entity which he seemed to have recreated fell apart within a year of his death. His widow Francesca for a while enjoyed the title of *basilissa* to which she had every right as the wife of a Despot. But his nephew Carlo II and his contentious bastard sons had no more right to call themselves Despots than had the sons and heirs of Gjin Boua Spata. The Venetians and the Ragusans thought it polite to address Carlo II as Despot or 'Despot of Arta', though they also knew him as 'duke of Cephalonia'. He himself adopted the circumlocution of 'Dominus Despotatus' or Lord of the Despotate. Pope Eugenius IV addressed him as such in 1432, adding the title of duke of Leucadia and Cephalonia. Spandounes reports that Carlo had it in mind to go to Constantinople for an investiture so that he could properly style himself Despot; but he had to be content with the title of lord of Arta.[5]

The unity which Carlo I had superficially imposed upon Epiros was shattered by the terms of his will. His widow Francesca received as her dower the island of Leukas with its castle of Santa Mavra and the mainland fortress of Vonitsa. For the rest the seeds of discontent had been sown many years before when Carlo and his brother Leonardo had made their plans for the future of the Despotate. Leonardo's son Carlo II inherited the islands of Cephalonia, Ithaka and Zante, as well as the cities of Ioannina and Arta. The southern portion of Aitolia and Akarnania was divided among the eldest of Carlo's illegitimate sons, Ercole, Menuno and Torno.[6] They had done, and enjoyed, much of the fighting for their late father in Epiros and the Morea. They were not content to let the best part of his legacy pass to their pampered cousin, simply because he bore the name of Tocco without the bar sinister. As early as March 1430 it was known in Venice that two of them, probably Ercole and Menuno, had imprisoned Carlo II. The Venetians at first welcomed this evidence of discord among the heirs of the late Despot. They might reap the profit by painlessly acquiring the islands of Cephalonia, Leukas and Zante. They sent an agent to negotiate with the *basilissa* Francesca at Santa Mavra. Troops and warships were to be put at the agent's disposal by the baillie of Corfu; and the islands, if and when annexed, were to be administered by a Corfiote governor.[7]

[5] *ActAlbVen*, II, 14, no. 3375, pp. 80–2 (June 1430); Mertzios, 'Trois lettres inédites de Charles Tocco', 354 (June 1432). *Bullarium Franciscanum continens Constitutiones Epistolas Diplomata ... Eugenii IV et Nicolai V*, nova series, I (*1431–1455*), ed. U. Hüntermann (Quaracchi, 1929), no. 85, p. 48: '...dilecto filio nobili viro Carolo II domino Despotatus et Leucatae ac Cephaloniae duci'. Spandounes, ed. Sathas, p. 150, ll. 15–19. Cf. Ferjančić, *Despoti*, pp. 84–6.

[6] Chalk. II, p. 15 (ed. Darkó). Hopf, *GG*, II, p. 107.

[7] *ActAlbVen*, II, 14, no. 3327, pp. 30–1 (3 March 1430); Thiriet, *Régestes*, II, no. 2186; Jorga, *Notes et extraits*, I, pp. 513–15.

As more news reached them, the Venetians lost some of their enthusiasm. The Turks too were making the most of the quarrels between the heirs to the Tocco estate. In June 1430 the baillie of Corfu reported that the Turks had plundered Leukas and taken many prisoners, and that the inhabitants were panic-stricken. The Venetians were not willing to fight to obtain the islands. With greater caution they now decided that they would take them over only if the 'Despot', Carlo II, seemed to be in danger of surrendering. If he was holding his own then they would get no further involved and would limit their action to giving him encouragement. As to the 'Lady of Santa Mavra', she could count on the protection of Venice and be persuaded to leave her island of Leukas to the Republic in the event of her death.[8]

A few weeks, later, on 6 July 1430, the senators considered the propositions put to their agents by Francesca. It appeared that she was not to be so easily dispossessed, despite the offer of safe asylum in any Venetian territory that she cared to choose. She would part with her island only on certain conditions. She asked for the annulment of any outstanding debts incurred by herself, her late husband or her father. She asked for protection for her nephew Carlo II and an assurance that his islands of Cephalonia, Zante and Ithaka (Val di Compare) would revert to her in case of his death; they would then pass to Venice by terms of her will. She asked for an annual pension of six hundred ducats for herself, to be payable to her nephew when she died. Finally, she asked that Vonitsa ('Bendeniça') and its dependencies should be considered as her personal property which would in due course pass to Carlo and his heirs and to Venice only by default. On such conditions the senators voted to proceed no further in acquiring the island of Leukas. The noble lady was advised to look to the defence of her own property, which she had so manfully defended in the past; though Venice would always be ready to give her and her family refuge in an emergency.[9]

Francesca had a mind of her own. She could also afford to look elsewhere for the defence of her possessions. In September 1430 the Venetians were disturbed to hear that one of their own galleys had been pirated by a Catalan ship in the pay of the *basilissa* of Santa Mavra and that its captain had been taken prisoner.[10] The same fate had already befallen the distinguished historian and statesman, George Sphrantzes. In March 1430 Carlo II had appealed to his brother-in-law, the Despot Constantine Palaiologos in the Morea, to mediate between himself and

[8] *ActAlbVen*, II, 14, no. 3375, pp. 80–1 (17 June 1430); Thiriet, *Régestes*, II, no. 2201.

[9] *ActAlbVen*, II, 14, nos. 3377, 3378, pp. 82–6 (6 July 1430); Sathas, *Monumenta*, I, pp. 191–2; Thiriet, *Régestes*, II, no. 2206.

[10] *ActAlbVen*, II, 14, no. 3405, pp. 108–9 (7 September 1430); Thiriet, *Régestes*, II, no. 2214.

his cousins, Ercole and Menuno. Constantine had sent Sphrantzes as his minister to effect a reconciliation and an arrangement which all parties would swear to accept. But on his way to Epiros, on 26 March, he had been captured with several others and all their treasure by a Catalan ship off the island of Leukas. That this ship too was in the pay of Francesca seems clear enough, for Sphrantzes knew that his captors' intention was to take him off to Naples by way of Cephalonia. He was, as it happened, spared this long voyage; for after a while he was delivered back to Clarentza on payment of a ransom.[11]

The reconciliation which he had been sent to achieve between the claimants to Epiros never occurred. It would have been difficult in any case to reconcile the third of Carlo's bastards, Menuno. Chalkokondyles describes Menuno as the most talented of them; he was also no doubt the least contented with the settlement that confined him and his brothers to Aitolia and Akarnania.[12] His sights were set on the cities of Ioannina and Arta. Almost as soon as Sphrantzes had disappeared, he and his brother Ercole went to see the sultan to beg the help of a Turkish army for the recovery of their inheritance. The sultan was Murad II, son of Mehmed I with whom their father had been on friendly terms. But he was a different man with a different view of how to deal with the petty princes of the Greek world. In March 1430 he directed the assault that led to the second and final Turkish capture of Thessalonica. The city had been a Venetian colony since 1423. The Venetians had taken it over from its Byzantine governor with high hopes of realising its commercial potential and turning it into a second Venice. Their hopes had never been fulfilled. Thessalonica had become an expensive liability. On 29 March 1430 the Turks broke in. Its citizens had been given the option of surrender. Many of them would have taken it. But their leaders thought otherwise and, as a consequence, all alike suffered the plunder, slaughter and destruction visited on their city by the conquering Turks.[13] The Tocco brothers must have known that the cities of Epiros would suffer the same treatment if they chose to resist instead of surrendering. But they had gone to seek the sultan's help and it was now too late. They were his vassals and they must take the consequences.

The attack on Thessalonica had been led by Sinan Beg, the Beglerbeg of Rumelia. As soon as he was free, the sultan ordered him to take his

[11] Sphrantzes, *Chron. Minus*, XXI. 1: p. 48; *Chron. Majus*, IX: p. 298. The *Majus* adds the figure of 5,000 gold pieces – 'a ransom', as William Miller puts it, 'such as no archaeologist would now fetch' (Miller, *Latins in the Levant*, p. 396).

[12] Chalk. II, p. 15, lays the blame solely on Menuno (Memnon). The Venetians, however, thought that Ercole was the chief culprit.

[13] A. E. Vacalopoulos, *A History of Thessaloniki*, translated by T. F. Carney (Thessaloniki, 1963), pp. 65–75; Nicol, *Last Centuries of Byzantium*, pp. 365–7.

army west into Epiros. Menuno and Ercole Tocco went with him. They marched through Aitolia, attacking Leukas on the way; but their main objective was Ioannina, where Carlo II was to be found. In May and June 1430 word reached Venice and Ragusa that the Turks had launched a massive attack on Ioannina with the object of taking it and other places belonging to the 'Despot' Carlo.[14] The operation took longer than they expected. The fragmentary Greek chronicle records that the people of Ioannina occupied the passes in the Pindos mountains and twice foiled the enemy's attempt to break through. The Turks suffered heavy casualties and were forced to return to Thessalonica. The sultan then addressed a letter to Ioannina, written in Greek and urging its citizens to avoid their own destruction by surrendering. He reminded them that God had set no limits to his empire; that he was already master of the Orient and of nearly all the West; and that by resisting they would only bring upon themselves the obliteration of their city in a welter of bloodshed from which the survivors would be sold into slavery. If they submitted and paid him homage he promised on oath that they would never be driven out of their city so long as they remained his loyal subjects. The men of Ioannina were suitably impressed by the tone of the sultan's letter. They compared his strength, as lord of so many castles in east and west, with the weakness of their own isolated little fortress. They had heard of the fearful destruction of Thessalonica by the Turks. They knew that Murad meant what he said and would accomplish what he threatened. Rather than run that risk they elected to surrender. A delegation went to the sultan taking with them the keys of the city of Ioannina. They found him outside Thessalonica; and there oaths were exchanged and a settlement was made about the submission of their city. Murad provided them with the charter of their rights which they had requested, and they handed him the keys of Ioannina and did him homage as their lord. The suburb of Thessalonica where the ceremony was enacted was thereafter known as Kleidi, the Key.[15]

[14] *ActAlbVen*, II, 14, no. 3375, pp. 80–2 (17 June 1430); Thiriet, *Régestes*, II, no. 2201. Text reproduced with a Greek translation by K. D. Mertzios, Ἡ ἅλωσις τῶν Ἰωαννίνων, *Ep. Chron.*, XII (1938), 121–2. The Venetians believed that the Turks had come on the invitation of 'Hercules' (Ercole), bastard son of the former Despot. In Ragusa it was reported on 3 June 1430 that the sultan had left only a part of his army to fight the Despot of Ioannina and had returned to Adrianople. Jorga, *Notes et extraits*, II, pp. 272, 273; Krekić, *Dubrovnik*, no. 775.

[15] This is the account given in *Epirotica. De Rebus Epiri Frag. III* (*CSHB*), pp. 242–4, where one version of the sultan's letter is to be found. Another version of the same letter, shorter and in more demotic Greek, also existed in the nineteenth century. Both versions were first printed by F. C. H. L. Pouqueville, *Voyages dans la Grèce*, I (Paris, 1820), p. 115; V (Paris, 1821), pp. 274–6. A 'translation' (or rather a paraphrase) of the letter was printed by T. S. Hughes, *Travels in Sicily, Greece and Albania*, II (London, 1820), pp. 19–20. See Sp. Lambros, Ἡ ἑλληνικὴ ὡς ἐπίσημος γλῶσσα τῶν Σουλτάνων, *NH*, V

Chalkokondyles gives an account of the capture of Ioannina which, though less detailed, is perhaps in some respects more trustworthy. The Turkish general, whom he calls Karatzias, laid siege to the city without success for some time, until its lord Carlo II and its inhabitants called on him to make terms. Carlo asked that he should be allowed by the sultan to retain and rule over the rest of Akarnania and Epiros. On this condition he would surrender the city.[16] There is, however, no reason to doubt the authenticity of the sultan's letter to Ioannina. It must have had its effect in persuading Carlo and his people to give in. But another and a more important document survives which makes it clear that the decision to submit was taken not by Carlo Tocco but by the bishop, the army commanders and the city fathers. While he was still conducting the siege, Sinan Beg issued a decree addressed to the metropolitan, the archons, the captain Strategopoulos and his son the captain Paul, the *protostrator* Voisavos and the *protoasekretes* Stanitzes. This document, written in Greek, is known as the *horismos* of Sinan Pasha.[17]

As captain of captains and lord of all the West, or Beglerbeg of Rumelia, Sinan explained that he had been sent by his master the Sultan to occupy the land and castles of the duke (Carlo). His orders were to do no harm to those places that paid homage without demur but to raze to their foundations those that resisted, as he had done at Thessalonica. Wherefore he advised the men of Ioannina to surrender and not to be deceived by the false promises of the Franks who were out not to help but to destroy them, as they had destroyed Thessalonica. He swore by all that was holy, by God above and the Prophet Mahomet, by the seven copies of the Koran (*mousaphia*), by the 124,000 prophets of God, by his own soul, his head and the sword in his belt, that they need have no fear that they

(1908), 40–78, especially 57–61; A. Bombaci, 'Il "Liber Graecus", un cartolario veneziano comprendenti inediti documenti ottomani in Greco (1481–1504), *Westöstliche Abhandlungen, R. Tschudi zum siebzigsten Geburtstag* (Wiesbaden, 1954), 288–9.

[16] Chalk. II, pp. 15–16. The Χρονικὸν περὶ τῶν Τούρκων Σουλτάνων, ed. G. T. Zoras (Athens, 1958), p. 61, following Chalk., wrongly calls the Turkish commander Καραγγία (for Καρατζίας). Cf. *PLP*, v, no. 11092.

[17] The best editions of the *horismos* of Sinan Pasha are contained in Lambros, *NH*, v (1908), 62–4, and in K. Amantos, Ἡ ἀναγνώρισις ὑπὸ τῶν Μωαμεθανῶν θρησκευτικῶν δικαιωμάτων τῶν Χριστιανῶν καὶ ὁ ὁρισμὸς τοῦ Σινᾶν πασᾶ, *Ep. Chron.*, v (1930), 208. The latter of these is reproduced in A. E. Vakalopoulos, Πηγὲς τῆς Ἱστορίας τοῦ Νέου Ἑλληνισμοῦ, I (*1204–1669*) (Thessaloniki, 1965), 289–90. Cf. K. Amantos, Οἱ προνομιακοὶ ὁρισμοὶ τοῦ μουσουλμανισμοῦ ὑπὲρ τῶν Χριστιανῶν, *Hellenika*, IX (1936), 118. The earliest edition appears to have been that published by G. Ainian in a little-known periodical called Ἀθηνᾶ published in Nauplion in 1831 (pp. 118–19). Cf. Vranousis, Χρονικὰ Ἠπείρου, pp. 36–9. This text was reproduced by Mustoxidi, *Hellenomnenon* (1847), pp. 576–7; again by Aravantinos, Χρονογραφία, II (1856), pp. 315–17; again by P. Uspenskij, *Putešestvie v Meteorskie i Osoolimpijskie monastyri v Thessalij v 1859 godu*, ed. P. A. Syrku (St Petersburg, 1896), pp. 426–7; and finally by *MM*, III, p. 282. Cf. Vranousis, Χρονικὰ Ἠπείρου, pp. 88, 104, 162. For the surviving manuscripts of the document, see Lambros, *NH*, v (1908), 62.

would be taken captive, that their children would be abducted, or that their churches would be demolished or turned into mosques. Their church bells would continue to ring as they had always done. Their metropolitan would retain his judicial authority and all his ecclesiastical prerogatives. Their archons who held fiefs would be allowed to keep them. Their ancestral holdings, their properties and their personal possessions would be guaranteed without question; and any other requests that they might make would be granted. If, however, they refused to submit and bow the knee to him, Sinan warned them that he would subject them, their church and their property to a devastation and annihilation such as he had brought to Thessalonica; and their blood would be on their own heads.

The pointed references to the destruction of Thessalonica had their effect. The promise that the church and the aristocracy would be permitted to retain their properties and privileges made the prospect of surrender tolerable if not attractive. Sinan had judged the situation well by addressing himself to the bishop and to the Greek and Serbian leaders of Ioannina. He ignored the young Carlo Tocco and his cousins who had helped to precipitate the Turkish invasion. They could be counted among the perfidious 'Franks'. The real authorities in Ioannina were the same men who had taken charge of the city after the death of the Despot Esau nineteen years before and who had been rewarded by the first Carlo Tocco when they had helped him to power in 1411. They were the Greek governor, Symeon Strategopoulos, and his son Paul, and the Serbian *protostrator* of the army, Stephen Voisavos. With their long experience, they had the good sense to see that Carlo II could never emulate his uncle, that the Turks had now come to stay, and that they had best accept the generous terms offered them by Sinan Beg. Led by their bishop they surrendered their city of Ioannina on 9 October 1430.[18]

Nothing is known of the fate of the army that had defended Ioannina or of its commanders. Later tradition, however, enshrined in the fragmentary chronicle about the fall of the city, preserves a fanciful tale about how the Turks ensured possession of it. There were at first only eighteen of them sent there as settlers. They announced their presence by a salute of

[18] Sphrantzes, *Chron. Minus*, XXI. 7: p. 50, ll. 3–4, sets the capture of Ioannina by Sinan Pasha in October in the context of the year 1430. A chronological note at the end of *Epirotica. De Rebus Epiri Frag. III* (*CSHB*), p. 246, records that 'the Turks took Ioannina in the year 6939, indiction 9, A.D. 1431, October 9th. Others, however, say that they took it in the same year as Thessalonica, in 6938, A.D. 1430'. *Epirotica. De Rebus Epiri Frag. V* (*CSHB*), p. 253, also gives the option of 6939 (= 1431) or 6938 (= 1431). The correct date, however, is 1430. Cf. Hopf, *GG*, II, p. 107; Romanos, *Despotate*, p. 86; Sp. Lambros, Ἡ παράδοσις τῶν Ἰωαννίνων, in Lambros, Ἱστορικὰ Μελετήματα (Athens, 1884), pp. 167–72; Mertzios, *Ep. Chron.*, XII (1938), 117–22; Schreiner, *Chron. Brev.*, I, nos. 58/5, 60/14, 62/5, 69/11, 71/6, 76/2, 77/1, 92/3, 101/5, 102/10, II, pp. 443–4.

guns from the castle and then, in defiance of the terms of surrender, demolished the cathedral church of the Archangel Michael. Later they built themselves a Turkish quarter outside the castle walls in the district later called Tourkopaloukon. They then looked for wives among the Christian families of the city; but none would have them. The sultan was consulted and he sent a deputy who authorised them to make their own arrangements about marriage. This they contrived by ambushing the Christian community one feast day as they were coming out of church and kidnapping the girls who took their fancy. The Christians not unnaturally lamented this authorised rape, but in time they resigned themselves to it and the fathers of the victims provided dowries for their daughters. 'Thus', says the chronicler, 'before long the infidel race of Agarenes increased its population.' This story was concocted probably no earlier than the seventeenth century.[19] Much more reliable and factual evidence about the Turkish occupation of at least one part of Epiros is contained in an Ottoman document of 1431–2 concerning the *sandjak* or province of Arvanid (Albania). The Turkish governor, Umur Beg, son of Sarutza Beg, compiled a *defter* or cadastral survey of this newly constituted province which extended from Kroia in the north down to the valley of the Kalamas river in the south. The names of all taxable villages are here listed as well as lands held by feudal lords or timariots, who were in the nature of things mainly Turks or Albanians. The document is informative about the topography and demography of the Turkish occupation of northern Epiros. But unfortunately little of its information can be referred back to an earlier age since the territory that it covers had long before ceased to belong to the Despotate.[20]

Ercole and Menuno Tocco had achieved their treacherous purpose of humiliating their cousin Carlo, but in so doing they had irretrievably lost one of the two chief cities of the Despotate, which can hardly have been their intention. Carlo escaped by buying his freedom. He was allowed to remain as lord of Arta and the islands on payment of tribute to the Turks and as the sworn vassal of the sultan. His troublesome cousins continued to make things difficult for him until he agreed that each of them should have a portion of territory to call his own. They too were held in fee by the Turks. In 1436 Ercole seems to have been lord of Angelokastron, Menuno was in the Morea and Torno was probably at Riniasa. Menuno tried to get the best of all worlds by asking the Emperor Sigismund of

[19] *Epirotica Frag. III*, pp. 244–6. Aravantinos, I, pp. 166–7. Cf. Vranousis, *Kastron*, pp. 3–4 (462–6).

[20] H. Inalcik, *Hicrî 835 Tarihli Sûret-i defter-i Sancak-i Arvanid* (Türk Tarih Kurumu Yayinlarandan, XIV/I: Ankara, 1954); idem, 'Arnawutluk', *Encyclopedia of Islam*, I (1960), pp. 650–8. Cf. A. E. Vacalopoulos, *Origins of the Greek Nation*, pp. 149–50; Soustal–Koder, p. 76.

Hungary to confer on him and his heirs the title to Ioannina and Arta, a request which the emperor was pleased to grant in view of Menuno's 'Christian character'.[21] The capture of Ioannina was indeed the beginning of the end. The Tocco family were soon to be driven back to the islands from which they had initiated their adventure on the Greek mainland. The sultan would see to it as soon as he had time to spare from greater projects.

The Despot 'Carolus secundus', as the Venetians styled him, had little of the spirit of his father Leonardo or of his formidable aunt, the *basilissa* Francesca, who had adopted him. Francesca's name disappears from the records after 1430. Left to his own devices, Carlo turned to Venice. Early in 1433 he sent an embassy to explain his problems. Now that the Turks had deprived him of Ioannina and a large part of the Despotate, he was afraid that they would shortly take Arta and the rest of his ancient heritage and would then attack the islands of Leukas, Cephalonia and Zante. He felt isolated with no other friends in the world. The Genoese, the Catalans and the Turks had no time for him. He therefore looked to Venice to help him preserve at least his islands, in which they had a lively commercial interest and which they would not want to see either in Turkish or in Greek hands. The Venetians were sympathetic but non-committal. They reminded Carlo that they had always held his family in high esteem. Like his ancestors, he too was a citizen of Venice and so entitled to the respect and protection of the Republic. To boost his confidence they declared him to be an honorary member of their highest council, the Maggior Consiglio.[22]

This empty honour cannot have brought Carlo much comfort. The Turks were closing in and he had good reason to be apprehensive. But Arta was perhaps not quite so isolated as he complained. Merchants from Venice and increasingly from Ragusa continued to come and go; and early in 1436 Carlo was able to play host to a distinguished scholar from Italy. His aunt Francesca many years before had deplored the fact that the only visitors to Cephalonia were boorish business men. It must have been much the same in Arta, until the arrival there of the Italian humanist,

[21] Chalk. II, p. 16. Spandounes, p. 150, says that some of the bastards went to the Sultan Murad, some to the Despots of the Morea and one to Venice. It has been supposed that the 'frère du duc de Chifalonie nommé Magnoly', whom Bertrandon de la Broquière saw at the Sultan's court at Adrianople in 1433 was Menuno. *Le Voyage d'Outremer de Bertrandon de la Broquière*, ed. C. Schefer (Paris, 1892), p. 195. Hopf, *GG*, II, p. 107. But by 1436 Menuno had settled in the Morea. See below, p. 206. For his request to Sigismund, see Jorga, *Notes et extraits*, V, pp. 318–19 (14 December 1433).

[22] *ActAlbVen*, II, 15, nos. 2549, 3550, pp. 4–6; II, 17, no. 3549 *bis*, p. 129 (14–15 March 1433); Sathas, *Monumenta*, III, no. 1007, pp. 416–17; Thiriet, *Régestes*, III, no. 2313. Hopf, *GG*, II, p. 107. Carlo neglected to tell Venice that he was on very cordial terms with the government of Ragusa, who sold him a brigantine in March 1436. Krekić, *Dubrovnik*, nos. 857, 859.

Ciriaco de' Pizzicolli of Ancona, at the start of one of his antiquarian tours of Greece. He had meant to put in at Corfu, but pestilence was raging there and he spent Christmas of 1435 at Butrinto. From there he sailed down the coast by way of Parga, Phanarion and 'Arnatium' (? Riniasa), past the site of Nikopolis and into the Ambracian Gulf. His ship carried him up the Arachthos river to the city of Arta, or as he calls it the ancient Akarnanian Arachthea, which he had longed to see.[23] Ciriaco seems to have known Carlo's secretary, Giorgio Ragnarolo of Pesaro, who made him welcome and introduced him to his employer. On 10 January 1436 Ragnarolo's son Prospero took him to visit Rogoi, whose real name he believed to be Astacora. There he saw the famous relic of St Luke as well as the head of St Anne, the Virgin's mother, and a foot of St John Chrysostom. Two days later he toured the ruins of Nikopolis and what he thought was Dodona. He also went hunting in the woods of Aktion with 'Jacobo Rufo', then governor of Leukas. His journey south took him by the ruins of Ambrakia ('Fidokastro') and Stratos to Vonitsa. But before he left Arta he dedicated a copy of his *Naumachia regia* to his host Carlo Tocco, and submitted to him an account of his travels and observations in Epiros. Carlo must have enjoyed being addressed as 'the most excellent Despot of the Romans, duke of Leukas and Zakynthos, most noble scion of the famous house of Tocco of Naples and illustrious and most serene emperor of the Epirotes'.[24]

Ciriaco has nothing to say about Carlo's troubles with his cousins. But in May 1436 he revisited Arta. On his way there he was entertained as a guest by Ercole Tocco at Angelokastron, which he describes as being in Aitolia by the river Acheloos. By way of thanks to his host he wrote a pretty little poem in Greek, in which he compares the two sons of Ercole, Carlo and Leonardo, with the godlike sons of Priam. From Arta he went on to be a guest at the wedding of a daughter of Torno, to whom he had been given a letter of introduction. The wedding took place at 'Orionatium', which may have been Riniasa on the coast, since Ciriaco sailed on from there to Corfu. In the following year he came back to Greece by way of Zante; and it was perhaps while he was there that Carlo provided him with a letter of introduction to his other cousin, Menuno,

[23] *Kyriaci Anconitani Itinerarium*, ed. Laurentius Mehus (Florence, 1742), pp. 59–64 (Letter III: to Franciscus and Crassus, dated 29 September [1435]). E. W. Bodnar, *Cyriacus of Ancona and Athens* (Collection Latomus, XLIII: Brussels, 1960), pp. 27–9; E. Ziebarth, Κυριακὸς ὁ ἐξ 'Αγκῶνος ἐν 'Ηπείρῳ, *Ep. Chron.*, I (1926), 110–19; K. Simopoulos, Ξένοι ταξιδιῶτες στὴν 'Ελλάδα, I: *333* μ. *X. –1700*, 2nd ed. (Athens, 1972), pp. 301–15.

[24] *Kyriaci Itinerarium*, ed. Mehus, pp. 66–7 (Letter IV: Georgio Ragnarolio Pisaurensi Inclyti Epirotarum Regis Secretario). Ziebarth, *Ep. Chron.*, I (1926), 114–15. 'Jacobo Ruphu' is probably Jacopo Rosso (or Russo) who became one of the regents after Carlo's death. See below, p. 209. Bodnar, *Cyriacus of Ancona*, pp. 29–32.

who was then living at Charpigny in the Morea.[25] These pleasantries suggest that some of the edge had been taken off the animosity between Carlo and his rival; and for a few years the fragments of the Despotate coexisted in peace. So long as Carlo and his cousins paid their *haradj* regularly and made no trouble, the sultan left them alone. He had bigger things in mind than the annexation of Arta and Aitolia.

At the end of 1443 Constantine Palaiologos went back to the Morea as despot in succession to his brother Theodore II. In the spring of the following year he supervised the reconstruction of the Hexamilion wall at the isthmus of Corinth and began to prepare for war against his neighbours to the north. He chose his moment well. Plans were being laid in western Europe for a crusade that was to march to the relief of Constantinople. In the mountains of Albania, George Kastriotes, a renegade Muslim whom the Turks called Skanderbeg, was at the same time organising an uprising from the fortress of Kroia which he had made his own. The Venetians, detecting a wind of change, contemplated acquiring, by purchase if necessary, Valona, Kanina and even Argyrokastron. The crusade from the west came to grief at Varna on the Black Sea in November 1444. But Skanderbeg's rebellion in Albania worried the Turks; and the Despot Constantine's offensive in Greece was a surprising success. Athens, Thebes and much of central Greece came under his control.[26]

The spirit of revolt was infectious. Carlo II was inspired to think that he too could defy the Turks and regain his independence. He had a powerful ally. Carlo had married Ramondina di Ventimiglia, daughter of Giovanni, count of Gerace. She was his cousin, for one of his father's sisters had married the previous count, Enrico di Ventimiglia. Giovanni of Gerace was in the service of king Alfonso V of Aragon and Naples, whose expansionist plans in the east included a restoration of the former Catalan regime in Greece. Alfonso strongly disapproved of the Despot Constantine's occupation of Athens. It was his belief that Athens belonged by ancestral right to the crown of Aragon and that the Ionian

[25] *Kyriaci Itinerarium*, ed. Mehus, pp. 68–70 (Letter V: Karulo Inclyto Epirotarum Regi: De suo Itinere ex Astacore ad Dodonaeum Orionatium, XIII Kal. Juniarum [1436]); pp. 71–2 (Letter VI: S. D. Danieli Sacerdoti optumo, & amico dulcissimo suo. Memnonem se vidisse scribit, ac Lacedaemona esse profecturum). Bodnar, *Cyriacus of Ancona*, pp. 47–8. His poem to Ercole is printed in Ziebarth, *Ep. Chron.*, I (1926), 117. Miller, *Latins in the Levant*, pp. 417–18, 420–1. Charpigny, which Ciriaco transcribes as χερπινιας is perhaps to be identified with Kerpini, a little to the north of Kalavryta. Bon, *Morée*, pp. 108–10, 464–5.

[26] Jorga, *Notes et extraits*, III, p. 145 (23 December 1443); pp. 179–80, 188 (14 July and 19 October 1444); Thiriet, *Régestes*, III, nos. 2623, 2659, 2670. 'Janina' in these documents must stand for Kanina. Cf. Hopf, *GG*, II, p. 124; Zakythinos, *Despotat grec de Morée*, I, pp. 226–32.

Islands belonged to the crown of Naples. As wearer of both crowns he would defend his rights.[27]

Carlo II was for a short while a beneficiary of the imperialist schemes of Alfonso V. The count of Gerace was detailed to go to his aid with a small cavalry force and sailed to Arta. The episode alarmed the Venetians, who regarded the Catalan ships that appeared in the Ambracian Gulf as pirates; and it provoked the Turks, who are said to have suffered many casualties in an encounter with Carlo and his father-in-law.[28] But it was a momentary episode. As soon as the count had left for Italy the Turks came back to take their revenge. Carlo was defeated and captured. He was forcibly reminded that he was a tribute-paying vassal of the Sultan and, according to one account, was made to hand over his son Leonardo as a hostage.[29] The Venetians were now so annoyed that they disowned him, for all that he was a citizen of Venice and an honorary member of their council. In March 1446 they gave orders that the property which he had deposited with their government in Corfu was to be sequestered. Carlo was informed of this decision and declared that he would send a messenger to explain his conduct. But no messenger appeared and his goods, to the value of five hundred ducats, were confiscated. Some of them were used to indemnify Venetian merchants who claimed that they had been robbed or wronged in Epiros and the islands. The last Venetian document to mention Carlo II deals with this very matter, on 7 August 1447. He died just over a year later, on 30 September 1448; and so far as Venice was concerned he died under a cloud, as his uncle Carlo had died before him.[30]

Carlo I Tocco had been the last Despot of Epiros. His nephew Carlo II was the last Christian ruler of the Despotate. Ioannina was already

[27] Ibid., p. 232. Carlo II was in touch with Alfonso V as early as 1437. Jorga, *Notes et extraits*, v, p. 37. F. Cerone, 'La politica orientale di Alfonso di Aragona', *ASPN*, xxvii (1902), especially 425–6, 594–5; Hopf, *GG*, ii, p. 119.

[28] *ActAlbVen*, iii, 18, no. 4792, p. 11 (7 March 1443); no. 5005, pp. 229–30 (14 July 1444). Jorga, 'Notes et extraits', *Revue de l'Orient latin*, vii (1900), 421 (11–25 August 1444), and 424 (20 August 1444), in which the Senate orders the Captain of the Gulf to hand back two galleys to the Aragonese Giovanni of Ventimiglia, who has written and sent an envoy to explain that he was only on his way to Arta to support the Despot Carlo, his son-in-law, and that he had orders not to attack Venetian subjects.

[29] Carlo's rescue by his father-in-law 'Ioannes Vintimilius' is recorded by Aeneas Sylvius. *Aeneae Sylvii Pii II. Pontificis Maximi, in Europam sui temporis varias continentem historias*, in *Aeneae Sylvii Piccolominei Senensis... Opera* (Basle, 1571), c. xiii, p. 406. Spandounes, p. 150, l. 27, reports the taking of Leonardo as a hostage.

[30] *ActAlbVen*, iii, 19, no. 5203, p. 161 (22 March 1446); no. 5266, pp. 218–20 (14 September 1446); no. 5323, pp. 272–3 (7 August 1447). Thiriet, *Régestes*, iii, nos. 2716, 2730, 2754. Stefano Magno, *Annali*, ed. Hopf, p. 196. The exact date of Carlo's death is provided by Ciriaco of Ancona. He was in Arta at the time and attended a requiem for Carlo in the church of St Luke at Rogoi. Bodnar, *Cyriacus of Ancona*, pp. 64–5; Setton, *Papacy*, ii, pp. 97–8; Hopf, *GG*, ii, p. 120.

Turkish. Arta was to become so six months after Carlo's death. The rebellion inspired by Constantine Palaiologos in the Morea had by then been ruthlessly suppressed and punished by the Sultan Murad and his general Turachan Beg; and in October 1448 Murad had routed the last resistance of the western Christian powers at Kossovo. His armies were free to attend to less urgent matters. On Monday, 29 March 1449 they marched into Arta.[31] No historian or chronicler was on hand to record the final Turkish conquest of the original capital of the Despotate or the name of its conqueror. Some say that there was a short siege. But no doubt Arta surrendered without offering too much resistance, for there is no evidence that the Turks punished its citizens by the wanton destruction of their city.[32] With Carlo II dead, there was in fact no one to organise armed resistance. He left three sons, but in 1449 they were all still young. His widow Ramondina had already made what arrangements she could by appointing four regents or deputy governors. All that was left to govern after the loss of Arta were the islands and, on the mainland, Vonitsa, Angelokastron and Barnako ('Varnazza'), or Kandeles, which the Turks allowed them to keep for the time being. The mainland possessions were probably held by some of Carlo's cousins, who appear to have made no bid for power after his death. The four governors were in charge of the islands.[33]

Jacopo Rosso, who was responsible for Leukas and Santa Mavra, quickly concluded that the only hope of survival now lay in a new appeal to Venice. In 1449, soon after the fall of Arta, he began negotiations with the influential Corfiote nobleman, Adam de S. Ippolito, for the transfer of Leukas to direct Venetian rule. The Venetians were interested. They could find no awkward restrictions or conditions on the deal such as those proposed by the late Francesca Tocco. In April they ordered their baillie of Corfu to make plans for the occupation of the island and for the payment of pensions to its leading men. The governor of Zante also expressed the desire of his people to be united with Venice. Some of the other islanders, however, perversely supposed that they would be safer under the protection of Alfonso V of Aragon and Naples.[34]

[31] The full date is given only in *Epirotica. De Rebus Epiri Frag. V*, p. 253. Cf. Schreiner, *Chron. Brev.*, I, no. 58/8; II, p. 476.

[32] Hopf, *GG*, II, p. 120, writes of a short siege of Arta but gives no supporting evidence.

[33] Stefano Magno, ed. Hopf, p. 196. Hopf, *GG*, II, p. 120, names the four governors as: Jacopo de' Rossi, Captain of Leukadia; Andrea de' Guidi de Strione; Galeazzo de Sta Colomba; and Marino Migliaresi. He equates three of them with the Rocco (or Rosso), Guido and Meliaresi mentioned as companions of Carlo I by Chalk. I, p. 196, l. 13. See above, p. 170. Jacopo Rosso is known from Ragusan documents of 1436 as 'procurator' of the Despot of Arta, Carlo II; as 'captain of Arta' in 1441; and as being in Santa Mavra in 1443. Krekić, *Dubrovnik*, nos. 882, 886, 963, 1021; cf. nos. 1136, 1250.

[34] *ActAlbVen*, III, 20, no. 5469, pp. 111–12 (26 April 1449); Thiriet, *Régestes*, III, no. 2797.

Matters did not go as smoothly as the Venetians would have wished. It emerged that Jacopo Rosso was not after all in a position to transfer his island of Leukas. All that he could promise was that he would offer no resistance if the Venetians were to send a fleet to occupy it. They tried to tempt him with the offer of an annuity of five hundred ducats and of various guarantees to the islanders, some of whom were known to be in touch with the count of Gerace.[35] In August 1449 the Senate had to consider a request from the bishop of Cephalonia that steps should be taken to defend his island on behalf of the heirs of the late Carlo Tocco who were still of tender years. Leone Venier was appointed to proceed from Corfu to Cephalonia and to Leukas to protect the islands and to make the four governors sign a treaty which would formally place them under the suzerainty of Venice. The terms of this treaty were clearly not observed. But the Venetians felt sure that fear of the Turks would soon bring the islanders round to accepting them. They rejected a motion proposed by one of their senators that Zante and Cephalonia should be occupied by force and that the late Carlo's sons should be brought to Venice and held there until they reached the age of twenty. But they rather unkindly impounded some goods belonging to the Tocco family to pay damages to one of their merchants who had been wronged by Carlo. The sins of the father were being visited on his children.[36]

Carlo's three sons were Leonardo (III), Giovanni and Antonio. Leonardo, as the eldest, became heir to his father's estate when he came of age. He continued to call himself Despot, or Despot of Arta, even though Arta was Turkish and his 'Despotate' on the mainland was reduced to three castles.[37] He was a violent man and much disliked by the people whom he tyrannised. He is said to have rewarded the deputy governors whom his mother had appointed by putting all four of them to death.[38] In December 1458, by which date he was evidently master in his own house, he suggested that the Venetians might now be ready to take over Cephalonia, Ithaka and Zante. They were no longer interested. In January 1459 they graciously confirmed that Leonardo and his brothers were citizens of Venice and left it at that; although three years later, in October 1462, they voted to give him four hundred ducats and one

On Adam of S. Ippolito and his family, see D. Jacoby, *La Féodalité en Grèce médiévale. Les 'Assises de Romanie'* (Paris-La Haye, 1971), p. 261.

[35] *ActAlbVen*, III, 20, no. 5482, pp. 122–4 (8 July 1449); Thiriet, *Régestes*, III, no. 2805.

[36] *ActAlbVen*, III, 20, nos. 5486–88, pp. 126–30; no. 5512, p. 148 (7, 8 and 11 August, 9 December 1449); no. 5569, pp. 213–14 (4 July 1450). Thiriet, *Régestes*, III, nos. 2808, 2809, 2814, 2825. Cf. Hopf, *GG*, II, p. 120.

[37] Stefano Magno, ed. Hopf, p. 196: 'Questo Lunardo si scriveva Arte Dispotus Dux Leucate comesque Cephalonie Palatinus'. Cf. Ferjančić, *Despoti*, pp. 86–7.

[38] Stefano Magno, ed. Hopf, p. 201.

hundred men to serve in the defence of his islands.[39] Meanwhile he had looked elsewhere for support. In September 1458 Aeneas Sylvius Piccolomini was elected to the papacy as Pius II. He announced to the world that he would hold a congress at Mantua of all the Christian powers to organise a new crusade against the Turks. Leonardo Tocco felt that he was already in the front line. He sent an ambassador to Mantua to report this fact directly to the pope and the congress and to make them aware of the casualties that he and his people were suffering at the hands of the infidel. Pius II replied exhorting him to stand firm. Help was on its way in the great crusade. To tide him over the pope authorised that one warship be sent to Leonardo with a grant of three thousand florins.[40]

On 1 May 1463 Leonardo married Milica, daughter of Helena Palaiologina, who had retired to a convent on Leukas after the death of her Serbian husband Lazar. Milica was a granddaughter of Thomas Palaiologos, the last Byzantine despot of Mistra. He died a few months before her marriage. But he died as a refugee in Rome.[41] By 1463 the Turkish conquest of the Morea, as of the Byzantine Empire, was complete. Constantinople had fallen on 29 May 1453. Mistra, capital of the despotate of the Morea, fell exactly seven years later, on 29 May 1460. In his island of Leukas Leonardo was still relatively secure. But his tenuous hold on the mainland, the last remnant of the Despotate of Epiros, could not last much longer. Very soon after the conquest of Mistra, perhaps in the same year 1460, the Turks crossed over to Akarnania and occupied Angelokastron and Barnako. One account has it that Leonardo was captured somewhere near Corinth and only escaped back to Leukas with the help of a friendly corsair. Only Vonitsa was now left. The Tocco inheritance had shrunk to its original little measure of the Ionian islands.[42]

[39] *ActAlbVen*, III, 23, no. 6733, pp. 400–1 (23 December 1458); III, 24, no. 6740, pp. 1–3 (3 January 1459); nos. 7233, 7236, pp. 478, 480 (16 and 26 October 1462). Cf. Setton, *Papacy*, II, p. 242 n. 39.

[40] L. F. A. von Pastor, *Acta Inedita Historiam Pontificum Romanorum praesertim saec. XV, XVI, XVII illustrantia*, I: *1376–1464* (Freiburg im Breisgau, 1904), nos. 88, 89, 95, pp. 119, 122 (16 and 25 November 1459; 13 April 1460). Cf. Setton, *Papacy*, II, pp. 212–13.

[41] Spandounes, ed. Sathas, p. 166; Musachi, ed. Hopf, p. 303. Papadopulos, *Versuch*, no. 99, pp. 66–7; Zakythinos, *Despotat grec de Morée*, I, p. 240. Thomas Palaiologos died on 12 May 1465. Sphrantzes, *Chron. Minus*, XLII. 10: p. 130; Schreiner, *Chron. Brev.*, I, nos. 34/31, 55/23; II, p. 528. In November 1467 Sphrantzes visited Leukas at the invitation of Leonardo's mother-in-law Helena and received some compensation from Leonardo for the suffering he had endured as a prisoner on behalf of Carlo II in 1430. Sphrantzes, *Chron. Minus*, XLV. 1: pp. 134–6; *Chron. Majus*, IV. 15: p. 568.

[42] Stefano Magno, ed. Hopf, p. 201. Three of the Short Chronicles record the fall of Angelokastron to the Turks. Schreiner, *Chron. Brev.*, I, nos. 58/12, 69/17, 77/4. But only the second of them places it in 1460, in agreement with Stefano Magno. The others date it to 1466 and 1457–8. Cf. Schreiner, *Chron. Brev.*, II, p. 496.

Without the goodwill of Venice the islands too were in peril. In 1463 Leonardo was still accounted as a faithful ally of the Republic.[43] It was in July of that year that the Venetians formally declared war on the Turks. Sixteen years later, poorer and wiser, they gave up the unequal struggle. A peace treaty was arranged between the Serenissima and the Porte in January 1479. But the 'faithful ally' Leonardo III Tocco was not a party to it nor was he included in its terms. He had been of some service to Venice during the war. His islands had accommodated thousands of refugees from the mainland. But he had caused offence by seeking the friendship and support also of the royal house of Naples, to which his forbears had owed allegiance. In 1477, after the death of his first wife Milica, he married Francesca Marzano of Aragon, a niece of Ferdinand I of Naples. The Venetians had always disputed the Neapolitan claim to suzerainty over the Ionian islands. In an outburst of indignation they disowned Leonardo, as they had ultimately disowned his father. Left out of account in the peace negotiations of 1479, his territories became an easy and a legitimate prey to the Turks. The Sultan was contemplating an invasion of the south of Italy. What better base could he find than the islands of Cephalonia, Ithaka and Zante?[44]

A paltry pretext was soon found for adding this last substantial fragment of Christian Greece to the Ottoman Empire. Leonardo had been able to hold out only by paying an annual tribute of four thousand ducats to the Turks. There was an irksome addition to this burden. Every time that a new *sandjak beg* or provincial governor arrived at Arta and Ioannina, Leonardo had to make him a present of five hundred extra ducats. The latest such governor to arrive was one of his own relatives who had gone over to the Turks, probably a son of one of Carlo Tocco's bastards. He was not yet seventeen years old, though he had already disgraced himself and been demoted from the rank of pasha. Leonardo refused to take him seriously and presented him with a hamper of fruit instead of his five hundred ducats. The matter was reported to the sultan, along with other complaints against Leonardo; and the *casus belli* was provided.[45] In the summer of 1479 the Ottoman beg of Valona, Gedik

[43] *ActAlbVen*, III, 25, no. 7347, pp. 87–8 (17 May 1463); Thiriet, *Régestes*, III, no. 3180.

[44] Spandounes, p. 166. Miller, *Latins in the Levant*, pp. 483–5. Milica is said to have been buried in the church of Santa Mavra on Leukas built by her mother Helena. E. Lunzi, Περὶ τῆς πολιτικῆς καταστάσεως τῆς Ἑπτανήσου ἐπὶ Ἑνετῶν (reprinted Athens, 1969), p. 80. On the Albanian refugees from the Morea settled in Zante, see P. Topping, 'Albanian Settlements in Medieval Greece: Some Venetian Testimonies', *Charanis Studies. Essays in Honor of Peter Charanis*, ed. Angeliki E. Laiou-Thomadakis (New Brunswick, N. J., 1980), 266–7.

[45] Spandounes, p. 166, where (line 33) the governor is named as 'Fait bassa, et era parente al detto Leonardo'. Niccolò Serra, *Storia di Zante*, ed. Hopf, *Chroniques*, p. 345, has it that the incident occurred due to Leonardo's rudeness to 'Ibraim Pasha', who had arrived with

Ahmed Pasha, was ordered to sail for the Ionian Islands with twenty-eight ships. Leonardo did not wait for them to arrive. He had fallen foul of Constantinople as well as Venice. There was no one to come to his rescue. Collecting as much of his treasure as he could carry on one ship, a hired Venetian merchantman, he fled with his family and brothers. From Leukas they made first for the castle of St George on Cephalonia and from there to Taranto and Naples. At the court of his wife's uncle, Ferdinand I, he found the haven denied him elsewhere. Lands were assigned to him in Calabria with an annuity of five hundred florins.[46]

His islands, so abruptly abandoned, were occupied by Ahmed Pasha's troops within a matter of weeks. The Turkish ships entered the Gulf of Arta and captured Vonitsa first. Leukas fell on 17 August 1479, Cephalonia on 26 August and Zante on 8 September.[47] The islanders were made to pay for Leonardo's mistakes. Those who had served him as officials were slaughtered; the castle of St George was burnt; and most of the inhabitants, men and women, were carried off to Constantinople and confined to the islands in the Sea of Marmora. There the sultan used them for a biological experiment. The husbands and wives were separated and forced to mate with Ethiopians, to see if they would produce a generation of grey-skinned slaves.[48]

Shortly after the death of the conquering Sultan Mehmed in 1481, Leonardo's brother Antonio borrowed some ships from Ferdinand of Naples and briefly occupied Cephalonia and Zante. The Venetians disapproved of this breach of their peace with the Turks. They sent a fleet to chase him out; and Antonio was killed at Cephalonia in 1483. Leonardo, who had to support one son and three daughters by his first marriage to Milica, persuaded Pope Alexander VI to supplement his annuity from Naples. He and his son Carlo both died in Rome. The subsequent history of the house of Tocco belongs not to Epiros, nor to the

a naval squadron, and that 'Ibraim was the son of a princess who was related to the Tocchi'. F. Babinger, *Mehmed the Conqueror and his time*, transl. R. Manheim, ed. W. C. Hickmann (Bollingen ser., XCVI: Princeton, N. J., 1978), p. 383, describes him as 'a cousin (of Leonardo III), that is, one of the five bastard sons of Leonardo's uncle Carlo I . . . who had gone over to the Turks and who under the name of Karlizadeler long played a part in Turkish politics'. If this were so he would have been a great deal older than seventeen.

[46] Spandounes, pp. 166–7. Miller, *Latins in the Levant*, pp. 485–6; Setton, *Papacy*, II, p. 341.

[47] Stefano Magno, ed. Hopf, p. 208; ed. Sathas, *Extrait d'un recueil sous le nom de Stefano Magno*, in *Monumenta*, VI (Paris, 1885), pp. 215–16, where the number of Turkish ships is given as forty-two ('galie 2 e fuste 40'). The dates are provided by a number of Short Chronicles. Schreiner, *Chron. Brev.*, I, nos. 40/11, 53/27, 54/22, 58/22, 66/8, 69/17, 70/33, 72/10, 77/6, pp. 315, 383, 390, 422, 514, 531, 547, 556, 576; II, pp. 520–1. Cf. W. Miller, 'Ithake under the Franks', in Miller, *Essay on the Latin Orient*, pp. 263–4.

[48] Spandounes, pp. 166–7. Miller, *Latins in the Levant*, p. 486; Babinger, *Mehmed the Conqueror*, pp. 383–4.

Ionian islands, but to the land of its origin, although its sons continued to call themselves Despots of Arta until the seventeenth century.[49] In southern Epiros, however, the name of Carlo Tocco was remembered for centuries to come. After the Turkish conquest, the district of Aitolia and Akarnania came to be known as Karli-eli, the land of Carlo. It may have been held in the sultan's name by one or more of Carlo I's bastards, for, as Spandounes observes, 'the Turks made no distinction between legitimate and illegitimate sons'.[50] When the last of them died, however, Karli-eli was allotted to a Turkish *sandjak beg* who had his headquarters at Angelokastron. In the days of Suleiman the Magnificent the *sandjak beg* of Karli-eli ruled from his capital at Angelokastron over Preveza, Santa Mavra, Vonitsa and Xeromera – all the country which had formed the first mainland province of the first Carlo Tocco.[51]

One by one the cities of the Despotate of Epiros went down in the fifteenth century. Naupaktos, already Albanian, became Venetian in 1407. Ioannina fell to the Turks in 1430, Arta in 1449. Vonitsa was the last to go, in 1479. The fortunes of Vonitsa may be taken to exemplify the fortunes of Epiros from the time of the Fourth Crusade until the Turkish conquest. By 1204 it was well established as the seat of a bishop of the Orthodox Church and as a prosperous little market town frequented by Venetian merchants. As such it became one of the cities of the separatist Greek state set up by Michael I Doukas. It was to Vonitsa that Michael II returned from the islands after the disaster at Pelagonia in 1259, to march on Arta and so open the new chapter in the history of Epiros where this volume begins. It was his son Nikephoros who, in 1294, made it over to the Angevins as part of the dowry of his daughter Thamar, along with Naupaktos and Angelokastron. Thereafter Vonitsa was no longer a Greek city for more than a few months at a time; though its inhabitants were Greek, and the subsistence of its foreign ruling class was provided by Greek farmers and fishermen.

Vonitsa served as base camp for the French and Italian forces, from the Morea and Cephalonia, who tried to bully Nikephoros's widow Anna into submission in 1305. Twice it was briefly retaken by the Despots of Epiros, first by Anna's son Thomas, and then, in the 1320s, by John Orsini, who survived the attempt of John of Gravina to do him down in 1325. But in 1331 it was recovered by Walter of Brienne and for many years was held by him, together with Leukas, as a fief from the kingdom of

[49] Lunzi, Περὶ τῆς πολιτικῆς καταστάσεως, pp. 83–6. Miller, *Latins in the Levant*, pp. 487–8; idem, 'Balkan Exiles in Rome', in Miller, *Essays on the Latin Orient*, pp. 512–13; Babinger, *Mehmed the Conqueror*, p. 384; Setton, *Papacy*, II, pp. 514–15.

[50] Spandounes, p. 150, ll. 21–2.

[51] F. Babinger, 'Beiträge zur Geschichte von Karli-eli vornehmlich aus osmanischen Quellen', Εἰς μνήμην Σπυρίδωνος Λάμπρου (Athens, 1935), pp. 140–9.

Naples. It was he who made Leukas, and with it perhaps Vonitsa, over to Graziano Giorgio of Venice in 1355. Then in 1362 it was acquired by Leonardo Tocco, whose widow invited the Knights Hospitallers to defend it in 1377. Their regime was short; and for the last hundred years of its survival as a Christian city, from 1380 to 1479, Vonitsa was held by the Tocco family. Like the city of Ioannina, but unlike that of Arta, it never succumbed to the Albanians. But its destiny had been determined for nearly two centuries by the act of its Greek Despot Nikephoros in handing it over to the French royal house of Naples.

Two marriage alliances did more to shape the character of the Despotate of Epiros than all the fighting and diplomacy of its ruling families. The first was the marriage of Helena to Manfred of Sicily in 1259. The second was the marriage of Thamar to Philip of Taranto in 1294. Each contract signed away a large portion of the country to foreign powers. Neither brought any noticeable benefits to the natives of that country. It would be pleasant to think that these unions between the Greek East and the Latin West, between two such close neighbours as Epiros and Italy, fostered some hybrid flowers in the fields of culture, literature and the arts. But there is no sign that this was so. They were engineered by hard-headed men for purely material ends, and neither country was the richer by the fusion of two cultures.

11

The administration and the economy

The history of Epiros in the middle ages is ineluctably the history of its ruling families. Contemporaries would not have expected otherwise. The Byzantines were conditioned to expect their historians to record the deeds of their ruling class. The modern historian of Epiros has to work with the records that have survived, whether in narrative or in documentary form. The Byzantine historians in Constantinople, such as Pachymeres, Gregoras or Cantacuzene, who wrote sophisticated narratives of the age in which they lived, regarded the Epirotes at worst as rebels and at best as provincials. There are no historians to put the other side of the story, until the fifteenth century when the Chronicles of Ioannina and of the Tocco family were composed. These are highly informative and very entertaining. But they were written by devoted local patriots who have little or nothing to say about the state of Epiros in its earlier years.

Not many documents have survived to illuminate the administrative, social or economic life of the Despotate. There are a few charters or fragments of charters issued by the Despots, and there are some issued by the emperors and patriarchs in Constantinople to reward the Epirotes for renouncing their rebellious ways or to chastise them for not doing so. Local documents there must have been in the archives of Arta and Ioannina, tax returns, censuses, church registers and the like. But almost the only continuous series that remain are the documents in the well-kept archives of Venice and of Ragusa (Dubrovnik); and these tell a tale, not of Greek patriotism, but of the persistence of foreigners in exploiting the markets of Epiros and protecting their business interests. One of the irreparable tragedies for the historian of Epiros was the loss during the Second World War of the Angevin archives of Naples. But they too told much the same tale. Charles of Anjou and his successors were only interested in Epiros as a stepping stone to greater things and for what they could get out of it.

The social system prevailing in Epiros must have been affected by the various changes of rulers, Greek, Italian, Serbian and Albanian. Its ethnic composition also became increasingly mixed. But society was always ordered on something close to a feudal system. Even before the thirteenth century Epiros and Thessaly were noted for their great landed estates which were virtually the private property of leading Byzantine families. The business of the Despots was to secure the unanimous loyalty of the landowners who constituted the ruling class. The very word Despotate, first found in Latin form, is a geographical rather than an institutional term, indicating an extended estate or appanage entrusted to one who held the Byzantine rank and title of Despot. Such was the Greek despotate of the Morea after the middle of the fourteenth century. None of the rulers of Epiros, of whatever ethnic origin, appropriated the title of Despot without due ceremony, which required that it be conferred by an emperor. Its conferment therefore always implied some form of participation in the imperial structure, however remote or reluctant. But it also implied, or came to imply, that its holder had some limited imperial status of his own.

The Despots in Epiros from Michael II onwards referred to their realm as their *basileia* (ἡ βασιλεία μου). Their wives were known by the title of *basilissa*, as prescribed by the etiquette of the Byzantine court; and they issued chrysobulls signed in red ink after the manner of local emperors and composed in the Greek formulae of the chancellery of Constantinople. Theodore Komnenos Doukas, as emperor in Thessalonica, did so in his own right. Michael II of Arta set the pattern for the future with his chrysobulls of 1236 and 1246 in which he confirmed the privileges and immunities of the people and clergy of Corfu.[1] The Despots enjoyed rewarding local magnates for their loyalty with grants of land and property, grants which invariably carried a hereditary title. At the end of the thirteenth century John Signorinos the *sebastos* and another Greek called Stasinos complained that their hereditary rights over landed property granted to them by the Despots in Akarnania had been infringed by the Angevin governors.[2] Foreigners as well as Greeks who served and supported the regime were also rewarded. The best attested case is that of the Venetian Jacopo Contareno who was the beneficiary of a chrysobull from the Despot Thomas in 1303; though the document expressly confirmed the fact that Contareno had already been granted a hereditary title to his estate at Vrastova.[3]

In later years, under the Italian Despots of the Orsini and Tocco families, the feudalisation of the Despotate was an accepted fact. Whole

[1] P. Lemerle, 'Trois actes du Despote d'Epire Michel II concernant Corfu connus en traduction latine', *Hellenika*, pt. IV (Προσφορὰ εἰς Στ. Κυριακίδην: Thessaloniki, 1953), 405–26; Nicol, *Despotate*, pp. 132–3, 142–3.

[2] See above, p. 64.

[3] See above, pp. 72–3.

villages and castles became the private and hereditary property of loyal soldiers or administrators, some Greek, some Italian, and some Serbian or Albanian. Such local barons seem to have raised and commanded their own armies. In 1337 Nikephoros Basilitzes and Alexios Kabasilas seized control of the castles of Arta and Rogoi. Thirty years later, in revolt against Thomas Preljubović, John Kapsokavades was able to seize and hold Arachobitsa, while Bardas took control of Hagios Donatos.[4] The most important walled cities, such as Arta and Ioannina, had their own standing armies and garrisons of a more regular nature. There are passing references to the office of *protostrator* or commander of the troops. Theodore Tzimiskes was *protostrator* in 1281, and Michael Zorianos about 1300. One Kabasilas had been *epi tou stratou* before 1321.[5] Stephen Voisavos was appointed as *protostrator* by Carlo Tocco in 1411 and remained as military commander in Ioannina until the surrender in 1430.[6]

Carlo Tocco began his career, however, by raising an army of his own. He recruited men by offering them properties on the island of Leukas; and he distributed the castles of his domain among his sons, his Italian officers and his Albanian allies with a liberal hand. In every case the donation was said to be made in perpetuity, to be held by the recipient as a hereditary property; and with it went the peasants who lived on and worked the land as well as the taxes that had formerly been paid to the central treasury of the Despotate. The Serbian and Albanian invasions of Epiros resulted in the division of the country into three, the Despotates of Arta, Acheloos and Ioannina. The *monaphentia* or single sovereignty allegedly reestablished by Carlo Tocco after his capture of Arta was no more than a fiction. The fragmentation of Epiros into a number of petty baronies was well under way before Tocco appeared on the scene. Whatever centralised administration and economy there may have been in earlier years had broken down long before 1400.

Documents of the thirteenth and fourteenth centuries continue to employ terms which had probably ceased to have any real significance. References are made to the 'theme' of Ioannina, or the 'theme' of Vagenetia, as though such military and administrative units existed as they had before 1204.[7] An added reason for distrusting the chrysobull of Symeon Uroš for John Tsaphas Orsini of 1361 is its anachronistic use of the word 'theme'. There had once been a theme of Nikopolis and a theme

[4] See above, p. 144.

[5] For Theodore Tzimiskes and Michael Zorianos, see below, pp. 221, 241–2. Kabasilas *epi tou stratou* is mentioned in the chrysobull for Ioannina of 1321: *MM*, v, p. 87, and above, p. 88.

[6] See above, pp. 177, 202–3.

[7] See above, pp. 76, 87, 141.

of Dyrrachion or Durazzo, each controlled by a *strategos* who levied the troops and collected the taxes of his province. But those days were over by the thirteenth century. The Byzantine government was for long unwilling to recognise that the domain of the rebellious Despots in Epiros could be classified as a *despotaton*. It could, however, be designated in general terms as 'the west'. From the standpoint of Constantinople both Macedonia and Epiros were undoubtedly western provinces. Syrgiannes was appointed 'commander of the castles and towns in the west' in 1330; and in the same year one George Strategos was described as 'Domestic of the western themes'.[8] But in a more particular sense the term 'west' was often used to define the state of Epiros.

Pachymeres calls Michael II 'the western Despot' or 'the Despot in the west'; and he describes Michael's son Nikephoros and his wife Anna as 'the Despot in the west' and 'the *basilissa* in the west'.[9] Manuel Philes describes Michael II as 'military commander of the western forces';[10] while one fourteenth-century document refers to the whole district of northern Epiros as 'the theme of the west', defining that area as being bounded by the towns of Kleisoura, Papingo, Libisda, Korousa and Koloneia.[11] Korousa is unidentifiable, but the other places encompass a recognisable region between Argyrokastron in the north and Konitsa in the south; though the text complicates matters by referring to Libisda as a separate 'theme'. The authenticity of this peculiar document, which purports to be a chrysobull, is not sufficiently established to allow for any conclusions. The use of the words 'theme of the west' is unique and probably fictitious. A much better authenticated document of 1315, however, coming from the patriarchate of Constantinople, refers to the monastery of St Nicholas at Mesopotamon as being located 'in the west in the (district of) Vagenetia'.[12]

It was quite natural that the emperors and patriarchs should think of Epiros as being in the west. When Philes described Michael II as 'commander of the western forces' he may simply have been implying that the Despot held an authority in the west which had been delegated to him by the emperor. But it is interesting that the Despots thought of

[8] Syrgiannes: κεφαλὴ τῶν κατὰ τὴν δύσιν κάστρων καὶ χωρῶν (text in Binon, *BZ*, XXXVIII (1938), 136). Strategos: δομέστικος τῶν δυσικῶν θεμάτων (text in Hunger–Kresten, *Register*, I, pp. 568–78; *MM*, I, pp. 151–4). Cf. Zakythinos, *Despotat grec de Morée*, II, p. 57.

[9] E. g., Pach., *De Mich. Pal.*, i. 13: I, p. 36, l. 2: τοῦ δυσικοῦ δεσπότου Μιχαήλ; i. 30; I, p. 81, l. 19: ὁ ἐν τῇ δύσει δεσπότης Μιχαήλ. Pach., *De Andron.* Pal., iii. 4: II, p. 200, l. 17; v. 30: II, p. 450, l. 6: ἡ κατὰ δύσιν βασίλισσα Ἄννα.

[10] Philes, ed. Miller, I, p. 253, ll. 18–19: ...Μιχαὴλ ὁ δεσπότης, / ὁ τῆς δυτικῆς ταγματάρχης ἰσχύος.

[11] D. A. Zakythinos, Ἀνέκδοτον βυζαντινὸν κτιτορικὸν ἐκ Βορείου Ἠπείρου, *EEBS*, XIV (1938), 277–94, especially 285–7, 293.

[12] Hunger–Kresten, *Register*, I, p. 114; *MM*, IV, p. vii: ... περὶ τὴν δύσιν ἐν τῇ Βαγενιτίᾳ.

themselves as rulers or commanders of 'the west'. In the early days the champions of the independence of the Epirote church from the patriarchs at Nicaea clearly distinguished what they called their 'western' church and society from those of 'the east'.[13] In an inscription on one of the tombs in the church of the Blachernai at Arta the Despot Michael II is described as *dysmokrator*, which may be interpreted as 'holder of sovereign power in the west'.[14] In the church at Boulgareli the Despot Nikephoros and the *basilissa* Anna are entitled σκηπτροκρατούντων τῶν δυτικῶν φρουρίων.[15] Michael Zorianos, one of the founders of a church at Mokista in Aitolia about 1300, is named as an officer of the Despot Thomas and *protostrator* of 'the western phalanx'.[16] And the poet Constantine Hermoniakos described his patron John Orsini as τὴν δύσιν δεσποτεύων.[17] When Stephen Dušan entitled himself 'emperor of the Serbs and Romans and of the Despotate of the western lands' he may have been following a long established and local usage that described Epiros as 'the west'.[18]

Nearly all that can be discovered about the administration of Epiros after the middle of the thirteenth century derives from documents emanating from Constantinople, notably the imperial chrysobulls for Kanina in 1307 and for Ioannina in 1319 and 1321. These documents naturally reflect a changed situation, when Byzantine authority had been reimposed in the areas concerned. Thus Kanina and Valona in the years after 1281 were administered by a *kephale* or κεφαλιτικεύων, though there was also a *dux* or δουκεύων of the *kastron*.[19] The case was the same in the city of Ioannina after 1318, and again about 1337 when John Angelos was appointed as *kephale* by Andronikos III.[20] This was the title which John Orsini adopted in 1323 to seduce the people of Ioannina into

[13] D. M. Nicol, 'Refugees, mixed population and local patriotism in Epiros and Western Macedonia after the Fourth Crusade', *XVe Congrès International d'Etudes Byzantines: Rapports*, I: *Histoire* (Athens, 1976), pp. 30–1.

[14] A. K. Orlandos, Βυζαντινὰ Μνημεῖα τῆς Ἄρτης. II: Ἡ παρὰ τὴν Ἄρταν Μονὴ τῶν Βλαχερνῶν. Ἀρχεῖον Βυζαντινῶν Μνημείων Ἑλλάδος (Athens, 1937), pp. 47–9: δεσπότης δυσμοκράτωρ.

[15] A. K. Orlandos, Μνημεῖα τοῦ Δεσποτάτου τῆς Ἠπείρου. Ἡ Κόκκινη Ἐκκλησία (Παναγία Βελλᾶς), *Ep. Chron.*, II (1927), 166.

[16] Zorianos: Ὁ ταξιάρχης τοῦ Μιχαὴλ Δεσπότου / καὶ δυσμικῆς φάλαγγος ὁ πρωτοστράτωρ / ὁ Ζωριανὸς Μιχαήλ.... G. Soteriades, Βυζαντιναὶ ἐπιγραφαὶ ἐξ Αἰτωλίας, Ἐπετηρὶς Παρνασσός, VII (1903), 208–15, especially 211. See below, p. 242.

[17] E. Legrand, *La Guerre de Troie ... par Constantin Hermoniakos*, in Legrand, *Bibliothèque Grecque Vulgaire*, V: (Paris, 1890), p. 3, ll. 6–9: εἰς ἀξίωσιν δεσπότου / Κομνηνοῦ Ἀγγελοδούκα / Ἰωάννου τοῦ ἥρωου, τοῦ τὴν δύσιν δεσποτεύων....

[18] See above, p. 129.

[19] P. J. Alexander, *B*, XV (1940–1), 181, l. 73: ...ὁ κατὰ καιροὺς δουκεύων εἰς τὴν εκεῖσε χώραν: ll. 79–80: ...τῶν κατὰ καιροὺς κεφαλιτικευόντων εἰς τὴν ἐκεῖσε χώραν Βαλλαγράδων καὶ Κανίνων.

[20] *MM*, V, pp. 80, 81, 86: I, p. 173.

accepting him not as their lord but as the deputy of their emperor in Constantinople.[21] It was a title that defined its holder as a servant of the imperial government, and as such it seems not to have been conferred by the Despots in Epiros.

The walled city or *kastron* was the administrative and military centre of each particular district of the Despotate. Every *kastron* was large enough to accommodate the surrounding population in time of emergency; and each had its own commander or *prokathemenos*, who exercised civil as well as military jurisdiction. The *prokathemenos* of Kanina in 1332 was Michael Malagaris.[22] In Ioannina in 1321 the *prokathemenos* was the *sebastos* Sgouros; and it seems likely that Symeon Strategopoulos held the same office in Ioannina in the fifteenth century, even though the Chronicle of Tocco regularly calls him 'captain'.[23] Doubtless each castle also had its *kastrophylax*, but none seems to be named in the sources. The most important *kastra* were Arta and Ioannina, the strength and extent of whose fortifications can still be seen. But there are many more such castles scattered around Epiros dating from the days of the Despotate. That at Rogoi, being among the best preserved, gives a good idea of what constituted urban life in the smaller cities of the Despotate in the fourteenth and fifteenth centuries. It can have differed little from the kind of life lived in and around the Angevin châteaux of Vonitsa, Angelokastron, or Naupaktos.

There is little record of the names and functions of other officers of the administration in the Despotate. One George Philanthropenos was *protoasekretes* or first secretary in Ioannina before 1357, and one Stanitzes held the same office in 1430.[24] Michael Zorianos was ἐπὶ τῆς τραπέζης for the Despot Thomas about 1300.[25] Michael Apsaras was *protobestiarios* for Thomas Preljubović in Ioannina.[26] John Tsaphas Orsini is said to have been Grand Constable in 1361 and his son-in-law to have held the rank of *protospatharios*.[27] Finally, two gentlemen are credited with the title or the rank of *kaballarios*, Nicholas Apsaras about 1330, and Myrsioannes Amirales in 1367–9.[28] Sparse though this information is it helps to reinforce the conclusion that the Despots gathered around them a few

[21] *MM*, I, p. 171. See above, p. 93 and n. 41.

[22] See above, p. 100. On the office of *prokathemenos*, see Zakythinos, *Despotat grec de Morée*, II, pp. 57–8; H. Ahrweiler, 'L'histoire et la géographie de la région de Smyrne', *TM*, I (1965), 155.

[23] Sgouros: *MM*, I, p. 86. Strategopoulos: *Chron. Tocco*, IV, c. 5, ll. 1217–18; at IV, c. 4, l. 1202, he is called ... τὸν καπετάνιον, τὴν κεφαλὴν τῆς χώρας. But the chronicler seems to use the Greek work *kephalē* in a very general sense.

[24] Philanthropenos: see below, p. 242. Stanitzes: see above, p. 202

[25] See below, p. 242.

[26] See above, p. 144.

[27] See above, pp. 140–1.

[28] Apsaras: see below, p. 244. Amerales: see above, p. 144.

well-established and wealthy Greek families who belonged to the ranks of the *eugenestatoi*. Prominent among them were the families of Apsaras, Kabasilas, Philanthropenos and Strategopoulos, some of whose descendants were to continue to play an influential part in the affairs of Ioannina long after the Turkish conquest.

The historians and chroniclers give the impression that the survival of Epiros as an independent state was assured by more or less constant warfare relieved by occasional exercises in diplomacy. But the government of the Despotate was sustained also by taxation and by trade. This required a currency which could be collected and which was acceptable to potential dealers and merchants. In this respect Epiros was not autonomous. Before 1261 its rulers had satisfied their pride by minting coins of their own, first at Arta and then for a while at Thessalonica as well. It is hard to believe that they were ever produced in sufficient quantities either for commerce or for taxation; and after the death of Michael II in 1267–8 the mint at Arta seems to have closed. There are no known coins of the Despot Nikephoros or of his son Thomas.[29] The common currency of the Despotate at least until 1318 was that in use elsewhere in the Byzantine world, the gold *hyperpyron* and its smaller silver or copper denominations. When the princess Thamar married Philip of Taranto in 1294 the financial element in her dowry was assessed in *hyperpyra*.[30] It was with *hyperpyra* that her mother Anna bribed her Latin enemies, first Duke Guy of Athens and then Philip of Savoy, to leave her in peace in 1303 and 1304.[31] It was in *hyperpyra* that the Despots settled their debts or their damages to Venice.[32] The chrysobull for Ioannina of 1319 stipulated that the coinage of the city should be that currently in circulation and no other; and that was evidently the *hyperpyra* of Andronikos II known as *trikephala*.[33]

The law relating to treasure trove as the property of the state rather than of the finder was strictly enforced. Not even the over-privileged Jacopo Contareno was exempt, nor were the citizens of Ioannina. Such treasure would usually consist of hoards of coins hurriedly buried by their owners in time of crisis. It would therefore have a special value when money was in short supply. The word *hyperpyron*, however, seems to have lost its particular significance. More and more it was used to mean simply currency or 'money of account'. By the fourteenth century the

[29] P. Protonotarios, Ἡ νομισματοκοπία τοῦ βυζαντινοῦ κράτους τῆς Ἠπείρου (1204–1268), *Ep. Chron.*, XXIV (1982), 130–50. A seal has, however, been attributed to Nikephoros. It bears the legend: σφραγὶς σεβάστου Νικηφόρου τοῦ Δούκα. V. Laurent, *Les Bulles métriques dans la sigillographie byzantine* (Athens, 1932), p. 428.

[30] See above, p. 47.

[31] See above, pp. 54, 59.

[32] See above, pp. 76, 100.

[33] See above, pp. 85, 88.

Byzantine *hyperpyron* had been so devalued that it was no longer universally acceptable even in the Greek world. In the markets of Epiros as elsewhere it had been superseded by the Venetian gold ducat and silver *grosso*. The going rate of exchange in Arta in 1324 seems to have been 12 silver *grossi* to the *hyperpyron*.[34] In other places the rate fluctuated between 10 and 12 *grossi*, presumably depending on the purity of the *hyperpyron*. In 1319 it appears that the ducat was worth about 1½ *hyperpyra*. By the middle of the fourteenth century it was worth 2; and by the end of the century it was worth 3 or possibly 4 *hyperpyra*.[35] In 1395 the Venetians claimed damages of 30,000 ducats from Carlo Tocco. In 1396 he offered to pay them the sum of 20,000 *hyperpyra*. This they agreed to accept, while pointing out that his debts really amounted to more than 5,000 ducats. If by this statement they were equating 20,000 *hyperpyra* with 5,000 ducats, then they were working on an exchange rate of 4 *hyperpyra* to the ducat.[36]

Other species of coins were also in circulation in the Despotate. The Despot John Orsini took to minting coins modelled on the *tornesi* or *deniers tournois* of the French Principality of Achaia, no doubt to facilitate trade with the Latins. His mint was at Arta and his coins depict the *kastron* with the legend: – IohS DESPOTVS / DE ARTA CASTRV. They bear a striking resemblance to the *tournois* struck by Philip of Taranto at Corfu and Naupaktos after 1294.[37] The Serbian occupation of Epiros and Thessaly probably introduced some Serbian currency into the Despotate. But it is hard to know in what form Thomas Preljubović raised his exorbitant taxes in Ioannina. The Chronicle of Ioannina fails to specify the nature of the currency in use, except in one passage where it is said that 200 *aspra* were collected to save the abbot of Metsovon from the Despot's clutches. The Byzantine *aspron* was a coin generally associated with Trebizond and Tana in the Crimea. The chronicler, who was writing some ten years after the Turkish conquest of his city, must here be guilty of an anachronism in referring the use of the Ottoman *asper* (akçe) back to an earlier period. The demotic version of the Chronicle not very helpfully translates the sum of 200 *aspra* into '150 *phlouria*' or

[34] *DVL*, I, no. 98, p. 201: 'de yperperis duobus milibus quadringentis decem ad grossos duodecim pro yperpero'. See above, p. 99 and n. 60.

[35] Cf. Thiriet, *Régestes*, I, pp. 226–7, and nos. 328, 388 (of 1358 and 1362); idem, *La Romanie vénitienne au moyen age* (Paris, 1959), p. 307.

[36] See above, p. 168 and n. 39. Thiriet, *Régestes*, I, no. 905. For the correct interpretation of this document (Senato, Misti 43, f. 120ᵛ), misleadingly summarised by Thiriet, I am indebted to Miss Julian Chrysostomides.

[37] G. Schlumberger, *Numismatique de l'Orient latin* (Paris, 1878), pp. 374–5, Pl. XIII, 16; pp. 388–9, Pl. XIII, 24, 26. C. P. Seltman, 'A hoard of coins of Frankish Greece', *Numismatic Circular*, LXXII, 6 (1964), 135; T. Gerasimov, 'Moneti na frankskija vladetel Ioan II Orsini', *Izvestija na muzeja v Trnovo*, II (1964), 29–34.

florins, though this too was a species of currency not unknown in Epiros by the fifteenth century.[38] The Albanian Despot of Arta, Gjin Spata, was quite happy to accept 8,000 florins as ransom money for the Grand Master of the Knights in 1378. Similarly, Gjin Zenevesi accepted 10,000 florins for the release of Esau Buondelmonti in 1399.[39] In both cases the ransom money came from Florence, but it would hardly have been acceptable if it could not be used. In 1411 Carlo Tocco is said to have ingratiated himself with the people of Ioannina by distributing 'ducats and florins'.[40] One cannot be so certain about the tale told in the demotic version of the Chronicle of Ioannina, that Thomas Preljubović bribed Gjin Spata to go away by giving him three horses and 5,000 florins.[41]

Most of the evidence for taxation in the Despotate comes from documents itemising various exemptions and immunities. In 1302 the inhabitants of the Angevin colony in Akarnania were declared to be exempt from payment of all taxes except the *kapnologion* and the *biologion* payable on their houses and their livestock. The document indicates that they had been paying these taxes for sixty or seventy years.[42] In other words the *kapnologion* and *biologion* must have been imposed in this area at least from the time of the Despot Michael II. The imperial chrysobull for Ioannina of 1319 lists eight taxes which had been imposed by the Despots in the past and from which the citizens were for the future to be exempt. Among them are the *kapnologion* and the *biologion*, as well as more specialised taxes which can only have been payable by such as fishermen, bee-keepers and pig-owners. The citizens were also to be freed from payment of the *kastroktisia* or contribution to the building and upkeep of castles, except for their own *kastron* of Ioannina. The state, however, retained its rights over treasure trove.[43]

The chrysobull for the Metropolis of Ioannina which the Despot John Orsini issued in 1330 seems also to have itemised a number of specific taxes from which the church's property was to be exempted. Among them were the *nomistron*, the *choirodekatia*, the *kapnologion*, the *orikē* and the *melissoennomion*, all of which are listed in the chrysobull of 1319. Also mentioned, however, are the πρεβέντα μετὰ τοῦ οἴνου δόσεως and the σιταρκεία τοῦ κάστρου. The *sitarkeia* was a tax levied, presumably in kind, for the provisioning of the garrison in the *kastron*. The *prevenda* (or *provenda*) is mentioned again in John Orsini's chrysobull for the monastery of Lykousada in Thessaly, and appears to have been an

38 *Chron. Ioann.*, c. 23, p. 91, ll. 29, 44.

39 See above, pp. 147–8, 163–4.

40 *Chron. Tocco*, c. 17, l. 1587:

41 *Chron. Ioann.*, c. 21, p. 89.

42 See above, p. 66. Cf. Zakythinos, *Despotat grec de Morée*, II, p. 233.

43 See above, pp. 85, 86 and n. 18.

adaptation of a form of levy imposed in the west.[44] Such exemptions must have benefited the local economy of Ioannina, but they cannot have brought much benefit to Epiros as a whole, still less to the central government in Constantinople when they were granted by the emperors.

The charters of exemption, however, suggest that the Despots had a quite elaborate system of taxation; and this fact implies that they must from time to time have taken a census or survey for purposes of assessing and raising it. Nothing further is known of the cadastral survey of the area which was ordered by Charles II of Anjou about 1298.[45] But the citizens of Ioannina were specifically excused this form of registration (*apographē*) in 1319.[46] Many if not most of the taxes levied must have been paid in kind and not in money. The priests of Ioannina in 1321 seem to have received their stipend mainly in wheat and barely (*sitokrithon*) and hogsheads of wine, with only fifty *hyperpyra* in cash.[47] On the other hand, the *mitaton* or enforced sale of grain to the governors or officers of a *kastron* at prices fixed by them, presupposes transactions in currency; and the Kanina chrysobull clearly mentions *hyperpyra*, even though the word may have meant no more than monetary currency.[48]

In the matter of taxation, most of the evidence is provided by documents concerned with Ioannina. There are no comparable documents for the city of Arta. This is partly because no charter of privileges has survived that might have been presented to it by an emperor or a Despot. In the matter of trade, on the other hand, it is Arta and not Ioannina which provides the information, nearly all of it from Venetian and Ragusan sources. The commercial life of Ioannina was more restricted than that of Arta. In 1319 its merchants were given the right to trade duty free (*akommerkeutoi*) in their own city and in all the cities and *kastra* of the Byzantine Empire as far as Constantinople itself. On paper this appears to be an extensive privilege. But there is little evidence to show that the merchants of Ioannina traded very far afield and none to suggest that they were active in Constantinople.

Trade in Ioannina was local, as befitted what was principally a market town. It had its wealthy aristocracy, the *eugenestatoi archontes*; and it had its rich business men, who seem to have had their houses in the *kastron*.[49]

[44] See above, p. 96. Romanos, *Despotate*, p. 66. On the *prevenda*, which is also mentioned in the chrysobull of Symeon Uroš for John Tsaphas Orsini, see G. Ostrogorsky, 'Das Chrysobull des Despoten Johannes Orsini für das Kloster von Lykusada', *ZRVI*, XI (1968), 213. See also *Chron. Mor. gr.*, l. 2696. On the *sitarkeia*, see Zakythinos, *Despotat grec de Morée*, II, pp. 236–7.

[45] See above, p. 64.

[46] See above, p. 86.

[47] See above, p. 88.

[48] Alexander, *B*, XV (1940–1), 203–4.

[49] *Chron. Ioann.*, p. 81, ll. 23–5, 59–60.

It was against these two classes of citizens that Thomas Preljubović directed his venom, exiling them and confiscating their property. The taxes that he imposed or invented are rather haphazardly listed by the chronicler, but most of them affected the market in foodstuffs. He monopolised the sale of wine, wheat, meat, cheese, fruit and fish. This meant that he or his agents stock-piled these commodities and forbade the city merchants to sell them until the stocks were exhausted.[50] But one hears nothing of imports or exports. The trade of Ioannina was no doubt brisk and profitable. But it was largely a retail trade, for the most part conducted by barter and probably not very widely spread. There was an annual fair (*panegyri*) held in October and November. This may have attracted traders from other parts of Greece, from Macedonia and Thessaly, and perhaps from Serbia and Ragusa. A Ragusan document of February 1436 records the creation of a merchant company for purposes of trade in Ioannina as well as in Arta; but nothing is heard of its success or failure.[51] Merchants from Arta are known to have lived in Ragusa; but the only people from Ioannina known to have lived there were in domestic service.[52] The chronicler of the Tocco family, a proud citizen of Ioannina, is eloquent about its beautiful countryside, its clear air and pure water; but he has nothing to say about its commercial life.[53]

The Venetians seem to have done no business at Ioannina. In almost every case where the word 'Janina' appears in a Venetian document it is fairly certain that it stands for Kanina. Kanina was on the coast. The city of Ioannina was too far inland to be of interest to Venice. Nor did it produce commodities that the Venetians required, except perhaps wheat. They had other and more accessible sources of wheat and grain. It was with the islands and the coastal cities of Epiros that they did their business, not least with Arta. There were Venetian trading stations all along the Albanian and Epirote coast, from Durazzo to Valona and Kanina, at Chimara, Butrinto, Saiata, and latterly at Parga and Phanarion at the mouth of the Acheron river. But Arta was their main centre. There they often maintained their own consul, as they did at Thessalonica, to oversee the affairs of the Venetian residents who seem to have been quite numerous in the late thirteenth and early fourteenth centuries, as

[50] *Chron. Ioann.*, p. 83, ll. 21–32. Cf. Angeliki E. Laiou-Thomadakis, 'The Byzantine economy in the medieval trade system; thirteenth–fifteenth centuries', *Dumbarton Oaks Papers*, XXXIV–XXXV (1982), 177–222, especially 209.

[51] Krekić, *Dubrovnik*, no. 852. For the fair at Ioannina, see above, p. 87.

[52] 'Rana' (?), a Greek, daughter of 'Raphta' of Ioannina was the servant of a Ragusan gentleman in 1324. 'Nicolas de Janina', who was in the service of 'Chiriacus Maropoulos', a Corfiote Greek at Ragusa, made off with his master's goods in 1428. Krekić, *Dubrovnik*, nos. 124, 758.

[53] *Chron. Tocco*, VIII, c. 1.

bankers, money-lenders, merchants and agents.[54] Some of them, notably the families of Moro and Contareno, became great landlords; others, like Bertuccio de Mazarolo in 1320, served as ambassadors to Venice on behalf of the Despots.[55]

Politics and warfare often interfered with business, and the Senate found it necessary to place an embargo on trade with Arta. This occurred in 1284, in 1318 and again in 1319.[56] In 1330 Venetian dealings in Arta were suspended for two years and in 1391 for as long as five years.[57] But as a rule business was resumed as soon as possible after the payment of damages or the settlement of debts. The greatest setback to Venetian interests in Arta seems to have been caused by the intervention of the Byzantine army about 1315. It was after that event that the Senate addressed its long list of complaints to the Emperor Andronikos II, giving details of the damage done to their agents and their property by the soldiers of Syrgiannes. They emphasised that they were law-abiding and non-partisan merchants whose affairs prospered in time of peace and suffered in the circumstances of war.[58]

The Republic of Ragusa was to do even more business with Arta and other ports of Epiros, though its merchants came later on the scene than the Venetians. They had been accorded privileges by the Despot Michael II; and by 1301 they had their own consul in Spinaritsa and the Valona district.[59] Not until 1358, however, did Ragusa become fully free to trade on its own account, when its dependence on Venice was broken after the Venetian war with Hungary. From about 1400 Arta became one of the Ragusans' principal trading centres. They had their own agents and residents there and imported much of their grain from there. Ragusa was much nearer to Arta than Venice. A letter written in Arta could reach Ragusa in about a week or ten days.[60] Their merchant ships could put in at Phanarion or Riniasa on their journey south and would sometimes sail on to Vonitsa and Kordobitsa on the further side of the Ambracian Gulf.[61] But they did most of their trade at Arta. Thanks to their special

[54] Venetian consuls in Arta: Thiriet, *Assemblées*, I, no. LXXXXI, p. 48 (1284); *ActAlbVen*, I, I, no. 24 (1315); see above, p. 77 n. 49.

[55] Bertuccio de Mazarolo: see above, p. 89.

[56] See above, pp. 72, 78–9. 89.

[57] See above, p. 168.

[58] See above, pp. 78–9.

[59] Krekić, *Dubrovnik*, nos. 5, 7 (1237 ?, 1251); nos. 62, 65, 67; p. 151 (1301, 1302).

[60] Krekić, *Dubrovnik*, no. 704 (a letter written at Arta on 17 August 1424 arrives in Ragusa on 24 August); no. 1133 (a letter written at Arta on 8 January 1448 reaches Ragusa on 18 January). For the burgeoning of Ragusan trade after 1358, see Krekić, pp. 39–65.

[61] Krekić, *Dubrovnik*, no. 528 (a Ragusan ship sails to Arta by way of 'Castrum Fanari' and 'Rinez' in February 1406). Krekić, *Dubrovnik*, nos. 873, 876 (ships sailing to Arta, 'Cerdovixa' or 'Corduuiza', and 'Vondiça' or 'Labodiza' in 1436). For Kordobitza, see Soustal–Koder, pp. 184–5.

relationship with the Turks, the Ragusans were still in business at Arta as late as 1460. In 1458 they were confidently negotiating with the sultan for the trade franchise in numerous places then within the Ottoman Empire, including Arta. By then they had all but excluded the Venetians from the Epirote market.[62]

Arta was at the centre of a rich agricultural area with good communications. It had harbours or anchorages at Kopraina and at Salagora, though ships seem occasionally to have stopped at the harbour of St Nicholas by Preveza.[63] The river Arachthos, which flowed by the castle walls, was navigable at least for small ships, as was the river Louros up as far as the castle of Rogoi.[64] The flatlands in the valleys of both rivers provided excellent pasture and grazing for horses, sheep, cows and buffaloes, and good soil for crops and vines. There was also plentiful wildfowl to be caught in the coastal districts. Carlo and Leonardo Tocco disported themselves hunting at Arta in the winter; and Ciriaco of Ancona was taken hunting in the woods at Aktion in 1436.[65] The market area of Arta, the μπόριο or *emporio,* was in the fields just outside the city walls and surrounded by merchants' houses. A Ragusan document calls it the 'burgus' of Arta. Being undefended it was vulnerable to attack and pillage, as Carlo Tocco proved on at least two occasions.[66]

The main exports or commodities most in demand by foreign traders in the Despotate were grain and salt, and the main outlets were Arta and Santa Mavra or Leukas. Most of the trade was done with Venice and later with Ragusa, though in 1331 John Orsini agreed to supply wheat to the Principality of Achaia.[67] Millet was also exported from Arta to Ragusa. By the fifteenth century Arta, Patras and Corinth were the three main sources of grain for Ragusa. Carlo I Tocco, who frequently vexed and disappointed the Venetians, always maintained friendly relations with Ragusa and its merchants, some of whom set up house in Arta.[68] One of them, Nalchus or Naleschus de Georgio (Djurdjević), lived and traded there on and off for more than thirty years, from 1393 to 1424, though just before his death he fell out with Carlo's right-hand man, Matteo

[62] Krekić, *Dubrovnik,* no. 1364 (January–May 1458); cf. no. 995 (January 1443). Ducellier, *TM,* VIII (1981), 123–4.

[63] In July 1418 ships went to load up salt at Santa Mavra, 'ad Sanctum Niccolam', or 'in Chopernam'. Krekić, *Dubrovnik,* nos. 644, 648.

[64] Ciriaco of Ancona sailed up the Arachthos river in 1436 (see above, p. 206). For the navigability of the Louros river (Rogon potamos), see Soustal–Koder, pp. 97, 252–3.

[65] *Chron. Tocco,* X, c. 12, ll. 2884–6; XII, c. 10. Ducellier, *TM,* VIII (1981), 114; see above, p. 206

[66] *Chron. Tocco,* I, c. 27, ll. 366–8; IX, c. 5, l. 2250; IX, c. 15, ll. 2553–8. Krekić, *Dubrovnik,* no. 1011: 'in burgo de Larta' (July 1443).

[67] See above, p. 98.

[68] Krekić, *Dubrovnik,* pp. 52–3, 58, 94; Ducellier, *TM,* VIII (1981), 120.

Landolfo.[69] There were also Florentine merchants doing business at Arta, mainly as middlemen acting for Venice or Ragusa. No doubt they came in the wake of Esau Buondelmonti and the Acciajuoli bankers; but the time of their greatest activity was in the fifteenth century, after Esau's death. Francesco 'Pitthi' of Florence resided at Arta as a member and a representative of a Ragusan wheat-importing company. The company was created in 1435 and registered at Ragusa on 1 February 1436, having bought from the Despot Carlo the right to collect the customs dues at Arta for one year. Some years later Francesco and his nephew Thomas were involved in a brawl at Arta.[70] Another Florentine merchant was 'Johannes Richi', who was exempted from paying duty at Ragusa on two cases of botargo or taramosalata, which Carlo had sent him as a friendly gesture in 1428.[71]

The second most important export from Epiros was salt. There were saltpans at Leukas and near Arta itself, but also along the coast in the north, at Valona and Saiata and elsewhere. Once the Venetians had acquired Corfu in 1368, they assumed a proprietorial right to the saltpans at Saiata and Butrinto on the mainland opposite the island, even though Corfu provided salt in greater quantities. In this matter too Carlo Tocco annoyed the Venetians by deliberately favouring trade with Ragusa.[72] In 1418 a Ragusan ship was sent to load salt at Santa Mavra, at 'Sancto Nicolo' or St Nicholas by Preveza, and at 'Choperno' or Kopraina within the Gulf of Arta.[73] Sometimes Ragusan ships sent to Arta for wheat were ordered to load salt as a substitute, if there was no wheat available.[74] Salt was also to be found at Naupaktos, which the Venetians acquired in 1407. Here again they had to contend with Carlo Tocco after he had seized the neighbouring tower of Anatoliko with its saltpans.[75]

Other goods exported from Arta to Ragusa included animal produce such as lard, salted meat, ham and cheese. Wax, tallow, hides and chestnuts are also mentioned; but the wine of Epiros seems not to have been to Ragusan or Venetian tastes. Not all of these commodities were locally produced.[76] Much was brought to Arta for onward shipment from the interior of the country. Arta provided a market for linen and cotton

[69] Krekić, *Dubrovnik*, pp. 85, 154–5, and nos. 704, 722; Ducellier, *TM*, VIII (1981), 117–18.

[70] Krekić, *Dubrovnik*, nos. 848, 852, 876, 921, 961, 983, 985, 1074, 1101; Ducellier, *TM*, VIII (1981), 118.

[71] Krekić, *Dubrovnik*, no. 763. For other Florentines trading with Arta, Krekić, *Dubrovnik*, nos. 937, 1090, 1343; Ducellier, *TM*, VIII (1981), 118.

[72] Thiriet, *Régestes*, II, no. 1660; Krekić, *Dubrovnik*, pp. 96–7; Ducellier, *TM*, VIII (1981), 120–1.

[73] Krekić, *Dubrovnik*, no. 648.

[74] Krekić, *Dubrovnik*, nos. 826, 828 (January 1435).

[75] See above, pp. 172, 194.

[76] Krekić, *Dubrovnik*, nos. 737 (salted meat), 726 (cheese), 854, 1343 (wax), 1404 (tallow), 968 (hides and chestnuts).

which was brought from elsewhere. Indigo too was to be found there.[77] After the late fourteenth century money rarely played much part in the transactions in the market at Arta. Barter was the normal procedure. Things had changed since the days when Venetians banked, lent or exchanged money there. Ships coming from Ragusa would unload their cargo, generally of cloth, in exchange for an equivalent load of wheat or salt or a mixed cargo. In 1452 one Ragusan ship loaded up with a cargo of grain, hides, indigo, flour, linen and ham.[78] Textiles and cloth from Ragusa were much sought after in Epiros, as they were in other parts of the eastern Mediterranean; and the Venetians, who had earlier cornered the market in Italian cloth, showed their displeasure by sending out ships from Corfu to plunder the Ragusan merchantmen heading for Arta. This may have been legitimate trade warfare. But piracy, official or unofficial, was a constant hazard.[79]

There is little evidence of overseas trade being conducted by the Epirotes themselves. It seems unlikely that the Despots maintained a regular fleet of merchant ships. The Orsini and Tocco rulers introduced a maritime element into the Despotate from their islands of Cephalonia, Leukas and Zante, and they did some trade with the Morea and with Ragusa. In 1441 a Greek business man called Dimus (or Dimcho) Kaballaropoulos was granted a licence for one year to export merchandise of all kinds from Arta to Ragusa on 'ships of the subjects of the Despot of Arta and other persons'.[80] The ships with which Carlo and Leonardo Tocco raided and occupied Clarentza came from the islands. Their achievements were hailed as heroic by their Greek chronicler but deplored as blatant piracy by the Venetians. Venice, the serene republic with a well-ordered system of shipping and agencies, looked on the Epirotes as troublesome children. There were on the other hand merchants and other citizens of Arta who lived in Ragusa from time to time, though not all of them were Greeks. 'Nicola de Calemani' (? Kalamanos), a merchant from Arta who was there in 1336, was probably a Greek.[81] 'Georgius Fumo', described as a Greek from Arta, was in Ragusa in 1428, and 'Georgius Teucer Cani' in 1438.[82] But others staying there in the fifteenth century seem to have been either Italian or Catalan.

[77] Krekić, *Dubrovnik*, pp. 100–1, and nos. 762, 1242 (linen and cotton), 1250 (indigo). Ducellier, *TM*, VIII (1981), 121.

[78] Krekić, *Dubrovnik*, no. 1250.

[79] Krekić, *Dubrovnik*, pp. 104–6; Ducellier, *TM*, VIII (1981), 122–3. The import into Arta of Ragusan cloth is particularly described in Krekić, *Dubrovnik*, nos. 1108 (September 1446), 1152 (October 1449), 1191 (November 1450), 1309 (August 1454).

[80] Krekić, *Dubrovnik*, no. 963; cf. no. 939. On the name 'Cavalaropulo' (Kaballaropoulos), see *PLP*, v, nos. 10046–10056.

[81] Krekić, *Dubrovnik*, no. 173.

[82] Ibid., nos. 762, 926.

'Antonellus Barges (or Barghis)', procurator of Carlo II at Ragusa in 1436 and 1438, is named as a Catalan; and 'Galasius Rubeus' from Arta who was in Ragusa in 1443 was the son of Jacopo 'Rubeus' or Rosso, Tocco's Italian captain of Arta, who went to Ragusa himself as an ambassador in 1448.[83]

There were others from Arta who lived in or visited Ragusa in a diplomatic capacity. 'Helisey' or 'Helisei', who was procurator of Carlo Tocco in 1423, could have been a Greek with the name of Elissaios.[84] Dimus 'Amirali' or 'Amiralius' was the representative at Ragusa of (Matteo) Landolfo, captain of Arta, in 1424 and 1436. He may have belonged to the same family as the *kaballarios* Amirales who was imprisoned in Ioannina by Thomas Preljubović.[85] Finally, Arta had the singular distinction of providing a whole family of trumpeters for Ragusa. Theodore, son of Theodore of Arta, and his brother John, began their careers there in 1424, employed by the Ragusan government on an annual contract. They did some business on the side and brought their families from Arta in 1427. Their sister Francha was also married to a trumpeter, Antonios of Arta, who died in 1430 leaving her with a daughter. Theodore was killed in battle while on service with the Ragusan army in 1430, and his brother John was then rewarded and honoured with citizenship of the Republic. John of Arta served Ragusa as a trumpeter for thirty-three years, from 1424 to 1457. But he retained possession of some fields and vineyards at Arta which he left to his sisters when he died. His son Mark entered the same service in 1445 and stayed as a trumpeter in Ragusa until his death in 1463.[86]

[83] Ibid., nos. 873, 918, 921, 1021, 1136.

[84] Ibid., no. 683. For the name Elissaios, see *PLP*, III, no. 6022.

[85] Krekić, *Dubrovnik*, no. 704 (September 1424). In 1436 he received loans of 300 and 100 *hyperpyra*. He died at Ragusa before April 1437. Krekić, *Dubrovnik*, nos. 870, 879, 904. For Myrsioannes Amirales, see above, p. 144.

[86] Krekić, *Dubrovnik*, p. 131. Other citizens of Arta who visited or lived in Ragusa were: Marinus, a priest, in 1372 (ibid., no. 134); an unnamed ambassador of Carlo Tocco in April 1433 (ibid., no. 806); a secretary of the Despot of Arta in February 1436 (no. 858); an unnamed ambassador of Carlo Tocco in March 1436 (nos. 859, 862); a representative of the Despot of Arta in May 1436 (no. 867); Benedictus, representing the Despot of Arta, in May 1443 (nos. 1004, 1006, 1010); Nicholas, a merchant of Arta, in May 1459 (no. 1391).

12

The church and cultural life

The status of the church within the Despotate often belied the political pretensions of its secular rulers. In the great days before and after the short-lived Empire of Thessalonica, Theodore Komnenos Doukas had actively encouraged his bishops to form their own synod irrespective of the patriarch at Nicaea who claimed jurisdiction over them. Under Theodore's guidance the synod appointed its own bishops without reference to Nicaea and behaved as though the church in Epiros, like the state, was wholly autocephalous and autonomous. This position had to be abandoned when Theodore's empire collapsed after 1230. The patriarch at Nicaea was then quick to send an exarch to northern Greece to remind the Orthodox bishops there and their rebel synod that they belonged to one undivided church under his authority; and this truth or fiction seems to have been generally understood in the Despotate thereafter.

Whatever the politics or the nationality of its secular rulers, the church of Epiros was technically a province of the patriarchate of Constantinople. For a while after 1261 the Emperor Michael VIII drove some of the bishops in Epiros and Thessaly into schism once again by enforcing his policy of union with the Roman church. But once Orthodoxy had been restored by Andronikos II, the patriarchs were able to reassert their authority over the Epirote church. That they did so is evident from the number of documents in the patriarchal registers of the fourteenth century referring to the appointment of bishops to such places as Durazzo, Ioannina and Naupaktos, and to the privileges of stavropegiac or patriarchal monasteries well within the boundaries of the Despotate. The political independence of Epiros was often asserted by its rulers and was often a fact; but in ecclesiastical matters the Patriarchs of Constantinople kept a firm hold. And on every occasion when a Despot sought to have his title recognised or confirmed by an emperor, it was the church which was the agent of the emperor's will by performing the solemn act of investiture, as the bishop of Ioannina and his colleagues invested first Thomas Preljubović and then Esau Buondelmonti in the fourteenth century.

In the time of John Apokaukos, in the 1220s, his metropolitan see of Naupaktos comprised ten bishoprics: Acheloos, Aetos, Arta, Belas, Vonitsa, Butrinto, Chimara, Dragameston, Dryinoupolis and Ioannina. Even in those days the metropolitan of Naupaktos, as heir to the ancient diocese of Nikopolis, was always held to be superior in rank to the bishop of Arta, for all that Arta was the seat of the Despot and the capital of his dominions. The ecclesiastical history of Arta between 1267 and the Turkish conquest in 1449 is better illustrated by its surviving churches and monasteries than by its documents. Not even the names of its bishops are recorded. Naupaktos is much better documented. In 1294 it became one of the mainland possessions of Philip of Taranto. Thirteen years later, in 1307, a Latin archbishop was installed there.[1] This event necessitated some rearrangement in the hierarchical order of the Greek Church. The metropolis of Naupaktos, now no more than titular, was relegated from the 35th to the 42nd place in the diocesan lists. Then in 1318 Ioannina, which had just submitted to the emperor, was raised to the status of a metropolis whose incumbent was to be known as *hypertimos*. Ioannina was no longer one of the ten suffragan bishoprics of Naupaktos, and in the lists as revised by Andronikos II it took its place as no. 53.[2] In the so-called *Ekthesis* of Andronikos III Naupaktos was restored to its 35th rank, but Ioannina with two other bishoprics was upgraded to no. 43.[3]

The emperor's chrysobull of 1321 accounts for four suffragan bishoprics of the new metropolis of Ioannina, though without naming them. They were most probably Belas (Vellas), Butrinto, Chimara and Dryinoupolis, all previously dependent upon Naupaktos.[4] In the fourteenth century it was the newly created metropolis of Ioannina and not the bishopric of Arta that took the place of Naupaktos so far as the patriarchs were concerned. It seems frequently to have been vacant. The synodal act of the Patriarch Philotheos of 1365, which wrongly dates the elevation of the see of Ioannina to 1285, accounts for only three metropolitans in eighty years. Two of them were able to officiate, but the third was prevented from doing so by the prevailing disorder. The first of

[1] See above, p. 67.

[2] J. Darrouzès, *Notitiae Episcopatuum Ecclesiae Constantinopolitanae. Texte critique, introduction et notes* (Paris, 1981), Notitia 17, nos. 42, 53, pp. 396, 397; Notitia 18, nos. 42, 53, p. 407. G. Parthey, *Hieroclis Synecdemus et Notitiae Graecae episcopatuum* (Berlin, 1866), Notitiae 11 and 12, nos. 43, 54, pp. 228, 229, 239. H. Gelzer, *Ungedruckte und ungenügend veröffentlichte Texte der Notitiae episcopatuum* (Abhandlungen der philosophisch-philologischen Classe der k. bayerischen Akademie der Wissenschaften, XXI/3: Munich, 1901), VII, nos. 43, 54, p. 598.

[3] Darrouzès, *Notitiae*, 19, nos. 46, 58, p. 413; 20, nos. 35, 47, pp. 417, 418. Gelzer, *Texte*, VIII, no. 49, 61, p. 608.

[4] See above, p. 87, and n. 23.

these may have been appointed in 1318, when the metropolis was created. The second may have been appointed in 1340 when, after the penance imposed on the disloyal citizens by the patriarch, a new metropolitan of Ioannina was ordered to proceed to the election of bishops.[5] He could thus have been the priest and *oikonomos* Michael Philanthropenos, founder of the monastery of St Nicholas Spanos on the island at Ioannina. The inscription in his church describes Philanthropenos as *hypopsephios* or bishop-elect; and he died in 1341–2 before his election had been confirmed.[6] The outbreak of civil war in 1341 might well have prevented him from travelling to Constantinople to be consecrated by the patriarch. The third metropolitan of Ioannina could have held office in the years between 1347, when the Patriarch John Kalekas was deposed, and 1364 when Philotheos became patriarch for the second time.

It was Philotheos who appointed Sebastian to Ioannina in 1365. In March of that year Sebastian and his successors were also accorded the title to the see of Naupaktos, for as long as that city remained in Latin hands.[7] In May of the same year Sebastian was further commissioned to take charge of the then vacant archbishopric of Leukas.[8] These arrangements did not last, for less than two years later, in 1367, a new archbishop was found for Leukas in the person of Matthew. This too proved to be a temporary measure. Matthew appeared at the patriarch's synod in Constantinople in June 1367. He had been expelled from Leukas by the 'Italians', presumably by Leonardo, father of Carlo Tocco, who had taken over the island in 1362. In July 1367 it was finally agreed with the patriarch and the emperor that Matthew should be given the title and the rights of the see of Naupaktos, though he would have to reside in Arta, whose bishop would become his suffragan. He would have jurisdiction over all the former bishoprics of Naupaktos, with the stated exceptions of Dryinoupolis and Belas.[9]

The patriarchs had a hard time trying to preserve the old order of things in the changing circumstances of Epiros in the later fourteenth century. There is no means of knowing how the Albanian Despot of Arta reacted to the imposition upon him of a Greek metropolitan bishop whose

[5] Asdracha, *REB*, XXXV (1977), 159–74 (text: 161); Darrouzès, *Regestes*, V, no. 2181. For the date (1340 and not '1347'), see O. Kresten, 'Marginalien zur Geschichte von Ioannina unter Kaiser Andronikos III. Palaiologos', *Ep. Chron.*, XXV (1983), 128–31.

[6] A. Xyngopoulos, Μεσαιωνικὰ Μνημεῖα 'Ιωαννίνων, *Ep. Chron.*, I (1926), 137–8; and see below, p. 242.

[7] *MM*, I, pp. 468–72; Darrouzès, *Regestes*, V, no. 2488. This act overruled the arrangement made by the Patriarch Kallistos in 1362, by terms of which the bishop of Cephalonia had been given the title of and the rights over Naupaktos. *MM*, I, pp. 413–15; Darrouzès, *Regestes*, V, no. 2446. Cf. Asdracha, *REB*, XXXV (1977), 171–2.

[8] *MM*, I, p. 472; Darrouzès, *Regestes*, V, no. 2490. Leukas ranked 15th in the list of archbishoprics in the fourteenth century. Gelzer, *Texte*, VIII, no. 16, p. 612.

[9] *MM*, I, pp. 490, 493–4; Darrouzès, *Regestes*, V, nos. 529, 2530.

title was that of Naupaktos. The Serbian Despot of Ioannina, Thomas Preljubović, would tolerate no such imposition. In 1367 he sent the new Metropolitan Sebastian into exile and turned his palace to secular uses.[10] Sebastian took refuge in a monastery in Thessaly. In 1371 the Patriarch Philotheos ordered him, under pain of excommunication, to go back to his see or to present himself in Constantinople. He could, if he wished, bring the metropolitan of Naupaktos with him from Arta. Sebastian knew better than the patriarch the problems of ministering to a flock whose ruling ascendancy were either Serbian or Albanian. He chose to obey the summons to Constantinople. His presence there is attested between 1372 and 1374 and again in 1381, by which date he had been transferred to the diocese of Kyzikos.[11]

From 1367 to 1381 there is no record of any metropolitan of Ioannina, whether Greek or Serbian. But in March 1381 the patriarch appointed a new incumbent. He was Matthew, bishop of Kernitza in the Morea. The former bishop Sebastian was present at the synod which approved Matthew's transfer to Ioannina and may have advised him about the difficulties he would encounter.[12] Matthew was installed in Ioannina on 8 September 1382 and, if the Chronicle tells the truth, he was promptly banished to Arta by the tyrant Preljubović. But the tyrant had already opted to seek the stamp of legitimacy from the Byzantine emperor at Thessalonica. He needed a bishop for the ceremony. Matthew was recalled to assist at the investiture of Preljubović as Despot in Ioannina.[13] Two years later, however, he was driven into exile again. When the tyrant was dead and gone he was reinstated by Esau Buondelmonti; and he had the satisfaction of assisting the bishops of Belas and Dryinoupolis at the investiture of Esau as Despot in Ioannina towards the end of 1385. Matthew died soon afterwards; and on 1 January 1386 Esau nominated as his successor Gabriel, abbot of the Archimandreion.[14] For two years Gabriel remained elected but not consecrated. When he finally reached Constantinople in 1388 the patriarchate was vacant. He was obliged to wait until the vacancy had been filled by the appointment of the Patriarch Antonios IV in January 1389. He got back to his church in Ioannina on 21 March of that year.[15]

Gabriel died in August 1406. He was succeeded in August of the same year by Joseph, who is the last properly attested metropolitan of Ioannina before the Turkish conquest, and to whom Esau Buondelmonti issued a

[10] See above, p. 144.
[11] *MM*, I, p. 594; II, pp. 24, 135; Darrouzès, *Regestes*, V, nos. 2649, 2657; VI, no. 2714.
[12] *MM*, II, pp. 23–4; Darrouzès, *Regestes*, VI, no. 2714.
[13] See above, p. 153.
[14] See above, p. 159.
[15] See above, p. 159 and no. 8.

charter of privileges in 1408.[16] When Carlo Tocco entered the city on 1 April 1411 we are told that he was greeted by the bishop and the clergy. But the bishop is not named. Esau probably professed the Orthodox faith while he was Despot in Ioannina. Carlo Tocco may have pretended to do the same. His first act in Ioannina was to pay his respects to the Archangel Michael in the cathedral. But it was an act of public relations more than of piety. In the Ionian islands from which he came the Roman faith prevailed, and his father Leonardo seems to have banished the Orthodox bishop from Leukas. On the other hand, Carlo never persecuted or harried his Orthodox subjects in Ioannina or later in Arta. Had he done so, the pious Greek chronicler of his deeds would never have so idolised him. In the end, in March 1430, it was to the metropolitan of Ioannina that Sinan Pasha addressed his declaration of the terms for surrender, and it was the metropolitan who led the delegation that handed the city over to the Turks. But his name is not recorded.

Of the other former suffragans of Naupaktos, Acheloos is known to have had a bishop called John in 1302. He was sent on a mission to the court of Naples by the *basilissa* Anna, widow of Nikephoros.[17] In December 1370, when the local Despot was the Albanian Gjin Spata, the patriarch's synod transferred a bishop of Acheloos to the metropolitan see of Corinth. The same bishop had for a time been excommunicated by his superior at Ioannina, but inquiries established that he had purged himself of whatever misdeed he had committed.[18] Belas and Dryinoupolis were detached from the jurisdiction of Naupaktos by the arrangements made by the patriarch in 1367 and assigned most probably to Ioannina, to which metropolis they belonged in the fifteenth century. Both of their bishops were present at the investiture of Esau Buondelmonti as Despot in 1385; though five years later the bishop of Belas thought it prudent to make terms of his own with the Albanians rather than see his diocese devastated.[19]

The diocese of Bouthrotos (Butrinto) on the mainland opposite Corfu had a chequered history. In 1337–8 the Patriarch John Kalekas intervened in a dispute between the monks of an unnamed monastery and the bishop of 'Bouthrotos and Glyky'.[20] This is the first mention of such a

[16] *Chron. Ioann. Oxon.*, fols. 269^{v}–270^{r}. See above, pp. 175–6. Some authorities list one Proklos of Ioannina in 1410. See, e.g., I. E. Anastasiou, in *ThEE*, VII (1965), cols. 65–9; P. G. Oikonomos, 'Η ἐν Ἰωαννίνοις Ἐκκλησία (Athens, 1966), p. 41; B. G. Ateses, Ἐπισκοπικοὶ Κατάλογοι τῆς Ἐκκλησίας τῆς Ἑλλάδος ἀπ' ἀρχῆς μέχρι σήμερον, Ἐκκλησιαστικὸς Φάρος, XXVI (1974), 440.

[17] See above, p. 65.

[18] *MM*, I, pp. 534, 540; Darrouzès, *Regestes*, V, nos. 2599, 2602.

[19] See above, pp. 159, 161.

[20] Asdracha, *REB*, XXXV (1977), 162–5 (text: 160); Darrouzès, *Regestes*, V, no. 2713; Kresten, *Marginalien*, 115–20. Asdracha (163) suggests that the unnamed monastery may have been that of Geromeri, on which see below, pp. 243–4.

combined bishopric. In 1320 Butrinto had still been Greek, when Nicholas Orsini offered to cede it to Venice. But ten years later it was back in Angevin control as an appendage to the island of Corfu; and Cantacuzene indicates that it was still so in 1339.[21] It was probably because of this change of fortune that the bishop of Bouthrotos was moved to the inland and less vulnerable site of Glyky, while retaining his former title.[22] The bishop of Chimara was in trouble with the patriarch in 1315 for trespassing on the rights of the stavropegiac monastery of St Nicholas at Mesopotamon.[23] In 1280 Chimara had been one of the coastal cities claimed by Charles of Anjou. But it must have reverted to Byzantine rule after the battle at Berat in 1281. In the fourteenth century it fell within the Serbian Despotate of John Komnenos Asen, whom Stephen Dušan made governor of Berat, Valona and Kanina. About 1360, however, it had a Latin bishop whose title was bishop of Chimara and Kozyle. He was a Dominican who, for reasons unknown, renounced his office and his Catholic faith and abjured his dogmatic errors in a submission to the Patriarch Kallistos.[24] Vonitsa too was a Latin bishopric, certainly by 1371, and probably long before.[25]

Dragameston is not heard of as an Orthodox bishopric after the early thirteenth century. Dryinoupolis, on the other hand, figures in the episcopal lists of Michael VIII. Alexios of Dryinoupolis was among the bishops who signed the dispensation for the marriage of Michael II's son to Anna Palaiologina in 1278.[26] The bishopric seems, however, to have been detached from Naupaktos and made dependent on Ioannina in 1367. The see of Kanina was evidently held by a Greek bishop in 1307, though the emperor's chrysobull confirming his rights does not give him a name. The patriarchs in the fourteenth and fifteenth centuries appear to have created some new bishoprics in Epiros. Rogoi had its own bishop by the time of the Turkish conquest. Pogoniani acquired a special importance as an archbishopric. It first appears as such, occupying the 25th rank, in the *Ekthesis* of Andronikos III. The archdiocese was probably centred on Depalitsa, the modern Molyvdoskepastos, where the church of the Holy Apostles lays claim to having been the cathedral from 1298.[27]

The church in Epiros seems usually to have managed to trim its sails to all the prevailing political winds and so to have sought or accepted

[21] See above, p. 90. A. Luttrell, 'Guglielmo de Tocco, Captain of Corfu: 1330–1331', *BMGS*, III (1977), 47, 50–6. Cantac. ii. 37: I, p. 529.

[22] On Glyky in Thesprotia, see Soustal–Koder, p. 158.

[23] See above, pp. 76–7.

[24] *MM*, I, p. 411; Darrouzès, *Regestes*, V, no. 2439.

[25] R. -J. Loenertz, 'Athènes et Neopatras, II', *BFG*, II, p. 371, no. 175.

[26] See above, pp. 21–2.

[27] For Kanina, see above, pp. 69–70. Darrouzès, *Notitiae*, 18, no. 158, p. 410; 21, no. 81, p. 420.

patronage from emperors and Despots alike. As a result it was one of the largest landowners and a most jealous guardian of its rights and privileges. Andronikos II's chrysobull of 1307 lists the extensive landed and other properties of the bishopric of Kanina. They included saltpans, fishing rights, mills, acreages of land and whole villages and farms. His chrysobulls of 1319 and 1321 confirmed the right of the church of Ioannina to possession of numerous estates and properties, together with the peasants who lived on them and worked them. The Despot John Orsini in his chrysobull for Ioannina in 1330 put the protection of the church's property above all other considerations. Esau Buondelmonti was equally considerate to the church of Ioannina in 1408. Only Thomas Preljubović presumed to treat his church like any other department of state and to relieve it of some of its wealth and worldly goods. For this if for no other reason he earned the enmity of his chronicler. Most of the Greek, Italian or Serbian Despots of Epiros were conscious of the powerful influence and popular appeal of the church and its monasteries. The Serbians had no need to advertise their Orthodoxy. But it is significant that Nicholas Orsini and his Italian successors embraced the Orthodox faith. This set them apart from most of the Latin rulers of Achaia, Athens and the Aegean islands. It emphasised their wish to be accepted by the local inhabitants of Epiros as the heirs of the Greek Despots.

The Despot Michael II and his saintly wife Theodora had set an example for their successors in building and restoring churches and monasteries in and around Arta. Among them are the church of the Panagia of Bryoni and that of St Demetrios Katsouri, both of which became patriarchal foundations in the thirteenth century; the monastery church of the Kato Panagia, on whose wall the monogram of Michael II is set in brick; and the church of St Theodora herself, which stands in the centre of Arta and contains her tomb. The monastery church of the Metamorphosis at Galaxidi on the bay of Itea in the Corinthian Gulf was, like the Kato Panagia, reputedly built by the Despot Michael II as an act of penance for his ill-treatment of his wife Theodora. It was here that the eighteenth-century Chronicle of Galaxidi was discovered.[28] Other churches built by

[28] On the churches in and around Arta built in the first half of the thirteenth century, see especially A. K. Orlandos, Βυζαντινὰ Μνημεῖα τῆς Ἄρτης (Ἀρχεῖον τῶν Βυζαντινῶν Μνημείων τῆς Ἑλλάδος), III, 1–2 (Athens, 1936–7); Nicol, *Despotate*, pp. 197–203; Soustal–Koder, pp. 114–15 (and the literature there cited). The late Byzantine monuments of Epiros as a whole are listed and described by D. I. Pallas, 'Epiros', *Reallexikon zur byzantinischen Kunst*, II (1968), cols. 257–304. For those in Aitolia and Akarnania, see A. D. Paliouras, Αἰτωλοακαρνανία. Συμβολὴ στὴ μελέτη βυζαντινῶν καὶ μεταβυζαντινῶν μνημείων (Ioannina, 1981). See also T. Paliouras, Βιβλιογραφία γιὰ τὴν Ἤπειρο (1969–79): Βυζαντινὴ ἀρχαιολογία καὶ τέχνη, *Ep. Chron.*, XXII (1980), 256–66.

Michael II were that of St Demetrios, near Kypseli or Tourkopaloukon in Thesprotia, and that of the Pantanassa near Philippiada.

St Demetrios, the katholikon of a small monastery on the bank of the river in the Kokytos valley, has the name Michael set in brick on the south wall of its transept, together with a date which appears to read 1242. In its original form it must have looked very like the church of the Kato Panagia. But about the end of the thirteenth century domed side chapels were added to the structure on north and south and a narthex spanning the whole west end. These additions may have been made by Michael's son Nikephoros.[29] The now ruined church of the Pantanassa is mentioned in the Life of St Theodora as one of the pious foundations of her husband. But it had an older history. An early Christian ambon has been discovered on the site. And it was still a church of the Despots at the end of the fourteenth century. The name 'Ιω[άννης] Δεσπότ[ης] Σπάτας is somewhat crudely carved on one of its columns. This is the only known material evidence, apart from that provided by the chroniclers and historians, for the Albanian regime at Arta of the Despot Gjin Boua Spata, between the years 1374 and 1399.[30]

The monastery church of the Blachernai or Blachernitissa, which stands across the river from Arta, was restored and partially rebuilt by Michael II. It seems to have served as the burial place of some of the Despots of Arta and their families. Two marble tombs stand in it, on one of which there is a long but now fragmentary inscription; and there are fragments of inscriptions from other tombs. One appears to have contained the bodies of two of the sons of the *basilissa* Theodora, wife of Michael II. It has been suggested that they were Demetrios-Michael and John, though the former died in prison in Constantinople some time after 1304.[31] It was at this monastery that the young Despot Thomas awaited the outcome of the attack on Rogoi by Philip of Savoy and his allies in 1304. Thomas's parents, the Despot Nikephoros and Anna, followed the lead set by Michael II. It was they who built the largest and the most unusual of all the churches of the Despotate, the Paregoritissa in Arta. The inscription over its entrance door records their names as:

On the church of St Theodora at Arta see also A. K. Orlandos, Τὸ τέμπλον τῆς 'Αγίας Θεοδώρας ᾽Άρτης, *EEBS*, XXXIX–XL (1972–3), 476–92.

[29] St Demetrios at Tourkopaloukon: A. Chatzinikolaou, *AD*, XXI (1966), B, 295–6; Pallas, 'Epiros', cols. 289, 291; Sp. Mouselimis, 'Η Μονὴ Τουρκοπαλούκου, *Ep. Hest.*, XIX (1970), 693–700; Soustal–Koder, p. 140.

[30] Pantanassa: P. L. Vokotopoulos, ᾽Ανασκαφὴ Παντανάσσης Φιλιππιάδος 1976, *AAA*, X (1977), 149–68, especially 162–3, 166; idem, in Πρακτικὰ τῆς 'Αρχαιολογικῆς 'Εταιρείας (1977), 149–53. Soustal–Koder, p. 225.

[31] Pach., *De Andron. Pal.*, V. 18–19: II, pp. 407–9. Blachernitissa: Orlandos, Βυζαντινὰ Μνημεῖα, III, 2, pp. 1–50; Nicol, *Despotate*, pp. 197–8; M. Acheimastou-Potamianou, Βυζαντινὲς τοιχογραφίες στὴ Μονὴ Βλαχερνᾶς τῆς᾽Άρτας, *AAA*, VIII (1975), 208–16; Soustal–Koder, pp. 125–6.

Komnenodoukas the Despot Nikephoros, Anna Palaiologina, and their Komnenian offspring ('Komnenoblastos'), who is described as Despot. Their offspring must be Thomas, who was born in 1288–9 and was made Despot by Andronikos II in 1294. The church of the Paregoritissa can thus be fairly precisely dated between 1294 and 1296, the year of the death of Nikephoros. Tradition has it that, in its present form, it was built by a pupil of the architect who had designed the Blachernitissa and that the achievement so angered his master that he cast his pupil down from the dome.[32]

The building of churches and monasteries in the Despotate was not confined to members of the ruling family. As in other parts of the Byzantine world in the thirteenth and fourteenth centuries, and in Constantinople itself, there were still private benefactors prepared to invest their money in the cause of saving their own souls. The church of the Virgin known as the Kokkine Ekklesia or Panagia Bellas at Boulgareli was built and decorated in 1281. The donors were the *protostrator* Theodore Tzimiskes and his brother John, along with their wives Maria and Anna. The fact is recorded in a long inscription above the west door of the nave; and portraits of the founders presenting their church to the Virgin are painted on the walls of the narthex. The inscription states that the church was built during the reign of the Despots Nikephoros and Anna, 'who then held sway over the western fortresses' (σκηπτροκρατούντων τῶν δυτικῶν φρουρίων).[33] Theodore Tzimiskes, who is otherwise unknown, must thus have been *protostrator* of the Despot's army about the time of the battle at Berat in 1281. It is surely no accident that the church at Boulgareli stands like a halfway house on one of the two main routes between Arta and Trikkala, Epiros and Thessaly. On the Thessalian side the route comes down from the hills at Pyli; and there stands the church of the Porta Panagia built by the half-brother of Nikephoros, the *sebastokrator* John Doukas, at almost the same time, in 1283.[34]

At Ioannina two of the little monastery churches on the island in the lake were built by private benefactors in the thirteenth century. That of St Nicholas *tou Ntiliou* is traditionally associated with the family of Strategopoulos.[35] That of St Nicholas Spanos is more certainly con-

[32] Paregoritissa: A. K. Orlandos, Ἡ Παρηγορίτισσα τῆς Ἄρτης (Athens, 1963); P. L. Vokotopoulos, *AD*, XXVII (1972 [1977]), B, 460–3, 465; Pallas, 'Epiros', cols. 249, 266–75, 277; Soustal–Koder, pp. 114–15.

[33] Boulgareli, near Drosopigi, some 30 km north-east of Arta. See A. K. Orlandos, Μνημεῖα τοῦ Δεσποτάτου τῆς Ἠπείρου. Ἡ Κόκκινη Ἐκκλησία (Παναγία Βελλᾶς), *Ep. Chron.*, II (1927), 153–69; Pallas, 'Epiros', cols. 275–6; Soustal–Koder, p. 131; K. A. Petronikolos, Τὸ Βουργαρέλι (Δροσοπηγή) Τζουμέρκων (Athens, 1977), pp. 43–8.

[34] Koder–Hild, *Hellas*, pp. 245–6.

[35] St Nicholas *tou Ntiliou*: A. Xyngopoulos, Μεσαιωνικὰ Μνημεῖα Ἰωαννίνων, *Ep. Chron.*,

nected with the family of Philanthropenos. An inscription above the entrance to the nave of the church refers to its foundation in 1292 by Michael Philanthropenos, priest and *oikonomos* of the metropolis of Ioannina. Another inscription in the narthex dates the death of this Michael to 1341–2, by which time he had himself been elected as metropolitan of Ioannina. Portraits of five members of the founding family in supplication to St Nicholas accompany the inscription; and among them is George Philanthropenos, once *protoasekretes* of Ioannina, who died in 1357. The others portrayed are sixteenth-century members of the family.[36]

Another military commander of the Despotate put up the money to build a church in Aitolia about 1300. Of the three Byzantine churches at Mokista, near the ancient Thermon, that of the Taxiarchai was built at the expense of the *protostrator* Michael Zorianos and his friend or relative Kosmas Andritsopoulos. Zorianos also held the rank of ἐπὶ τῆς τραπέζης of Thomas Doukas Komnenos of Epiros.[37] Both men are known from other sources to have been writers.[38] In the same district of Mokista an inscription was found recording the name of the *basilissa* Anna Cantacuzene, mother of the Despot Thomas; and the church of the Dormition at Zapanti (Megale Chora) also in Aitolia once contained another inscription relating to Anna.[39]

Another private benefactor of the church in Epiros may have been the *protobestiarios* Andronikos Palaiologos, the eldest son of Demetrios-Michael and grandson of the Despot Michael II. Andronikos was governor of Berat and district for Andronikos II in 1326 and may have served there some years earlier.[40] A later manuscript copy of what

I (1926), 133f. M. Acheimastou-Potamianou, Νέα στοιχεῖα περὶ τῆς Μονῆς τοῦ ‘Αγίου Νικολάου τοῦ Ντίλιου εἰς τὴν νῆσον τῶν ’Ιωαννίνων, *AD*, XXIV (1969), A, 152–75; S. I. Dakaris, Τὸ Νησὶ τῶν ’Ιωαννίνων. ‘Ιστορία, Μνημεῖα, Μουσεῖο, 2nd ed. (Athens, 1982), pp. 35–45; Soustal–Koder, pp. 205–6.

36 St Nicholas Spanos: Xyngopoulos, *Ep. Chron.*, I (1926), 53–62. M. Acheimastou-Potamianou, Νέα στοιχεῖα περὶ τῆς Μονῆς τῶν Φιλανθρωπηνῶν εἰς τὴν Νῆσον τῶν ’Ιωαννίνων, *AAA*, VI, 3 (1973), 457–63; Pallas, ‘Epiros’, cols. 295–7; Dakaris, Τὸ Νησὶ τῶν ’Ιωαννίνων, pp. 27–35; Soustal–Koder, pp. 205–6. Michael Philanthropenos is known to have presented a manuscript of the Gospels to the monastery, which he calls that ‘of St Nicholas called of Kyr Iakobos’. E. K. Chrysos, ‘Ιστορικὰ στοιχεῖα γιὰ τὴν ”Ηπειρο σὲ σημείωμα τοῦ κώδικα Cromwell 11, *Ep. Chron.*, XXII (1980), 58–65, especially 64–5.

37 Mokista: P. Lazarides, in *AD*, XVI (1960), B, 198; P. Vokotopoulos, in *AD*, XXVII (1972), B, 441. The inscription in the church was originally published by G. Soteriades, Βυζαντιναὶ ἐπιγραφαὶ ἐξ Αἰτωλίας, ’Επετηρὶς Παρνασσός, VII (1903), 208–15. A. D. Paliouras, Αἰτωλοακαρνανία, pp. 178–88; Soustal–Koder, p. 208.

38 See below, p. 247.

39 Sp. Lambros, ”Αννα ἡ Καντακουζηνή. Βυζαντιακὴ ἐπιγραφὴ ἐξ Αἰτωλίας, *NH*, I (1904), 36–42. Zapanti: Paliouras, Αἰτωλοακαρνανία, pp. 117–20; Soustal–Koder, p. 280.

40 See above, pp. 93–4.

purports to be a founder's inscription refers to the creation of three monasteries 'in the theme of the west' by one 'Komnenos Palaiologos', his wife Helena and his sons Simon and Nikephoros, with the blessing of the Emperor Andronikos of Constantinople.[41] There are many reasons for suspecting the truth of this document as it now stands; and the location of two of the alleged monasteries, that of St Nicholas at 'Seltzi' and that of St Athanasios at 'Bougresi', cannot be determined. The third, however, is described as that of the Theotokos in the 'theme of Libisda'. It has been suggested that this was the monastery church of the Virgin at Molyvdoskepastos or Depalitsa on the Albanian frontier, which bears an inscription relating to its reconstruction by 'Andronikos Komnenos and Megas Doukas Palaiologos'.[42] Molyvdoskepastos was the seat of the archbishop of Pogoniani, a place associated with Libisda by John Cantacuzene.[43] But the inscription in the church is not wholly reliable. It was not written until 1561; and it seems more probable that it refers not to the *protobestiarios* Andronikos but to the Emperor Andronikos II, who so liberally extended his favours to the church of Ioannina in 1319 and 1321. The church of the Holy Apostles at Molyvdoskepastos was also first built about the end of the thirteenth century, though in its present form it dates from the sixteenth and seventeenth centuries. A list of the archbishops of Pogoniani gives the year 1298 as the date of its foundation and consecration as the cathedral.[44]

A better-substantiated foundation of the fourteenth century is the monastery of Geromeri or Geromerion, which stands in the hills above the modern town of Philiates to the north of Igoumenitsa. As it now stands, the monastery church dates from its renovation in 1568, by which time it had become a *stavropegion* dependent on the patriarch alone and free from the jurisdiction of the metropolitan of Ioannina. But it was first founded by a monk called Neilos Erichiotes about the year 1330.[45] Among the manuscripts in the monastery library are the Life of St Neilos, in the form of a *synaxarion*, and his last will and testament. The Life survives in a sixteenth-century copy, the original text having been written by a monk called Job, who could conceivably be the same monk Job who composed the Life of St Theodora of Arta. The testament exists in a copy made in the nineteenth century.[46]

[41] D. A. Zakythinos, 'Ανέκδοτον βυζαντινὸν κτιτορικὸν ἐκ Βορείου Ἠπείρου, *EEBS*, XIV (1938), 277–94 (text: 293–4).

[42] Ibid., 289–91; Pallas, 'Epiros', cols. 298–303.

[43] Cantac. iii. 12: II, p. 81.

[44] Molyvdoskepastos: D. M. Nicol, 'The Churches of Molyvdoskepastos', *Annual of the British School at Athens*, XLVIII (1953), 141–53; Soustal–Koder, pp. 140–1 (s.v. Depalitsa).

[45] Geromeri: L. I. Vranousis, Γηρομερίου, μονή, *ThEE*, IV (1964), cols. 496–502; D. Triantaphyllopoulos, *AD*, XXIX (1973–4), B, 624–5: Soustal–Koder, pp. 156–7.

[46] The Life and the Testament of Neilos were printed in part by P. Aravantinos, Περὶ τοῦ

Neilos, who was later to be revered as a local saint, came of the family of Laskaris and he was born about 1250. As a young monk in Constantinople he suffered for his opposition to the union of Lyons in the late 1270s and was sent into exile. After the restoration of Orthodoxy in 1282, he came back to be acclaimed as a martyr for the true faith. He then went to the Holy Land and spent a total of thirty-one years at Mt Sinai, Mt Carmel, Jericho, and in a monastery by the Jordan. Late in his life he felt impelled to travel again. He sailed by way of the Aegean islands to the Morea, to Corfu, and then over to the mainland of Epiros. He landed at Erichos or Hierichos, near Valona, and there built himself a hermit's cell, becoming known and respected in the district as Neilos Erichiotes. Before long he was persuaded to move further inland, to a cave in a mountain glen at Geromeri. His fame attracted disciples. Two of them, Kallinikos and Gerasimos, helped him to make a clearing in the hillside opposite his cave and to render it, as he says, serviceable and fit for monastic tranquillity. There he erected a church dedicated to the Mother of God, which became the katholikon of the monastery of Geromeri.

One of its first benefactors was a local nobleman (*paneugenestatos*) called John Apsaras (or Opsaras) who donated a vineyard to the monastery. Neilos also commemorated in his will the archons of the district, the *kaballarios* Nicholas Apsaras and Aristarchos Kapandrites. In particular he prayed that the Despot John Angelos Doukas and his 'most Christian' wife the *basilissa* Anna Palaiologina might enjoy long life, a peaceful reign and victory over their enemies visible and invisible. He prayed too that their children should, under God's protection, succeed to the government of their Despotate (*despoteia*) and enlarge its territory. The Despot John is without doubt John Orsini, husband of Anna and father of Nikephoros and Thomais. Neilos must surely have been unaware that John had made himself master of Epiros by murdering his own brother Nicholas; and it was as well that he died before his 'most Christian' *basilissa* disposed of her husband by poisoning him in 1337. The will and testament of Neilos with regard to the future of his monastery was confirmed by a charter of John Orsini in December 1336, declaring that its terms would be respected for ever by himself and by all his successors in the Despotate.[47]

The monastery of St Nicholas at Mesopotamon near Delvino, to the

῾Οσίου Νείλου τοῦ ᾿Εριχιώτου, Νέα Πανδώρα, xv (1865), 470–4; more fully by B. Krapsites, Θεσπρωτικά, II (Athens, 1972), pp. 160–78 (texts: pp. 161–2, 163–7).

[47] ed. Krapsites, p. 167. Krapsites, like Aravantinos and Vranousis, assumed that the confirmation of the will of Neilos was made by the emperor and not by the Despot John. In its existing form of a nineteenth-century copy it bears no signature. But the references in it to the *basileia* of its author and to the heirs of his *despoteia* are quite consonant with the terminology used by the Despots of Epiros. The date, December 1336, if correct, may provide a *terminus ante quem* for the death of John Orsini. See above, p. 105.

north of Geromeri, was an older foundation whose rights as a *stavropegion* were confirmed by the patriarch in 1315. Its abbot went to Naples in 1302 as an ambassador of Anna, widow of Nikephoros. Later in the fourteenth century one of its monks, Niphon, was to spend some time as a hesychast at the monastery of Geromeri. St Nicholas is the largest of the Byzantine churches in Albania, notably similar in architectural style and in some of its decorative features to the church of the Blachernai near Arta. It probably dates from the time of the Despot Nikephoros, when the region of Mesopotamon was under Angevin occupation, before 1286. The fleurs de lys to be seen on the floor of the narthex of the church were the arms of Charles of Anjou; and the fact that the nave had two apses and two altars may indicate that it was used for the Catholic as well as for the Orthodox rite.[48]

A few other churches bear inscriptions which make it possible to date them to a precise period in the history of the Despotate. The church of the Metamorphosis at Chrysobon in the hills above the Mornos river to the north-east of Naupaktos has fragments of wall-paintings dated to the year 1270.[49] That of the Holy Apostles at Neromanna near Agrinion has wall-paintings dated to 1372–3; and the monastery church at Vitsa (Besetza) near Monodendri in Zagori has an inscription recording its foundation in 1413–14 by the 'voivode' Michael Therianos in the reign of Carlo Tocco.[50] There are many more churches in Epiros which can be assigned to the time of the Despotate by reason of the style of their architecture or their decoration. Notable among them are the little church at Kostaniani, between Ioannina and Dodona, which appears to belong to the thirteenth or fourteenth century. It bears much resemblance to the church of the Kato Panagia at Arta and the church at Boulgareli.[51] That of St Nicholas Rodias near Arta, a small and probably private chapel dependent on a monastery of the Virgin called Rodia, also dates from the second half of the thirteenth century and contains frescoes of the fourteenth century.[52]

In Thesprotia, on the foothills of the Paramythia mountains on the east side of the Kokytos valley, there are thirteenth-century churches at

[48] See above, pp. 76–7. F. Halkin, 'La vie de Saint Niphon, ermite au Mont Athos (XIVe siècle)', *Analecta Bollandiana*, LVIII (1940), 12–13. On the church at Mesopotamon, see A. Meksi, 'Arkitektura e kishës së Mesopotamit (L'architecture de l'église de Mesopotame)', *Monumentet*, III (1972), 47–95; idem, 'Të dhëna të reja për kishën e Mesopotamit (Nouvelles données sur l'église de Mesopotame)', *Monumentet*, X (1975), 151–9.

[49] Chrysobon: P. Lazarides, in *AD*, XXI (1966), B, 269–72; Soustal–Koder, p. 138.

[50] Neromanna: Paliouras, Αἰτωλοακαρνανία, pp. 173–7; Soustal–Koder, pp. 109–10. Vitsa (Monodendri): see above, pp. 194–5 and n. 60; Soustal–Koder, p. 125.

[51] Kostaniani: D. Evangelides, in *Ep. Chron.*, VI (1931), 258–74; Pallas, 'Epiros', cols. 297–300; Soustal–Koder, p. 186.

[52] St Nicholas Rodias: Orlandos, in Ἀρχεῖον Βυζαντινῶν Μνημείων, III, 2 (1936), 131–47; Soustal–Koder, p. 213.

Gardiki and at Zerbochori. The former, dedicated to St Kyriaki, has typical thirteenth-century brickwork on its apse and a round window above its west entrance. The latter stands at Kaminia, above the village of Zerbochori (or Dragomi) and is dedicated to St Demetrios. It has been much overbuilt and only its apse can be assigned to the thirteenth century.[53] Further north, near Konitsa, the church known as the Kokkine Panagia has frescoes which may date to the early fifteenth century;[54] while down in Aitolia the church of St George near the village of that name and that of the Virgin at Palaiokatouna near Katochi, both in the district of Mesolonghi, are said to date in part at least from the end of the thirteenth century.[55] Finally, the churches known as the Soter *ton Spheton* and the Panagia Alichniotissa, both in the neighbourhood of Vonitsa, belong to the thirteenth and fourteenth centuries respectively.[56]

A pleasing local legend has it that the monastery of the Dormition called Dourachani, across the lake from the city of Ioannina, was founded or enriched in the fifteenth century by the Turkish commander Turachan, Beglerbeg of Rumelia. It is said that on one dark winter's night, after he had crossed the Pindos mountains from Thessaly, he led his army over the frozen water of the lake in happy ignorance of its existence. When he discovered how near to death he had been, he attributed the miracle to the Virgin and as a thankoffering refurbished her monastery on the lakeside. Thereafter it was known as Dourachani or Turachan's monastery.[57] Turachan Beg certainly passed through Epiros about 1436 on his way north to suppress an Albanian revolt and to relieve the siege of Argyrokastron.[58] But it seems unlikely that he would have been ignorant of the fact that Ioannina had a lake; and the monastery as it now stands gives no sign of being as old as the fifteenth century.

Culturally the Despotate was something of a backwater. The church might have inspired and promoted literary and scholarly activity, and to begin with it undoubtedly did. In the early years of the thirteenth century

[53] Gardiki: D. Evangelides, Ἡ βυζαντιακὴ ἐκκλησία τῆς Ἁγίας Κυριακῆς τοῦ Γαρδικίου (Παραμυθίας), Ἀφιέρωμα εἰς τὴν Ἤπειρον. Εἰς μνήμην Χρίστου Σούλη (1892–1951) (Athens, 1956), 129–36; Pallas, 'Epiros', cols. 291–2; Soustal–Koder, p. 154. Zerbochori: Vokotopoulos, *AD*, XXI (1966), B, 295; XXII (1967), B, 351; Triantaphyllopoulos, *AD*, XXIX (1973–4), B, 625–6; Pallas, 'Epiros', col. 292; Soustal–Koder, p. 145.

[54] Kokkine Panagia: Pallas, 'Epiros', col. 298; Soustal–Koder, p. 183.

[55] Paliouras, Αἰτωλοακαρνανία, pp. 139–41, 271–4; Soustal–Koder, pp. 156, 220.

[56] Paliouras, Αἰτωλοακαρνανία, pp. 257–60, 275–6; Soustal–Koder, pp. 128, 262–3.

[57] Dourachani: The story is recorded most fully by Aravantinos, Χρονογραφία, I, p. 162, n. 2. Cf. Sp. Lambros, Ἡ λίμνη τῶν Ἰωαννίνων καὶ αἱ ἐπὶ τῆς νησίδος αὐτῆς μοναί, *NH*, XI (1914), 4–5; idem, Σύμμικτα, *NH*, XI (1914), 315–16; P. G. Oikonomos, Ἡ ἐν Ἰωαννίνοις Ἐκκλησία (Athens, 1966), pp. 102–3.

[58] Chalk. V: II, p. 30; *Chron. Turk.*, ed. Zoras, p. 66, ll. 7–13. Gegaj, *L'Albanie et l'invasion turque*, pp. 52–3.

the church could boast of the presence of a number of learned bishops, such as John Apokaukos of Naupaktos, George Bardanes of Corfu, and Demetrios Chomatianos of Ochrida. But these cultured men were all products of the Constantinopolitan schools and the tradition of learning that had existed before 1204; and that tradition was not perpetuated after they were dead. Schools there must have been and libraries too, but neither Arta nor Ioannina seems to have produced scholars of distinction; nor did any of the Despots found institutions of higher learning. It could be said that their deliberate isolationism cut them off from the mainstream of the continuing tradition of education in Constantinople.

The monk Job Melias Iasites, who composed the Life of St Theodora of Arta and perhaps also that of St Neilos Erichiotes of Geromeri, may have had local connexions in Epiros. But he lived and wrote in Constantinople; and, apart from hymns, his literary output consisted mainly of anti-Latin, anti-unionist polemics. Like St Neilos, Job was sent into exile by Michael VIII about 1275. His interest in Epiros may well have been stirred by the fact that there the true Orthodox faith was preserved unsullied during the dark days before and after the union of Lyons.[59] In later years Epiros contributed nothing to the remarkable revival of classical scholarship and of interest in the Hellenic past which flourished at the court of Andronikos II and at Thessalonica in the early fourteenth century. One of the scholar-monks of that revival, Joseph the Philosopher, who died about 1330, is said to have come from Ithaka. But he got his education in Thessalonica and Constantinople.[60]

Very few names of authors or scribes in the Despotate are known, though this must be partly due to the chance survival of manuscripts. Rare exceptions are the two gentlemen who endowed one of the churches at Mokista in Aitolia about 1300, Michael Zorianos and Kosmas Andritsopoulos. Zorianos, who was *protostrator* of the Despot Thomas, was the author of some verses addressed to St Matthew the Evangelist. Andritsopoulos wrote a short but curious prophetic work about the fall of the empire and the coming of the Antichrist.[61] At about the same time a *notarios* composed for the bishopric of Ioannina a Sticherarion with musical notation, which is now in the British Museum.[62] Michael Philanthropenos, priest and *oikonomos* of Ioannina, put together a Gospel book which he presented to the monastery of St Nicholas Spanos on the

[59] On Job, see Vranousis, Χρονικὰ Ἠπείρου, pp. 49–54; *PLP*, IV, no. 7959.

[60] On Joseph the Philosopher, see D. M. Nicol, *Church and Society in the Last Centuries of Byzantium* (Cambridge, 1979), pp. 57–8.

[61] On Michael Zorianos, see M. Vogel and G. Gardthausen, *Die griechischen Schreiber des Mittelalters und der Renaissance* (Leipzig, 1909), p. 312; *PLP*, III, no. 6666. On Andritsopoulos, see Sp. Lambros, Ἡ πρόρρησις τοῦ Ἀνδριτζοπούλου, *NH*, III (1906), 474–6; *PLP*, I, no. 940.

[62] Cod. BM Add. 27865.

island; and two noblemen, the *megalepiphanestatoi* Constantine Melitas and Nicholas Mesarites, presented a book of canon law, which may or may not have been written in Ioannina, to the cathedral of the Archangel Michael before 1319.[63]

The Italian ascendancy in Epiros never inspired anything like the hybrid literature and poetry that was later to be produced in Venetian Crete. The Orsini family tried hard to become hellenised, but they seem to have contributed little in the way of Italian or western culture to their surroundings. John Orsini commissioned a very second-rate poet called Constantine Hermoniakos to compose a collection of tales from Homer. This tedious compilation of 9,800 lines of trochaic octosyllabic verses reveals some pedantic ingenuity but it can hardly be said to have much literary merit.[64] Nor did Epiros produce any native historians to carry on the Byzantine tradition of Greek historiography in the classical style, as George Akropolites had done in the Empire of Nicaea. The Chronicle of Ioannina and the Chronicle of the Tocco family, both composed in the fifteenth century, are uniquely informative and sometimes vividly descriptive works. But neither of them could be classed as monuments of great literature. There were certainly architects, artists and craftsmen in Epiros under the Despots and some of their work is original in style and inspiration and of high quality. The evidence for literary and scholarly creativity is by comparison disappointingly small; and even the few manuscripts known to have been of Epirote provenance are mainly religious in content and unoriginal in form.

[63] Cod. Mus. Benaki 53; Cod. Sinait. gr. 1641. See Vranousis, *Kastron*, p. 28 (460); Chrysos, *Ep. Chron.*, XXII (1980), 64–5.

[64] E. Legrand, *La Guerre de Troie . . . par Constantin Hermoniakos*, in Legrand, *Bibliothèque Grecque Vulgaire*, v (Paris, 1890). H. -G. Beck, *Geschichte der byzantinischen Volksliteratur* (Munich, 1971), pp. 168–9; Elizabeth M. Jeffreys, 'Constantine Hermoniakos and Byzantine Education', Δωδώνη, IV (1975), 81–109.

Epilogue

Modern historians regard the Despotate of Epiros as a chapter in the mediaeval history of Greece. Its inhabitants between the thirteenth and the fifteenth centuries would not have shared this view. They did not think of themselves as citizens of a country called Greece or Hellas. Nor did they think in terms of a Greek nation of which Epiros was a province. The French and Italians who exploited or colonised Epiros considered it to be part of 'Romania', their generic term for the Byzantine Empire. The Chronicles of Ioannina and of the Tocco family described its Greek-speaking inhabitants as 'Romaioi', not as Hellenes. The Epirotes of the middle ages were not accustomed to being called Hellenes, for the world to which they belonged by tradition, culture and religion was the Romaic world of Byzantium. Their rulers jealously defended their political independence from that world, for which the Byzantines of Constantinople castigated them as rebels against the divine order of things. Having been born and bred in the Byzantine tradition they ought to have known better than to defy the authority of God's vicegerent in the Queen of Cities.

The Despotate of Epiros, at least after the Byzantine restoration in 1261, might be defined as part of the Byzantine Commonwealth, that community of eastern European peoples who, though living beyond the bounds of the empire, yet shared a common cultural and religious wealth, the source of which was Constantinople. The Balkan kingdoms of Bulgaria and Serbia belonged to that commonwealth; and there is much about the geography as well as the history of Epiros which links it more to eastern Europe than to Greece. To this day the city of Ioannina retains an appearance and an atmosphere which are more Balkan than Greek, though its citizens are among the proudest and the hardiest of Hellenes. But in the middle ages Epiros was also perforce linked to western Europe because of its proximity to Italy. The Normans had sailed across in the eleventh century. The same route was taken by Manfred of Hohenstaufen and then by Charles of Anjou in the thirteenth century. The history of Epiros thereafter was much interwoven with that of the expansionist

Drang nach Osten of the Angevin kingdom of Naples. It was at first a stepping-stone on the way to Constantinople; and when that dream faded it was treated as a poor relation of the larger French colony in the Morea to the south. But, so far as can be seen, the Epirotes gained almost nothing in the way of material or spiritual benefit from their western neighbours. They remained Byzantines by tradition and by faith.

Epiros played its part also in the enrichment of the commercial Republics of Venice and of Ragusa. For the Venetians too it was a stepping-stone or landing stage on their trade route to Constantinople and the east. Not that they ever sought to dominate or to colonise it. They were content eventually to acquire the island of Corfu, a substantial prize, which helped to assure their command of the Adriatic and Ionian Seas and which they held against all comers until 1797. Epiros thus attracted the attention of Italian and Slav merchants as well as of Frankish colonists; and in the fourteenth century, thanks to the growing wealth and investments of the banking houses of Florence, it attracted Florentines as well, one of whom, Esau Buondelmonti, became Despot of Ioannina in 1385. The Italian families of Orsini and of Tocco, whose sons made themselves Despots of Epiros in the fourteenth and fifteenth centuries, maintained a tenuous link with Italy; though their power base was the Ionian islands offshore and they looked to Byzantium rather than to the west for legitimisation of their acts of piracy on the mainland. Unlike the Venetians and the French, they believed that the way to win the hearts of the Greek-speaking people of Epiros was to adopt the Byzantine way of life, thought and religion.

Some modern Greek historians claim that the Despotate of Epiros illustrates an early revival of the Greek national spirit and that its rulers were champions of Hellenism before their time. The evidence hardly supports such a claim. The Despotate can, however, be seen to illustrate the decline and fall of the Byzantine Empire. Its continuing existence as a separatist state after 1261 is one of the symptoms of that decline. The fragmentation of the empire, which had begun even before the Fourth Crusade, had gone so far that a whole province could defy the central government for eighty years. In 1340, when the 'rebels' finally gave in, it was too late to reassemble the pieces of the once integrated Empire of Constantinople. Its own rulers were at daggers drawn with each other. The Byzantine despotate of the Morea, established in 1348 when the struggle for the throne was over, might have set a pattern for the government of Epiros. But again it was too late. The Serbians had found and seized their opportunity to add Epiros and Thessaly to their own empire. The Serbian conquest and occupation emphasised the Balkan connexion of northern Greece. The Serbians swept Epiros into their part of the Byzantine commonwealth. The Chronicle of Ioannina has nothing good to say of them; though in Thessaly they were comparatively well received. The church and the monasteries had cause to be grateful, for the Serbians made much of the fact that they were pious Orthodox Christians in the Byzantine tradition. The excesses of the tyrant Thomas Preljubović in Ioannina, probably exaggerated by the chronicler, were perhaps not typical of the behaviour of the Serbian ascendancy in Greece. The researches of the late George C. Soulis, now being prepared for publication, will surely shed more light on this episode of Serbian history.

Finally there came the Albanians and the Turks. The first rulers of separatist Epiros in the thirteenth century had made treaties and alliances with the Albanian chieftains to the north of their domain. The Byzantine emperors had seen them as a threat to the peace and granted them privileges to buy them off. But in the fourteenth century they began to infiltrate into Epiros and Thessaly. Many found their way down into the Morea, where, by 1400, there was reckoned to be about 10,000 Albanians, and by 1450 as many as 30,000. The history and the demography of Epiros were to be permanently affected by the invasion and settlement of the Albanians. The city of Ioannina never succumbed to them. But the city of Arta and most of Akarnania were in Albanian control for over fifty years, from 1359 to 1416; and it was to protect their land against the Albanians that the Despots of Epiros first called on the help of the Turks. The Turkish conquest of Epiros would surely have happened sooner or later. But it is a melancholy fact that the triumph of Islam was more helped than hindered by the actions of the last Christian rulers of Epiros. Carlo Tocco was persuaded that only the Turks could put the fear of God into the Albanians. But the Turks themselves knew, and were soon to prove, that only they could put a stop to the internecine feuds among the Christians. The squabbling Byzantine despots of the Morea in the fifteenth century brought the Turkish conquest upon themselves. The same was true in Epiros. The sons of Carlo Tocco, by their petty disputes and jealousies, accomplished the Turkish conquest of Ioannina in 1430 and hastened the absorption of Epiros into the Ottoman Empire. The chronicler of their father's deeds was in prophetic mood when he observed: Οἱ Τοῦρκοι πάντα ἠγαποῦν τῶν Χριστιανῶν τὸ σχίσμα.[1]

[1] *Chron. Tocco.* XIV, c. 12, l. 3738: 'The Turks were always gratified when the Christians were divided.'

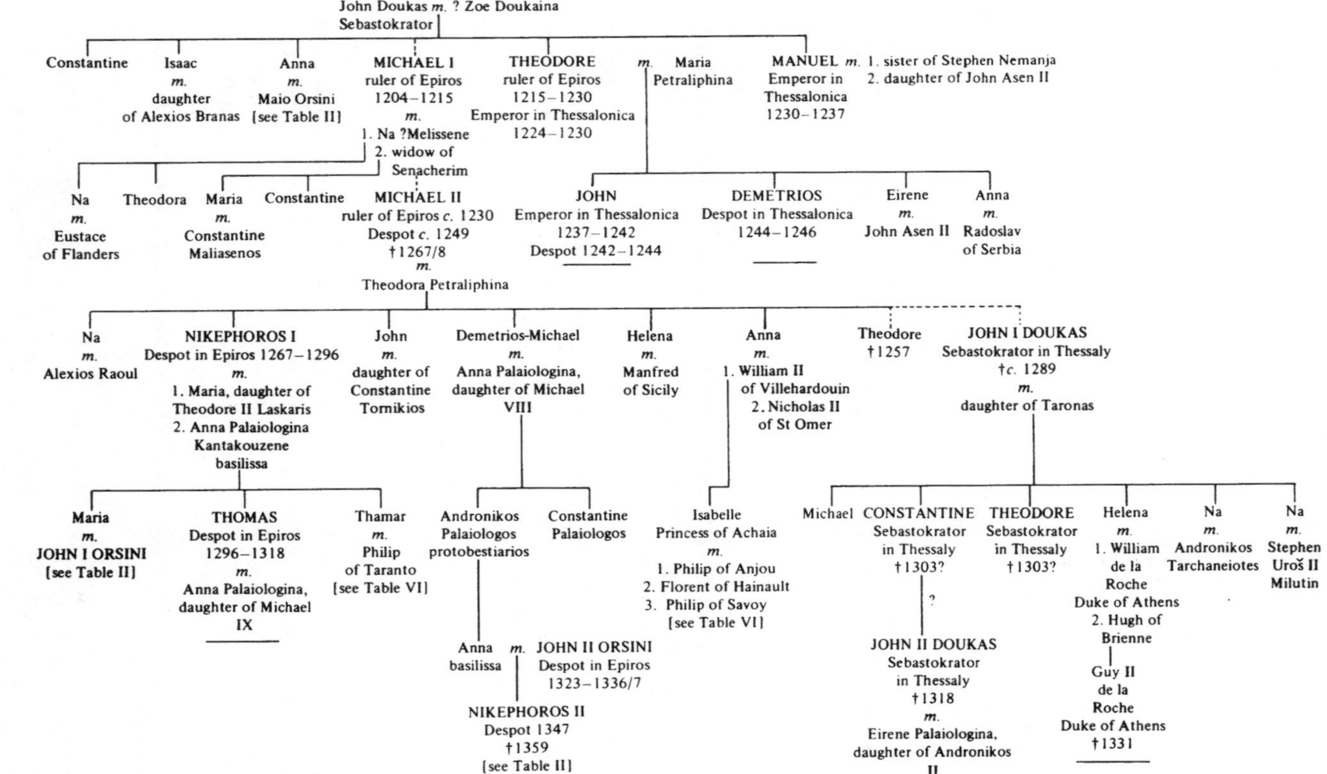

1. Greek rulers of Epiros and Thessaly 1204–1318

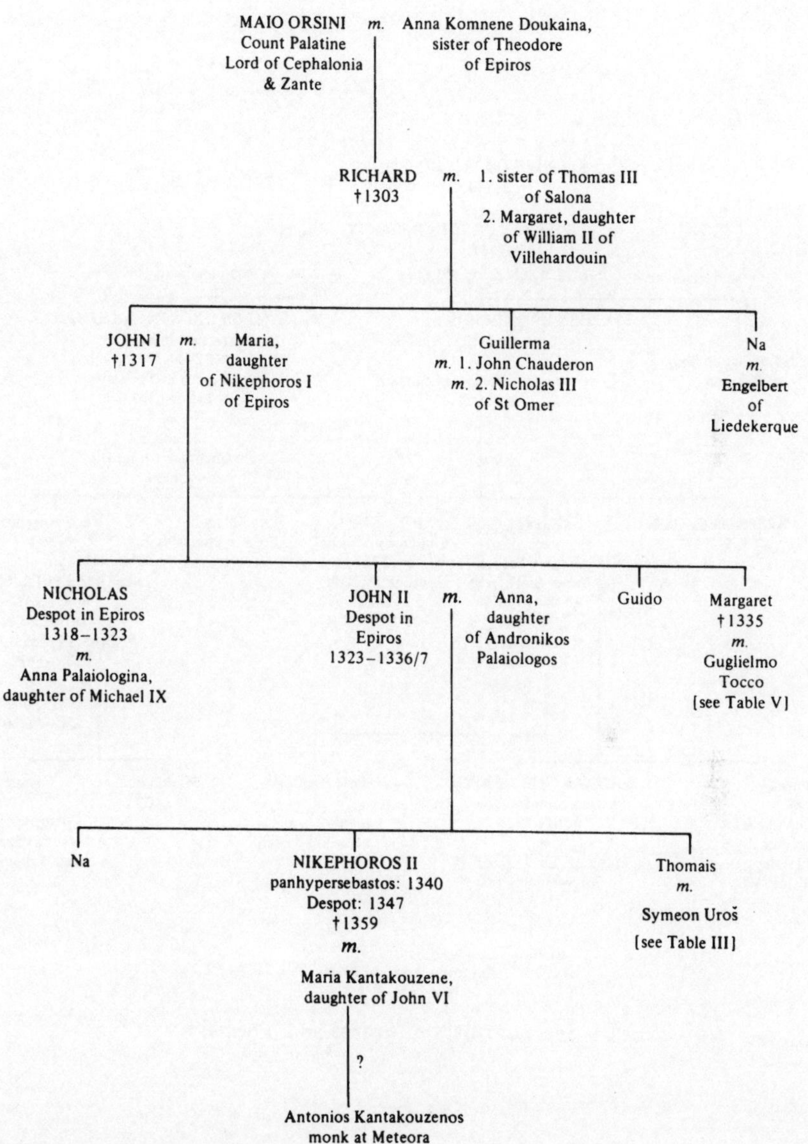
MAIO ORSINI
Count Palatine
Lord of Cephalonia
& Zante
m.
Anna Komnene Doukaina,
sister of Theodore
of Epiros
RICHARD
†1303
m.
1. sister of Thomas III
of Salona
2. Margaret, daughter
of William II of
Villehardouin
JOHN I
†1317
m.
Maria,
daughter
of Nikephoros I
of Epiros
Guillerma
m. 1. John Chauderon
m. 2. Nicholas III
of St Omer
Na
m.
Engelbert
of
Liedekerque
NICHOLAS
Despot in Epiros
1318–1323
m.
Anna Palaiologina,
daughter of Michael IX
JOHN II
Despot in
Epiros
1323–1336/7
m.
Anna,
daughter
of Andronikos
Palaiologos
Guido
Margaret
†1335
m.
Guglielmo
Tocco
[see Table V]
Na
NIKEPHOROS II
panhypersebastos: 1340
Despot: 1347
†1359
m.
Maria Kantakouzene,
daughter of John VI
Thomais
m.
Symeon Uroš
[see Table III]
?
Antonios Kantakouzenos
monk at Meteora

2. The family of Orsini. Counts of Cephalonia and Zante: Despots in Epiros

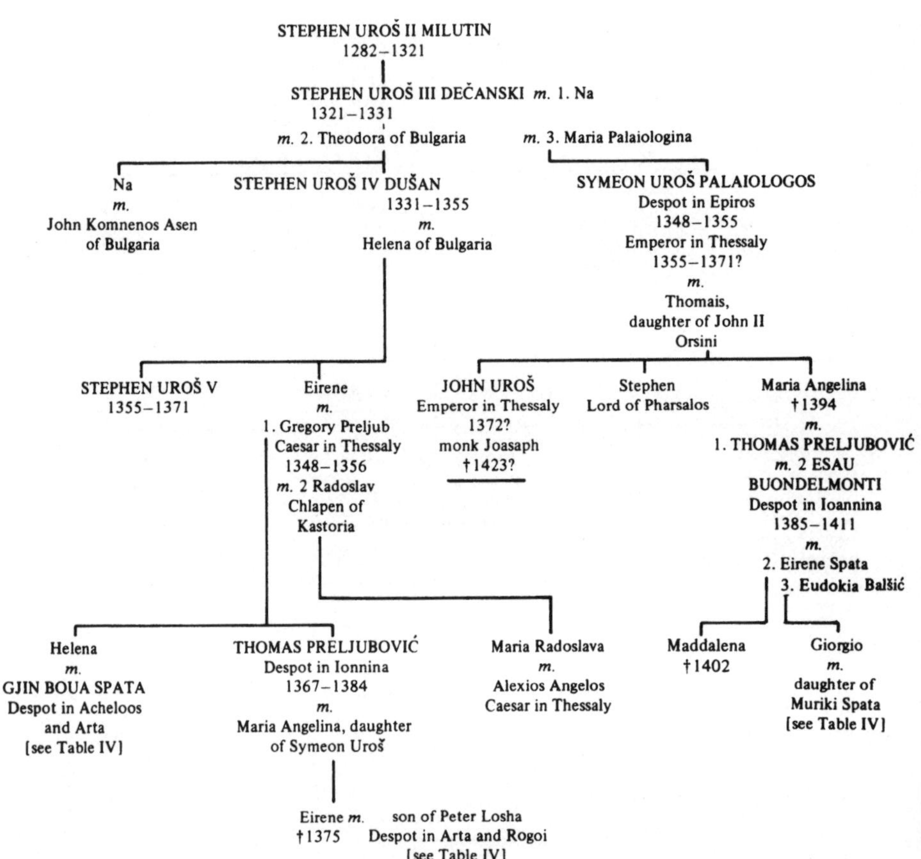

3. Serbian rulers of Epiros and Thessaly

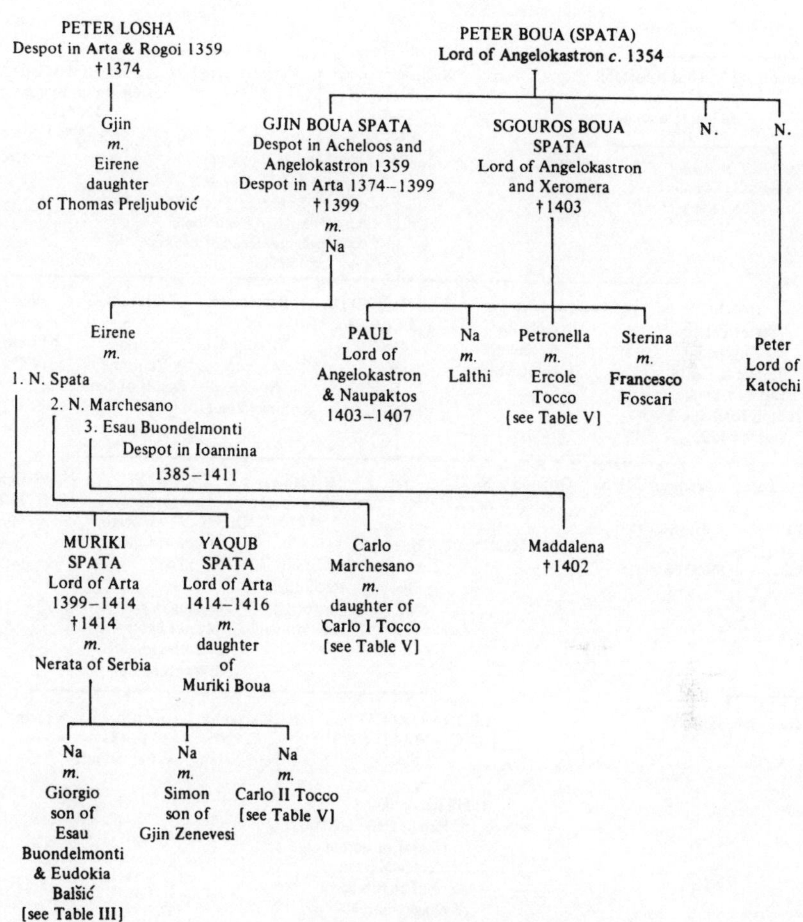
PETER LOSHA
Despot in Arta & Rogoi 1359
†1374
Gjin
m.
Eirene
daughter
of Thomas Preljubović
PETER BOUA (SPATA)
Lord of Angelokastron c. 1354
GJIN BOUA SPATA
Despot in Acheloos and
Angelokastron 1359
Despot in Arta 1374–1399
†1399
m.
Na
SGOUROS BOUA
SPATA
Lord of Angelokastron
and Xeromera
†1403
N.
N.
Eirene
m.
1. N. Spata
2. N. Marchesano
3. Esau Buondelmonti
Despot in Ioannina
1385–1411
PAUL
Lord of
Angelokastron
& Naupaktos
1403–1407
Na
m.
Lalthi
Petronella
m.
Ercole
Tocco
[see Table V]
Sterina
m.
Francesco
Foscari
Peter
Lord of
Katochi
MURIKI
SPATA
Lord of Arta
1399–1414
†1414
m.
Nerata of Serbia
YAQUB
SPATA
Lord of Arta
1414–1416
m.
daughter
of
Muriki Boua
Carlo
Marchesano
m.
daughter of
Carlo I Tocco
[see Table V]
Maddalena
†1402
Na
m.
Giorgio
son of
Esau
Buondelmonti
& Eudokia
Balšić
[see Table III]
Na
m.
Simon
son of
Gjin Zenevesi
Na
m.
Carlo II Tocco
[see Table V]

4. Albanian rulers of Epiros

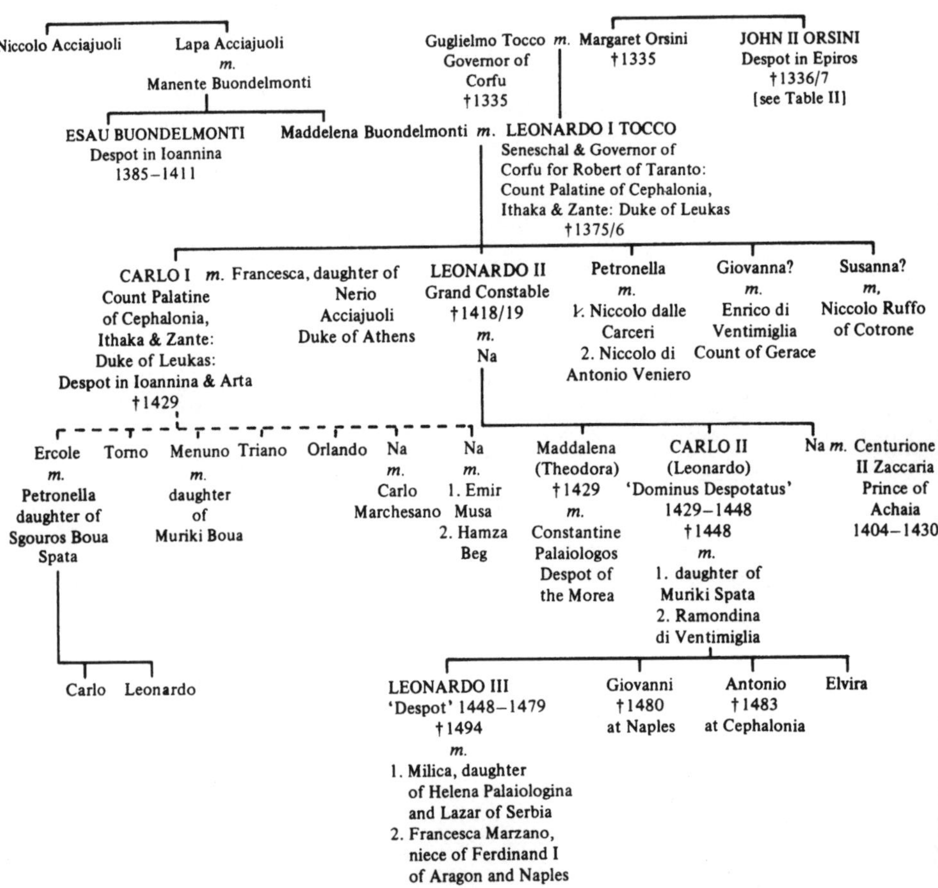

5. The family of Tocco. Counts of Cephalonia: Dukes of Leukas: Despots in Epiros

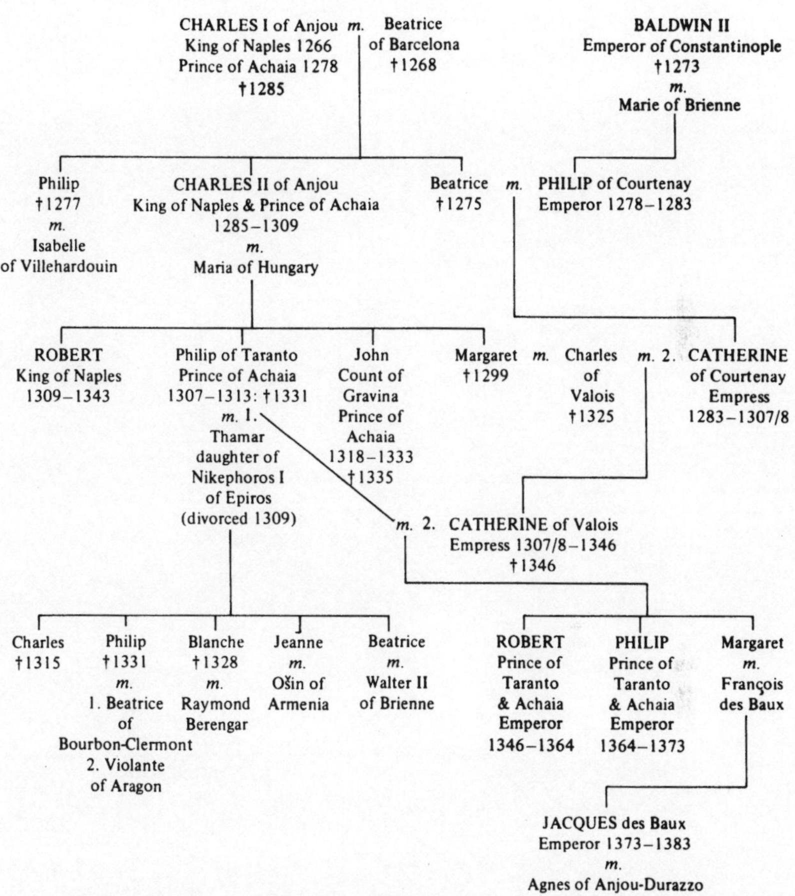

6. The house of Anjou–Naples and titular Latin emperors of Constantinople

Bibliography

COLLECTIONS OF SOURCES

A: Greek
B: Angevin
C: Venetian
D: Other

LITERARY SOURCES

A: Greek
B: Other

MODERN WORKS

COLLECTIONS OF SOURCES

A: Greek

Actes de Lavra, III: *de 1329 à 1350* (Archives de l'Athos, x), ed. P. Lemerle, A. Guillou, N. Svoronos, Denise Papachryssanthou (Paris, 1979).

Bees, N. A. Συμβολὴ εἰς τὴν ἱστορίαν τῶν Μονῶν τῶν Μετεώρων, Βυζαντίς, I (1909), 191–331.

Σερβικὰ καὶ Βυζαντιακὰ γράμματα Μετεώρου, Βυζαντίς, II (1911), 1–100.

BHG Bibliotheca Hagiographica Graeca, ed. F. Halkin (Subsidia Hagiographica, 8[a]), I–III (3rd ed., Brussels, 1957).

CFHB Corpus Fontium Historiae Byzantinae (Berlin–Rome–Vienna–Washington, 1967–).

CSHB Corpus Scriptorum Historiae Byzantinae (Bonn, 1828–97).

Darrouzès, J. *Les Regestes des Actes du Patriarcat de Constantinople*, I: *Les Actes des Patriarches*, fasc. v: *Les Regestes de 1310 à 1376* (Paris, 1977); fasc. VI: *Les Regestes de 1377 à 1410* (Paris, 1979).

Notitiae Episcopatuum Ecclesiae Constantinopolitanae. Texte critique, introduction et notes (Paris, 1981).

Dölger, F. *Regesten der Kaiserurkunden des oströmischen Reiches*, III: *1204–1282* (2nd ed., P. Wirth: Munich, 1977); IV: *1282–1341* (Munich–Berlin, 1960); V: *1341–1453* (Munich–Berlin, 1965).

Gedeon, M. Νέα βιβλιοθήκη εκκλησιαστικῶν συγγραφέων, I (Constantinople, 1903).

Gelzer, H. *Ungedruckte und ungenügend veröffentlichte Texte der Notitiae episcopatuum: ein Beitrag zur byzantinischen Kirchen- und Verwaltungsgeschichte* (Abhandlungen der philosophisch-philologischen Classe der königlich bayerischen Akademie der Wissenschaften, XXI/3: Munich, 1901).

'Ungedruckte und wenig bekannte Bistümerverzeichnisse der orientalischen Kirché, *BZ*, I (1892), 245–82; II (1893), 22–71.

Hunger, H. and Kresten, O. *Das Register des Patriarchats von Konstantinopel*, I: *Edition und Übersetzung aus den Jahren 1315–1331* (*CFHB*, XIX/1: Vienna, 1981) [in progress].

Lambros, Sp. Ἔγγραφα ἐκ τοῦ ARCHIVIO CAPITOLINO, *NH*, XX (1926), 297–315.

Ἐνθυμήσεων ἤτοι χρονικῶν σημειωμάτων: συλλογὴ πρώτη, *NH*, VII (1910), 8–313.

Παλαιολόγεια καὶ Πελοποννησιακά, I–IV (Athens, 1912–26).

Laurent, V. *Les bulles métriques dans la sigillographie byzantine* (Athens, 1932).

Les Regestes des Actes du Patriarcat de Constantinople, I: *Les Actes des Patriarches*, fasc. IV: *Les Regestes de 1208 à 1309* (Paris, 1971).

and Darrouzès, J. *Dossier grec de l'Union de Lyon (1273–1277)* (Archives de l'Orient chrétien, XVI: Paris, 1976).

MM Miklosich, F. and Müller, J. *Acta et Diplomata graeca medii aevi sacra et profana*, I–VI (Vienna, 1860–90).

MPG Migne, J. P. *Patrologiae cursus completus. Series graeco-latina* (Paris, 1857–66).

Parthey, G. *Hieroclis Synecdemus et Notitiae Graecae episcopatuum. Accedunt Nili Doxopatrii Notitia patriarchatuum et locorum nomina immutata* (Berlin, 1866).

Papadopoulos-Kerameus, A. Ἀνάλεκτα Ἱεροσολυμιτικῆς Σταχυολογίας, I–V (St Petersburg, 1891–8).

Ἱεροσολυμιτικὴ Βιβλιοθήκη, I–IV (St Petersburg, 1891–9).

Rhalles, K. and Potles, M. Σύνταγμα τῶν θείων καὶ ἱερῶν κανόνων, I–VI (Athens, 1852–9).

Sathas, C. N. Μνημεῖα Ἑλληνικῆς Ἱστορίας. *Monumenta Hellenicae Historiae. Documents inédits relatifs à l'histoire de la Grèce au moyen âge*, I–IX (Paris, 1880–96).

Schreiner, P. *Chronica Byzantina Breviora. Die byzantinischen Kleinchroniken* (*CFHB*, XII/1, XII/2, XII/3: Vienna, 1975, 1977, 1979).

Solovjev, A. and Mošin, V. *Grčke povelje srpskich vladara* (Greek documents of the Serbian rulers) (Belgrade, 1936).

B: Angevin

Del Giudice, G. *Codice Diplomatico del Regno di Carlo I.° e II.° d'Angiò ... dal 1265 al 1309*, I (Naples, 1863); II, part I (Naples, 1869); III (= II, part 2: Naples, 1902).

Filangieri, R. *I Registri della Cancelleria Angioina*, ricostruiti da Riccardo Filangieri (Testi e Documenti di Storia Napoletana pubblicati dall' Accademia Pontaniana: Naples, 1950–) [in progress].

Minieri-Riccio, C. *Alcuni Fatti riguardanti Carlo I di Angiò dal 6 di Agosto 1252 al 30 Decembre 1270* (Naples, 1874).

Genealogia di Carlo I. di Angiò (Naples, 1857).

Genealogia di Carlo II. di Angiò (Naples, 1882); also in *ASPN*, VII (1882), 5–67, 203–62, 465–96, 653–84; VIII (1883), 5–33, 197–226, 381–96.

Il Regno di Carlo I di Angiò negli anni 1271 e 1272 (Naples, 1875).

Il Regno di Carlo I° d' Angiò, dal 2 gennaio 1273 al 7 gennaio 1285 (Florence, 1875–81); from *ASI*, ser. 3, XXII (1875), 3–36, 235–63; XXIII (1876), 34–60, 223–41, 423–40; XXIV (1876), 226–42, 373–406; XXV (1877), 19–42, 181–94, 404–16; XXVI (1877), 3–25, 204–24, 417–26; ser. 4, I (1878), 1–13, 225–47, 421–44; II (1878), 192–205, 353–64; III (1879), 3–22, 161–70; IV (1879), 3–18, 173–83, 349–60; V (1880), 177–86, 353–66; VII (1881), 3–24, 304–12.

Notizie storiche tratte da 62 registri angioini (Naples, 1877).

Saggio di Codice Diplomatico formato sulle antiche scritture dell' Archivio di Stato di Napoli, Supplemento, parte prima (88–1299); parte seconda (1300–26). (Naples, 1882, 1883).

Studii storici fatti sopra 84 registri angioini (Naples, 1876).

Studî storici su' fascicoli angioini dell' Archivio della regia zecca di Napoli (Naples, 1863).

Perrat, C. and Longnon, J. *Actes relatifs à la principauté de Morée, 1289–1300* (Collection de documents inédits sur l'histoire de France, VI: Paris, 1967).

C: Venetian

ActAlb Acta et Diplomata res Albaniae mediae aetatis illustrantia, I–II [see below under D].

ActAlbVen Acta Albaniae Veneta Saeculorum XIV et XV, ed. J. Valentini, S. J. Part I, vols. 1–7: *Saeculum XIV complectens*; Part II, vols. 8–17: *Saeculi praescenderbegianam periodum complectens*; Part III, vols. 18–24: *Scanderbegianam periodum complectens* (Palermo–Milan–Rome, 1967–77).

Cessi, R. *Deliberazioni del Maggior Consiglio di Venezia*, III (Bologna, 1934).

Cessi, R. and Sambin, P. *Le Deliberazione del Consigilio dei Rogati (Senato) serie Mixtorum* (Deputazione di Storia Patria per le Venezie: Monumenti Storici. Nuova serie, XV), I (Libri I–XIV) (Venice, 1960); II (Libri XV–XVI), ed. R. Cessi and M. Brunetti (Venice, 1961).

DVL Diplomatarium Veneto-Levantinum, sive Acta et Diplomata res Venetas, Graecas atque Levantis illustrantia a 1330–1454, I-II, ed. G. M. Thomas and

R. Predelli (Monumenti Storici pubblicati dalla R. Deputazione Veneta di Storia Patria, ser. prima. Documenti, vols. v, ix: Venice, 1880, 1889).

Giomo, G. *Rubriche dei libri perduti dei Misti* (Venice, 1887); also in *Archivio Veneto*, xvii (1879), 126–32; xviii (1879), 40–338; xix (1880), 90–117; xx (1880), 81–95.

Predelli, R. *I Libri Commemoriali della Republica di Venezia: Regesti*, i–vi (Venice, 1876–8).

Tafel, G. L. F. and Thomas, G. M. *Urkunden zur älteren Handels- und Staatsgeschichte der Republik Venedig mit besonderer Beziehungen auf Byzanz und die Levante*, i–iii (Fontes rerum Austriacarum, Abt. ii: Diplomata, xii–xiv: Vienna, 1856–7).

Thiriet, F. *Délibérations des Assemblées Vénitiennes concernant la Romanie*, i, ii (Documents et Recherches, viii, xi: Paris-La Haye, 1966, 1971).

Régestes des Délibérations du Sénat de Venise concernant la Romanie, i–iii (Documents et Recherches, i, ii, iv: Paris-La Haye, 1958–61).

D: *Other collections of sources*

ActAlb Acta et Diplomata res Albaniae mediae aetatis illustrantia, i–ii, ed. L. de Thallóczy, C. Jireček, E. de Šufflay (Vienna, 1913, 1918).

Acta Romanorum Pontificum ab Innocentio V ad Benedictum XI (1276–1304), ed. F. M. Delorme and A. L. Tăutu (Pontificia Commissio ad redigendum Codicem Iuris Canonici Orientalis: Fontes, ser. iii, vol. v, tom. ii: Vatican City, 1944).

Benedict XI, Pope. *Le Registre de Benoit XI*, ed. C. Grandjean (Paris, 1905).

Bullarium Franciscanum continens Constitutiones Epistolas Diplomata Romanorum Pontificum Eugenii IV et Nicolai V, nova series, I (1431–1455), ed. U. Hüntermann, O. F. M. (Quaracchi, 1929).

Clement V, Pope. *Acta Clementis PP. V (1303–1314)*, ed. F. M. Delorme and A. L. Tăutu (Pontificia Commissio ad redigendum CICO: Fontes, ser. iii, vol. vii, tom. i: Vatican City, 1955).

Dokumente të periudhës bizantine për historinë Shqipërisë (Shek. vii–xv) (Byzantine documents on the history of Albania [7th to 15th centuries]), ed. K. Bozhori (Akademia e Shkencave e RPSSH, Instituti i Historisë: Tirana, 1978).

Hopf, C. *Chroniques gréco-romanes inédites ou peu connues* (Berlin, 1873).

John XXII, Pope. *Lettres secrètes et curiales du pape Jean XXII (1316–1334)*, ed. A. Coulon, i (Paris, 1900).

Jorga, N. *Notes et extraits pour servir à l'histoire des Croisades au XVe siècle*, i–vi (Paris–Bucharest, 1899–1916); also in *Revue de l'Orient latin*, iv (1896), 25–118, 226–320, 503–622; v (1897), 108–212, 311–88; vi (1898), 50–143, 370–434; vii (1900), 38–107, 375–429; viii (1900–1), 1–115, 267–310.

Krekić, B. *Dubrovnik (Raguse) et le Levant au Moyen Age* (Documents et Recherches, v: Paris-La Haye, 1961).

Muratori, L. A. *Rerum Italicarum Scriptores*, i–xxv (Milan, 1723–51) [new series in progress].

Pastor, L. F. A. von. *Acta Inedita Historiam Pontificum Romanorum praesertim saec. XV, XVI, XVII illustrantia*, I: *1376–1464* (Freiburg im Breisgau, 1904).

Raynaldus, O. *Annales ecclesiastici ab anno MCXCVIII ubi desinuit Cardinalis Baronius auctore Odorico Raynaldo*, V (Lucca, 1750).

Rubió i Lluch, A. *Diplomatari de l'Orient Català (1301–1409)* (Barcelona, 1947).

LITERARY SOURCES

A. Greek

Akropolites, George, *Historia. Georgii Acropolitae Opera*, I, ed. A. Heisenberg (Leipzig, 1903); ed. P. Wirth (Stuttgart, 1978).

Cantac. Cantacuzenus (Kantakouzenos), John, *Historiae. Ioannis Cantacuzeni eximperatoris Historiarum Libri IV*, ed. L. Schopen, I–III (*CSHB*, 1828–32).

Chalk. Chalkokondyles, Laonikos. *Laonici Chalcocandylae Historiarum Demonstrationes*, ed. E. Darkó, I–II (Budapest, 1922–7).

Chronicle of Galaxidi. Χρονικὸν ἀνέκδοτον Γαλαξειδίου, ed. K. N. Sathas (Athens, 1864 and 1914); Χρονικὸ τοῦ Γαλαξειδίου, ed. G. Valetas (Athens, 1944).

Chron. Ioann. Chronicle of Ioannina, ed. S. Cirac Estopañan, *Bizancio y España. El legado de la basilissa María y de los déspotas Thomas y Esau de Ioannina*, I (Commentary), II (Text) (Barcelona, 1943); ed. L. I. Vranousis, Τὸ Χρονικὸν τῶν 'Ιωαννίνων κατ' ἀνέκδοτον δημώδη ἐπιτομήν, 'Επετηρὶς τοῦ Μεσαιωνικοῦ 'Αρχείου, XII (1962), 57–115 (text and demotic version).

Chron. Ioann. Oxon. Codex Aedis Christi 49, fols. 251–71: *Chronicle of Ioannina* with additional chronological notes; partially edited by L. I. Vranousis, Ἱστορικὰ καὶ τοπογραφικὰ τοῦ μεσαιωνικοῦ κάστρου τῶν 'Ιωαννίνων (Athens, 1968).

Chron. Mor. Τὸ Χρονικὸν τοῦ Μορέως, ed. P. P. Kalonaros (Athens, 1940); ed. J. Schmitt, *The Chronicle of the Morea* (London, 1904).

Chron. Tocco. Cronaca dei Tocco di Cefalonia di anonimo. Prolegomeni, testo critico e traduzione, ed. G. Schirò (*CFHB*, X: Rome, 1975).

Chron. Turk. Χρονικὸν περὶ τῶν Τούρκων Σουλτάνων, ed. G. T. Zoras (Athens, 1958).

Doukas, *History*. Ducas, *Istoria Turco-Byzantină (1341–1462)*, ed. V. Grecu (Bucharest, 1958).

Epirotica. De Rebus Epiri, in *Historia politica et patriarchica Constantinopoleos*, ed. I. Bekker (*CSHB*, 1849), pp. 205–79.

Greg. Gregoras, Nikephoros, *Byzantina Historia*, ed. L. Schopen, I–III (*CSHB*, 1829, 1830, 1855).

Greg. (van Dieten). Nikephoros Gregoras, *Rhomäische Geschichte, Historia Rhomaike*, übersetzt und erläutert von J. L. van Dieten, I, II/1, II/2 (Stuttgart, 1973, 1979) [in progress].

Gregoras, Nikephoros. *Speech* to the Emperor Andronikos III Palaiologos: Τοῦ σοφωτάτου καὶ λογιωτάτου κυρίου Νικηφόρου τοῦ Γρηγορᾶ λόγος προσφωνηματικὸς εἰς τον βασιλέα, ed. L. Westermann, *Certamina Eruditionis... in annum MDCCCLXV. Excerptorum ex bibliothecae Paulinae Lipsiensis libris manu scriptis pars prima* (Leipzig, 1865), pp. 21–6.

Hermoniakos, Constantine. E. Legrand, Ἰλιάδος Ῥαψωδίαι ΚΔ'. *La Guerre de Troie, poème du XIV*[e] *siècle en vers octosyllables, par Constantin Hermoniakos*, in Legrand, *Bibliothèque Grecque Vulgaire*, v (Paris, 1890).

Job monachus. (Job Melias Iasites), *Life of St Theodora of Arta, MPG*, CXXVII, cols. 901–6.

Pachymeres, George, *History. Georgii Pachymeris De Michaele et Andronico Palaeologis libri tredecim*, ed. I. Bekker, I–II (*CSHB*, 1835) [cited as Pach., *De Mich. Pal.*; Pach., *De Andron. Pal.*].

Philes, Manuel. *Manuelis Philae Carmina*, I–II, ed. E. Miller (Paris, 1855, 1857); *Manuelis Philae Carmina Inedita*, ed. Ae. Martini (Naples, 1900).

Planoudes, Maximos. *Maximi monachi Planudis epistulae*, ed. M. Treu (Breslau, 1890).

Pseudo-Kodinos, *De Officiis*. Ed. J. Verpeaux, *Pseudo-Kodinos, Traité des Offices* (Paris, 1966).

Sphrantzes, George, *Chronicon Minus* and *Chronicon Majus*. Georgios Sphrantzes, *Memorii 1401–1477. În anexă Pseudo-Phrantzes: Macarie Melissenos, Cronica 1258–1481*, ed. V. Grecu (Bucharest, 1966).

Thomas Magistros. F. W. Lenz, *Fünf Reden Thomas Magisters* (Leiden, 1963).

B: Other

Aeneas Sylvius. *Aeneae Sylvii Pii II. Pontificis Maximi, in Europam sui temporis varias continentem historias*, in *Aeneae Sylvii Piccolominei Senensis... Opera* (Basle, 1571).

Anon. *Anonymi Descriptio Europae Orientalis* "Imperium Constantinopolitanum, Albania, Serbia, Bulgaria, Ruthenia, Ungaria, Polonia, Bohemia" anno MCCCVIII exarata, ed. Olgierd Gorka (Cracow, 1916).

Bertrandon de la Broquière. *Le Voyage d'Outremer de Bertrandon de la Broquière*, ed. C. Schefer (Paris, 1892).

Buondelmonti, Cristoforo. *Christoph. Bondelmontii, Florentini, Librum Insularum Archipelagi*, ed. L. de Sinner (Leipzig–Berlin, 1824); *Description des Iles de l'Archipel par Christophe Buondelmonti. Version grecque par un anonyme*, ed. E. Legrand, I (Paris, 1897).

Chron. Mor. arag. Libro de los Fechos et Conquistas del Principado de la Morea. Chronique de Morée aux XIIIe *et XIV*[e] *siècles*, ed. A. Morel-Fatio (Geneva, 1885).

Chron. Mor. fr. Livre de la Conqueste de la Princée de l'Amorée. Chronique de Morée (1204–1305), ed. J. Longnon (Paris, 1911).

Chron. Mor. ital. Versione Italiana inedita della Cronaca di Morea, ed. C. Hopf, *Chroniques gréco-romanes*, pp. 414–68.

Ciriaco of Ancona. *Kyriaci Anconitani Itinerarium*, ed. Laurentius Mehus (Florence, 1742).

Froissart, Jean, *Les Chroniques de Jean Froissart*, XVI, ed. J. A. Buchon (Collection des chroniques nationales françaises: Paris, 1826); *Oeuvres de Froissart: Chroniques*, XVI, ed. K. de Lettenhove (Brussels, 1871).

Muntaner, Ramon. L. Nicolau d'Olwer, *Ramon Muntaner. L'expedició dels Catalans a Orient* (Barcelona, 1926); *The Chronicle of Ramon Muntaner*, translated by Lady Goodenough, I–II (Hakluyt Society: London, 1920, 1921).

Musachi, Giovanni. *Breve Memorie de li discendenti di nostra casa Musachi*, ed. C. Hopf, *Chroniques gréco-romanes*, pp. 270–340.

Ptolemy of Lucca. *Ptolemaei Lucensis Historia Ecclesiastica*, in Muratori, *Rerum Italicarum Scriptores*, XI (Milan, 1727), cols. 741–1242.

Sanudo Torsello, Marino. *Istoria del Regno di Romania*, ed. C. Hopf, *Chroniques gréco-romanes*, pp. 99–170.

Secreta Fidelium Crucis, ed. J. Bongars, *Gesta Dei per Francos*, II (Hanover, 1611).

A. Cerlini, 'Nuove lettere di Marino Sanudo il vecchio', *La Bibliofilia*, XLII (1940), 321–59.

Spandounes, Theodore. *Theodoro Spandugnino, Patritio Constantinopolitano, De la origine deli Imperatori Ottomani, ordini de la corte, forma del guerreggiare loro, religione, rito, et costumi dela natione*, ed. C. N. Sathas, *Monumenta Hellenicae Historiae*, IX (Paris, 1890), pp. 133–261.

Stefano Magno. *Estratti degli Annali Veneti di Stefano Magno*, ed. C. Hopf, *Chroniques gréco-romanes*, pp. 179–209.

Evènements historiques en Grèce (1479–1497). Extraits d'un recueil sous le nom de Stefano Magno, ed. C. N. Sathas, *Monumenta Hellenicae Historiae*, VI (Paris, 1885), pp. 214–43.

Symon Semeonis. *Itinerarium Symonis Semeonis Ab Hybernia ad Terram Sanctam*, ed. M. Esposito (Scriptores Latini Hiberniae, IV: Dublin, 1960).

Villani, Giovanni. *Cronica di Giovanni Villani* a miglior lezione ridotta, I–VIII (Florence, 1823).

MODERN WORKS

Acheimastou-Potamianou, Myrtale. Βυζαντινὲς τοιχογραφίες στὴ Μονὴ Βλαχερνᾶς τῆς Ἄρτας, *AAA*, VIII (1975), 208–16.

Νέα στοιχεῖα περὶ τῆς Μονῆς τοῦ Ντίλιου εἰς τὴν Νῆσον τῶν Ἰωαννίνων, *AD*, XXIV (1969), A, 152–75.

Νέα στοιχεῖα περὶ τῆς Μονῆς τῶν Φιλανθρωπηνῶν εἰς τὴν Νῆσον τῶν Ἰωαννίνων, *AAA*, VI (1973), 457–63.

Ahrweiler, Hélène. 'L'histoire et la géographie de la région de Smyrne entre les deux occupations turques (1081–1317) particulièrement au XIIIe siècle', *TM*, I (1965), 2–204.

Alexander, P. J. 'A chrysobull of the Emperor Andronicus II in favor of the See of Kanina in Albania', *B*, XV (1940–1), 167–207.

Amantos, K. Ἡ ἀναγνώρισις ὑπὸ τῶν Μωαμεθανῶν θρησκευτικῶν δικαιωμάτων τῶν Χριστιανῶν καὶ ὁ ὁρισμὸς τοῦ Σινᾶν πασά, *Ep. Chron.*, V (1930), 197–210.

Οἱ προνομιακοὶ ὁρισμοὶ τοῦ μουσουλμανισμοῦ ὑπὲρ τῶν Χριστιανῶν, *Hellenika*, IX (1936), 103–66.
Angold, M. *A Byzantine Government in Exile. Government and Society under the Laskarids of Nicaea (1204–1261)* (Oxford, 1975).
Aravantinos, P. Χρονογραφία τῆς Ἠπείρου τῶν τε ὁμόρων Ἑλληνικῶν καὶ Ἰλλυρικῶν χωρῶν, I–II (Athens, 1856; reprinted Athens, 1969).
Περὶ τοῦ Ὁσίου Νείλου τοῦ Ἐριχιώτου, Νέα Πανδώρα, XV (1865), 470–4.
Arnakis, G. 'The names of the months in the History of Georgios Pachymeres', *BNJ*, XVIII (1960), 144–53.
Asdracha, Catherine. 'Deux actes inédits concernant l'Epire. La métropole de Janina et l'évêché de Bouthrotou-et-Glykéos', *REB*, XXV (1977), 159–74.
Atesis, B. G., of Lemnos. Ἐπισκοπικοὶ κατάλογοι τῆς Ἐκκλησίας τῆς Ἑλλάδος ἀπ' ἀρχῆς μέχρι σήμερον, Ἐκκλησιαστικὸς Φάρος, XXVI 1974), 105–80, 417–96; XXVII (1975), 111–73, 447–550.
Babinger, F. *Beiträge zur Frühgeschichte der Türkenherrschaft in Rumelien: 14.–15. Jahrhundert* (Sudosteuropäische Arbeiten, 34: Munich, 1944).
'Beiträge zur Geschichte von Karli-eli vornehmlich aus osmanischen Quellen', Εἰς μνήμην Σπυρίδωνος Λάμπρου (Athens, 1935), pp. 140–9.
Mehmed the Conqueror and his Time, translated by R. Manheim, edited by W. C. Hickman (Bollingen Series, XCVI: Princeton, N. J., 1971).
Baçe, A. 'Qyteti i fortifiknar i Beratit (La ville fortifiée de Berat)', *Monumentet*, II (1971), 43–58.
Barišić, F., 'Mihailo Monomach, eparch i veliki konostavl', *ZRVI*, XI (1968), 215–34.
Barker, J. W. 'On the chronology of the activities of Manuel II Palaeologus in the Peloponnese in 1415', *BZ*, LV (1962), 39–55.
Manuel II Palaeologus (1391–1425): A Study in Late Byzantine Statesmanship (New Brunswick, N. J., 1969).
Barone, N. 'La Ratio Thesaurariorum della Cancelleria Angioina', *ASPN*, X (1885), 413–34; XI (1886), 5–20, 175–97, 415–32, 577–96.
Bartusis, M. C. 'Brigandage in the Late Byzantine Empire', *B*, LI (1981), 386–409.
Beck, H.-G. *Geschichte der byzantinischen Volksliteratur* (Munich, 1971).
Bees, N. A. Συμβολὴ εἰς τὴν ἱστορίαν τῶν Μονῶν τῶν Μετεώρων, Βυζαντίς, I (1909), 191–331.
Σερβικὰ καὶ Βυζαντιακὰ γράμματα Μετεώρου, Βυζαντίς, II (1911), 1–100.
'Sur les tables généalogiques des despotes et dynastes médiévaux d'Epire et de Thessalie', *Zeitschrift für osteuropäische Geschichte*, III (1913), 209–15.
'Übersicht über die Geschichte des Judentums von Janina', *BNJ*, II (1921), 159–77.
'Fragments d'un chrysobulle du couvent de Lycousada (Thessalie)', *Mélanges offerts à Octave et Melpo Merlier*, III (Athens, 1957), 479–86.
Bees-Sepherles, Eleni. 'Aus dem Nachlass von N. A. Bees (Ἐκ τῶν καταλοίπων τοῦ N. A. Βέη): Unedierte Schriftstücke aus der Kanzlei des Johannes Apokaukos des Metropoliten von Naupaktos (in Aetolien)', *BNJ*, XXI (1971–6), Supplement, pp. 1–243.

῾Ο χρόνος στέψεως τοῦ Θεοδώρου Δούκα ὡς προσδιορίζεται ἐξ ἀνεκδότων γραμμάτων ᾽Ιωάννου τοῦ ᾽Αποκαύκου, *BNJ*, XXI (1971–6), 272–9.

Belting, H., Mango, C., Mouriki, Doula. *The Mosaics and Frescoes of St. Mary Pammakaristos (Fethiye Camii) at Istanbul* (Dumbarton Oaks Studies, XV: Washington, D.C., 1978).

Bertaux, E. 'Les Français d'Outre-mer en Apulie et en Epire au temps des Hohenstaufen d'Italie', *Revue Historique*, LXXXV (1904), 225–51.

Bibliography. Βιβλιογραφία γιὰ τὴν ᾽Ήπειρο (1969–1979), *Ep. Chron.*, XXII (1980), 235–305.

Bierbrier, M. L. 'Modern descendants of Byzantine families', *Genealogists' Magazine*, XX, 3 (1980), 85–96.

Binon, S. 'A propos d'un prostagma inédit d'Andronic III Paléologue', *BZ*, XXXVIII (1938), 133–55, 377–407.

Bodnar, E. W. *Cyriacus of Ancona and Athens* (Collection Latomus, XLIII: Brussels, 1960).

Bogiatzides, I. K. Τὸ Χρονικὸν τῶν Μετεώρων, *EEBS*, I (1924), 139–75; II (1925), 149–82.

Συμβολὴ εἰς τὴν μεσαιωνικὴν ἱστορίαν τῆς ᾽Ηπείρου, *Ep. Chron.*, I (1926), 72–80.

Bombaci, A. 'Il "Liber Graecus", un cartolario veneziano comprendenti inediti documenti ottomani in Greco (1481–1504)', *Westöstliche Abhandlungen, R. Tschudi zum siebzigsten Geburtstag* (Wiesbaden, 1954), 288–300.

Bon, A. *La Morée franque* (Bibliothèque de l'école française d'Athènes et de Rome, 213: Paris, 1969).

Borsari, S. 'La politica bizantina di Carlo I d'Angio dal 1266 al 1271', *ASPN*, n. s., XXXV (1956), 319–49.

Bratianu, G. I. 'Notes sur le projet de mariage entre l'empereur Michel IX et Catherine de Courtenay', *RHSEE*, I (1924), 59–63.

Buchon, J. A. C. *Recherches et matériaux pour servir à une histoire de la domination française dans les provinces démembrées de l'empire grec.* I–II (Paris, 1840).

Nouvelles Recherches historiques sur la principauté française de Morée et ses hautes baronnies à la suite de la 4me Croisade, I–II (Paris, 1843).

Recherches historiques sur la principauté française de Morée et ses hautes baronnies, I–II (Paris, 1845).

Buschhausen, H. and H. *Die Marienkirche von Apollonia in Albanien* (Vienna, 1976).

Caggese, R. *Roberto d'Angio e i suoi tempi*, I–II (Florence, 1922, 1930).

Carabellese, F. *Carlo I d'Angio nei rapporti politici e commerciali con Venezia e l'Oriente* (Bari, 1911).

Carile, A. and Cavallo, G. 'L'inedito crisobollo di Andronico III Paleologo per il monastero di Licusada', *Atti dell' Accademia di Scienze dell' Istituto di Bologna*, Classe di Scienze morali, Rendiconti, LXVIII (1974–5), 86–101.

Cerone, F. 'La politica orientale di Alfonso di Aragona', *ASPN*, XVII (1902), 425–56, 555–634, 774, 852.

Charanis, P. 'The Phonikon and other Byzantine taxes', *Speculum*, XX (1945), 331–3.

'Town and Country in the Byzantine possessions of the Balkan peninsula during the Later Period of the Empire', *Aspects of the Balkans. Continuity and Change*, ed. H. Birnbaum and S. Vryonis (La Haye, 1961), 117–37.

Cheetham, N. *Mediaeval Greece* (New Haven–London, 1981).

Chionides, G. C. Ἱστορία τῆς Βεροίας τῆς πόλεως καὶ τῆς περιοχῆς, II (Thessaloniki, 1970).

Chiotes, P. Ἱστορικὰ Ἀπομνημονεύματα τῆς νήσου Ζακύνθου, I–III (Kerkyra, 1849, 1858, 1864).

Chrysos, E. K. Ἡ προαγωγὴ τῆς ἐπισκοπῆς Ἰωαννίνων σε μητρόπολη, Δωδώνη, V (Ioannina, 1976), 337–48.

Ἱστορικὰ στοιχεῖα γιὰ τὴν Ἤπειρο σε σημείωμα τοῦ κώδικα Cromwell 11, *Ep. Chron.*, XXII (1980), 58–65.

Chrysostomides, Julian, 'Corinth 1394–1397: some new facts', *Byzantina*, VII (1975), 81–110.

Dade, E. *Versuche zur Wiedererrichtung der lateinischen Herrschaft in Konstantinopel* (Jena, 1938).

Dakaris, S. I. Τὸ Νησὶ τῶν Ἰωαννίνων. Ἱστορία, Μνημεῖα, Μουσεῖο (Athens, 1982).

Darrouzès, J. 'Ekthésis Néa. Manuel des pittakia du XIVe siècle', *REB*, XXVII (1969), 5–127.

Le registre synodal du patriarcat byzantin au XIVe siècle. Etude paléographique et diplomatique (Archives de l'orient chrétien, 12: Paris, 1971).

Delaville le Roux, J. *Les Hospitaliers à Rhodes jusqu'à la mort de Philibert de Naillac, 1310–1421* (Paris, 1913).

Del Giudice, G. 'La famiglia di Re Manfredi', *ASPN*, III (1878), 3–80; IV (1879), 35–110; V (1880), 21–95, 262–323, 470–547.

De Lellis, C. *Regesta Chartarum Italiae. Gli Atti perduti della Cancelleria Angioina*, ed. R. Filangieri, part I: *Il Regno di Carlo I*: I–II, ed. B. Mazzoleni (Rome, 1939, 1942).

Dendias, M. Ἑλένη Ἀγγελίνα Δούκαινα, βασίλισσα Σικελίας καὶ Νεαπόλεως, *Ep. Chron.*, I (1926), 219–94.

Dennis, G. T. *The Reign of Manuel II Palaeologus in Thessalonica, 1382–1387* (Orientalia Christiana Analecta: Rome, 1960).

Dinić, M. 'Za chronologiju Dušanovich osvajana vizantijskich gradova (Pour la chronologie des conquêtes des villes byzantines par l'empereur Dušan)', *ZRVI*, IV (1956), 1–11.

Djurić, I. 'Svetovni dostojanstvenici u "Ektesis Nea" (The laic nobles in the "Ekthesis Nea")', *ZRVI*, XVIII (1978), 189–211.

Dölger, F. *Beiträge zur Geschichte der byzantinischen Finanzverwaltung besonders des 10. und 11. Jahrhunderts* (Byzantinisches Archiv, 9: Leipzig-Berlin, 1927).

'Zum Gebührenwesen der Byzantiner', in Dölger, *Byzanz und die europäische Staatenwelt* (Ettal, 1953), pp. 232–60.

DuCange, C. Du Fresne. *Histoire de l'empire de Constantinople sous les empereurs français jusqu'à la conquête des Turcs*, ed. J. A. Buchon, I–II (Collection des chroniques nationales françaises... du treizième au seizième siècle: Paris, 1826).

Ducellier, A. *La Façade maritime de l'Albanie au moyen âge. Durazzo et Valona du XIe au XVe siècle* (Documents et Recherches, XII: Thessaloniki, 1981).

'Aux frontières de la Romanie: Arta et Sainte-Maure à la fin du moyen âge', *TM*, VIII (1981), 113–24.

Durrieu, P. *Les Archives angevines de Naples. Etude sur les registres du roi Charles Ier (1265–1285)*, I–II (Bibliothèque des écoles françaises d'Athènes et de Rome: Paris, 1886, 1887).

Eszer, A. K. *Das abenteuerliche Leben des Johannes Laskaris Kalopheros* (Wiesbaden, 1969).

Evangelides, D. Βυζαντινὰ Μνημεῖα τῆς 'Ηπείρου. I. Κωστάνιανη, *Ep. Chron.*, VI (1931), 258–74.

῾Η βυζαντιακὴ ἐκκλησία τῆς ῾Αγίας Κυριακῆς τοῦ Γαρδικίου (Παραμυθίας), 'Αφιέρωμα εἰς τὴν 'Ήπειρον. Εἰς μνήμην Χρίστου Σούλη *(1892–1951)* (Athens, 1956), 129–36.

Failler, A. 'Chronologie et composition dans l'Histoire de Georges Pachymère', *REB*, XXXVIII (1980), 5–103; XXXIX (1981), 145–249.

Fassoulakis, S. *The Byzantine Family of Raoul-Ral(l)es* (Athens, 1973).

Ferjančić, B. *Despoti u Vizantiji i južnoslovenskim zemljama* (Die Despoten in Byzanz und den südslavischen Ländern) (Belgrade, 1960).

'Sevastokratori u Vizantiji (Les sébastokratores à Byzance)', *ZRVI*, XI (1968), 141–92.

Tesalija u XIII i XİV veku (La Thessalie aux XIIIe et XIVe siècles) (Belgrade, 1974).

'Solunski Car Manojlo Angeo (1230–1237) (The Thessalonican Emperor Manuel Angelos (1230–1237))', *Zbornik filosofskog fakulteta*, XIV (Belgrade, 1979), 93–101.

Forges-Davanzati, Domenico. *Dissertazione sulla seconda moglie del Re Manfredi e su' loro figliuolo* (Naples, 1791).

Foss, A. *Epirus* (London, 1978).

Frances, E. 'La féodalité et les villes byzantines au XIIIe et au XIVe siècles', *BS*, XVI (1955), 76–96.

Geanakoplos, D. J. *Emperor Michael Palaeologus and the West 1258–1282. A study in Byzantine–Latin relations* (Cambridge, Mass., 1959).

Gegaj, A. *L'Albanie et l'invasion turque au XVe siècle* (Louvain, 1937).

Gerasimov, T. 'Moneti na frankskija vladetel Ioan II Orsini' (Coins of the Frankish ruler John II Orsini), *Izvestija na muzeja v Trnovo*, II (1964), 29–34.

Germanos of Sardis, 'Επισκοπικοὶ κατάλογοι τῶν ἐν 'Ηπείρῳ καὶ 'Αλβανίᾳ ἐπαρχιῶν τοῦ πατριαρχείου Κωνσταντινουπόλεως, *Ep. Chron.*, XII (1937), 11–103.

Grégoire, H. 'Imperatoris Michaelis Palaeologi De Vita Sua', *B*, XXIX–XXX (1959–60), 447–75.

Gregorovius, F. ῾Ιστορία τῆς πόλεως 'Αθηνῶν κατὰ τοὺς μέσους αἰῶνας ἀπὸ τοῦ 'Ιουστινιανοῦ μέχρι τῆς ὑπὸ τῶν Τούρκων κατακτήσεως, translated from the German by Sp. Lambros, III (Athens, 1906).

Grierson, P. *Byzantine Coins* (London–Los Angeles, 1982).
Grumel, V. *La Chronologie* (Traité des Etudes Byzantines, I: Paris, 1958).
Halkin, F. 'La Vie de saint Niphon ermite au Mont Athos (XIVe siècle)', *Analecta Bollandiana*, LVIII (1940), 5–27.
Hammond, N. G. L. *Epirus. The geography, the ancient remains, the history and the topography of Epirus and adjacent areas* (Oxford, 1967).
Hendy, M. F. *Coinage and Money in the Byzantine Empire, 1081–1261* (Dumbarton Oaks Studies, XII: Washington, D. C., 1969).
Hoeck, J. M. and Loenertz, R.-J. *Nikolaos-Nektarios von Otranto Abt von Casole. Beiträge zur Geschichte der ost-westlichen Beziehungen unter Innozenz III. und Friedrich II.* (Ettal, 1965).
Holland, H. *Travels in the Ionian Isles, Albania, Thessaly, Macedonia, &c. during the years 1812 and 1813* (London, 1815).
Hopf, K. *Geschichte Griechenlands vom Beginn des Mittelalters bis auf unsere Zeit*, I–II, in J. S. Ersch and J. G. Gruber, *Allgemeine Encyklopädie der Wissenschaften und Künste*, LXXXV, LXXXVI (Leipzig, 1867, 1868) [cited as Hopf, *GG*, I, II].
Hughes, T. S. *Travels in Sicily, Greece and Albania* by the Rev. Thomas Smart Hughes, I–II (London, 1820).
Hunger, H. 'Urkunden und Memoirentext: Der Chrysoboullos Logos des Johannes Kantakuzenos für Johannes Angelos', *JÖB*, XXVII (1978), 107–25.
Inalcik, H. *Hicrî 835 Tarihli Sûret-i defter-i Sancak-i Arvanid* (Türk Tarih Kurumu Yayinlarindan, XIV/I: Ankara, 1954).
'Arnawutluk', *Encyclopedia of Islam*, I (1960), pp. 650–8.
'Ottoman methods of conquest', *Studia Islamica*, II (Paris, 1954), 104–29.
Jacoby, D. *La féodalité en Grèce médiévale. Les "Assises de Romanie", sources, application et diffusion* (Documents et Recherches, X: Paris-La Haye, 1971).
'Catalans, Turcs et Vénitiens en Romanie (1305–1332): un nouveau témoignage de Marino Sanudo Torsello', *Studi Medievali*, serie terza, XV (1974), 217–61.
Jeffreys, Elizabeth M. 'Constantine Hermoniakos and Byzantine Education', Δωδώνη, IV (1975), 81–109.
Jervis, H. J.-W. *History of the Island of Corfu, and of the Republic of the Ionian Islands* (London, 1852).
Jireček, K. *Geschichte der Serben*, I–II (Gotha, 1911, 1918); *Istorija Srba*, I–II, ed. J. Radonić (Belgrade, 1978).
'Albanien in der Vergangenheit', in *Illyrisch-Albanische Forschungen*, ed. L. von Thallóczy, I (Munich–Leipzig, 1916), pp. 63–93.
'Die Lage und Vergangenheit der Stadt Durazzo in Albania', ibid., pp. 152–67.
'Valona im Mittelalter', ibid., pp. 168–97.
'Die Witwe und die Söhne des Despoten Esau von Epirus', *BNJ*, I (1920), 1–16.
Jochalas, T. 'Über die Einwanderung der Albaner in Griechenland (Eine zusammenfassende Betrachtung)', *Dissertationes Albanicae* (Munich, 1971), pp. 89–106.

Karpozilos, A. D. *The Ecclesiastical Controversy between the Kingdom of Nicaea and the Principality of Epiros (1217–1233)* (Thessaloniki, 1973).

'The Date of coronation of Theodoros Doukas Angelos', *Byzantina*, VI (1974), 197–202.

Katsaros, B. Συμβολὴ στὴν ἱστορία καὶ μνημειακὴ τοπογραφία τοῦ χωρίου Κατοχὴ 'Ακαρνανίας, *Hellenika*, XXX (1977–8), 307–21.

Každan, A. P. 'Some notes on the "Chronicle of the Tocco"', *Bisanzio e l'Italia. Raccolta di studi in memoria di Agostino Pertusi* (Milan, 1982), 169–76.

Kirsten, E. 'Die byzantinische Stadt', *Berichte zum XI. Internationalen Byzantinisten-Kongress München 1958*, V, 3 (Munich, 1958).

Koder, J. and Hild, F. *Hellas und Thessalia* (*TIB*, I: Vienna, 1976).

Kordoses, M. S. Σχέσεις τοῦ Μιχαὴλ 'Αγγέλου Δούκα με τὴν Πελοπόννησο, *Ep. Chron.*, XXII (1980), 49–57.

Kourouses, S. Μανουὴλ Γαβαλᾶς εἶτα Ματθαῖος Μητροπολίτης 'Εφέσου *(1271/2–1355/60)*, I: Τὰ Βιογραφικά (Athens, 1972).

Krapsites, B. Τὸ Μοναστῆρι Γηρομερίου, in Krapsites, Θεσπρωτικά, II (Athens, 1972), pp. 160–78; 2nd ed. (Athens, 1973), pp. 328–46.

Kresten, O. 'Marginalien zur Geschichte von Ioannina unter Kaiser Andronikos III. Palaiologos', *Ep. Chron.*, XXV (1983), 113–32.

Kyrris, K. 'The social status of the archontes of Phanari in Thessaly', *Hellenika*, XVIII (1964), 73–8.

Laiou (-Thomadakis), Angeliki E. *Constantinople and the Latins. The Foreign Policy of Andronicus II, 1282–1328* (Cambridge, Mass., 1972).

'The Byzantine Economy in the Medieval Trade System; Thirteenth-Fifteenth Centuries', *Dumbarton Oaks Papers*, XXXIV–XXXV (1982), 177–222.

Lambrides, I. 'Ιωάννου Λαμπρίδου *(1839–1891)*, Α': 'Ηπειρωτικὰ 'Αγαθοεργήματα καὶ ἄλλα δημοσιεύματα (Ioannina, 1971).

'Ιωάννου Λαμπρίδου *(1839–1891)*, Β': 'Ηπειρωτικὰ Μελετήματα, 1–10 (Ioannina, 1971).

Lambros, Sp. 'Ανέκδοτον χρυσόβουλλον τοῦ αὐτοκράτορος 'Ανδρονίκου τοῦ Παλαιολόγου, *DIEE*, I (1833–4), 116–19.

῾Η παράδοσις τῶν 'Ιωαννίνων, in Lambros, ῾Ιστορικὰ Μελετήματα (Athens, 1884), pp. 167–72.

᾿Άννα ἡ Καντακουζηνή. Βυζαντιακὴ ἐπιγραφὴ ἐξ Αἰτωλίας, *NH*, I (1904), 36–42.

῾Η ὑπὸ τοῦ Ριχάρδου 'Ορσίνι παραχώρησις τῆς 'Ιθάκης, *NH*, X (1913), 492–3; XI (1914), 414–16.

῾Η λίμνη τῶν 'Ιωαννίνων καὶ αἱ ἐπὶ τῆς νησίδος αὐτῆς μοναί, *NH*, XI (1914), 3–27.

῾Η ἑλληνικὴ ὡς ἐπίσημος γλῶσσα τῶν Σουλτάνων, *NH*, V (1908), 40–78.

Laskaris, M. Θεόδωρος ᾿Άγγελος, υἱὸς τοῦ σεβαστοκράτορος τῆς Θεσσαλίας 'Ιωάννου, *EEBS*, III (1926), 223–4.

'Byzantinoserbica saeculi XIV. Deux chartes de Jean Uroš, dernier Némanide (Novembre 1372, indiction XI)', *B*, XXV–XXVII (1955–7), 277–323.

Lazzarini, V. 'L'acquisto di Lepanto (1407)', *Nuovo Archivio Veneto*, XV (1898), 267–87.

Leake, W. M. *Travels in Northern Greece*, I–IV (London, 1835).

Legrand, L. 'Relation du pèlerinage à Jérusalem de Nicolas de Martoni notaire italien (1394–1395)', *Revue de l'Orient latin*, III (1895), 566–669.

Lemerle, P. 'Le privilège du Despote d'Epire Thomas I pour le Vénitien Jacques Contareno', *BZ*, XLIV (1951: *Festschrift Franz Dölger*), 389–96.

'Trois actes du Despote d'Epire Michel II concernant Corfu connus en traduction latine', *Hellenika*, pt IV (Προσφορὰ εἰς Στ. Κυριακίδην: Thessaloniki, 1953), 405–26.

L'Emirat d'Aydin. Byzance et l'Occident. Recherches sur "La Geste d'Umur Pacha" (Paris, 1957).

Léonard, E. G. *Les Angevins de Naples* (Paris, 1954).

Loenertz, R.-J. *Byzantina et Franco-Graeca*, I–II (Storia e Letteratura, Raccolta di Studi e Testi, 118, 145: Rome, 1970, 1978) [cited as *BFG*].

'Pour l'histoire du Péloponnèse au XIVe siècle (1382–1404)', *Etudes Byzantines*, I (1943), 152–96; reprinted in *BFG*, I, pp. 227–65.

'Hospitaliers et Navarrais en Grèce (1376–1383). Regestes et documents', *OCP*, XXII (1956), 319–60; reprinted in *BFG*, I, pp. 329–69

'Notes sur le règne de Manuel II à Thessalonique – 1381/2–1387: I. La restauration grecque en Epire et en Thessalie. 1381–1383', *BZ*, L (1957), 390–4.

'Athènes et Néopatras, I. Regestes et Notices pour servir à l'histoire des duchés catalans (1311–1394)', *AFP*, XXV (1955), 100–212, 428–31; Athènes et Néopatras, II. Regestes et documents pour servir à l'histoire ecclésiastique des duchés catalans (1311–1395)', *AFP*, XXVIII (1958), 5–91; reprinted in *BFG*, II, pp. 183–303, 305–393.

'Ordre et désordre dans les Mémoires de Jean Cantacuzène', *REB*, XXII (1964), 222–37; reprinted in *BFG*, I, pp. 113–30.

'Mémoire d'Ogier, protonotaire, pour Marco et Marchetto, nonces de Michel VIII Paléologue auprès du Pape Nicholas III (1278, printemps–été)', *OCP*, XXXI (1965), 374–408; reprinted in *BFG*, I, pp. 537–72.

'Lettre de Georges Bardanès, métropolite de Corcyre, au patriarche oecuménique Germain II (1226–1227 c.)', *EEBS*, XXXII (1964), 87–118; reprinted in *BFG*, I, pp. 467–501.

'Aux origines du Despotat d'Epire et de la Principauté d'Achaie', *B*, XLIII (1973), 360–94.

Longnon, J. *L'Empire latin de Constantinople et la principauté de Morée* (Paris, 1949).

Loverdo-Costi, J. *Istoria dell' Isola di Cefalonia*, translated into Greek with notes by P. K. Gratziatos, Ἱστορία τῆς νήσου Κεφαλληνίας δοκίμιον συγγραφὲν ἰταλιστί... (Kephallenia, 1888).

Lunzi, E. Περὶ τῆς πολιτικῆς καταστάσεως τῆς Ἑπτανήσου ἐπὶ Ἑνετῶν (Athens, 1856; reprinted Athens, 1969); translated into Italian as: *Della condizione politica delle Isole Ionie sotto il dominio Veneto, preceduta da un compendio della storia delle isole stesse dalla divisione dell' Impero Bisantino..., versione con note di Marino Dr Typaldo-Foresti e N. Barozzi* (Venice, 1858).

Luttrell, A. 'Interessi fiorentini nell' economia e nella politica dei Cavalieri Ospedalieri di Rodi nel Trecento', *Annali della Scuola Normale Superiore di Pisa*, Lettere, Storia e Filosofia, ser. II, XXVIII (1959), 317–26.

'The Principality of Achaia in 1377', *BZ*, LVII (1964), 340–45.

'Vonitza in Epirus and its Lords: 1306–1377', *RSBN*, n.s., I (XI) (1964), 131–41.

'Aldobrando Baroncelli in Greece: 1378–1382', *OCP*, XXXVI (1970), 273–300.

'Guglielmo de Tocco, Captain of Corfu: 1330–1331', *BMGS*, III (1977), 45–56.

Machairas, K. G. Τὸ ἐν Λευκάδι φρούριον τῆς ῾Αγίας Μαύρας (Athens, 1956).

Magdalino, P. 'Notes on the last years of John Palaiologos, brother of Michael VIII', *REB*, XXXIV (1976), 143–9.

'The History of Thessaly, 1266–1393' (unpublished dissertation: Oxford, 1976).

Maksimović, Lj. 'Poslednie godine protostratora Teodora Sinadena (The Last years of the Protostrator Theodore Synadenus – Prosopographic Notes)', *ZRVI*, X (1967), 177–85.

'Grčki i Romania u Srpskoj vladarskoj tituli (The Greeks and Romania in the Serbian sovereign title)', *ZRVI*, XII (1970), 61–78.

Vizantijska provinzijska uprava u doba Paleologa (The Byzantine provincial administration under the Palaeologi) (Belgrade, 1972).

'Poreski sistem u grčkim oblastima Srpskog Carstva (Le système fiscal dans les provinces grecques de l'Empire Serbe)', *ZRVI*, XVII (1976), 101–25.

'Charakter der sozial-wirtschaftlichen Struktur der spätbyzantinischen Stadt (13.–15. Jh.)', *XVI. Internationaler Byzantinistenkongress, Akten* I/I (Vienna, 1981), 149–88.

Maltezou, Chrysa. Οἱ ἱστορικὲς περιπέτειες τῆς Κορίνθου στὰ τέλη τοῦ ΙΔ'αἰῶνα, Σύμμεικτα, III (Athens, 1973), 17–23.

Προσωπογραφικὰ βυζαντινῆς Πελοποννήσου καὶ ξενοκρατουμένου ἑλληνικοῦ χώρου (μὲ ἀφορμὴ τὸν φάκελο Foscari τῆς Βενετίας), Σύμμεικτα, V (Athens, 1983), 1–27.

Marinescu, C. 'Tentatives de mariages de deux fils d'Andronic II Paléologue avec des princesses latines', *RHSEE*, I (1924), 139–43.

Marmora, A. *Historia di Corfu* (Venice, 1672).

Mavromatis, L. 'A propos des liens de dépendance en Epire à la fin du XIVe siècle', *ZRVI*, XIX (1980), 275–81.

Mazal, O. *Die Prooimien der byzantinischen Patriarchenurkunden* (Byzantina Vindobonensia, VII: Vienna, 1974).

Mehus, L. *Kyriaci Anconitani Itinerarium* (Florence, 1742).

Meksi, A. 'Arkitektura dhe datimi i kishës së manastirit të Apollonisë (L'église du monastère d'Apollonie, son architecture et le problème de sa datation)', *Monumentet*, III (1972), 103–17.

'Arkitektura e kishës së Mesopotamit (L'architecture de l'église de Mesopotame)', *Monumentet*, III (1972), 47–95.

'Tri kisha bizantine të Beratit (Les trois églises byzantines à Berat)', *Monumentet*, IV (1972), 59–102.

'Të dhëna të reja për kishën e Mesopotamit (Nouvelles données sur l'église de Mesopotame)', *Monumentet*, X (1975), 151–9.

Ménage, V. L. 'Beglerbegi', *Encyclopaedia of Islam*², I (London–Leiden, 1960), pp. 159–60.

Mercati, G. *Scritti d'Isidoro il cardinale Ruteno* (Studi e Testi, 46: Rome, 1926).

Merendino, E. 'Federico II e Giovanni III Vatatzes', *Byzantino-Sicula*, II (1974), 1–15.

'Quattro lettere greche di Federico II', *Atti dell' Accademia di Scienze Lettere e Arti di Palermo*, ser. iv, XXXIV (1974–5), part ii, 291–344.

'Manfredi fra Epiro e Nicea', *Actes du XV*[e] *Congrès International d'Etudes Byzantines*, IV. *Histoire* (Athens, 1980), 245–52.

Mertzios, K. D. Ἡ ἅλωσις τῶν Ἰωαννίνων, *Ep. Chron.*, XII (1938), 117–22.

Τὸ ἐν Βενετίᾳ κρατικὸν Ἀρχεῖον, *Ep. Chron.*, XV (1940), 23–4.

Τὸ δεύτερον χρυσόβουλλον Ἀνδρονίκου τοῦ Β′ Παλαιολόγου ὑπὲρ τῆς ἐκκλησίας τῶν Ἰωαννίνων, *Ep. Hest.*, I, 2 (1952), 115–18.

Μία ἀνέκδοτη ἐπιστολὴ τοῦ Καρόλου Α′ τοῦ Τόκκου πρὸς τὸν Δόγην Βενετίας γραφεῖσα ἐξ Ἰωαννίνων τὸ 1425, Πεπραγμένα τοῦ Θ′ Διέθνους Βυζαντινολογικοῦ Συνεδρίου (Θεσσαλονίκη) (1953), II (= *Hellenika*, pt. 9: Athens, 1956), 556–9.

'Trois lettres inédites de Charles Tocco en 1427, 1428 et 1432', *Akten des XI. Internationalen Byzantinistenkongresses* (Munich, 1960), 352–4.

Mihaljčić, R. 'Bitka kod Acheloja (La bataille d'Acheloos)', *Zbornik filosofskog fakulteta*, XI (Belgrade, 1970), 271–6; Greek translation by K. Sotiriou, in Ἐπετηρὶς Ἑταιρείας Στερεοελλαδικῶν Μελετῶν, III (1974), 365–71.

Mijović, P. 'O ikonama s portretima Tome Preljubovića i Marije Palaeologove (Les icones avec les portraits de Toma Preljubović et de Marie Paléologine)', *Zbornik za likovne umetnosti*, II (Matica Srpska: Novi Sad, 1966), 183–95.

Miller, W. *The Latins in the Levant. A History of Frankish Greece (1204–1566)* (London, 1908).

Essays on the Latin Orient (Cambridge, 1921).

'Valona', *Journal of Hellenic Studies*, XXXVII (1917), 184–94; also in *Essays*, pp. 429–41.

'Ithake under the Franks', in *Essays*, pp. 261–5.

'Balkan Exiles in Rome', in *Essays*, pp. 497–515.

Minieri-Riccio, C. 'Genealogia di Carlo II d'Angiò Re di Napoli', *ASPN*, VII (1882), 5–67, 201–62, 465–96, 653–84; VIII (1883), 5–33, 197–226, 381–96, 587–600.

Miola, A. 'Notizie d'un Codice della Biblioteca Nazionale di Napoli', *ASPN*, V (1880), 394–412.

Monti, G. M. *La Espansione Mediterranea del Mezzogiorno d'Italia e della Sicilia* (Istituto Nazionale di Cultura Fascista. Studi Giuridici e Storici: Bologna, 1942 – XXI).

Moravcsik, Gy. *Byzantinoturcica*. I: *Die byzantinischen Quellen der Geschichte der Türkvölker*; II: *Sprachreste der Türkvölker in den byzantinischen Quellen*. 2nd ed. (Berlin, 1958).

Moritz, H. *Die Zunamen bei den byzantinischen Historikern und Chronisten* (Programm des k. humanistischen Gymnasiums in Landshut, II [1897–8]).
Morrisson, Cécile. 'La découverte des trésors a l'époque byzantine: théorie et pratique de l'εὕρεσις θησαυροῦ', *TM*, VIII (1981), 321–43.
Mouselimis, Sp. Ἡ Μονὴ Τουρκοπαλούκου, *Ep. Hest.*, XIX (1970), 693–700.
Ἡ Λάκκα τοῦ Μπότσαρη (Ioannina, 1976).
Mpara, B. Τὸ Δέλβινο τῆς Βορείου Ἠπείρου καὶ οἱ γειτονικὲς τοῦ περιοχές (Athens, 1966).
Mustoxidi, A. *Delle Cose Corciresi* (Corfu, 1848).
Ἑλληνομνήμων ἢ Σύμμικτα Ἑλληνικά, I–XII (1843–53); reprinted Athens, 1965. [cited as Mustoxidi, *Hellenomnemon*].
Nicol, D. M. 'The Churches of Molyvdoskepastos', *Annual of the British School at Athens*, XLVIII (1953), 141–53.
The Despotate of Epiros (Oxford, 1957).
The Byzantine Family of Kantakouzenos (Cantacuzenus) ca. *1100–1460. A genealogical and prosopographical study* (Dumbarton Oaks Studies, XI: Washington, D.C., 1968).
The Last Centuries of Byzantium, 1261–1453 (London, 1972).
Meteora. The Rock Monasteries of Thessaly, revised ed. (London, 1975).
'The relations of Charles of Anjou with Nikephoros of Epiros', *BF*, IV (1972), 170–94.
'Refugees, mixed population and local patriotism in Epiros and Western Macedonia after the Fourth Crusade', *XVe Congrès International d'Etudes Byzantines, Rapports*: I. *Histoire* (Athens, 1976), 1–33.
Church and Society in the Last Centuries of Byzantium (Cambridge, 1979).
'The date of the death of Nikephoros I of Epiros', *Rivista di Studi Bizantini e Slavi*, I (= *Miscellanea Agostino Pertusi*, I: Bologna, 1981), 251–7.
Πρόσφατες ἔρευνες γιὰ τὶς ἀπαρχὲς τοῦ Δεσποτάτου τῆς Ἠπείρου, *Ep. Chron.*, XXII (1980), 39–48.
Nikarouses, A. Χρονολογικαὶ ἔρευναι Β'. – Πότε ἀπέθανε Μιχαὴλ Β' ὁ Ἄγγελος ὁ δεσπότης τῆς Ἠπείρου, *DIEE*, n.s., I (1928), 136–41.
Oikonomos, P. G. Ἡ ἐν Ἰωαννίνοις Ἐκκλησία (Athens, 1966).
Ἡ Ἐκκλησία ἐν Βορείῳ Ἠπείρῳ (Athens, 1969).
Ἡ ἐν Ἄρτῃ Ἐκκλησία ἀπὸ ἱδρύσεως τῆς μέχρι τῶν καθ'ἡμᾶς χρόνων (Athens, 1972).
Orlandos, A. K. Μνημεῖα τοῦ Δεσποτάτου τῆς Ἠπείρου. Ἡ Κόκκινη Ἐκκλησία (Παναγία Βελλᾶς), *Ep. Chron.*, II (1927), 153–69.
Ἡ Πόρτα Παναγία τῆς Θεσσαλίας, Ἀρχεῖον τῶν Βυζαντινῶν Μνημείων τῆς Ἑλλάδος, I (1935), pp. 5–40.
Βυζαντινὰ Μνημεῖα τῆς Ἄρτης. Ἀρχεῖον τῶν Βυζαντινῶν Μνημείων τῆς Ἑλλάδος, III, 1–2 (1936–7).
Τὸ τέμπλον τῆς Ἁγίας Θεοδώρας Ἄρτης, *EEBS*, XXXIX–XL (1972–3), 476–92.
Ἡ Παρηγορίτισσα τῆς Ἄρτης (Athens, 1963).
Ostrogorsky, G. *Pour l'histoire de la féodalité byzantine* (Brussels, 1954).
Quelques problèmes de la paysannerie byzantine (Brussels, 1956).
'Pour l'histoire de l'immunité à Byzance', *B*, XXVIII (1958), 165–254.

'Problèmes des relations byzantino-serbes au XIVe siècle', *Proceedings of the XIIIth International Congress of Byzantine Studies* (Oxford, 1967), pp. 41–55.

'Das Chrysobull des Despoten Johannes Orsini für das Kloster von Lykusada', *ZRVI*, XI (1968), 205–13.

History of the Byzantine State (Oxford, 1968).

Ostrogorsky, G. and Schweinfurth, P. 'Das Reliquiar der Despoten von Epirus', *Seminarium Kondakovianum*, IV (1931), 165–72.

Paliouras, A. D. Αἰτωλοακαρνανία· Συμβολὴ στὴ μελέτη βυζαντινῶν καὶ μεταβυζαντινῶν μνημείων (Ioannina, 1981).

Paliouras, T. Βιβλιογραφία γιὰ τὴν Ἤπειρο (1969–79): Βυζαντινὴ ἀρχαιολογία καὶ τέχνη, *Ep. Chron.*, XXII (1980), 256–66.

Pallas, D. I. 'Epiros', *Reallexikon zur byzantinischen Kunst*, II (1968), cols, 257–304.

Paoli, C. 'Nuovi documenti intorno a Gualtieri VI di Brienne duca d'Atene e signore di Firenze', *ASI*, ser. 3, XVI (1872), 22–62.

Papachryssanthou, Denise. 'A propos d'une inscription de Syméon Uroš', *TM*, II (1966), 483–8.

Papadopoulos-Kerameus, A. Περὶ συνοικισμοῦ τῶν Ἰωαννίνων μετὰ τὴν Φραγκικὴν κατάκτησιν τῆς Κωνσταντινουπόλεως, *DIEE*, III (1891), 451–5.

Papadopulos, A. Th. *Versuch einer Genealogie der Palaiologen 1259–1453* (Munich, 1938: reprinted Amsterdam, 1962).

Papageorgiou, K. Οἱ δύο Τουρκικὲς κατακτήσεις τοῦ Γιαννιωτικοῦ κάστρου, *Ep. Hest.*, IV (1955), 419–26.

Parisot, V. *Cantacuzène, homme d'état et historien* (Paris, 1845).

Petritzopoulos, D. *Saggio storico sull' età di Leucadia sotto i Romani e successivi conquistatori* (Venice, 1824).

Petronikolos, K. A. Τὸ Βουργαρέλι (Δροσοπηγὴ) Τζουμέρκων (Athens, 1977).

Philippson, A. and Kirsten, E. *Die griechischen Landschaften*, I–IV (Frankfurt am Main, 1950–9).

Polemis, D. I. *The Doukai. A Contribution to Byzantine Prosopography* (London, 1968).

Politis, L. Ἡ κτιτορικὴ ἐπιγραφὴ τῆς Μονῆς Ἁγίας Παρασκευῆς Βίτσας καὶ ἡ χρονολογία της, *Hellenika*, XX (1967), 421–6.

Pouqueville, F. C. H. L. *Voyages dans la Grèce*, I–V (Paris, 1820–1).

Prinzing, G. 'Studien zur Provinz- und Zentralverwaltung im Machtbereich der Epirotischen Herrscher Michael I. und Theodoros Doukas', *Ep. Chron.*, XXIV (1982), 73–120; XXV (1983), 37–112.

Prosopographisches Lexikon der Palaiologenzeit, ed. E. Trapp, R. Walther and H.-V. Beyer, I–VI (Vienna, 1976–83) [in progress].

Protonotarios, P. Ἡ νομισματοκοπία τοῦ βυζαντινοῦ κράτους τῆς Ἠπείρου (1204–1268), *Ep. Chron.*, XXIV (1982), 130–50.

Remondini, Balthassar Maria, Episcopus Zacynthi, et Cephaleniae &c. *De Zacynthi Antiquitatibus, et Fortuna Commentarius* (Venice, 1756) [see also Serra, Nicolò].

Rodd, Sir Rennell. *The Princes of Achaia and the Chronicles of Morea. A Study of Greece in the Middle Ages*, I–II (London, 1907).

Romanos, I. A. Περὶ τοῦ Δεσποτάτου τῆς Ἠπείρου ἱστορικὴ πραγματεία (Kerkyra, 1895); reprinted in Ἰωάννου Ῥωμανοῦ ἱστορικὰ ἔργα, ed. K. Daphnes (Kerkyra, 1959), pp. 1–87.

Γρατιανὸς Ζώρζης αὐθέντης Λευκάδος ἱστορικὴ πραγματεία τοῦ καθ. Καρόλου Χόπφ (Kerkyra, 1870); reprinted (1959), pp. 127–330 [Greek translation with extensive commentary of the article 'Giorgio' by K. Hopf, in Ersch and Gruber, *Allgemeine Encyklopädie der Wissenschaften und Künste*, LXVII (Leipzig, 1858), pp. 382–4].

Ἀνδηγαυικὸν Δίπλωμα τοῦ Ταραντινοῦ ἡγεμόνος Φιλίππου τοῦ Β'. περιέχον μετάφρασιν χρυσοβούλλου Μιχαὴλ τοῦ Β'. δεσπότου τῆς Ἠπείρου, *DIEE*, II (1885), 587–608; reprinted (1959), pp. 89–106.

Περὶ Βουθρωτοῦ, *DIEE*, III (1889), 548–59; reprinted (1959), pp. 107–15.

Rouillard, G. 'Le mot χάραγμα dans les actes des Paléologues', Εἰς μνήμην Σπ. Λάμπρου (Athens, 1935), pp. 375–80.

Runciman, S. *The Sicilian Vespers. A History of the Mediterranean World in the Later Thirteenth Century* (Cambridge, 1958).

Schirò, G. 'Manuele II Paleologo incorona Carlo Tocco Despota di Gianina', *B*, XXIX–XXX (1959–60), 210–17.

'Evdokia Balšić Vasilissa di Gianina', *ZRVI*, VIII, 2 (= *Mélanges G. Ostrogorsky*, II: 1964), 383–91.

'La genealogia degli Spata tra il XIV e XV sec. e due Bua sconosciuti', *RSBN*, XVIII–XIX (1971–2), 67–85.

Cronaca dei Tocco di Cefalonia di anonimo (*CFHB*, X: Rome, 1975).

'Il Ducato di Leucadia e Venezia fra il XIV e XV secolo', *BF*, V (1977), 353–78.

Ἡ Κέρκυρα καταφύγιον Ἠπειρωτῶν δυναστῶν κατὰ τὸν ΙΔ'–ΙΕ' αἰῶνα, Κερκυραϊκὰ Χρονικά, XXIII (= Δ' Πανιόνιο Συνέδριο, Πρακτικά, I [Kerkyra, 1980]), 307–14.

Schlumberger, G. *Numismatique de l'Orient latin* (Paris, 1878).

'Le tombeau d'une impératrice byzantine à Valence en Espagne', in Schlumberger, *Byzance et Croisades. Pages medievales* (Paris, 1927), pp. 57–86.

Schmid, H. F. 'Byzantinisches Zehntwesen', *JÖBG*, VI (1957), 45–110.

Schreiner, P. 'Zur Geschichte Philadelpheias im 14. Jahrhundert (1293–1390)', *OCP*, XXXV (1969), 375–431.

'Ein Prostagma Andronikos' III. für die Monemvasioten in Pegai (1328)', *JÖB*, XXVII (1978), 203–28.

Seltman, C. P. 'A hoard of coins of Frankish Greece', *Numismatic Circular*, LXXII, 6 (1964), 135.

Serra, Nicolò. *Estratto dalla storia inedita, antica e moderna della citta e isola di Zante, scritta gia in Latino da Monsr. Baldassar Maria Remondini ed ora tradotta in italiano e riformata, coretta ed arrichita di molte considerabili aggiunte, studio e fatica di Nicolo Serra nobile Zacintio 1784*, ed. Hopf, *Chroniques gréco-romanes*, pp. 341–5.

Setton K. M. *Catalan Domination of Athens 1311–1388*, revised ed. (London, 1975).

The Papacy and the Levant (1204–1571), I: *The Thirteenth and Fourteenth*

Centuries (Philadelphia, 1976); II: *The Fifteenth Century* (Philadelphia, 1978).

Simopoulos, K. Ξένοι ταξιδιῶτες στὴν Ἑλλάδα, I: *333* μ.Χ.–*1700* 2nd ed. (Athens, 1972).

Solovjev, A. 'Thessalijskie archonty v XIV veke (Thessalian archons in the fourteenth century)', *BS*, IV (1932), 159–74.

'Un beau-frère du Tsar Douchan', *Revue Internationale des Etudes Balkaniques*, I (Belgrade, 1935), 180–87.

Soteriades, G. Βυζαντιναὶ ἐπιγραφαὶ ἐξ Αἰτωλίας, Ἐπετηρὶς Παρνασσός, VII (1903), 208–15.

Sotiriou, G. Τὸ κάστρο τῶν Ῥωγῶν, *Ep. Chron.*, II (1927), 98–109.

Soulis, G. C. Ἡ πρώτη περίοδος τῆς Σερβοκρατίας ἐν Θεσσαλίᾳ, (1348–1358), *EEBS*, XX (1950), 56–73.

Περὶ τῶν μεσαιωνικῶν Ἀλβανικῶν φύλων τῶν Μαλακασίων, Μπουΐων, καὶ Μεσαρίτων, *EEBS*, XXIII (1953) [Κανίσκιον Φαίδωνι Ἰ. Κουκουλέ], 213–16.

'Byzantino-Serbian Relations', *Proceedings of the XIIIth International Congress of Byzantine Studies* (Oxford, 1967), pp. 57–61.

Soustal, P. 'Die griechischen Quellen zur mittelalterlichen historischen Geographie von Epirus' (unpublished dissertation: Vienna, 1975).

'Sybota und Sopotos', *Ep. Chron.*, XXII (1980), 35–8.

Soustal, P. and Koder, J. *Nikopolis und Kephallēnia* (TIB, III: Vienna, 1981) [cited as Soustal–Koder].

Stiernon, L. 'Les origines du Despotat d'Epire. A propos d'un livre récent', *REB*, XVII (1959), 90–126.

'Les origines du Despotat d'Epire (suite). La date du couronnement de Théodore Doukas', *Actes du XIIe Congrès International des Etudes Byzantines*, II (Belgrade, 1964), 197–202.

Šufflay, M. von 'Die Grenzen Albaniens im Mittelalter', in *Illyrisch-Albanische Forschungen*, ed. L. von Thallóczy, I (Munich–Leipzig, 1916), pp. 288–93.

Städte und Burgen Albaniens hauptsächlich während des Mittelalters (Denkschriften der Akademie der Wissenschaften in Wien, phil.-hist. Klasse, LXIII/1: Vienna, 1924).

Svoronos, N. G. *Recherches sur le cadastre byzantin et la fiscalité au XIe et XIIe siècles: Le cadastre de Thèbes* (Ecole française d'Athènes: Paris, 1959).

Taeschner, F. and Wittek, P. 'Die Vezirfamilie der Ğandarlyzade (14–15 Jahrht.) und ihre Denkmäler', *Der Islam*, XVIII (1929), 60–115.

Thallóczy, L. von *Illyrisch-Albanische Forschungen*, zusammengestellt von Dr. Ludwig von Thallóczy, I–II (Munich–Leipzig, 1916).

and Jireček, K. 'Zwei Urkunden aus Nordalbanien', ibid., pp. 125–51.

Thallóczy, L. von and Jireček, K. 'Zwei Urkunden aus Nordalbanien', *Archiv für slavische Philologie*, XXI (1899), 96–8.

Theocharides, G. I. Προβλήματα τῆς μεσαιωνικῆς Ἱστορίας τῆς Ἠπείρου, Δωδώνη, I (Ioannina, 1972), 1–18.

Thesprotos, Kosmas and Psalidas, Athanasios Γεωγραφία Ἀλβανίας καὶ Ἠπείρου, ed. A. Ch. Papacharisis (Ioannina, 1964).

Thiriet, F. *La Romanie vénitienne au moyen âge. Le développement et l'exploitation du domaine colonial vénitien (XIIe–XVe siècle)* (Paris, 1959).

'Les interventions vénitiennes dans les îles Ioniennes au XIV siècle', *Actes du IIIme Congrès Panionien, 1965* (Athens, 1967), 374–85.

Topping, P. 'Albanian settlements in medieval Greece: some Venetian testimonies', *Charanis Studies. Essays in Honor of Peter Charanis*, ed. Angeliki E. Laiou-Thomadakis (New Brunswick, N. J., 1980), 261–71.

Tourtoglou, M. Παρθενοφθορία καὶ ευρεσις θησαυροῦ (Athens, 1963).

Triantaphyllopoulos, D. D. Ἡ ἐπισκοπὴ καὶ ἡ μονὴ Κοζίλης στὴν Ἤπειρο (Συναγωγὴ στοιχείων – προβλήματα), *Actes du XVe Congrès International d'Etudes Byzantines*, II: *Art et Archéologie. Communications* (Athens, 1981), pp. 839–62.

Trojanos, S. 'Καστροκτισία. Einige Bemerkungen über die finanziellen Grundlagen des Festungsbaues im byzantinischen Reich', *Byzantina*, I (1969), 39–57.

Tzannetatos, T. S. Τὸ πρακτικὸν τῆς λατινικῆς ἐπισκοπῆς Κεφαλληνίας τοῦ *1264* καὶ ἡ ἐπιτομὴ αὐτοῦ (Athens, 1965).

Uspenskij, P. *Putešestvie v Meteorskie i Osoolimpijskie monastyri v Thessalij v 1859 godu* (Travels to the monasteries of the Meteora and of Ossa and Olympos in the year 1859), ed. P. A. Syrku (St Petersburg, 1896).

Vacalopoulos, A. E. *A History of Thessaloniki*, translated by T. F. Carney (Thessaloniki, 1963).

Πηγὲς τῆς Ἱστορίας τοῦ Νέου Ἑλληνισμοῦ, I (*1204–1669*) (Thessaloniki, 1965).

Origins of the Greek Nation. The Byzantine Period, 1204–1461 (New Brunswick, N. J., 1970).

Ἱστορία τοῦ Νέου Ἑλληνισμοῦ, I: Ἀρχὲς καὶ διαμόρφωσή του, 2nd ed. (Thessaloniki, 1974).

Vatopedinos, Alexandros Ἐπιγραφαὶ ἱερᾶς Μονῆς Βατοπεδίου, Μεσαιωνικὰ Γράμματα, II (1934–5), 219.

Vlantes (Blantes), Sp. A. Ἡ Λευκὰς ὑπὸ τοὺς Φράγκους, τοὺς Τούρκους καὶ τοὺς Ἐνετούς. Ἱστορικὸν Δοκίμιον (Leukas, 1902).

Vogel, M. and Gardthausen, G. *Die griechischen Schreiber des Mittelalters und der Renaissance* (Leipzig, 1909).

Vokotopoulos, P. L. Ἀνασκαφὴ Παντανάσσης Φιλιππιάδος 1976, *AAA*, X (1977), 149–68.

Vranousis, L. I. Ἱστορικὰ καὶ τοπογραφικὰ τοῦ μεσαιωνικοῦ κάστρου τῶν Ἰωαννίνων (Athens, 1968); also in Χαριστήριον εἰς Ἀ. Κ. Ὀρλάνδον, IV (1968), pp. 439–515.

Χρονικὰ τῆς μεσαιωνικῆς καὶ Τουρκοκρατουμένης Ἠπείρου (Ioannina, 1962).

'Deux historiens byzantins qui n'ont jamais existé: Comnénos et Proclos', Ἐπετηρὶς τοῦ μεσαιωνικοῦ Ἀρχείου, XII (1962), 23–9.

Γηρομερίου, Μονή, in *ThEE*, IV (1964), cols. 496–502.

Xenopoulou-Serapheim (Σεραφεὶμ ὁ Βυζάντιος, Μητροπολίτης Ἄρτης). Δοκίμιον ἱστορικῆς τινος περιλήψεως τῆς ποτε ἀρχαίας καὶ ἐγκρίτου

Ἠπειρωτικῆς πόλεως Ἄρτης καὶ τῆς ὡσαύτως.. Πρεβέζης, (Athens, 1884); reprinted with additions by G. Tsoutsinos (Arta, 1962).

Xyngopoulos, A. Μεσαιωνικὰ Μνημεῖα Ἰωαννίνων, *Ep. Chron.*, I (1926), 53–62, 133–47, 295–303.

Νέαι προσωπογραφίαι τῆς Μαρίας Παλαιολογίνας καὶ τοῦ Θωμᾶ Πρελιούμποβιτς, Δελτίον Χριστιανικῆς Ἀρχαιολογικῆς Ἑταιρείας, ser. 4, IV (1964–5), 53–70.

Zachariadou, Elizabeth A. Οἱ χίλιοι στίχοι στὴν ἀρχὴ τοῦ Χρονικοῦ τῶν Τόκκο, *Ep. Chron.*, XXV (1983), 158–81

Zakythinos, D. A. Ἀνέκδοτον βυζαντινὸν κτιτορικὸν ἐκ Βορείου Ἠπείρου, *EEBS*, XIV (1938), 277–94.

Μελέται περὶ τῆς διοικητικῆς διαιρέσεως καὶ τῆς ἐπαρχιακῆς διοικήσεως ἐν τῷ Βυζαντινῷ κράτει: I. *EEBS*, XVII (1941), 208–74, XVIII (1948), 42–62; II. *EEBS*, XXI (1951), 179–209.

'Crise monétaire et crise économique à Byzance du XIIIe au XVe siècle', *L'Hellénisme contemporain* (Athens, 1948), 1–149; reprinted in Zakythinos, *Byzance: état–société–économie* (London, 1973), no. XI.

Le Despotat grec de Morée, I: *Histoire politique*; II: *Vie et institutions*. Edition revue et augmentée par Chryssa Maltézou (London, 1975).

Ziangos, N. G. Φεουδαρχικὴ Ἤπειρος καὶ Δεσποτάτο τῆς Ἑλλάδας. Συμβολὴ στὸ Νέο Ἑλληνισμό (Athens, 1974).

Ziebarth, K. Κυριακὸς ὁ ἐξ Ἀγκῶνος ἐν Ἠπείρῳ, *Ep. Chron.*, I (1926), 110–19.

Index

Printed in Great Britain
by Amazon.co.uk, Ltd.,
Marston Gate.